GET OUT

Dedicated to all the men who've wondered if
I am writing about them.
I am.

GET OUT

The Gay Man's Guide To Coming Out and Going Out

Aniruddha Mahale

HarperCollins *Publishers* India

First published in India by HarperCollins *Publishers* 2022
4th Floor, Tower A, Building No. 10, Phase II, DLF Cyber City,
Gurugram, Haryana – 122002
www.harpercollins.co.in

2 4 6 8 10 9 7 5 3 1

P-ISBN: 978-93-5357-823-7
E-ISBN: 978-93-5357-824-4

Typeset in 11/15 Minion Pro at
Manipal Technologies Limited, Manipal

Printed and bound at
Thomson Press (India) Ltd

FSC MIX Paper FSC® C010615

This book is produced from independently certified FSC® paper
to ensure responsible forest management.

Disclaimer

Before you dive-deep into this book and get lost in its many pages, here's a quick reminder that this is not a self-help book. It might *sound* like a self-help book. It might *look* like a self-help book. It might even *call* itself a self-help book once or twice – but it's probably drunk, lying or mistaken.

The contents of this book are solely based on the author's ~~dating misadventures~~ lived experiences (and the occasional anecdote he *might have been told* by an *unsuspecting* date). What might have worked for him might not work for you. It's pure science: just as two snowflakes are never alike, two gay men will never live the same story (side note: it's probably not great advice to call gay men 'snowflakes' because it's a derogatory term. See, I did tell you that you can't take this book seriously).

The author would also like you to know that he has many red flags (writing funny books is not one of them) and you should take everything he says with a pinch of salt. Just a pinch though. He doesn't want you to develop hypertension or high blood pressure.

Contents

An Honest Introduction to the Best Guide in the World

Hello there, beautiful person who enjoys reading dating books. Welcome to the most comprehensive one yet. If you picked this book up because it has a gorgeous cover and you thought it would make for a great read, then I hate to break it to you, but – CONGRATULATIONS! You made the right choice!

Or, like most others, if you gave it a sneak peek because it *looks* like a guide for queer men and you thought you needed that little nudge to go live your best gay life this side of the Indian Ocean, then CONGRATULATIONS AGAIN! You are *really* getting good at this.

Down the nearest shot you find, because you deserve it. (If you don't find any alcohol within arm's length, or are a minor (or ~~choose to not make the mistakes I made~~ don't drink) – just grab a glass of water. Most guides will not tell you how important it is to get your daily quote of H_2O, but LESSON #1 – hydration is the key to mental and physical fitness. I told you this book was different, didn't I? You're already learning new things.)

Now that you've ~~got your daily reminder to drink more water~~ finished your first lesson, let's not test your patience and dive right in. Are you ready?

This one's going to be a fun read.

A Personal Note from the Writer's Desk: Why Do You Need This Book, Boys?

I've always had a lot of questions in my head.

Is ketchup better than mustard? Did man *really* walk on the moon? How do you eat crème brulée? Should I really have that fourth cup of espresso? What's twenty-nine times seventy-two? Are gay men any different from the straight ones? Does true love exist for either?

Let's set something straight.

Unlike the typical gay stereotype, I might not know the right spoon to eat my crème brulée with (just pick a damn spoon), or what colour shirt goes with a leather jacket (most people have you at the leather jacket), but I *do* know that when it comes to finding love, the entire concept of the One™ is a myth – there'll be a Two™, Three™ or Four™, and probably more. It will work out with some of them, and sometimes it will not. (Side note: White shirts work with everything.)

Sound familiar, my straight-brethen-who-are-sneaking-a-peek-at-this-introduction-when-their-friends-aren't-looking?

WELL, DUH. It obviously does, because – LESSON #2: there is no difference between gay and straight folks when it comes to romance, sex or relationships.

Some men love women. Some men love men. Some men love men and women. Some men love minds. Some men love souls. Some men love everyone. Some men love no one. Love is love is love. Heartbreak is heartbreak is heartbreak. There's no mathematical formula, no chemical reaction that must be balanced to find true, eternal love. No LHS = RHS when it comes to making a connection. Contrary to popular belief and popular magazines, dating isn't easy for *anybody*. Put simply, it's … *tough*.

Think about it. Spending hours trudging through traffic to reach your date, only to trudge through hours of monotonous conversation. Picking the right clothes to make the best first impression, but having no luck getting picked up at the bar. Text-dancing with a man for months with no end goal in sight, when you can be dancing to the latest Bollywood remix at your favourite club. Dating is, if you've been paying attention to what I just said, tough. So what do we do? Do we just give up and start following meme accounts? Or worse, *start* a meme account?

Why hello, boys. You've come to the right place.

But What Makes Me the Expert?

'Why should we listen to you?' gay men will yell. 'How are you *different* from every other dating blog out there?'

I agree. Dating blogs and relationship columns are all the same. Formulas to find love. Rules of a relationship. Hacks to get over heartbreak. The dos and don'ts of dating. Lists and lists of information meant to increase your chances of lucking out. Yada yada, you've reached the limit of your patience (much before you reach the end of this book).

We all get it. Dating can be awkward and exasperating, and if you could fall in love just by reading a book, the world wouldn't need Disney's live-action fairy tales. So why should you listen to me (or read my book)? What makes *me* the expert?

Here's where I tell you a tiny little secret, reader. I have extremely credible on-the-field research on my side. Over the past nine years, I've been on a total of sixty-nine first dates (there were many, many more, but I had to stick to the ones that follow because these have the ~~funniest~~ best highlights), and I can safely say that I've seen the world (and the insides of its pants). Was it fun? Was it sad? Was it exciting? Was it disturbing? Was it a constant trip to the STD clinic? Or the therapist's couch?

Honestly, it has been one giant adventure (but thankfully, not one that's taken me to the urologist). Each date was a different story. There were good dates. There were bad dates. There were fantastic dates. There were dates that could have been something more, and dates that *should have been avoided altogether.*

There were writers and there were stylists. There were designers and there were actors. There were photographers, chefs and lawyers. There were socialites, editors and expats. There were consultants, entrepreneurs and bankers. There was a whirlwind of artists. There was the occasional model, as well as a couple of men I can't name without the fear of being sued. But wait … is this a book or my personal LinkedIn profile?

Well no, because there were also a couple of psychopaths. Each date left behind a lesson; ~~a little parting gift~~ personal insights that I got to take back home and frame on my enormous wall of ~~case studies~~ fantastic dates. The stylists taught me how to dress. The teachers taught me how to behave. The actors taught me how to be attractive. The writers taught me how to talk attractive. The models taught me how to walk attractive. The entrepreneurs taught me what to say. The editors taught me what I shouldn't say. The socialites taught me how to charm. The lawyers taught me how to bail myself out. The optimists taught me why I need to believe in myself. The pessimists taught why we need this book.

When you go on so many dates with so many (mostly nice and gorgeous) men, you *sort of* become an expert. You end up knowing how to spot the assholes (and more importantly, not end up becoming one). Over the past decade, I created my little black book (of instructions) on 'how to behave' as a single gay man.

And now I am going to pass on some of that knowledge to all of you.

So How Will This Book Help?

Have you ever wondered why we love rollercoasters so much?

Rollercoasters are scary and nauseating, and let's face it: your average amusement park ride isn't really doing your heart a favour. Every time you get on a rollercoaster, you let a part of that fear go, and (almost often) come out unscathed and exhilarated. You ride that high for a second, and then get right back in line to have another go. Dating is a lot like being on a rollercoaster. A rollercoaster of unsuitable (and occasionally suitable) men. I've been on this rollercoaster so many times, I know it like I know the back of my hand.

See, I've made a lot of mistakes. But every mistake has also been a lesson … a lesson in what *doesn't* work. I can't promise that this book will help you *find* the One™, but I can promise real (as real as the men mentioned over the course of the book), honest advice that will help you *become* him. If you came here looking for quick tips on acing the dating game, I want you to take a long, hard look at the cover, and then at yourself. The right men will teach you what you want from a relationship, but the wrong ones will teach you *who* you want to be in a relationship. LESSON #3: Every time a relationship doesn't work, you learn something about yourself. And bit-by-bit, you realize that going through a rut doesn't mean that you will never get it right.

This book is designed to help you GET OUT of that rut (or your comfort zone) by learning from my romantic (mis)adventures. I want to help you get out and live with the grace and ease (and technology) that I never had. You'll have that, plus a bonus: my personal track record.

I might not be able to hold your hand throughout your journey (LESSON #4: hello, it's a book), but I do promise to nudge you down the right path whenever you are confused.

How Do I Use This Book?

Like my extensive dating history, this book might seem complicated and all over the place, but bear in mind that it's also equally easy to navigate.

Think of it as two different books that have been rolled into one. The first is an interactive guide that tells you how to live the best gay life possible – an activity book that's brimming with personality tests, memory maps, tips and techniques to ~~find~~ be the Coolest Gay Person In India™. The second is a series of sixty-nine real-life encounters I've had over the past decade, giving you a first-person narrative of what dating in the real world actually looks like. My romantic escapades are interspersed throughout the course of this book; so do keep an eye out for all the insight (and a lot of guaranteed laughs) that I have to offer. DISCLAIMER #1: Please take what resonates with you, and take the rest of it with a pinch of salt. What worked for me might not necessarily work for you, but that doesn't mean that the knowledge I have to share is any further from THE REAL TRUTH™. Some of it might seem brutally honest. Some of it might come off as brash. Some of it might sound downright rude. To spare a few (obvious) awkward questions and (even more obvious) lawsuits, some of the details have been tweaked so that the men in question can't be identified.

The combination, however, is an introductory course in what IRL dating is all about: it's not always perfect; it's not always romantic. And it's mostly *never* glamorous. It's a long, winding road, and you'll wear many a pair of shoes out, but that doesn't mean you should *just give up on* finding your happy ending.

The only rule to finding your happy ending is LESSON #4: you don't *need* a significant other to find your happy ending. You don't need a significant other because you are lonely. (Hint: you need a friend.) You don't need a significant other because you are bored. (Hint: you need this book.) You need a significant other because they add value to your life. You need a significant other because you are ready. For everything else, there's a credit card and your phonebook of friends.

There might not be a pop-culture guidebook for *being* a homosexual – LESSON #5: no one can teach you how to be gay – but there is one to know how to *date* as one. It's *this* one. Think of this guide as a list of dos and don'ts or wills and won'ts for every question you might have regarding the fabulous world of being a single gay man in India.

And trust me, there *will* be questions.

How do I find love? Where do I meet men? How do I know if my crush is gay? How do I know if he likes me back? How do I ask someone out on a date? Where do I go for a date? What *is* a date? Am I ready to have sex? Do I know how to have sex? Am I expected to carry condoms for a nightcap? How do I make a clean exit (pun intended) the morning after? Can I wear loafers with my jacket on a date? *Should* I wear a jacket on a date? Where do I find that leather jacket you mentioned earlier? Where do I bump into my next excuse to get off Grindr? Is the gorgeous man at the gym someone I should pursue over protein supplements and Pilates? Do *I* need protein supplements to find love?

The Gay Man's Guide to (Coming Out &) Going Out answers all your unanswered questions and sets you on a path of self-discovery and sexual awakening. I might not have the answers to all my questions from earlier (a fourth cup of espresso, though, is never a good idea), but I do have answers for the ones here and more. Don't worry, boys. There's a light at the end of every tunnel, and I'm going to make life easier for you with this nifty handbook.

And we have all my mis(adventures) to be grateful for. They helped me find myself, just like I hope to help you find yourself. I promise to keep it 100 per cent real.

Who Is This Book For?

You don't need to be a gay man to read this book. In fact, you don't even need to be queer-identifying to read this book. Whether you identify as gay, straight, bi, pan, ace, demi, gender-fluid, non-binary, or even 'I'm-still-not-sure-what-any-of-these-terms-mean-and-I-might-be-slightly-confused-about-my-sexual-identity-so-is-it-okay-if-I-haven't-decided-yet', this book is for everyone. Yes, everyone (not including my mother). That includes you, person-holding-this-book-in-their-hand.

First things first, if you do identify as gay, then you've come to the right book. If you identify as anything else, the least I can promise is a scintillating read. As a gay man writing a book for a gay audience, the book might occasionally sound gendered – but the lessons will apply to everyone.

On the other hand, if you identify as my mother, um … hello mom. Kindly keep this book down. It's not for your (sensitive) eyes.

See, growing up gay a decade back was a lot less cathartic than it is today. I spent years in the closet, gnawing at the walls of self-doubt and self-hate. Would I ever be able to find myself, I would wonder. It took me years to realize that I had to get out of my head first, before I stumbled out into the real world.

And so do you.

But for that to happen, you need to get out of your shell. You need to get out of your house. You need to get out and smell the roses. You need to get out of your dating rut. You need to get out of your comfort zone. But most importantly, you need to get out and not make the same mistakes that I did. Like I said, this book has an HONEST, NO-NONSENSE APPROACH to help you navigate the complexity that is the LGBTQIA+ landscape once you've confidently stepped out of the closet.

There's a sea full of confident, queer men waiting for you out there.

Now get out, and be one.

What to Expect When You Are Expected to Come Out

✵✵

The Queer Man's Guide to Coming Out

a.k.a an introduction for the queer reader

Knock, knock.

Oh, hello again, reader. Didn't see you there. But do you see that closet door? Relax. It's not a literal door. It's a figurative one. Get back to the book now, I need your full attention. Okay? Okay.

Where were we? Yes, back to your (figurative) closet. Open it. Suddenly, it doesn't feel claustrophobic any more. You can breathe. You can see. You can move. You can smell something other than mothballs and sock sweat. You can do as you please. You feel … *free.*

That's what coming out feels like. Now, if you are holding this book as an out-and-proud gay person, then CONGRATULATIONS, because you've already crossed **The Biggest Milestone Of Your Queer Life**™. Coming out to yourself is the biggest challenge there is, and you've put the worst behind you.

Does That Mean I Have to Come Out Now?

NO, YOU BEAUTIFUL PERSON. THIS DOES NOT MEAN YOU HAVE TO COME OUT NOW. Read that in all caps. You can come out whenever (and however) you want. You can come out to your best friend, or your dog, your mother or even that stranger who accidentally stepped on your shoe at the supermarket. You can come out at home or on a vacation. You can come out at the bar or on a Facebook group. You can come out via text, a phone call or (if you can carry a note), even a song. There's no wrong way to come out. See, people will tell you that coming out is a special milestone in every queer person's life – a coming-of-age passage that we have to go through in this convoluted journey of trying to '*find ourselves*' – which makes it *your* story to tell. This book is here to help you make that story a bestseller.

Are We There Yet?

Coming out is tough. It's *really* tough. Mostly because it can be difficult for a variety of reasons – the fear of being ostracized, the multiple conflicts with your religious beliefs, the struggle for acceptance … to say nothing of the slew of *Queer Eye* references that will be constantly thrown at you.

But if you have the bandwidth and the support, coming out can also be honestly refreshing. Take this quick quiz to find out if you are ready to come out of the closet yet:

1. Do you want to come out?
YES: Head to question two.
NO: Well, don't worry. This is where the book will help you. Whether you choose to come out tomorrow, next year or never, it's completely cool. You do you, boo.

2. Is it safe for you to come out?
YES: Head to question three.
NO: Safe spaces are important, boys. Read the rest of the chapter to find out what this means.

3. Do you have a person you can come out to?
YES: Head to question four.
NO: Choosing the right person to come out to first is like choosing your favourite flavour at the ice-cream parlour. You know it's going to be just as delightful in the end.

4. Do you fear they won't accept you?
YES: Oh no, head back to question three and answer again (with someone nicer)!
NO: Head to question five.

5. Are you ready?
YES: PERFECT! WE HAVE A WINNER!
NO: Read on, bubs. This book is here to help you with that nudge.

Important note from the writer's desk

Generations of queer men have made great sacrifices so that you can read this book today. Use it wisely.

Think of this book as your best friend, but, more importantly, as every queer man's survival guide. That includes you. Now, contrary to popular belief, the first step of survival is not finding shelter (unless, of course, you are stranded in the middle of a torrential downpour or a zombie apocalypse), it's *acceptance*.

Coming out might seem taxing, but reading this book while you are *inside* the closet will be doubly so. (Maybe less so if you have in-built wardrobe lights.) The entire premise of this book is to help you get out and be the most authentic version of yourself, but for that, you need to first overcome your doubt.

Want to make this tome your personal pocketbook that'll help you handle all your (queer-related) problems?

Read on. Just make sure you have your bookmarks ready.

How do I make coming out as easy as it looks in a Netflix production?

The internet may have played the largest role in shaping our journey of self-discovery, and opening the doors to gender and sexual identity. For a generation that has meet-cutes on Snapchat and flirts entirely with memes, technology has revolutionized the coming-out experience. Coming of age isn't a celebration now; it's an Instagram post.

Nevertheless, for people who prefer the old-fashioned way, here's a step-by-step guide to coming out of the closet with confidence.

a) Accept yourself

The hardest part about coming out is accepting you as 'you' – which is also why the most important person to come out to is yourself. When you begin to realize that you are different, it's natural to experience feelings of shame, fear and self-hatred. If you can, tie it all together and courier it halfway across the world. And don't put a return address on it. The key is to be kind and patient with yourself, as you would with your neighbour's puppy. Remember that it's completely normal to have your own path of self-discovery. It might involve ice cream. It might involve a string of boys. It might involve a crate of wine. It might involve all of the above.

Once you can look in the mirror and confidently say, 'I'm gay' or 'I'm bisexual' or 'I'm trans', you've won half the battle. Now go win the other half.

b) Educate yourself

Make the internet your best friend, and go seek answers for all the questions you might have. Spend hours reading up about alternate sexuality. Look for LGBTQIA+ communities in your neighbourhood. Reach out to them. Reach out to others like you (because yes, the world is teeming with fabulous folk). Soak it all in.

Or, read this book.

c) Don't force yourself

If you don't think this is the right time to take the plunge into the fag end of the pool (pun intended), then don't. Trust your instincts every time. The key to coming out comfortably is to not *force* yourself out of the closet. There's always tomorrow. Or next month. Or even next year. Come out because you *want* to, not because you *have* to. Take the plunge when you feel like it.

Just know that it will be refreshing.

d) Start with someone who matters

Make a long list of all the people you love. Ask yourself who'd be the kindest and the most supportive. Ask yourself who won't punch you in the face. Ask yourself who'd plant a kiss on your cheek. It could be your sister. It could be your mother. It could be your best friend. It could be an uncle. It could be your favourite teacher from school or even your chemistry lab partner.

It doesn't matter who it is, as long as you trust them. Go ahead and tell them. Be honest and open about your feelings. Enjoy the moment. Repeat the process till you've told everyone who counts.

e) Have a safety plan ready

Coming out can be an emotionally charged experience, because you can't always predict how people will react. Sometimes people will support you with all their love, and sometimes they will not (at least in the beginning). Have a contingency plan ready for that worst-case scenario – what if you are thrown out of your home, cut off from your family, or cut off from your family inheritance?

Have your best friends on speed dial. Stall the process a bit if you think you are at high risk (especially when you're dependent on your family for food, shelter or education). Know your options (even though it *will* all work out in the end).

And if you're old enough, remember that this is what your savings are for.

f) Figure out the first conversation

Do you have the conversation at home or at a café? Should you do it on the phone or through a text? Should you be wearing your lucky socks or a bulletproof vest?

Just like there's no right way to eat a burger, there's no right way to come out – it's all about creating a comfortable environment where both of you can have an open, honest conversation and feel snug in a blanket of feelings. Ideally, you want the person to be relaxed – so try and avoid coming out to someone when they are stressed, busy or doing something that demands their full attention, like driving or saving a baby from a burning building. After that, all you have to do is …

g) Believe

Coming out can be stressful, so the least you can do is be nice to yourself. You might not believe in Santa Claus, global warming or the current government, but *you have to start learning* how to believe in yourself.

Only then will people believe in you.

Wait. There's a Quick PSA!

Remember that being out and proud is as expansive as the LGBTQIA+ community itself. There's no right or wrong way to be queer, just like there's no one way or right way to be out and proud. For some, it is as simple as having a profile picture up on their dating app profile; for some, it's a pride flag as a sticker on their work desk; while for others, it may be walking hand-in-hand with their partner in public or introducing their lover to close friends and family. Out and proud will never have a singular definition. No matter how being it looks for you, it is your personal story (and yours alone). Being out and proud, however you choose to be so, is your contribution to disrupting this heteronormative world.

Go ruffle it up.

The Ally's Guide to Acceptance
A.k.a an Introduction for the Straight Reader

Hello for the third time, reader. Now if you identify as a straight person who picked up this book, the chances are you probably skipped the earlier chapter. If you did no such thing, pat yourself on the back for a job well done and read on (like you, this book prides itself in being RATHER INCLUSIVE). But if you find yourself guilty of flipping through the past few pages, here's a quick bulletin for you:

WHAT WERE YOU THINKING?

Is a book *really* a book if you skip the introduction? Don't roll your eyes, I see you. 'But … I don't need to come out of the closet …' you nervously chuckle. 'So why does it even matter?'

Before you chide this book for being mildly passive-aggressive, think of the most nerve-wracking decision you've ever had to make. Working up the courage to propose to your significant other. Taking that ugly report card back home. Quitting your job to work on your startup. Throwing yourself off a cliff for that bungee-jumping experience. Now multiply that moment by a thousand, and imagine it playing out, as you are strapped to the dentist's chair for a root canal treatment.

That's what coming out feels like.

Every person has their own coming-out story, and it's different every time you tell someone new. It's a lot like getting a tattoo – sometimes it's exciting, sometimes it feels just right, sometimes it's a spur-of-the-moment decision and sometimes (though very rarely) mid-action, you wonder why you decided to do it in the first place. But once you decide to *actually* go through, there's no going back.

Kartik, 32, a copywriter from the suburbs of Bombay, has had it easy. He told his parents at the dinner table, over biscuits and lemon tea. He'd had this conversation many times before – over drunken texts, long-distance phone calls, drinks at the bar, long-winded emails and intimate dinners, and once even in the restroom of his favourite pub – but telling his parents was ... different. He had played out the scenario in his head eighteen times (with outcomes that ranged from being blasted off the family inheritance to a 'we love you so much let's find you a European boyfriend right away' family trip).

There was no going back after scenario eighteen. It had to be done.

There were a few seconds of awkwardness, before his mother looked up at him and asked, 'But what do we do with all the jewellery that we saved up for your wedding?'

Hugs were exchanged moments after, and they continued sipping their tea in silence. The biscuits tasted better, Kartik tells me, but he still only had two. No questions were asked; no answers were given.

Kartik's Netflix movie is the best-case scenario. Most coming out stories never play out, and the ones that do usually don't fare so well. Acceptance doesn't come that easy, because you can't find it *everywhere.*

A Quick Note on Acceptance

You don't find acceptance in gift-wrapped boxes or brown paper packages. It doesn't pop up out of Chinese takeout containers or unopened text messages. And I'm only telling you this because I've looked, but you definitely don't find acceptance in a tub of ice cream.

For Carl, a store manager at a high-end luxury store, coming out was a continuous loop that stretched out over several years. Every time he 'had the conversation', his parents would exchange looks of disappointment, tell him to get back to work and pretend they hadn't heard him. He would mull about it for days and then start all over again the next time.

'I just don't want you to go to hell. No mother wants that for her child,' his mother finally said to him, when he came out for the fourth time. He was taken to the church. He was taken to the therapist. He was even taken to a distant family friend's house for a marriage proposal.

'But it's okay now,' he says to me through a cloud of smoke at a friend's house party, 'they've reached a point of indifference. They know I am seeing someone, but they call him my "flatmate from Delhi".'

Calls are made from time to time, but random references are avoided and names are not dropped. No questions are asked; no answers are given.

For every Kartik, you have a thousand Carls – lovers become roommates, boyfriends become best friends, and your soulmate becomes that friend from out of town who comes over for Sunday lunch because he craves home-cooked food. No questions are asked; no answers are given.

And that's the problem.

For every coming-out story, the questions succeeding them never step up. Did you know that the solution to most problems is a conversation? Ask questions, but don't expect answers to each and every one of them. Like I said, coming out is not easy – so how about meeting the recipient halfway there?

If a close friend, a colleague or a sibling puts down his low-fat latte, looks you straight in the eyes and tells you that he's got 'something important to tell you', there's a high chance you are going to be privy to a coming-out story … unless you've got something stuck between your front teeth, that is (so before you put on your best understanding face, do check a mirror).

And the next time someone tells you that they are gay, talk to them. Be nice. Be polite. Be understanding. Carefully lay out some snacks and grab a pint. Make yourself comfortable, because you are not going to let your friend do this alone.

How Do I React When Someone Comes Out to Me?

1. **Stay calm.**
   This is not about you. This is not about you. This is not about you. Repeat after me till you believe it.

2. **Thank them for telling you.**
   'I'm really glad you decided to tell me,' is the best thing to hear when you come out to someone. Acknowledge their courage for speaking up. After all, not all heroes wear capes, right?

3. **Ask if they want to talk more.**
   Just make sure you don't bombard them with your own questions. Coming out can be emotionally exhausting. Let your friend talk (but only if they want to).

4. **Ask if they need somewhere safe to stay.**
   Coming out is mostly never easy, and sometimes there's a chance things might go downhill for a friend. In that case, offer your home as a safe space or help them find some place comfortable. A lot of doors shut when someone comes out of the closet, so open ones are always heartwarming and helpful.

5. **Ask if they need anything.**
   Sometimes, a shoulder is all they need. Make yours comfortable. And irrespective of what they say, give them a hug. They need it.

Even if you are the most well-meaning empath in the world, there's a high chance you'd mess up your reaction when a friend comes out to you. It happens to the best of us: messing up is a human tendency. Does that mean you don't react at all?

No. It just means you refrain from **heterosplaining**.

A Quick Note on Heterosplaining

Heterosplaining (also commonly referred to as straightsplaining or cis-splaining) is the irritating art of explaining LGBTQIA+ issues, people or behaviour to someone who is not of heterosexual orientation (i.e., a queer individual) in a condescending manner. In simpler terms, it's like telling a professional baker how to make the perfect cake.

This means that you should most certainly avoid saying something along the lines of ...

1. **'Have you thought about seeing a therapist about this?'**
   They probably have, and probably did – which is one of the main reasons this conversation is happening. Do you know how snug it is in the closet with the sweaters and the cardigans?

2. **'No, you are not.'**
   Do you know what *you* are not? A nice person.

3. **'Why are you telling me this?'**
   Being able to finally feel comfortable in your skin is the best feeling in the world. Someone wanting to share that feeling with

you is like wanting to share a large ice cream sundae on a hot summer day. Cherish it.

4. **'I am just really disappointed.'**
   No one needs such negativity in their life. Maybe *you* need to be disappointed in yourself.

5. **'I think you are too young to make this kind of a decision.'**
   I personally know men who realized that they were gay at the age of twelve and some who stumbled out at thirty-two. Everyone has their own journey that they start at different points in their life. It's your duty to hold their hand whenever they decide to start out.

6. **'Oh, that's great. But wait a minute, you won't hit on me now, will you?'**
   No, because you clearly aren't my type. If you were, we would not be friends in the first place. I'd just be gushing about you to my best friend.

7. **'I always knew it.'**
   When someone comes out to you, it's an exhilarating feeling – kind of like the giddiness that comes with riding a rollercoaster. Telling someone that you already knew (even if you did) is like pulling the handbrakes.

8. **'Well, duh!'**
   Read point seven, but slap yourself on the head this time.

9. **'So, are you the guy or the girl?'**
   Get out.

10. **'Haha, is this just because you've not had a girlfriend yet?'**
    Ditch the biology book when you are wondering what your gay friend does behind closed doors. Love has nothing to do with how things fit, because it's not the big 5,000-piece jigsaw puzzle that we all assume it to be.

11. **'I don't really know what to say right now.'**
    If you don't, a hug might do – there's nothing worse than radio silence. Be normal; the best reactions aren't even remembered because they feet so natural.

12. **'I think it's cool, but ... how did you decide you wanted to be gay?'**
    The same way you decided to be straight.

13. **'Why didn't you tell me sooner?'**
    Making someone's coming-out story about *you* is usually not the best idea. Focusing on them and their experience instead? Let's get out those medals of honour.

14. **'Maybe this is just a phase?'**
    These aren't your overly distressed denims from 2010. A person's sexuality is never a phase.

15. **'You mean you are bisexual, right?'**
    No. Gay. G-A-Y. Get that?

Parts of Section 377 might have been struck down with the Supreme Court verdict back in 2018, but the battle is far from over. So don't just watch your friend struggle to come out: hold the door open and help him out. Tip your hat as they walk by. Do you know why?

It's going to be clearance sale season soon, and we are going to need all that space in our closet for better things.

Number One: The Performance Artist
So How Do We Begin?

March 2011

A warm March afternoon. The world is sepia-hued and hazy, like a fading photograph from a forgotten album. It's what great stories with great beginnings are made of; ones we could have saved on our Instagram archives, but sadly, that doesn't exist yet.

And yet, this is just the beginning. This is my first date ever. I'm brand new, fresh out of the factory (just kidding, there's no factory). Over the years, I'll go on to date many men. I'll have multiple first encounters (and if you've been keeping a tab, you'll know that there are sixty-eight others). I'll break hearts. I'll have my heart broken. I'll perfect moves that I'll repeat on loop and say words that I don't mean with such honesty that even I'll believe them.

Eventually, I'll ace the Game™. In fact, (over the course of the pages to follow), I'll make the rules of this mythical game. But like most things, I don't know it yet (just like you don't know what the Game is, but more on that in chapter 3).

For now, I am a nervous wreck. What should I do? What do I wear? What should I say? How do I greet him? Should I go in for a handshake or a hug? Should I throw in a compliment?

Should I throw out all my questions?

I do.

I am sitting with him at an old-school drinking hole in the suburbs. It's full of screechy sixteen-year-olds with the weight of the world on their shoulders. The restaurant reeks of college gossip and stories of what your best friend did behind your back during Biology lab. But I am unconcerned. **One** is tall, gangly and has a rather large set of ears, but he also has the expressive face of a dancer. He's a friend of a friend, and I've had a crush on him for all of 2010 (in gay years, that's a lifetime). I don't notice the eyebrow piercing or the bottled-up insecurities: it's too early, and I am too infatuated.

For me, **One** could very well be the One™ (but if you've read the prologue, you know there are sixty-eight more of these, so he's obviously not).

For now, the two of us are drinking draught beer out of cheap plastic glasses – large, unpretentious and filled to the brim, unlike the thimble-sized glass jars of 2020. I find the pizza appetizing, just like my company. He's interning as a junior architect at a firm in Lower Parel, designing swanky homes for clients who wouldn't talk to him otherwise. Over a period of time, he will move on to other jobs. A product designer, a poet, an activist, a trophy boyfriend, a muse, a painter, an artist, a butcher, a baker, and a candlestick-maker ... maybe I am confusing his life for a nursery rhyme. But what does he *really* want to be?

A performance artist.

That's when I should laugh out loud, hold my head back with mirth and walk away. But I don't. Instead, I sit there, listening to him talk animatedly about his seemingly bleak future. I am new. I don't recognize a red flag when I see one. It could glide past me on a giant float with neon headlights, and I wouldn't bat an eyelid.

One would move to Dubai in three years, change his name and set up his own art space, but neither one of us knows that yet. Back in March 2011, he's simply the architect with the eyebrow piercing and dubious life plans. 'Doesn't the family mind the piercing?' I ask. He laughs loudly. They are back in Kerala, but he doesn't miss home. Over multiple dates, I find out that his relationships are strained, at home and otherwise. He has a father who doesn't acknowledge him, and a younger sister he doesn't acknowledge. The mother goes by unnoticed, as most mothers do. It's the stereotypical gay man's tale. But for now, there is only an awkward pause and an unfinished story.

'Has anyone ever told you that you have a beautiful smile?' he wonders aloud, and I blush on cue. Flash dimple. Look away. Smile. Repeat. I don't know it yet, but over the next decade or so, this is going to become my classic move, practised and perfected over subsequent meetings (and men). I'll bask in it on a bright, sunny day.

For now, I am a beginner at best and his words move me.

'Are you okay missing the World Cup?' I ask him as he guzzles his third glass of beer. We are a mere week away from winning the cricket championship, but like most other things, we don't know it yet.

He tells me that he doesn't follow cricket, and that he'd rather watch me. We smile at each other, while our feet engage in a deep conversation under the table. I look at him closely as he bites into his slice of pizza. He's everything I want. He's an architect, he's an old friend, he likes his beer and, most importantly, he likes me. We'd go on to date for five happy months.

I would eventually find out that he also has a girlfriend.

1
The Beginner's Guide to Being Queer

1.1 Where Do You Fall on the Queer Spectrum?

One long (pseudo) introduction later, you've finally made it to the very beginning of this book. Good job, folks. This is it. You are queer, and you are (a dozen pages later) here.

But before we dig deep into this book and begin our journey navigating the queer landscape, we must ask ourselves a very important question.

What Does the Word Queer Mean?

Kartik was twelve years old when someone asked him if he was queer. It was the very first time he had heard that word. It was 2000, and the world was learning new things.

He remembers going back home, opening the dictionary and flipping through its pages, hungry for the definition. And there it was, on page 783, comfortably sandwiched between *queen truss* and *quell*.

Strange, it screamed back silently, and Kartik remembers feeling disappointed. *Eccentric. Peculiar. Questionable. Sick. Worthless. Counterfeit*. Definition after definition, the dictionary sniggered and smirked, throwing words that were too heavy for his twelve-year-old brain to understand. And then, as an afterthought, it coughed out a succinct 'slang for homosexual'.

'I was a sight, yes, but did I ever identify as … *strange*?' he chuckles. 'Weird? Maybe. Eccentric? Possible. But … *strange*?' He slammed the dictionary shut and never opened it ever again. In the two decades since, the word queer has evolved into an *inclusive* word. Countless movements and multiple debates later, the word has become an umbrella term for sexual and gender minorities who are 'not heterosexual or not cisgender'. It's 2022, and personal identity is everything. The new Webster's dictionary would agree.

But what *really* is Kartik's queer identity?

The word 'identity' is so *fluid*. Who am I? Why am I? Where am I? What am I? These are questions we all (must) ask ourselves. It's not an existential crisis; it's an everyday struggle.

So what (or more importantly, who) do you identify as, reader?

Fluidity is quickly becoming an acceptable norm in the queer community. What advice would I give to someone who's still trying to figure out where they fit on the queer spectrum?

Just one word: don't. The *entire* point of the queer spectrum is to embrace inclusivity and acceptance, regardless of how you choose to identify yourself. Unlike your closets, there's no need for labels here.

You can identify as gay. You can identify as a trans man. You can identify as bicurious. You can identify as asexual. Genderqueer, Pansexual. Non-binary. Demiromantic. You can identify as anything you like (as long as it's not a douchebag), because it is *your* identity. It is what makes you who you are. It is what makes *you* unique.

There's no denying that labels are important, because they help people forge a sense of self in a world where they feel marginalized:

every letter in the LGBTQIA+ umbrella has fought tooth and nail to be here. But just as labels can reassure, they can also confine. We've spent our entire lives trying to fit into the heteronormative formula (spoiler alert: there's no heteronormative formula), so we must make it easier on ourselves to find our place on the rainbow.

But … I Still Want to Know?

You won't give up, will you? Can your place on the sexual spectrum really be stripped down to a basic quiz? Not at all, but we can try. Your sexual identity might not *need* a definition, but identities *do* come with definitions.

Men who are holding this book in their hands, answer the following questions to find out where you might land in the alphabet soup that is the LGBTQIA+ scale:

1. **You are a man who's attracted to …**
   a. only men
   b. only women
   c. both
   d. these options don't make sense to me
   e. um, I don't identify as a man

If your answer is option '**a**', you *probably* identify as a **gay** man.

What I've got to say: Congratulations! That was … *easy*. Well, if you read this book right, so is navigating the gay landscape. Hurry up and dive right into the next chapter!

If your answer is option '**b**', you *probably* identify as a **straight** man.

What I've got to say: Hello there, heterosexual man! If you accidentally picked up this book because you thought it was a guide to becoming the coolest woke bro in town, then … CONGRATULATIONS! You are CORRECT!

But if you picked it up because you want to gift it to your gay buddy, pat yourself on the back, because you just won the 'Ally of the

Year' award. Just kidding, there's no such thing, because this award doesn't need a pedestal.

If your answer is option '**c**', move on to **question 2**.

If your answer is option '**d**', move on to **question 3**.

If your answer is option '**e**', oops, sorry! Should we have a sequel?

What I've got to say: Hello, you beautiful person! While the queer spectrum might be ever-expanding, the page count of this book, unfortunately, is not.

But even though this guide has been written keeping in mind a male audience (because let's face it, men need *all* the help they can get in their journey of not screwing up as they navigate the dating landscape), feel free to brush through the following chapters for some general rules of modern love.

2. **When I say I am attracted to both sexes, I feel it is ...**
   a. my sexual identity
   b. something I've been thinking about

If your answer is option '**a**', you *probably* identify as **bisexual**.

What I've got to say: Bigots will say that bisexuality works like a switch; I say you switch the haters off and move on to the next chapter. Like our cover, the world is a lot better when it's not viewed in black & white.

If your answer is option '**b**', you *probably* identify as **bicurious**.

What I've got to say: You might still be exploring your labels and you probably never have to decide, but picking up this book is the first step in finding yourself, good man. Small baby steps.

3. **You are sexually attracted to ...**
   a. many people at the same time
   b. strong, emotional connections
   c. I don't feel sexual attraction
   d. I still need a little more clarity

If your answer is option '**a**', you *probably* identify as **polyamorous**.

What I've got to say: You desire intimacy with more than one partner, and yes, obviously with their consent. Which makes this book 2x important.[1]

If your answer is option '**b**', you *probably* identify as **demiromantic**.

What I've got to say: Someone call the fire department, because that heat you feel while experiencing a deep romantic attraction towards the object of your desire is hitting the roof! Now all you need is this book to hold those hoses.

If your answer is option '**c**', you *probably* identify as **asexual**.

What I've got to say: Like the quintessential Hallmark greeting card, you believe in relationships forged on romantic connections. Also, sex is highly overrated. Send a greeting card to everyone who doesn't agree with you, fellow.

If your answer is option '**d**', move on to **question 4**.

4. **Okay, then you are romantically attracted to ...**
    a. people, irrespective of gender
    b. strong emotional connections
    c. I don't feel romantic attraction

If your answer is option '**a**', you *probably* identify as **pansexual**.

What I've got to say: Love sees no shape, size, colour or age. And when you are pansexual, it doesn't even see gender.

If your answer is option '**b**', you *probably* identify as **demisexual.**

What I've got to say: Sex isn't given priority, but you feel a keen sense of attraction when you bond with a person romantically.

If your answer is option '**c**', you *probably* identify as **aromantic**.

---

1 You can also be attracted to many people at the same time *without* being polyamorous. Even monogamous people are attracted to multiple people; they are just not amorous with them at the same time!

What I've got to say: You don't need to take that arrow through the heart, because it's totally fine if you don't feel romantically attracted to anybody. 'Why do I need this book?' you'd ask. 'What does a dating guide have to do with me?'

Everything, actually. After all, this guide isn't just about falling in love with someone else.

It's more about falling in love with yourself.

Number Two: The Heterosexual Does Straight Come With A Setting?

July 2015

I match with **Two** on Tinder, a man with a boring corporate job who secretly wants to become a mountaineer, like every other person who has a boring corporate job but secretly wants to do something more exciting. **Two** is sinewy and smart, with eyes that quietly take you back to their room after buying you a drink at the bar.

Two is *also* straight. 'My friends changed my settings as a joke,' he explains when I send him a customary 'hello'. In the long list of ludicrous things I've heard on dating apps, this one's a first. Does your sexual orientation come with a toggle? How do I restore mine to factory settings?

I apologize, and almost write him off when he asks if he can buy me a beer to make up for the embarrassment. He's visiting town for a conference, and I am thirsty. I agree.

We meet the following Friday, and he greets me with half a hug and a thump on my back. He's *really* straight. We spend the next thirty minutes chuckling over all the confusion, when he casually mentions he has a girl in his room upstairs.

I can hear the silence. 'She's always wondered what it's like to be with two men at the same time,' he says. I sip on my beer and suggest using Tinder to find someone. He stares at me hard for five seconds, but I don't break eye contact.

'That's a good idea,' he says. We clink our pints noisily and say goodbye.

1.2 Your Personal Dictionary for Gay Slang

You've done it.

You've figured out your place on the queer spectrum. That's the tough part, isn't it? No more questions from here on. So you can safely immerse yourself in this book now, right?

WRONG.

When you are a queer man, you'll always be full of questions (when you are not full of self-doubt, that is) – but some will always be more important than the others. Take a few of these, for example.

Have you ever been confused when people ask you if you are a **bear** or a **cub**? Do you feel it's rude (and very inappropriate) when someone asks you whether you are a **slave**? Ever wondered why your friends laughed at you when you said you *loved* **vanilla**? Are you surprised that people could be *that* into **otters**? More importantly, *what* is an otter?

To understand the Universal Truth™ that is this book, you need to first get back to the basics. You can't be fluent in gay speak if you don't *speak* the language. It's what queer men have been using to converse with each other (without the knowledge of their unsuspecting straight brethren) for decades now.

As you use the following arsenal of words from here on, remember that your dictionary of gay slang will always be as varied as your little black book of boys. Some of them would seem glaringly obvious while others won't; some of them will be factual while some might also seem facetious. But that doesn't make their place in this cheat sheet any less important:

Barebacking: Having unprotected sex.

Bear: An older, broader, hairier man, who (unlike his namesake) does not need to hibernate.

Beard: A woman used as a cover for a gay partner.

Beefcake: A man who spends most of his time at the gym, and the rest of it scooping spoonfuls of protein supplement into his post-workout shakes.

BJ: A blowjob; an abbreviation used when someone wants to make a blowjob sound cool.

Bottom: The receptive sexual partner a.k.a 'someone who likes taking it in'.

Buns: Butt, used when someone wants to be cute about your butt.

Butt plug: Some definitions just write themselves.

Chem sex: Supplementing sexual acts with ~~catalysts~~ chemical substances.

Chubby chaser: A gay man who likes his partners just like he likes his pillows – soft and cuddly.

Cock ring: A ~~fashion statement~~ circular device that men wear around the base of their penis, to strengthen their erection.

Creampie: A type of pie made with cream. Were you expecting some type of pornographic definition?

Cruise: To seek casual gay sex encounters – usually in restrooms, pubs, trains or sometimes even on the internet – so that you can regret them the morning after.

Cub: A younger version of the **Bear**, but heavier than the **Otter**. May or may not deal with body issues.

Cum: A slang for semen and/or an orgasm.

Daddy: An older, established man who likes his scotch aged and his boys young.

Daddy chaser: A gay man who likes his partners older, but not necessarily wiser.

DDF: Disease- and drug-free. No guarantee the man will be drama-free.

DTF: Down to ~~fornicate~~ have some casual fun.

Discreet: A man who is either in a relationship or in denial, and wants sex on the side.

Dom/Dominant/Master: A person who likes to play *who's the Boss?* in bed.

Douche: The second stage of being a dick; between asshole and jerk.

Douching: The act of cleaning out your rectum with jets of water before indulging in anal sex.

Doucheing: The pattern of being emotionally invested in men who often turn out to be douches.

Drag: Wearing (and completely pulling off) clothes that are traditionally assigned to the opposite gender.

Edging: Purposefully stopping sexual stimulation just before reaching an orgasm to make your climax so intense it could land itself a starring role in an Anurag Kashyap movie.

Faggot: A rude thing to call a gay person.

Fairy: Another rude thing to call a gay person.

Fruit: Someone needs to stop coming up with homophobic slurs that begin with the letter F.

Friends with benefits: A relationship between two men who are too scared to be in an actual relationship.

FWB: Friends with benefits being lazy.

Faghag: A derogatory term for a woman who just happens to surround herself with gay men.

Fellatio: Fancy term for oral sex on a guy.

Fisting: The process of inserting a fist up someone's rectum to achieve sexual stimulation. Not to be confused with a fistfight, because the former won't happen at a pub brawl.

Gaydar: Inherent superpower gay men possess to identify other gay men in public.

GBF: A derogatory term for a best friend who also happens to be gay.

Golden shower: The sexual act of urinating on another person, usually for sexual gratification or as a consensual form of humiliation. Might need an actual shower after.

Host/Hosting: A man who can have a ~~hookup~~ date over at home; a rarity in India, where tight-knit families and exorbitant rents prevent people from staying by themselves.

High fun: An alternative term for chem sex.

Hi fun: Another alternative term for chem sex, but make it shorter.

HF: This is just men getting lazy now.

Iron closet: A gay man who is in such deep denial of his sexuality that he might never step out of the closet.

Kinky: Something that is not **vanilla** sexually, but peach apricot with hazelnuts.

Looking for networking: A man who travels a lot and is on the lookout for vacation flings.

Lube: Short for lubricant, a lifesaver for penetrative sex.

Masc4Masc: A term used by gay men attempting to frame their toxic masculinity (and prejudiced attitude) as a sexual preference.

Mask4Mask: A term used by gay men attempting to frame their pandemic-led obligation to be socially responsible as a sexual preference.

Meat cute: When two men meet on Grindr, but lie by saying they met each other at a Starbucks when their barista messed up their orders.

Muscle Mary: A gym bro who also happens to be gay.

NSA: No-strings-attached casual sex that doesn't involve feelings or goodbye messages.

Open relationship: A relationship between two people with an understanding that they have a free pass to sleep with other people.

Otter: A thinner, leaner version of the **Bear**. Has nothing to do with the animal.

Orgy: Group sex, but make it sound Greek.

Pig: A kinkier, more sexually experimenting bottom.

PnP (Party & Play): Drugs + Sex = Much rock and roll in the bedroom.

Power bottom: A bottom that ~~acts like he's a top~~ controls the narrative.

Poppers: Slang for amyl nitrate, a recreational inhalant that causes your muscles to relax, making your blood vessels dilate, which helps facilitate sex.

Poz: An HIV-positive man who's doing what a lot of men out there are not – telling us about his status.

Rim/Rimming: Imagine eating an ice cream, where the ice cream is someone's butt.

Sapiosexual: To be sexually attracted to intelligence above all qualities. A term (often loosely) used by gay men to describe themselves on dating apps, as a pretentious attempt at sounding intellectual.

Straight-acting: A queer man who prides himself for having 'traditionally masculine' characteristics.

Side: A queer man who is honest (and brave) enough to tell you that he's not into anal sex, but will engage in other forms of same-sex activity.

Slam: When someone wants to inject chemicals (usually a variant of MDMA) straight into their bloodstream to heighten their senses (but not their inhibitions) during sex.

Spooning: a endearing term for lying next to each other on your sides, bodies packed in tight. It's only mildly comforting for the person in the front – the little spoon – as they get to 1) breathe freely and 2) feel their partner's crown jewels pushing into their lower backs. The partner – the big spoon – gets a mouthful of hair, constricted breathing and an unaware lover crushing their genitals.

Sub/Submissive/Slave: A person who likes being bossed around in bed.

Threesome: A sexual act involving three people, where the level of awkwardness is directly proportional to the number of penises present.

The closet: A place where you keep all your ridiculously expensive clothes, your snug woollens and yourself, when you are not out to the world. In other words, queer folks who have not told everyone that they're queer.

Top: The inserting sexual partner, a.k.a 'someone who likes to put it in'.

TVB: The ~~lazy way~~ acronym for asking someone their preferences in bed.

Twink: A younger, smoother, spunkier gay man.

Vanilla: Someone who likes his sex just like he likes his family values, traditional.

Vax4Vax: Mask4Mask (see above), but make it a level higher.

Versatile: A gay man who likes it both ways, but is secretly a bottom.

Versatile bottom: A bottom with an identity crisis.

Versatile top: A bottom that pretends to be a top.

Wolf: A hairy gay man who is neither a **Bear** nor an **Otter,** but floats somewhere in between. Also, may not howl at the moon if you ask him to.

Number Three: The Side
Can I Have You For Main Course, Please?

July 2015

In the month and a half that I've known him, I can categorize my three dates with **Three** in three courses – fact, fiction and the foie gras that I will never end up having.

What I do know?

Three is a young up-and-coming entrepreneur, weeks away from launching his beauty services app. He's constantly stressed, which means he's also constantly avoiding me. I've bought him drinks, showered him with compliments, and even invited him to a friend's party – the queer man's equivalent of asking someone to go steady. But whenever I ask him out to dinner, he's always busy. He's always checking my texts ten hours too late.

What I don't know?

Buying drinks for someone doesn't serve as an appetizer for the main course – the insides of his pants.

... And what I'll eventually find out?

Three doesn't want to be my main course, because apparently, we are both sides.

1.3 How We Met Each Other: A (Very Brief) History of Finding Queer Love before We Found Love Online

Rizvaan, twenty, and Sumeir, twenty-two, met each other on Instagram.

Somewhere between their matching flower-crown filters and millennial names, they found and added each other, and (over after a series of Instagram stories and inappropriate GIFs) hopelessly (and very conveniently, I must say) fell in love. Rizvaan calls it fate; the other calls it public privacy settings.

Dating is that simple today. You leave a string of strategic likes on another gay man's Instagram profile, and you've *officially* made your first move. There's no denying the fact that Gen-Z'ers Rizvaan and Sumeir have had it easy.

Before Instagram became a phenomenon and a platform for guys to ~~leave hearts behind on other men's profiles and complain about why they won't follow you back~~ flirt with each other, the queer dating landscape was a very different place: this journey from the streets to sheets has been a long and hard one (pun intended), but it's been an interesting one nonetheless). So, how did men find each other before Instagram let us surreptitiously slide into each other's DMs?

To understand how modern dating really works, all we need is a swift lesson on how it all began. In fact, over the past few decades we've come a long way. But you don't need to dig out those dusty history textbooks, because what am I here for if not to give you a quick refresher? If it helps, I promise not to make it a boring one.

So ... Where Did It All Start?

It all started thousands of years ago.

Throughout our ancient texts, there have been various descriptions of saints, gods and demi-gods breaking gender norms (long before Jaden Smith even knew it was a thing) and myths about love being heteronormative. Gay, bisexual or transgendered – it's evident that queer-identifying men have always existed.

And they've been finding each other ever since.

Over the decades, we've gone past searching for each other under streetlights: we've fondled other men in unused washrooms; signalled to each other with colourful handkerchiefs at traffic signals; and bumped into one another at seedy, dingy bars (and then a few drinks later, in bed). Was it the whirlwind marathon that I make it out to be?

Not really. That's close to decades of gay *cruising*, squeezed down to four sentences. Vijay, a fifty-something friend who runs an NGO, has 'found' himself in a washroom multiple times over the past decade, and he still finds it beautiful. His definition of beauty is ambiguous, because a lot of men helped him over the years. A cab driver from Bhilai, a student from an arts college in town, two stockbrokers who work in Mumbai's financial district, a waiter from an Udipi restaurant down the road, and a television star (with a girlfriend) who stays in a high-rise by the sea.

It was difficult, yes, but there was an adrenaline rush every time you found someone new. Was he gay? Would he understand the signal? What if he told on you? What if someone walked in? The thrill of making a new connection was exciting.

And then, everything changed. **The 90s happened.**

In 1990, India saw its first LGBTQIA+ platform in the guise of *Bombay Dost*, a queer magazine that hit newsstands (and headlines), completely transforming how gay men met each other. The periodical welcomed men to write letters to others like them, making personals popular much before Shaadi.com. And as we excitedly filled in our classifieds (and preference), trends changed once again.

Online portals such as Yahoo Messenger and MSN Chat provided a substitute for the magazines from the mid-'90s, moving us from personals to chat rooms. We hid behind usernames and blank silhouettes, typing out our ASLs (age, sex, location) in anonymous chat rooms, slowly stepping into a world that's very reminiscent of the one we know today.

In many ways, this was the precursor to modern day-dating. So how did we get where we are today?

We evolved.

We've moved on from clandestine trysts in washrooms to ones on our phones in ways that were previously unimaginable, because the dating apps of today are a reflection of what mankind has been doing for ages – creating new forms of communication and then fine-tuning them into channels for finding sex, love and long-term relationships. Over the past few years, we've sent footprints to torsos on Planet Romeo, favourited boys on Grindr, woofed at hopefuls on Scruff and super-liked our way through a dozen profiles on Tinder.

Technology is revolutionizing romance, and we've even got the numbers to prove it. With more than ten million users worldwide, Grindr recorded a surge from 11,000 to 69,000 active new users per month, simply within a span of four years, and that was back in 2015. Numbers never lie … unless it's the phone number you pass on at the end of a drunken night.

Even though online dating has been in the headlines (of mostly trashy online magazines and internet sex columns) for 'hijacking modern love' and trivializing the concept of everyday romance, we are at the dawn of a new age. Every year, new dating apps and websites show face, making it easier for single gay men to find each other and fall in love. Your phone, unlike your laptop, is the most private thing you own, and something you don't easily share with anybody.

If you look closely, things haven't changed much. The previous generation called it 'cruising'; we call it 'communication'. We still scout the roads and send winks, only now we do it from our smartphones. Technology makes trysting easier, because you no longer need to explain to a policeman why two grown men are parked in a side alley at midnight, with their pants (and inhibitions) lowered all the way down to their knees.

Yet, we are nowhere near the finish line.

Like I said, this is just the beginning. All you need to do is break in.

But that's exactly where this book comes in.

Number Four: The Redux
Who Was I When You Found Me the First Time?

March 2014/October 2017

My eyesight isn't what it will be in the years to come, but I still spot him at the bar.

It's **Four**, a stylist with a high-profile fashion magazine who looks like he's walked straight out of a high-profile fashion magazine. Rumour has it that **Four** is going to be heading the production team at a clothing giant very soon, but for now, he's heading his troupe to the bar.

'Should I go say hello?' I ask myself tipsily. Dressed in a floral shirt and trousers made out of a material that I can't place, he looks dapper; meanwhile, I am desperately hoping that my flannel shirt and denims combo can pass off as 'effortless chic'.

Over my countless retellings of this story at dinners and birthday parties, I'll never really know why I did what I did next. Maybe it's the spotlight or maybe it's the three shots of Jager that I've just downed, because before I know it, I am making a beeline straight for the bar.

'Hi!' I introduce myself. He turns around with a frown. This isn't a great beginning.

'Hi!' he beams, as he taps me on my shoulder, a full three years later in 2017.

Back in 2014, I am not one to give up easily.

'I saw you from across the bar, and I thought I should come over ...' my words hollow out, washed over by Charlie XCX's '*Boom Clap*'.

'... and introduce myself!' he grins, in 2017. I stare at him for a full minute, my face frozen in a smile. Is this a joke? Is he trying to play me?

'Are you ... serious?' I ask suspiciously. He doesn't bat an eyelid, and then it hits me. He doesn't remember. But how would he? My face is thinner and my clothes fitter. My acne's gone and so is my self-doubt. All my scars have healed, physical and otherwise. Even I wouldn't recognize myself.

Is my failed romantic pursuit getting a redux? And if it is, why is it happening now? As queer men, are we conditioned to put the more toned, ripped men at the top of the pedestal, at the height of the LGBTQIA+ food chain?

We pump ourselves with protein supplements, count our meals by the calorie and choose our steps based on our fitness apps, while laughing at the ones who don't. Think of it this way: every time you do so, more and more men are pushed back into oversized cardigans and internet diets. More and more men are pushed into eating salad as actual meals.

Which is what I've been doing for the past three years. And here we are, our alternating timelines playing a quick game of exs and ohs. A cross here. A nought there. He's across here. I am not there.

'So,' we both say in unison, three years apart, our faces full of hope.

'Can I buy you a drink?' I ask him in early 2014.

'Can I buy you a drink?' he asks me in late 2017.

We both reply in the negative.

1.4 Fantastic Men and Where (Not) to Find Them

Yash and Raghav met in December 2015. It wasn't fate, it wasn't fortune. It was a cousin's birthday, and Yash had to force himself to go. In retrospect, it was a great idea. Somewhere over birthday cake and red solo cups of beer, they hit it off.

'Love is not something you find overnight. In fact, sometimes you don't even find it all. I guess we just got lucky,' Yash tells me. He runs his own wellness startup, and is only twenty-seven years old.

Yash is right. There are a great many places in this world where you can fall in love. The pub. The bookstore. Your friend's contact list. The standup show you've been meaning to attend. The supermarket. The airport. The beach. The pet adoption drive. The LGBTQIA+ fundraiser. Maybe, even the gym. No judgements here.

See, this list can go on, because the list of places where you can find your big romance is one bottomless pit. Multiple meet-cutes waiting to happen. But there's just one tiny problem.

Meet-cutes are a heteronormative concept. Sure, there are millions of us out there, and we are all hiding in plain sight. But the handsome lad you lock eyes halfway across the bar or bump into at the check-in line at the airport might end up being ... straight. Yeah, we have gaydar on our side, but that intuition is more of a gut feeling, it's not a superpower. Gay men don't mysteriously (or unfortunately) come attached with glow-in-the-dark bands or unicorn horns on their heads to set them apart; if they did, you wouldn't need this book.

So what do we do?

Well, we don't give up. The probability of finding love as a gay man out in the open might seem like a variable, yet what is love but the greatest variable of them all?

Remember that every location is a possibility. You can *literally* meet someone while you're checking this book out at the counter. But what if you chose to buy this book online? I'll give you another headstart.

Peruse this list of ten potential suggestions where the chances of you *accidentally*[2] bumping into your next love story feature across the probability scale:

1. Your friend's contact list

Chances of finding your big love: 8/10

Think about it. Your friend is the personal dating app that you need, but don't deserve – they've known you at your best, and they've seen each of your idiosyncrasies across the table, including that one

2 Only because gay men are not Pokemon, and there's no guarantee that you'll find them at designated places in the wild.

time that you were *actually* sprawled drunk across the table. Your friends know what ticks you and what turns you on. They know the personality traits that you value and the red flags you should avoid. They know you like your drinks mixed, your feelings, not so much. Your friend, thus, knows you better than any dating app ever will.

Yet, getting set up by a friend can be a disaster-in-the-making or a miracle-waiting-to-happen, depending on who you allow to be your matchmaker. The ideal matchmaker should be someone who holds you in high regard and knows of your (high) standards. The ideal matchmaker should also not try setting you up with another man because 1) you are the only two lone gay men they know or 2) they want to have some leverage on your social life

Otherwise, there's a chance you'll end up on a blind date with their never-mentioned-before 'buddy from school' who 'isn't on social media right now, but I can safely vouch that he was a great guy back in 2008. It's been more than a decade since I last saw him ...'

2. The gym
Chances of finding your big love: 4/10

The gym is a great place to ~~gawk at men~~ cruise for love, especially when it's packed with treadmill after treadmill of glistening muscle ... so it can be difficult to not let your mind stray, considering there's very little to look at apart from all the ~~available men~~ biceps, arms, pecs, triceps, or worse, men wearing tight vests (and tighter cycling shorts). But when more than three-quarters of your testosterone-charged mates are busy looking at their abdominal muscles, how can one look for love?

Sure, you might find a helpful hottie who gives you tips on everything from the best way to eat raw eggs to effectively holding a plank for longer than forty seconds, but there's a catch. Yes, Mr Gym Freak™ (read full entry below) just offered to split his protein shake with you after your workout, but he'd rather be splitting your legs in the showers instead. The only way you can spot your next big love at the gym is by spotting his reps in the free weights section.

And he'll probably tell you that you are doing it all wrong.

3. Volunteering

Chances of finding your big love: 8/10

Volunteering can be amazing. For starters, you are giving back to society and are also teaming up with other like-minded individuals, who, like you, are clearly the nicest people that make up a mere 2 per cent of the world. If this doesn't find you a good man, what will?

But don't just stop there.

Take up a cause that actually matters to you. Teach underprivileged kids. Help out at LGBTQIA+ NGO. Sign up for a queer-led pet adoption service. Join a gay beach cleaning drive.

Maybe as you clean up the shorelines of your city, you can clean up the mess your life is at that moment by meeting a much-needed positive influence on your life. How about giving a chance to the wavy-haired gentleman with the deep tan and deeper dimples who's picking up the plastic bags?

Sign me up, please.

4. Your gourmet supermarket

Chances of finding your big love: 3/10

Meet-cutes are a myth, but how can you *not* get your hopes up about meeting someone at your gourmet supermarket? A store that stocks up on organic diet food, protein supplements, exotic produce and off-the-counter alcohol, all within a few aisles of each other? It might as well be the stereotypical gay man's natural habitat.

Picture this. You are stocking up on your supply of chicken breasts (free range) for the week when you make eye contact with a tanktop-wearing hottie by the spices section. He's picking up parsley and pudina, while you are busy thinking ways of picking him up.

You dart past the counter selling organic olive oil, rush through stacks of multigrain pasta and scuttle over to the refrigerated area to help yourself to a spice trail (and a view of his well-defined buttocks). A quick peek into his shopping basket (a trolley would suggest he stays with more people – parents, a wife, or worse, a boyfriend who teaches French and holidays in Ladakh) reveals the following items:

1. Organic quail eggs *(ooh, a hipster)*
2. Kale and spinach *(he's getting his fibre)*
3. Almond milk *(a vegan?)*
4. A six-pack of Gatorade *(we've got ourselves an athlete!)*
5. A prescription for anti-diarrheal pills

Eww. You'll pass. You slide away from the spice section, far away from your five-second crush and his (possibly) soiled jockstrap. Aside from the fact that you can't really fall in love with someone over his shopping list, what else does this teach you?

That it's probably not a good idea to follow someone down the aisles of your neighbourhood grocery store; the only thing you are going to swipe off at the checkout counter is a restraining order. Now, how about you go get those avocadoes that you came here for in the first place?

5. The Pride parade

Chances of finding your big love: 9/10

What is Pride but a rainbow parade of sincere men who are out of the closet (and more importantly, out on the streets to support queer rights)?

Pride's always been the perfect excuse to be proud of your LGBTQIA+ identity and keep the inhibitions at bay. You can lay your gaydar at rest, because mostly everyone who shows up is queer and here – which makes it the perfect mating ground for like-minded out-and-proud men. You don't have to rummage around the dregs of online dating, sifting through the same pool of shirtless men any more. Can you imagine the possibilities of not having your heart broken by yet another torso that asks you for 'a dick pic'?

Well, now you can. How about you go say hi to the cute boy waving the pride flag across the road instead? You no longer need to lie to people about meeting your future boyfriend at Starbucks – make the most of it, because this is your once-in-a-year opportunity.

Side note: Don't want to limit your chances of meeting a man to a one-time-only offer every year? Pride brings with it a host of queer-themed events: gay stand-up comedy, queer bazaars, LGBTQIA+ panels and much, much, more. Line up the Pride schedule with your calendar, and who knows, maybe you'll be lining up dates pretty soon too.

6. A gay party

Chances of finding your big love: 6/10

Your Saturday night soiree might seem like the ideal place to pick up some loving, but it's probably a good idea to pick up the cheque instead.

Think about it. This is the same place where you played tonsil hockey with the bartender. Dirty danced with the Spanish expat who never called back. Did seven shots at the bar before ultimately passing out on the manager's chair. Cried into a stranger's breast pocket over a bad break-up (before ultimately going back home with him). Looking for your future plus-one in the same place you vaguely recall puking the contents of your vodka-lined stomach can leave a bad taste in your mouth. But how do you pass the chance for a second lease on your (dating) life, when you are packed like testosterone-filled sardines in such a tight space (with men in even tighter clothes)?

Chances are the suburban Greek god you are locking eyes with at the bar has already locked eyes (and more) with half the crowd on the dance floor – and even though he might grind with you for two whole dance numbers (including a slow Beyoncé track), there's something you should know. Do you see that meandering line of men that you assumed was the queue for the men's washroom? That's actually a string of hopefuls just waiting for you to be done (and done with) so that they get their chance with Prince Charming-me-out-of-my-pants-already.

That is why it's better not to pick up men at a gay soiree; because there's a high chance you might be picking up their bar tab instead. Now down your martini along with your hopes of finding love here.

Let's just go back home.

7. The therapist

Chances of finding your big love: 2/10

You are here for your 4 p.m. appointment.

As you wait for your 4 p.m. appointment, flipping through trashy magazine after trashy magazine (Is Taimur Ali Khan not the real deal? Who is Ranbir Kapoor dating *now*? Kylie Jenner does something rich people do!), he walks in with a five o' clock stubble and piercing brown eyes that have dark stories to tell.

Your eyes light up (for the first time in weeks), and you contemplate shifting seats to have a better look at him (and his inner demons). There's an empty seat right next to him – maybe he can help fill all the emptiness inside you? Why not heal your heart while you heal yourself?

But remember, boys, you came here to solve your problems, not create new ones. Unless you want the premise of your love story to be the poignant tale of how you mixed up your antidepressants with his, most stories that begin at the therapist's office don't have a happy ending. You should probably give him a hard pass; otherwise, you are just going to spend more hours (and more of your hard-earned cash) on another therapist's couch, wondering where it all went wrong.

8. Your commute to work
Chances of finding your big love: 7/10

Remember how they say that the journey is more important than the destination?

For most of us, commuting to work can be quite boring – travelling from point A to B can sometimes take several hours, which is time that you'd rather spend lifting weights at the gym or chugging shots at the bar. So what do we do with all those hours that would otherwise go waste?

It's time to leave your car at home and cross over to the public transport lane. Men have been ~~cruising for hookups~~ finding mates on their preferred mode of public transport for *decades* now, flagging each other down with newspapers, strategically placed handkerchiefs and body language. Yes, it was a huge risk ('what if he turns out to be straight?'), but it was a risk they were willing to take.

Thankfully, we have it a lot better than our (gay) ancestors ever did. You don't need to rely on our gaydar any more; we have Grindr (and other dating apps) for that. One quick scan of your neighbourhood, and your commute route lights up like a GPS tracker of gay-identifying men.

And they are all looking for others like them.

So, the next time you take the train, metro or UberPool to work, look up from your phones. You just might spot your next date. Hold on to the railings and let your body do the talking. You'll be taking the last train back (to his arms) in no time.

PS: Think about all the fuel (and money) you'll save taking public transport: that's where your gym membership and shots at the bar come from.

9. Your toxic ex's arms

Chances of finding your big love: 0/10

Stop.

Don't do it.

Trying to find love back in the arms of the (mostly toxic) ex is like trying to find a clean restroom on the highway: there's a very, very low chance you'll be happy with what you find, and a very, very high chance you'll end up feeling dirtier after.

You might find yourself at his doorstep with a bottle of his favourite gin as a peace offering, but don't forget that the last time this happened, you were the one who needed the tonic to calm your nerves. See, there's no magical end to this story wherein after fifteen break-up-to-make-ups and twice the number of fights, you go over to his apartment (in the rain, of course) and suddenly have a movie-worthy reuniting moment in his living room where you apologize to each other for all your mistakes and lick tears off each other's faces. No. You're just going to break up again. The only reason we like going back to an ex is that it feels familiar and easy.

But this is ultimately unfulfilling, and if it didn't work the first ten times, it won't work out now. That's why you are here. That's why you are reading this book at this very moment.

This leaves us with the last (but not the least) route to find romance …

10. Online

Chances of finding your big love: Infinite.

… Turn the page, reader. You've earned the final key.

1.5 So Wait … What About Dating Apps?
A.k.a is Online Dating the Masked Murderer of Modern Love?

In the long list of man-made techniques to find true love, online dating possibly has the worst reputation, a close second to that nagging aunt who wants to set you up with her neighbour's (very straight) daughter because she thinks you are a waste in the matrimonial grapevine.

Online dating is … desperate, you'd say: 'If I wanted to meet a stranger, I'd take chances with my nagging aunt, thank you very much.' But you are … queer, and your nagging aunt (probably) doesn't know any other gay men.

Here's the thing about dating. In an ideal world, you'd want to meet the love of your life as you lock eyes over a new art exhibit at the museum, but let's be honest, when was the last time you went to the museum? In fact, when was the last time you went out at all?

That's why we have the internet.

So that we don't have to go out.

Technology lets you find love with one click, but also get rid of him with another. It makes finding love simpler. Hence, you have to do whatever it takes to stay in the game, and yes, that includes giving online dating a chance. Take Urvaksh, for example.

Urvaksh, a thirty-something banker loves plaid, almond milk lattes and artisanal beer. Like most gay men I know, Urvaksh is on the lookout for slide-me-off-my-feet love.

But as is with most gay men, Urvaksh is also 'hopelessly' single. It's a status that stings more on weekends – suddenly, Netflix feels lonely and bar deals (two for the price of one) seem too taxing.

Some people call that 'self-improvement'; Urvaksh calls it 'self-actualization'. He takes 'finding love' very seriously – a trait that's equally heartbreaking and heartwarming in gay men across the country.

To further his quest, Urvaksh goes on a new date every week (while sleeping with thrice the number of people at the same time) and falls in love every fortnight. It's a tough life, but he survives (and so does his company-provided credit card). He pulls no stops when it comes to finding his soulmate either. Urvaksh has memberships with Grindr Xtra, Scruff Pro and Tinder Plus. That's a lot of money (and effort) to make sure he finds his Mr Right.

So can Mr Right get here *right now*?

Technically, he should. That's three times the boys (on Tinder), an infinite supply of blocks (on Grindr) and billboard-style exposure (obviously, on Scruff). This way, an unlimited crew of underwear models, upcoming fashion photographers, Type A consultants and highflying entrepreneurs can spot him before anyone else does. The stats are definitely on his side ... but the stars?

Not so much.

'It's *just* not working out,' Urvaksh tells me over a drink at a gay shindig in January. He's swiped right on all the cute boys on Tinder, favourited the nicest profiles on Grindr, woofed appropriately at hirsute men on Scruff and even looked around more than once on Happn (although he wasn't very happy).

'Why is it so hard to find someone who wants the same things you do?' he asks me, but doesn't give me time to respond.

Urvaksh doesn't have all the answers in life. He might not know what he's looking for in a man at the moment ('finding someone I can have a *real* conversation with would be nice'), but he knows exactly what he'*s not* looking for: men who don't take him seriously online.

The real question is: Does Urvaksh take himself seriously online?

'Why are all the nice boys not online (read: available)?' He blows smoke in my face. I'd offer words of support, but it's tough to empathize with someone (read: Urvaksh) who ends his Grindr bio with a conditional 'only 9"+ cocks apply'. It's only a domino effect of disappointment from there on.

But now is not the time for unsolicited advice. Instead, what I do tell him is that all the nice boys *are* online; they are just complaining about the fact that there are 'no nice boys online'.

'I think I should just go off the grid for a bit; I thought it would be easier,' Urvaksh reassures himself, and I wonder why I am even a part of this conversation.

The internet's biggest lie is the one that says dating apps make romance conveniently fast and easy. They make it sound like fast food: deliciously satisfying, but really, really bad for your health.

But here's the deal. Anyone who says that finding love on dating apps is easy has never spent hours trying to figure out what it means when a man sends you an ill-timed pig-face emoji. Is he feeling sloppy, or greedy, or kinky or does he just have an unhealthy obsession with bacon? It's a mindboggling maze of deciphering smiley faces.

And that myth about it being fast?

As someone who has spent *years* chatting up multiple mates in the search for a soulmate, let me tell you that online dating can seem like a continuous loop of regrets and rebuttals. Fuckboys, douchebags and dimwits aren't custom-made at a secret Grindr factory; they've been around forever.

Technology has been bearing the brunt for being the cause of most of our world's problems: the television stands with its head down in shame for its contribution to the rise in gun violence, the microwave regrets its hand in obesity, and the air-conditioner might as well have been the single reason for global warming.

'I wish I could meet someone the old fashioned way,' Urvaksh sighs, but he misses the gaping plot hole here. What exactly is the old fashioned way?

Being awkwardly set up by friends at a house party just so they don't have to listen to your scrambling single survival stories over scrambled eggs at brunch? Strangers meeting as they stumble out of a bar together to eventually stumble into seventeen-odd months of regret, slurred voicemails and alcohol-induced altercations? Bumping into someone while waiting in line at a coffee shop just to realize that they like their coffee with *milk* and *five* cubes of sugar?

Let me tell you something. We don't have safe spaces when it comes to finding love. Actually, we don't have safe spaces at all. If you think your next big love isn't hidden behind a grid of online dating profiles, there's a very big chance he's not waiting for you in your rom-com meet-cute. He's not waiting at the museum. He's not waiting at the airport. Conventional ways of finding love are dying out and for good reason: we just don't have the time.

Contrary to what we will tell you, gay men are obsessed with the idea of finding a sense of normalcy. Which means that gay men are obsessed with the idea of finding companionship.

Enter, online dating.

You know how they say when one door shuts, another one opens? Online dating is a revolving door of opportunities: Page after page, profile after profile, and thumbnail after thumbnail of men who are all looking for the same thing in life.

Mates and dates.

Sure, trying to find romance online can seem exasperating, but it is helping us reach out to people like never before. Plus, remember that a relationship built on a dating app is no less real than the one forged over mixed-up orders at your neighbourhood coffee shop.

It's an uphill journey of introspection. You just need to know where to find it, and who to find it with.

But more on that in the next chapter.

Number Five: The Investment Banker
Where Do Good Men Go When They Are Done?

June 2013

'Should I call for some more wine?'

There you go. Golden words to hear on a first date. It takes me only one dinner with **Five** to realize that the doctor-turned-banker is a catch. He laughs at all my jokes, is really attractive and his chest – straining beneath his shirt – looks like it's itching to be traced over. Plus, he paints oil pastels in his free time.

How can this ever go wrong?

Five is comfortably rich, goes on an exotic holiday every two months and his family lives in a city that is far away yet close enough. The only catch – he doesn't seem to want me as much as I want him.

There it is.

'I want to find someone I can fall in love with …' he sighs over steaks and sangria. I sit up in my chair. Most gay men will search high and low, but never fully realize what they want in (and from) their lives. Even if it's sitting right in front of them.

Maybe we could share a joint account. Maybe we could go on exotic vacations together. Maybe we could visit his family on weekends in the city that is far away yet close enough.

'Do you know anybody you can set me up with?' he asks. I stifle a cough, smile and tell him that I'll think about it.

Our steaks are done, and so are we. I grab the wine bottle to go.

1.6 The Gentleman's Guide to Every Gym Freak in the World: A Bonus Feature

Tushar, thirty-seven, is an architect who loves two things very dearly: design and the gym.

Tushar likes to believe that he's a self-aware, self-loving gay man. But like most self-aware, self-loving gay men I know, Tushar cares a little too much about how he looks. In fact, at the latest Secret Santa at his firm, all his colleagues chipped in and got him a full-length cheval standing mirror as a gift.

He says it's his most prized possession. Tushar is an out-and-proud Gym Freak.

What's a Gym Freak?

When every fourth guy on Grindr looks like he has stepped out of an underwear catalogue, you know you might have a problem. It's no surprise that we've been trained to come out of the closet and go straight to the gym, but now we are doing so on our yoga mats.

It's simple – if there's one thing you need as a gay man today, it's a body. You might want to think differently, but eight out of ten times, you are not going to get a great deal of interest from another gay man just because you *look* like you listen to Mozart and devour literary classics for breakfast. Sadly, muscles are in and they are *never* going to go out of style.

Now, most gay men like to remove their flimsy cotton V-necks at a moment's notice, showcasing their kilometre-wide chests and xylophone abs as if they were starring in an Indian remake of *Magic Mike*. They make other men gulp and vow to start going to the gym from the following Monday.

Enter, the **Gym Freak**.

How Do You Find a Gym Freak?

How do you sort the gym rats from those that scour the food court at the mall? Here's how you spot one, when he's not asking you to spot him as he weight-trains at the gym:

- The Gym Freak hates it when people call him a gym freak, or worse, a gym rat (he'll kill you if you dare call him a Muscle Mary). He prefers the term 'fitness enthusiast'. He has a vest with the same emblazoned on it.
- He has eye-popping biceps, billboard-worthy pecs, a tray of abs that can balance half a dozen eggs, and broad shoulders that are the shape of a cosy armchair. You can even sit on him, but only when he's doing a plank.
- He says he does not have a 'type', but will proudly put up #Masc4Masc on his Grindr profile.
- He follows it with a succinct 'no fats, no femmes' in his bio.
- And a photo of his glistening abs (more than six, less than eight) as his picture.
- He has a day for triceps. It's on Thursday.
- He dresses up sexily for the gym.

- The only time he cheated was when he cheated on his diet plan with a double-cheese hamburger five Sundays ago. He's still not forgiven himself.
- He doesn't need an alarm clock. He *is* the alarm clock.
- The Gym Freak counts his calories every day. He allows himself 500 calories for breakfast, 400 for lunch and a mere 300 for dinner.
- His protein shake accounts for 500 calories every serving.
- His gym face is his orgasm face.
- He spends two hours hitting the gym every day, and another two hours thinking about it.
- He hates it when people typecast gay men as gym-obsessed fitness freaks. He'll tell you *all* about it as you help him count his reps at the free weight section.
- He religiously records his home workouts for his Instagram audience. He watches them in his free time. While on the treadmill. On his way to work. At dinner. Just before he falls asleep. While jerking off. In the loo. At his best friend's wedding.
- He hates going on long vacations, because it breaks his strict regimen.
- But when he does, he looks for a hotel with a 24/7 gym and a heated indoor pool. He gets excited if they have a massage room.
- On more than one occasion, he's thanked the gods for great genes and grilled chicken. But he still goes on a juice cleanse twice every month.
- He takes a #TransformationTuesday picture every week. And every day of the week.
- He'll use any chance he gets to go shirtless. At the beach. In the sauna. By the swimming pool. On a run. When he's reading at home. While going grocery shopping.
- He'll tell you that your vodka-and-soda has eighty-five calories as you order it, while you are out on a date with him.
- He knows because he looked it up online.

- He'll then call for a Caesar salad with extra chicken. He'll tell the waiter to hold the croutons and the vinaigrette dressing.
- He has an app that reminds him to drink water every hour. He has an app that reminds him that he has to run every other day. He has an app that reminds him he's overshot his calorie intake for the day. He wishes he had an app that would tell him where he can find someone to go to the gym with.
- He will tell you that chocolate-chip protein shake tastes like chocolate-chip ice cream, but he knows that he's lying to you.
- He knows the *exact* benefits of whey protein.
- One night, over wheat crackers and low-fat cheese, he'll cry to his friends about how all the gay boys only love him for his body.
- But he'll forget to mention that his Grindr profile picture is an aesthetically pleasing shot of his chiselled torso.
- It also mentions that he's looking for 'gym-fit muscular men only'.
- He'll touch beer only if it's gluten free.
- He gets serious separation anxiety if he skips the gym one day. He skips dinner the same night.
- He hates flirting with other men at the gym, because how would he train otherwise?
- He uses the hashtag #NoPainNoGain, but he doesn't use it ironically.
- When he pictures his future with any potential plus-one, he pictures the two of them breaking into a sweat (both in and out of bed) and grabbing a protein smoothie afterwards. They exchange rings at the beach, after which they run off (literally) into the sunset.
- The Gym Freak is never going to be happy with the way he looks. He'll always have something to complain about. Too much fat. Too little muscle. Too much cardio. Too little sweat. He'll go to the gym the very next day and work on the part of his body that bothers him, even though he knows that spot reduction doesn't work.

Number Six: The Fashion Manager
We Found Platonic Love in a Hopeless Place?

October 2011

Grindr's geo-location tag says that **Six** stays three streets away. For gay men, that's the equivalent of being next-door neighbours. 'Three streets?' one might say. 'Think of that as three hundred and sixty-two metres to someone who could possibly be the next love of your life.' Any closer, and he could practically duck-walk his way home in thirty minutes or less. There's a pizza commercial in there somewhere. His name flashes on my phone.

'What are you doing now?'

Is that a question? Does it have an answer?

Staring into space. Thinking about free pizza. Pretending to work. Reading a book. Reciting Michael Faudet's poems. Saving the world. I see limitless possibilities for my reply, each an exciting beginning to a story.

'Nothing', I reply. Short and subtle. I like my love stories that way.

'Want to meet now? I am passing by,' my phone tweets. How does he know where I stay? How can he just assume I'd be free to meet at such short notice? Do I even want to meet a stranger? Am I ready to go make a first impression at such short notice? Where are my pants when I need them? These are questions I *don't* ask myself. Why not?

There's a certain adrenaline rush in meeting a complete stranger at 11 p.m. on a Tuesday night. Ask any gay man you know, he'll confirm. I pull on my pants and run down the stairs, two at a time.

He's already waiting, earning himself a swift brownie point. **Six** looks like James Franco (that's another brownie point), with eyes that sparkle (one more) and a gorgeous set of dimples (does this ever stop?). I wouldn't mind paying for the hypothetical pizza (that we'll eventually end up splitting) if he keeps piling me with these brownies. 'Did I keep you waiting?' I ask. He shrugs, and we walk into the night.

Six is the floor manager at a high-end fashion label – the first of many fashion stints he'll take up in the years to come. Waiting is second nature for him. He deals with society WAGs, expats and A-listers over slices of toast (whole wheat) and scrambled eggs (far-free), and every single time he has a client meeting, they are all *always* fifteen minutes away. Doesn't all that waiting get exhausting?

The job comes with perks – party invitations, supermodel friends and the occasional bottle of single-malt whisky. The parties and the models can be draining, but the single malt never is. How does he manage it all?

He leans closer. I can smell a wash of something remarkably expensive. 'The whisky helps.'

We both laugh. I suddenly understand where he gets his confidence and the undeniable charm. It's infectious.

'I make it sound like a lot more hard work than it actually is.' He smiles yet again. He smiles a lot. 'Why don't you tell me something about yourself?'

Where do I even begin?

'I have an idea. Do you want to play never-have-I-ever?' His dimples cut deeper than a Bukowski poem.

'But we don't have alcohol ...'

'Who needs alcohol? Do you want a smoke?' He offers me one. I accept, and he lights it. 'Have you never smoked a cigarette before?' He laughs as I stumble through mine. How can someone smile so much?

The boy smiles with his eyes. They twinkle in the moonless light, creating constellations in my mind. I realize he's someone who should smile more often, if not always. I let him begin.

Never have I ever stolen money from home? We both take puffs and giggle. Never have I ever cheated in an exam? Puff and puff.

Never have I kissed two boys on the same night? Slept with someone on the first date? Smoked pot at home? Fallen in and out of love with someone in a week? Hated a friend's boyfriend? Loved someone else's? Been in love with two people at once?

We tell each other ribald stories through cigarette fumes, letting a hundred skeletons loose from our closets with every puff of smoke. This puff is an ex-boyfriend I cheated on, that sliver there is his father who abandoned his family, this little wisp is the nine shots of tequila I downed (and regretted) at a friend's farewell, the one over there is a close friend he cheated with. Our cigarettes ash away, our stories don't. Nothing brings people together like a great story.

There's a possibility that I might fall for **Six** if I see him again; he's a kindred spirit, this one. I am already dreaming about getting matching towels (and a pet) as I ask him about his plans for the weekend. I don't want to sound too eager. 'Do you want to hang out this Saturday night? Only if you don't have any plans …'

How obvious is *too* obvious? I think it's evident, because he off-handedly tells me that he has a boyfriend in Delhi and that they've (unfortunately) scheduled a virtual date for then. **Six** shows me a quick photo of the two of them from a recent holiday. The boyfriend looks like Timothee Chalamet. In fact, they look like they could be brothers. There is no justice in this world.

'Did you not know?'

Time to throw the hypothetical towels away and give the pet up for adoption. I laugh derisively – the way I usually do when I am lying – and tell him that I'd rather have him as a friend. He smiles at me when I say that. I feel so far from him when he smiles like that. Like someone is taking a picture of him. I smile back. Our friendship has been sealed. My work here is done.

Eventually, I'll find out that not every gay man you meet has to be another notch on your belt. Some will find their way into your lives without finding a way into your bed.

But for now, the night is complete.

2

Online Dating 101: Finding You 2.0

2.1 The Dummy's Guide to the Ten Best Dating Apps There Are

How did gay men meet before smartphones?

If you want the gist, you probably missed the introductory class to Queer Culture 101. TLDR: Up until early 2000s, finding a mate for gay men was as difficult as finding a vegan-friendly birthday cake. And then along came the dating app, and it changed everything. Men moved their dalliances from seedy internet cafes to the safe confines of their smartphones. It was a revolution. Gay men had finally found their match, no right swipes necessary.

Now, a decade later, the stigma attached to online dating is disappearing faster than Rakhi Sawant's relevance. Technology has allowed us to finally come together and spread our glorious wings (and sometimes, even our legs) wide. If you can order a cab through your phone, why can't you find a man?

The gay dating app is thus every homosexual man's paradise: a one-way ticket to companionship, without the hassles of getting your friends or family involved (and unlike the latter, the dating app does not discriminate). But can you really enter the big, bad arena of online dating if you don't know your weapons of choice?

While there might be multiple apps that let you find your potential soulmate based on your picks and preferences (and sometimes, even fetishes), here are the ones that work best.

1. Grindr

What it is: Grindr, in its unfiltered GPS-based glory, is the It-Girl of online dating. Here, you can find every type of man represented within its 3x33 grid. Dom tops looking for kinky, pig bottoms; circuit queens seeking party favours at the club; PnP gays desperate for invite-only orgies; otters sniffing around for silver foxes; nubile twinks in search of sugar daddies ... the entire spectrum of gay culture. Astonishingly accurate and (equally) anonymous, Grindr isn't *just* an example when it comes to the dating app; it's the benchmark.

How it works: With Grindr, your facts and figures are presented like a protein bar's nutritional values; men are measured in dick pics and distances. We can't deny that Grindr demands supreme self-confidence. Here, torso after torso does the tango before your tired eyes, and charisma is squeezed into a short bio, 255 characters or less. If a guy doesn't have the necessary profile information, it means one of two things – there's probably nothing worth seeing or your subject is shy.

Urvaksh chanced upon Dylan's profile, the (latest) man of his dreams, just three months ago. Dylan was an investment banker, with a plush two-bedroomed sea-facing apartment in downtown Bombay and a face that could have been on a billboard. He was gorgeous, had dimples that were deeper than the Mariana trench and cheekbones so high they could be on meth. Rightly said, Dylan was thirty going on sixteen and everything a guy could ever want to be with (or be). They sent each other flames and devils and whatnots, texting continuously through the weekend.

There was only one *tiny* problem.

Dylan was five feet tall – a detail they had both overlooked. The banker forgot to mention it on his profile; Urvaksh forgot to ask. He never saw him again, and his digits were lost forever in Urvaksh's sea of deleted phone numbers, along with all thoughts of moving into his picturesque bachelor pad.

What we like about it: Finding instant gratification is as easy as making instant noodles.

What we don't like about it: Finding instant gratification is as easy as making instant noodles.

If you like Grindr, you'd also like: Hornet

Conventionally speaking, Hornet is an upgraded version of Grindr. Upgraded, only because the app isn't bound by Cartesian limits like its predecessor is. Hornet lets you match with anyone across the world, giving it a leg up over all its coordinate-bound competition. Gush over Hollywood with Ryan from Los Angeles, parley over pisco sours with Anthony from Peru, serenade Haruto from Japan with your mild obsession with sushi, or ramble over world politics with Vladimir from Russia – you don't need any flight tickets to get flirty on Hornet. Only visa on arrival.

Hornet also lets you 'follow' other users, search for men using hashtags and have multiple pictures up on your profile. Does that make it the 'Instagram' of the gay dating world?

Perhaps, but you don't need any filters here.

2. Scruff

What it is: Like Grindr, Scruff is a grid of available, attractive gay men with pictures in various stages of undress. It's infested with bears, otters, wolves and cubs. Is this an app or a zoo?

It's a mating ground, but more on that later. Scruff follows Grindr's tried-and-tested formula: scroll through a near-endless grid of thumb-sized profiles of men with not-so-thumb-sized dicks. Scruff's all-black, faux tough guy motif might not be all that memorable, but it comes with its own set of redeeming qualities – namely, a narrowed-down user base with millions of guys on the hairier side. And they are all looking for the same thing.

You.

How it works: While Scruff might not have the same critical mass of users as Grindr does (or the cultural clout), it comes with a purpose – letting scruffy men find their hairier halves. You 'woof' at people you like, leaving them little red notifications of love that they can sniff back to your account. However, Scruff's standard layout allows four profiles in a row (as opposed to Grindr's three) – so a guy who looks cute in a tiny thumbnail picture might not look the same blown up. After all, you don't want your thumbnail Rahul Khanna to look like Rahul Mahajan when you zoom in.

It allows you to search for like-minded men in other cities (and offer Airbnb-style travel accommodation for the same), making it ideal for that vacation fling that is hairier and smarter than your average bear. Why should (finding) love be marred by location settings?

One fine night, Kartik's phone screen lights up with a message from one such hirsute hottie. It's a thirty-two-year-old man from 1,200 miles away. He calls himself 'Entreflaneur'. His interests include art, design, film, aimless wandering and compulsive list-making. His photos include well-defined pecs.

Kartik sends out a woof before he can even open the message.

'Can I see how hairy you are?' asks the Amazonian demi-god, unlocking his (highly NSFW) private album on cue; here, each picture is an advanced biology lesson.

Kartik blinks at his phone. Is that the new 'Hello! Nice to meet you?'

'I don't have any shirtless pictures,' he pings back. The woof he sent two minutes ago has probably strangled itself in embarrassment. The UAE-based entrepreneur never texts back, leaving my friend to aimlessly wander by himself.

What we like about it: Are you a self-proclaimed pogonophile? Scruff takes the basic dating experience and tailors it for men of the older (and hairier) persuasion.

What we like about it: Scruff's exclusive match feature only seems to pair people based on what they're looking for – dates, relationships, fun – not deeper criteria, such as common interests or your views on Donald Trump's latest shenanigans.

If you like Scruff, you'd also like: Growlr

If you are looking to connect with men who have some hair on their chest and dirt in their nails, Growlr is perfect, because it's *exactly* like Scruff. Only, the former lets you send sweet nothings as voice notes to your (multiple) lovers. Don't get fooled by its cute teddy-bear logo, readers. This app is strictly not for kids.

Unless you are a bear cub.

3. Tinder

What it is: When an app uses a tagline that suggests that you 'start something epic', you need to know they take online dating very seriously.

Tinder isn't here to help you find a hookup; it's here to help you find a match. In fact, it's here to find you multiple matches. Like the nagging aunt, it shows you picture after picture of suitable men (and if you prefer, women), hoping that you find the One. Unlike the nagging aunt, Tinder also has a strict no-judgement policy when it comes to ~~matchmaking~~ online dating. It's currently open to people who identify with any of the twenty-three listed gender selections.

That's a definite pot of gold (star) at the end of this rainbow.

How it works: Tinder's mechanisms are easy to follow. You can swipe right to 'Like', turn left to 'Oh I don't think so'. Tinder is a clearance sale of Facebook profile pictures. You collect the ones you love and ignore the ones you don't. But then, the pile keeps on growing, and you don't know what to do. Tinder is smart, because it nudges you to start a conversation with strategically timed push notifications. It *wants* you to sift through your stockpile of profiles.

It wants you to make a match.

Not if you are Urvaksh.

Last month, the corporate banker came across Rajeev. Like Dylan from Grindr, Rajeev was handsome and ran his own startup, but unlike Dylan from Grindr, Rajeev's profile said that he was 6' 3", the right height for the kind of man Urvaksh was looking for. Was he the light at the end of the tunnel of douchebags and dimwits?

More importantly, could their mutual love for Rihanna, Banksy and 'Humans Of New York' account for total compatibility in the romance department? Probably not, but maybe Tinder could help them meet halfway.

Urvaksh super-liked and waited.

And waited. And waited. He waited for all of twenty-three days, seven hours and forty-two minutes. Rajeev never matched back. Obsessing over a text message is a little crazy, but when you're in an online relationship, that's really all you have. Are you allowed to feel heartbroken if you've never met someone in person?

Maybe for a little while.

Because there's always going to be more right swipes (and guys).

What we like about it: Unlike most gay dating apps, Tinder doesn't allow immediate, unfiltered communication. There's no space for sexts, dicks pics, or terrible introductions that go, 'I see that you are fifty metres away, wanna hook up?'

Chat (and ultimately cuddle) with only people you match with.

Although there's no guarantee a man won't turn out to be a douchebag after fifty texts full of witty prose.

What we don't like about it: Tinder's unfiltered communication is also a double-edged sword. Without the added stimuli of pictures (to send) and location pins (to drop), most conversations follow a textbook template and/or are doomed to die an early death, fizzling out faster than an opened Coca-Cola bottle.

Bonus feature: Remember how scores of gay men complain about the constant fear of being catfished on a dating app? Imagine spending hours talking to someone whose profile pictures look like they are straight out of GQ magazine, only to realize they've probably *been* copy-pasted *from* GQ magazine.

With its new profile verification feature, Tinder lets you sort out the cool cats from the catfishes. Now if it only had a feature to sort people out according to their douchiness.

If you like Tinder, you'd also like: OkCupid

Are you someone who makes all of their important life decisions based on personality tests – including (but not limited to) what your favourite kind of bread says about your dating life?

OkCupid is to dating what BuzzFeed is to ~~deep-scrolling on the internet~~ personality quizzes. The (often updated) app's compatibility feature is a combination of non-traditional questions and maths – the algorithm pairing people based on common interests, goals, ideas and opinions, instead of pairing them based on their preferences in bed. The interface is colourful and easy to use, but that doesn't mean you should let your four-year-old nephew use it. While this Disney-style method of matchmaking is important, there's one major loophole: people lie on their compatibility tests just like they do on their resumes.

So, the chances that the attractive architect who told you he believes in monogamous relationships and veganism is actually lying? As high as a groupie at an EDM concert after-party.

Like all the men I've ever dated (or mated with), OkCupid is extremely promising. Its interface is also equally attractive. An app that understands that the future is fluid? Hell yes. A portal that understands that 'dating deserves better' and makes it its core proposition? Here are my credit card details. A dating platform that (only) lets you talk to people who share the same interests (and quirks) as you? I'm looking for my chequebook right now. But the icing on the cake – a safe space to be (and love) queer. Inclusivity has never been so alluring.

SIGN ME UP ALREADY! But like all the boys I've loved, OkCupid has one *crucial* con –

It can get taxing. Sure, the questions are ridiculously liberal and fun, but for a world that believes in instant gratification, it can seem like a lot of effort, because by the time I've found my first (potential) match on OkCupid, I've already lined up three dates on Tinder.

And they are all 'seem to want the same things in life that I do'.

4. Hinge

What it is: Remember the nineties – when internet trolls, post-millennials and online dating didn't exist – the good old days when people would set each other up with their friends and ultimately get blamed for heartbreak (or worse, herpes)?

Well, there's an app for that now. Hinge calls itself the 'relationship app', and it leaves no stones unturned while trying to set you up with your soulmate.

How it works: Hinge pools all the singles in your extended friend circles (using Facebook as its underlying base) and pairs you with the most suitable of them, based on a series of questions and common interests, which you have to 'like' to initiate an interaction. This reduces your chances of running into a hopeless string of men who are just looking for no-strings-attached sex. Hinge believes that swiping keeps you single and instead focuses on creating more engaging profiles that reduce users from treating other men like 'a playing card they'd flick to the left or right'.

Instead, it'll ask you a set of questions, prod you for your interests and even bug you till you upload a picture. Some call it cute; others call it 'too much work to get into someone's pants'. I call it a great idea.

Do you both love dogs? Lovely.

Is your idea of the perfect date a walk on the beach? Bring it on.

Does hiking on a Sunday morning seem viable to you too? Let's get the wedding rings ready.

On paper, Hinge is like the Facebook of online dating. Profiles are peppered with gorgeous pictures, tongue-in-cheek answers, and captions that are so witty they could star in an AIB video. Too bad you can't send someone a friend request.

What we like about it: Unlike traditional dating apps, Hinge sets you up with people in your social circle – making sure that you have common interests (or friends) that you can talk about over a quick beer (or five, if the friend in question is interesting).

Also, it offers great prompts (read: icebreakers) for adding personality to your profile, making our low-pressure dating app a lot like that always-eager-to-set-you-up buddy you wished you had. In fact, the more you use Hinge, the better it gets to know you. It's like your best friend sans the unsolicited advice – finding you matches based on people you've previously matched with before. Goodbye catfish. Goodbye internet creeps. Goodbye boys who slide into your DMs with unsolicited dick pics.

What we don't like about it: Since all your matches are pulled from your friend's Facebook accounts (while obviously avoiding awkward ex and family ties), any match you encounter will already have someone in common with you – which can either be a great conversation starter or a deal-breaker, especially when the mutual is an estranged friend you don't talk to any more, or worse, your date is a man you can't wait to get rid of.

If you like Hinge, you'd also like: Jack'd

Jack'd is tailored specifically for people of colour.[3] When you are already in a minority group, finding someone with interests or expectations that match your own can be difficult. Sometimes, it feels like all the apps out there cater to only one type of man – the straight-acting, fit-bodied metrosexual.

Jack'd appears to have the most diverse community of users, broken down into what they refer to as 'scenes' – twinks, bears, big muscles, strictly friends, LTR (long-term relationships) and straight/bicurious. By choosing which scene you identify with, you make it easier for other people who are attracted to your ~~tribe~~ type to find you.

No more disappointments. No more douchebags who don't text back.

But most importantly, no more #Masc4Masc bros.

5. Planet Romeo

What it is: A German-based networking portal for LGBTQIA+ singles who are 'looking to mingle', Planet Romeo can rightly be called the deeper end of the online dating pool. Keep your flippers (and your condoms) ready.

---

3 Which means it's only used by expats and tourists in India.

How it works: Romeo is an online directory of men to sleep with – page after page of profiles of horny available men, looking for everything ranging from 'now' to 'why *not* now?'

As a user, you feel an odd adrenaline rush every time you log in: the 'ta-da-ding' message alert syncs with your heartbeat (or your libido) and urges you to open the app every thirty minutes (which you will). It's the Yahoo chat room of the new millennium. The rules are simple: send someone a 'footprint' (great butt, hot cock, handsome face), and leave them as souvenirs for the men you want to *keep* as souvenirs in your little black book. Once thoughts (and sexual preferences) match, people exchange numbers and, eventually, bodily fluids.

What we like about it: Flapping dicks (pics) aside, Planet Romeo really is very nonchalant about what it wants to do. In so many ways, it's like your cool aunt who knows about your sexual history and makes sure she buys you a pack of condoms before you step out for your hot date. Planet Romeo's info zone (called Ask Mother) shares free and reliable information about STDs, emphasizing the importance of safe sex and condoms. Just like how mothers help nurture a baby, this section also offers relationship tips and advice for gay men to nurture their relationships. Unlike your mother, it prods you to use the app more often.

What we don't like about it: The app (and the desktop version) is cluttered with ads, pop-up windows and profiles of 'boys who'd rather pick your bodies than your brains', making it more confusing to navigate than your quarterly Zara sale.

If you like Planet Romeo, you'd also like: Blued

With over forty million users worldwide (now more, because they've partnered with Hornet), China-based Blued is the largest gay social network in the world, and with good reason. It's got a bit of everything.

Blued calls itself 'a social life in one simple app', which means they've borrowed features from every app ever made: verified profiles (Tinder), disappearing texts (Grindr), GIF reactions (Scruff), free voice calls (Bumble) … the list goes on, but wait, there's more.

Blued adds friend requests and posts, and trending topics (and men) that you can like or leave comments on. It puts the social back in social networking. Yet, it's not Blued's cheerful interface or social media UI/UX that makes it so popular. The app goes where no other app has gone before.

It lets you broadcast LIVE to your audiences.

And that could be anyone (or everyone) from its forty million users around the world.

Suddenly, sex is not just about having sex. It's also about this idea that you *can* have (virtual) sex, or that someone *wants* to have (virtual) sex with you. In this way, the thrill of a conversation on Blued can seem almost pornographic, a kind of dopamine high you can acquire without ever leaving your house. What if that doesn't work?

Create an OnlyFans account. It's not free.

6. Happn

What it is: Love can be found in the most unexpected places. If you are the smart, suave Jane Austen novel-inspired hero, you can find love as you rummage through old classics at the bookstore. You might lock eyes with your future soulmate as you buy yourself an old fashioned at the bar. You can even fall hopelessly head-over-heels with a fellow patient in your doctor's waiting room (just make sure it's not your therapist). The train station? Obviously. The supermarket? Maybe. The world is your oyster, and you are its king.

But what happens when you are shy and mild mannered, and have the self-confidence of a prepubescent teenage boy?

Happn is an app that lets you reconnect with all those missed connections. It's your boost of confidence. Your (slightly creepy) wingman. Your second chance. Your 'other door' when the first one slams shut in your face.

How it works: Happn picks up everyone within a 250-metre radius and presents them to you like an open buffet of opportunities. It's every stalker's dream come true. Which brings us to June 2017.

As he was halfway through a chicken sandwich, Kartik saw the man pull over at the signal. He was inconspicuously tall and conventionally good-looking. Kartik was metres away from staging a meet-cute. He looked at Kartik through his window just as the traffic lights switched from red to green, and my friend's face switched from green to red. Tossing his floppy black hair away from his eyes, the man smiled and drove by. Kartik felt his heart race along, but it couldn't keep up – he'd already zoomed away into oblivion. Was this a burning heart or heartburn? Kartik threw the last bits of the sandwich away, just in case.

This is where Happn comes in.

Open the app and watch as it loads up everyone you've potentially crossed paths with in your life. Recognize someone you might have seen pass by and want to show him that you are interested?

Just send him a heart on Happn and hope that he sends one back – the secret way of letting a match know that you like them, so they won't know you are interested in them unless they're interested in you too. If you want to be more persuasive, you can even send a 'charm', sliding your way into their DMs, or in this case their match lists, with the flair of a self-proclaimed dating coach.

But do remember, Happn has the same probability of connecting you to the hunky model you saw at the bar last night as it does of setting you up with the creepy neighbour from across the street – the one who's always looking at you through his plastic drapes. Stay cautious, stay safe.

What we like about it: On Happn, matches include the company and job title of each user, which makes it easy to do your research if a guy seems particularly dodgy (not that anyone's career choices are a measure of their shadiness).

What we don't like about it: The more people you pass during the day, the higher your chances are of meeting the love of your life – which means it also automatically increases your chances of being pestered by creeps, douchebags and potential serial killers that you might have passed by (without looking twice) on the road.

7. Bro

What it is: Men have always had it easy. Gay or straight, the laws of online dating have always been balanced. Gay men have Grindr. Straight men have Tinder. But what about all the men who are sitting on the fence?

Bro promises that it 'goes beyond using labels, and is for men that are interested in meeting other guys – it's as simple as that'. It's for men seeking friendships, men who want to date, men who want casual hookups – all without the baggage of old labels that result in questions by older relatives.

How it works: Straight, gay or bisexual, Bro is an all-accepting men's-only club. In fact, it advertises itself as the app that welcomes men who don't feel welcome in the gay community. But beneath the blue-and-white, hetero-friendly exterior, does it really offer anything that other dating apps don't?

There are fewer torsos and more happy faces of people doing happy things. There's always been a grey area between the boundaries of sex, relationships and friendship, and when an app asks you whether you are looking to find friendship, fun or 'whatever', Bro wins, hands down.

What we like about it: Sexuality is a continuum and not a binary, and Bro recognizes that. It's online dating without typecasting itself as online dating. Bro is for men who don't want to commit to silly things like labels.

What we don't like about it: ... but then again, it's also for men who don't want to commit to a relationship.

If you like Bro, you'd also like: Bumble

Bumble was first founded to challenge the old-fashioned rules of dating: by letting women make the first move, it puts them in the driver's seat when it comes to navigating the dating scape. So what happens when the gays take over?

A lot of confusion. Who makes the first move? Is there a first move? Do we stop and ask each other 'who's the man and who's the woman in the relationship'? Is the app sensitive to not stereotyping gay men? Is the app *even* for gay men?

I'm not really sure about any of those answers, because Bumble has bigger problems at hand. Kartik tells me he spent all of a week sifting through a carousel of (very pretty) women only to realize that he had to change his settings to get his preferences (and his sexual orientation) right.

And once you've got that out of the way, it's the interface that packs quite a sting. The app comes with not one, but three *different* modes to explore: date eligible men with *Bumble Date*, meet new people with *Bumble BFF*, and network with aspiring entrepreneurs with *Bumble Bizz*.

But there's a catch (if there wasn't, would this even be a dating app?).

Once you've matched, you *only* have 24 hours to strike up a conversation before your prospective partner disappears into the dregs of deleted chats and long-forgotten matches. This is a problem, yes, because sometimes it takes me longer to decide what I want to have for dinner.

Now, Bumble might sound like the complete package when it comes to finding you your future soulmate/friend/job/Netflix original, but since it lists all your matches together, there's a high chance you'll be left looking like a bumbling idiot. Sure, the matches are colour coordinated so that you don't mix them up, but what if you mistakenly ask your (rather platonic and woefully straight) buddy out for a hookup? Or worse, what if you ask your date to write you a LinkedIn recommendation?

Rating someone according to their dating game? That's one testimonial no one wants to see.

8. Recon

What it is: As the biggest gay fetish app, Recon is exclusively for men looking to hook up with a kinky twist. It's bold, brash and bratty – sort of like the Samantha Jones (from *Sex and the City*) of gay dating apps. Recon doesn't *just* talk about gay sex; it defines gay sex. Leather, rubber, bondage or kink, there's no discrimination on the basis of desire or debauchery. Recon is here to deliver, and it'll probably bring along a pair of nipple clamps too.

How it works: After a quick profile set-up process that goads you for the tiniest of details from your personal stats to your preferences in bed, Recon does something that no app has done before. It says goodbye to the grid. No more Sudoku-like squares of glistening six-pack abs, no more screenshots of smiling faces.

Instead, profiles pop up as listings, chronologically stacked in order of proximity (and, not surprisingly, passivity in bed).

What we like about it: A lot of gay apps are very confused when it comes to finding their identity. They continue to make attempts at toeing the line between helping men discover their sexual identity and their sexual desires. There's no middle. Hence, some call themselves dating apps. Some call themselves matchmaking apps. Some even go to the extent of branding themselves as networking apps.

Recon slaps them all in the face and identifies itself as the biggest fetish app for men seeking kink with other men. It unabashedly lays out its purpose bare on the table, like the submissive men who love using the app.

Have a dark, kinky side that you are too embarrassed to talk about? Open up Recon. Love a bout of water sports on the side? This app is here to shower you with surprises. Looking to embrace the delicious world of S&M? Recon will welcome you with open arms (and if you like it, a leather harness too).

What we don't like about it: For an app that's obsessed with kinks, there's a lot of math involved. Am I 80% submissive or 20% dominant? If I say I am 50% active, does that make me 50% passive? What if I am 100% not interested?

Unless you have a fetish for solving elementary-level math problems, Recon is not an app you should toy with.

If you like Recon, you'd also like: DaddyHunt.

Contrary to its rather suggestive name, DaddyHunt is surprisingly not full of … daddies. Instead, it's primarily populated by men who are seeking older, rugged gentlemen (read: Hugh Jackman in every movie ever). Once you get past the loophole, DaddyHunt gets one thing right. Namely, a face-centric approach to profile pictures, giving the community a warmer, distinguished vibe.

Just like the daddies you came looking for.

Number Seven: The Video Editor
Bro, How Many Dating Apps Are You On?

May 2016

On a bright Sunday morning, I download Bro with the vigour and hope that I usually reserve for the first day of a clearance sale. The app's interface is bright, multi-racial and eye catching, which is great – because that's how I like my boys. After a quick sign up where it pesters me for my stats, preferences and HIV status, Bro does what no other dating app does. It asks me to distinguish myself.

Am I the beefy jock bro? A nerdy brogrammer? A muscular G.I bro? Casual bro? Suited bro? Or worse, a hipster bro?

I choose the casual bro because no hipster would ever admit to being one. Once I am set, a grid of hopefuls shows up.

It's a sea of men I've blocked on other dating apps, long-forgotten exs, a few friends and men I've seen around but never spoken to. I feel slightly disappointed. This is no clearance sale.

I dive in and start my day with a fresh fist bump in my push notifications. It's **Seven**, a bisexual video editor with whom I went on a few dates a couple of months ago. **Seven** and I have a complicated relationship: we've met more times online than we have in person. I've swiped right on him on Tinder; woof'd at him on Scruff and starred him as a favourite on Grindr. I do the only sensible thing that can be done. I send a fist bump back at him.

'What are you doing here?' he texts me.

'I was going to ask you the same question,' I text him back.

We share a laugh and make plans to meet soon, but we both know that it won't happen.

I see him two months later.

We match on Hinge.

2.2 The Different Kinds of Guys You'll Meet Online (… and How to Spot Them)

At the end of the day, online dating is what it is.

Whether you scroll past, woof at or swipe right, every app is a supermarket of available men. There are smart men, there are witty men, there are hot men, but most importantly, there are men who want to meet other men, no strings attached. But take note, reader. Whether you are shopping for abs or absolute love, you'll find some templates that'll never fade away, just like the hickey from last weekend.

There will always be the usual suspects – boys with pictures of them basking by the beach, blank-and-white portraits that were most likely taken professionally at a studio, or the occasional shirtless guy posing with his dog – but has there ever been a dearth of men (and stereotypes) when one's looking for a connection virtually?

Not really.

While you haggle over beets and biceps at your neighbourhood supermarket of sex, here's a broad overview of the kind of ~~templates~~ men you'd find prowling online. What if someone doesn't match one of these profiles?

Congratulations, that's because he's reading this book.

1. The Blank Profile

The Blank Profile prides himself in being the most commonly found kind of man on a dating app. But sadly, that's where his list of achievements comes to an end. He prowls behind the template grey silhouette (hiding from friends and family), with a sense of confidence that is inversely proportional to the amount of information you can find on his profile. With no name, age, height, or other such important details listed, the man has (only) one excuse for all your anxious questions.

He's discreet.

Any conversation with the Blank Profile is like a game of (extremely one-sided) dodgeball: he swerves past your questions while hitting you with his own.

Can he send you a picture? No.

Does he want you to send him nudes; your full address and the last four digits of your credit card? Obviously.

Whether Mr Profile (first name, Blank) is a secret agent or a serial killer, you'll never know, because he'll never tell you. He could be anyone. He could be your classmate from high school. He could be your food delivery guy. He could be your accountant. He could be your next-door neighbour's toddler *accidentally* creating a profile on his father's unattended phone.

You'll never find out, because you'll probably end up not meeting him, since it's unlikely that he looks like the Grindr logo.

Things you'd hear him say:
'Your pix plz.'
'I don't share pics.'
'Where do you stay?'
'H8 long convos, man.'
'Do u stay alone?'
'Can I come over?'

Where would you find him: In the closet, probably.[4]

2. The Druglord

The Druglord isn't here to meet men for friends, chat or fun; he's here to run his very own drug cartel on your friendly dating app. He's sort of like Pablo Escobar, but without the cigars or the

4 Unless he's at home with his wife and kids.

Netflix series to his name. The Druglord doesn't bother with stats or profile pictures, and skips the pleasantries to get straight to the point.

A quick sale.

The Druglord sells everything from poppers to crystal meth (and even weed, to the less adventurous), and for the record, will always promise 'stuff that has been imported from the hinterlands of Eastern Europe'. When you eventually agree to meet the Druglord ~~to buy recreational drugs~~ for research, you realize that he's marked by a characteristic glazed expression, eyes that dart all over the place, and a nose that constantly sniffles.

But here's a quick news flash, kids. At the end of a really fast (drug-fuelled) day, our resident thrill seeker can only promise you one of two things – three hours of happiness or a trip to the urologist.

Either way, you might need a one-way ticket to rehab.

Things you'd hear him say:
'Are you into HF?'
'Want to do poppers?'
'Have place for high fun?'
'It's per gram, not per tablet.'
'Don't waste my time, plz.'
'Do u wanna buy?'
'2000/- for MD.'

Where would you find him: In a back alley of the seedier parts of town, wearing loose pants, but not carrying any loose change.

3. The Torso

What has six-pack abs, an endearing belly button, muscular hands on toned hips, but no face?

Every third profile on every gay dating app ever. For the most part, Grindr can be described as an open buffet of men with beautiful bodies. In other words, it's a mash-up of six-pack after six-pack; a jigsaw puzzle of fifty shades of skin. The Torso is easy to spot; his profile picture is literally a photo of his … glistening torso. The Torso is a man on a mission; he's looking for right now, and he has the right tools at his disposal – three (or more) sets of rock-hard abs.

Some people might go as far as calling him 'every gay man's wet dream come true' – only, he's missing a head and the ability to converse in anything more than a monosyllable. For a gentleman with abs that are so well defined that they can be projected in HD, the Torso will forever be *shrouded* in mystery, solely because you'll never know what he really looks like – movie star Henry Cavill or much-married monarch Henry VIII.

Either way, it's a guarantee that he's no Superman.

Things you'd hear him say:
'Can I see a body pic?'
'Are you toned?'
'No pic, no place.'
'Into muscular, gym fit only.'
'Sorry! Only Masc 4 Masc.'
'NSA fun only.'

Where would you find him: Pumping iron at the gym and dreaming of pumping you later.

4. The Spambot

With his blonde hair, ripped body and good-natured face, the Spambot is your classic all-American frat boy. 'What's he doing on this side of the Indian Ocean?' you'd stop and ask yourself, but chances are that you'd get distracted midway. If he's not flashing his dentist-approved smile, he's probably flashing his washboard abs. His picture usually has him grinning cockily into a (surprisingly clean) bathroom mirror, with an expression that says, 'Hey! Are you ready for some lovin'?'

Some would call him the perfect fix for your weekend.

Only, he's not *real*. In fact, he isn't *even* human (although he could be termed as the 'human equivalent' of a virus). While there's no known cure for this man-shaped malady, the Spambot does come with some standard warning symptoms: he always begins with a crisp (yet cheerful) salutation, but makes the mistake of following it up with a series of increasingly #NSFW sexts, irrespective of how and what you respond. Here's a quick example:

Him: 'How do you do?'

You: 'I am fine, thanks! What about you?'

Him: 'Sweet, I've been working out a ton. It makes me hard lol.'

You: 'Um …'

Him: 'I've got a great big cock and I love to show it off!'

You: 'Are you … okay?'

As you continue playing this confusing game of textual table tennis, he asks you (very seductively) if you want to watch him jerk off on his webcam. You politely refuse, but he sends you a dubious link anyway – one that is sure to give your phone the digital version of herpes, incubation period not included.

The only giveaway in the Spambot's otherwise blank profile? His height, listed at a questionable 105 cm.

Things you'd hear him say:

'Hello! Wanna talk?'

'Want to see my cock?'

'You make me hot …'

'I am so horny right now, see me jerk off at this link here.'

Where would you find him: In the dark web, hidden between computer viruses and hacked firewalls.

5. The Masseur

The Masseur is your no-nonsense spambot effortlessly copy-pasting promotional massage offers, profile after profile, waiting till he strikes gold or the sore spot on your lower back. The Masseur's modus operandi is simple and 100% effective: it's a picture of him wearing the flimsiest of banana hammocks, and a flyer he made on *Canva*.

Do you want a relaxing massage with essential tree oils and organic balms? He's your guy. Desperately seeking a man to rub your blues away (extra charges for rubbing you the right way)? You've hit the right profile. Care to have a ripped professional take care of all your stress? Look no further; give him a quick call on +91-massage-me-right-now.

The Masseur does not beat around the bush when it comes to his profession. Like the Druglord, he's here strictly for work and he'll make it a point to tell you that he's *not* looking for sex (even if you didn't ask). When you eventually lather up (pun intended) the courage and call him over (because he can never host), he'll rub you down, do his thing and leave after talking about his hobbies for an hour.

But not before he gives you a happy ending on the house.

Things you'd hear him say:
'Body pic only on booking.'
'Extra charges for whole night fun.'
'I am paid.'
'Happy ending extra.'
'Are you looking for relaxing exotic Ayurvedic body massage?'

Where would you find him: In a makeshift massage parlour, which is usually his dingy bedroom.

6. The Celebrity

With his movie-star looks, manicured beard and twinkling eyes that deserve their own spot in the Hollywood Walk of Fame, the Celebrity looks like Fawad Khan. In fact, *if* his profile picture is to believed, it *is* Fawad Khan.

Unfortunately, it isn't, and no, this isn't your personal rom-com. For every five genuine profiles on Tinder, you come across the Celebrity, with his billboard-worthy face and a sparkling set of teeth that unfortunately don't belong to him. How do you spot him? He hides behind film-star silhouettes, stock paparazzi photos or the Google search result for 'Hot Men, Indian'.

But sadly, our master of disguise has nothing else up his sleeve. Barely three lines into a conversation, and the curtains fall: there's no encore, just a single-screen matinee that gets lost like a blink-and-miss role.

You'll never see him again, because he'll be out of the theatres (and your thoughts) almost immediately.

Things you'd hear him say:
'I dnt share pics.'
'Hy!'
'Gud mrng. Pic?'
'DP not mine.'
'No mate, I am not Rana Duggabatti. It's not my pic.'

Where would you find him: Slouching in his bedroom, sifting through page after page of search results for 'handsome desi guy'.

7. The Tourist

Suave, spiritual and always ready for an adventure (in your bed or otherwise), the Tourist is either here on business, visiting extended family, or backpacking across the country – living a life straight out of Elizabeth Gilbert's *Eat Pray Love.* Only, our friend from overseas isn't here to find himself; he's here to find *you*. How do you recognize the Tourist?

His profile name shows his country flag? Check.

His 'About me' says that he's visiting? Check.

His picture has him grinning away with a drink on an exotic beach? Check.

He's interested in meeting locals to show him around and explore? Check.

Any online liaison with the Tourist follows these three simple questions: Are you a local? Yes. Do you live near the airport? Great. Can I come over? Uh.

His thirst for vacation flings aside, the Tourist has only one motive: collecting souvenirs that you can't buy at the gift shop, and hopefully don't have to show the doctor back home. Usually staying at a hotel close to the airport, he prefers drinks at the 24/7 bar in the lobby and desserts back in his room.

Brownie points if you are the dessert.

Things you'd hear him say:
'I am bored. Wanna show me around?'
'Indian guys are spicy, right?'
'The bar at my hotel makes some really potent drinks ...'
'I have a weakness for brown skin.'
'I like *desi* men.'

Where would you find him: In a lonely luxury hotel room, with a double measure of scotch and a bowl of untouched salted peanuts.

8. The Nun

The Nun will tell you that he doesn't want to have sex with you because he wants to 'connect emotionally' – short for 'I want to get to know you before I see the colour of your underwear.' You believe him and sip freely on your fourth glass of wine.

The Nun is beautiful, and in a grid of half-naked torsos and unsolicited dick pics, he helps you see the light. You gush at his stories, laugh at his jokes and get turned on by his endearing sense of humour – before you know it, you are hopelessly falling in love (and into his bed). You feel safe with the Nun, and why shouldn't you?

The Nun wants to go slow, and be friends first. The Nun wants you to lead the way. The Nun wants you to know that he's not like the others.

But here's the holy truth. Chances are, if 'I don't want to hook up on the first date', ever comes up in conversation, he's already planned how to get you back to his, what he'll do to you in bed and how long it'll take before he very politely offers to book your Uber ride back home. And then he'll block you right after.

'But he wanted to be friends,' you'll cry to yourself that night. You won't realize that he conveniently skipped the addendum: He's 'looking for friends' yes, but he's largely looking for 'friends … with benefits'.

Things you'd hear him say:
'Can we be friends first?'
'Usually I like taking things slow, but with you …'
'This just feels right, doesn't it?'

Where would you find him: Sending you a follow request on Instagram, only to delete it when you don't follow him back.

9. The Grown Up

Although one might assume that the Grown Up is a dying rare breed of gentlemen, he sticks out like a sore thumb online with his one discerning feature.

His profile description: 'sane and sorted, looking for the same'.

Describing himself as 'drama-free', the Grown Up is attentive, always puts you first and is great with comforting hugs, so you decide to ignore the fact that he spews out inspirational quotes like a Pinterest board.

Why is he still single?

The Grown Up was waiting for you to ask, because he has his answer ready. He's tired of being up on this Ferris wheel of fuckboys, and is now looking for something 'real and mature'.

What is he looking for?

For one, he's done playing the game and is now consciously looking for a man who can swoop in and save him from an eternity spent alone (which is convenient, because he claims 'you just waltzed into my life as if it were a Christmas miracle').

The grown up makes the Sapiosexual look like a child. So you swoop in to save him and agree to spend all of (drama-free) eternity together. Life is a bed of roses.

Until you end things with him, and he sends you thirty-three vicious texts in a row.

More than half of them have typos.

10. The Supermodel

The Supermodel muddles up his vital stats like I muddle up my income tax returns (but only one of us is successful). On his profile, the Supermodel has it all. Rock hard abs that you can iron your clothes on. A jawline that you can cut toast with. A nose so linear it could be photoshopped. Pictures you can use to potentially catfish other unsuspecting men. The Supermodel looks like the kind of guy who walks the runway for breakfast.

But I'll tell you something. He's the one who adds a couple of inches to his height, knocks off a few pounds from his weight and multiples your body issues overnight. Whether he's used a picture that was taken back when Orkut was still relevant or added an assortment of filters, the Supermodel's body type will always be the biggest lie in the online dating world.

The harsh truth is that the Supermodel isn't here because he's looking for you; he's here because he's looking for his big break in Bollywood.

Things you'd hear him say:
'Thanks for the tap, buddy.'
'Do you know any casting directors?'
'I can act too …'
'Do you want to see the rest of my portfolio?'

Where would you find him: Waiting in line, for an audition.

11. The Catfish

The Catfish enters your life (and your dating app grid) with no prior warning. There you are, scrolling through the same boring set of thumbnails, when he pops up completely announced, a fresh new face in a grid full of ~~average men~~ hopelessness.

'How did I not see this gorgeous thing before?' you ask yourself, and send him a text.

The Catfish is handsome (but not unattainably hot so you know he's not the Celebrity), wise (but not patronizing so you know he's not the Grown Up), and great at constructing grammatically correct sentences (but he's not overbearing about it, so you know he's not the Nun). Our friend is the Ranveer Singh of gay dating apps – funny; not LOL funny, but actual laugh-out-loud funny. Sometimes, that's enough.

You text endlessly over the next few days, exchanging pictures by the dozen. He's prompt at sending them: here is a snap of him with his dog, there's a picture of him on a hike in Cambodia. He even agrees to send you nudes (but only after asking for your permission). The Catfish is perfect on paper, he's got everything you are looking for in a man online – and yet, you have *that* nagging feeling in your heart. Something seems amiss. He feigns deafness whenever you ask him for his Instagram handle, and his photos always look skewed. There's something wrong with the aspect ratio. Maybe they are cropped wrong. Maybe he doesn't have high-resolution pictures. Maybe Grindr is screwing it all up. Maybe you are thinking too much.

Not letting your cynicism get the better of you, you finally muster up the courage to ask him for his number. On cue, he goes offline.

'Hello?'

'Hello?'

'Hello?'

He's gone without a trace. 'Did I do something wrong?' you ask yourself, but also decide not to give up so easy. You generally won't do this (or so you would tell yourself), but desperate times call for desperate measures. Chiding yourself for taking a screenshot of one of his (many) pictures, you process it through a quick reverse image search on Google.

There he is. On Instagram. On Facebook. On LinkedIn. On his college alumni board. Page after page clarifying that he is, in fact, a real person. You scroll through his profile, and his photos stare right back at you. Photos he's sent you before. Photos you've discussed before. But something seems amiss, and you can't ignore the nagging feeling in your heart any more.

They all look different here. The aspect ratio is different. The resolution is different. You read his captions and realize that he sounds different. Supressing your anxiety, you slide into his DMs.

'Who is dis?' he replies, two days later. Your worst fears have come true.

It's not the guy you've been chatting with all this while; it's just the guy he was pretending to be. That night, as you cry yourself to sleep, you realize you'll never hear from him (or the man whose identify he so deftly stole) again.

Sorry, you've just been catfished.

Things you'd hear him say:
'Why don't we chat here instead of exchanging numbers?'
'Let me find you on Instagram when I am free?'
'I just need more time before I can share more details ...'
'I just saw all your messages now'
'Sorry, I logged out ...'

Where would you find him: Pretending to be the One online.

12. The One

The One is the man ~~you've been reading this book for~~ dreaming about, right since you bumped into your first Blank Profile. He's the light (you meet) at the end of a really dark, depressing tunnel of Torsos and Tourists.

And it's been a long ride indeed. The One's dating profile is the missing jigsaw piece. He's everything the Catfish was (mostly because he's 100 per cent real) and more. You click with him almost immediately and give him your number even before your first conversation is over. He pings you right away. The two of you furiously text over the next few days until you work up the courage to call him one night, having downed a few shots to calm your nerves.

His voice is the deep baritone you imagined. You giggle at all the right spots as he sets up a date (in a decently expensive restaurant, where they serve soup in small plates, but not *so* small that you complain about it over your entree). When you do meet each other, you realize why it took you so long to find him.

Because he's worth every bit of the wait.

Things you'd hear him say:
'Want to meet for a drink and see how it goes?'
'I feel like your smile would look great in person'
'I am going offline now. Do you want to exchange numbers?'

Where would you find him: On a dating app, after a lot of bad decisions, including (but not limited to) all the men above.

Some (Not So) Honourable Mentions

A.k.a Do These Templates Ever Stop?

1. The Escort

Scores of men have pushed the boundaries when it comes to their primary motive to be on a dating app. The Tourist wants a guide, the Druglord is looking to peddle drugs, and the Masseur needs a client. The Escort is here to sell sex.

Identifiable by his portfolio of pictures (because they all look like they've been shot by a professional) and a profile description/name that tells you he's 'paid', the escort will waste no time in telling you that he'll only unzip his pants when you'll unzip your wallets. When you'll try to ~~haggle over prices~~ argue, he'll point out that great things in life don't come free, at which point you'll exit the conversation.

Your wallet (much like your body) will remain untouched.

2. The Couple

Happily in love and looking for a third, although both of them have secret online dating profiles that the other doesn't know about.

3. The Straight Guy

He's probably married. He probably has kids. He's probably very discreet.

He's mostly here for a blowjob.

4. The Screenshotter

The Screenshotter regularly screen grabs his conversations with unsuspecting matches – chats that aren't offensive or shady, but merely lacking in syntax/basic grammar – to post on his social media, just to prove 'how funny he is'.

He's not that funny.

5. The Dick Pic

The Dick Pic pops into your messages with a blurred close up of his shrivelled genitals. No other introductions are given.

Disgusted, you'll choose to ignore his texts, only to be followed up with a string of new questions, needling you for your likes, location and a link to your Instagram profile. When you'll continue feigning a deaf ear to his messages, he'll end with the effervescent 'R u not interested?'

You'll block him shortly after.

6. The Anaconda

'9+ size. If you know what I mean'.

Yes, the whole world knows what you mean, including the Queen of England, your grand aunt's second cousin and your mother.

7. The Goldfish

The Goldfish's MO is to diligently send you the same set of salutations (and pictures) at regular intervals of time. Maybe he's bored or maybe he suffers from short-term memory loss, but he'll be quick to splutter out an apology when you point out that he's messaged you before ('and no, you are not interested, sorry').

That won't stop him from repeating the loop two months later.

Number Eight: The Ghost
Will You Binge Me When I Am Gone?

November 2013

The meteorological department predicted a sunny day with clear skies.

We were supposed to walk around the lake. We were supposed to get drinks after. We were supposed to talk about how nice the weather was. We were supposed to do a lot of things.

But it's raining. So we've traded all of the above for steaming mugs of coffee. **Eight** tells me that he's a sales executive for a paper company, and my eyes light up. 'You could be on *The Office*!' I exclaim, and he grins. The only exciting thing that's ever happened to him at work is the lone trip he made to Samarkand two years ago. There's no whimsical boss, no blithering assistant, and much to my secret delight, no rival sales representative that doubles as a love interest.

From there on, the date streams effortlessly, like a fresh new sitcom that you don't feel the need to skip through.

Suddenly, the rains don't seem that dampening. We spend the next eight hours bingeing on each other's company. Time has a funny way of rushing by when you're having fun. At some point, it stops raining, but we are too engrossed in each other's company to notice. Our conversation feels like a warm blanket: he tugs at one end, and I pull at the other. Nobody loses.

Can this love story get a full series order already?

As he boards his bus back home, we say goodbye and seal the deal with a momentous kiss under my yellow umbrella. I never meet him after, and my sitcom dies a pilot-only death.

Number Nine: The Tourist
Meat, Play and (Most Probably) Love?

December 2012

On a crisp December afternoon, I show **Nine**, a wandering tourist with a wandering libido, the sights and sounds of the city. He's thin and wiry; with a thick south Indian accent that drips down his pointed chin.

I am already besotted.

Nine has a dead-end job in a chemical plant overseas but makes up for it with his quirky sartorial taste. 'I love Bombay,' he squeals to me in his bright yellow outfit, and I grin. He's taken photos with the street kids, complained about the weather, eaten *chaat* on the streets, braved the local trains *and* managed to survive. He could be a veteran.

Like most visitors, **Nine** wants to 'soak in the local vibe' – but that's just code for a 'vacation fling'. I'm not complaining. Our pharmaceutical scientist is new here, which means that he's never popped up on my Grindr grid. He's practically a clean slate.

As he mulls over taking a souvenir back home, I resist the urge to ask him to take me instead. Wouldn't that be perfect? It could be my solution to leaving all the city boys behind. A 'get out of jail free' card for all my failed attempts at finding love.

Maybe we could start a life together, I think to myself. Square one. Ground zero. Two of us forever – not marred by stories of exes (we may both know) or trysts (we might have in common). A fresh start. I am so caught up in my dream of becoming a househusband in Singapore that I don't hear his question.

'Do you know this man?' he asks me, flashing a smiling picture of **One** on his phone screen. It's the performance artist from two years ago. My smile falters.

'Of course I do,' I giggle nervously. 'Why do you ask?'

'I have a date with him tomorrow night. Do you have any quick tips?'

An hour later, I leave the clean slate behind. Maybe they can use it to write the daily specials.

2.3 The Gentleman's Guide to Every Sapiosexual in the World: Another Bonus Feature

Ranvier, twenty-nine, is a high-profile accountant with a high-profile multinational corporation.

And yes, that's how he describes himself.[5]

Ranvier likes matcha tea and sourdough bread, and enjoys walking his dog on alternate weekends. He guffaws at racist jokes and occasionally ghosts people because 'things are moving too fast and I can't handle all the expectations'. Whereas the fact that he chooses to deliberately misspell his name might ring a warning bell, it's something much more sinister that usually knocks the final nail in the coffin.

Ranvier is a self-proclaimed *sapiosexual*.

What's a Sapiosexual?

The average eagle-eyed reader would remember (and make it a point to tell you) that the word 'sapiosexual' describes a person 'who is sexually attracted to intelligence above all qualities'. The average eagle-eyed reader would also draw a blank when asked to elaborate on said definition.

What is sapiosexuality then?

Is it a sexual orientation for people who think that they're too smart to have a sexual orientation? Is it a pretentious word people

---

5 And spells his name.

use to strengthen brain muscles? Is it a cause for all the rebels, misfits and rule breakers who prefer a book to a booty call?

Maybe it's all three, because no one wants to date an idiot.

Online dating in 2020 has led us to a constant barrage of new terms that help us navigate the uncertainties of modern love. And yet, no online dating term has garnered quite as much popularity (or criticism) as the sapiosexual. Now, the word is used so commonly (and loosely) on gay dating apps, it could be right up there with a man's vital stats – all muddled up – because by the time the term trickles down to dating bios and chat histories, it becomes a mere shadow of its dictionary meaning.

Some will say that 'sapiosexuality' is a security blanket used by gay men to keep the douchebags away, assuming it's going to draw in a string of smart, suave and eligible men straight to the bedroom (and beyond). But that's the thing.

All the smart, suave and eligible men are taken.

And they don't call themselves sapiosexuals.

How Do You Spot a Sapiosexual?

The beauty of identifying the Sapiosexual is that it's no brainteaser. You won't even have to ask, because the chances are really high that he'll tell you himself. If he doesn't, here are some ~~warning symptoms~~ signs that can help you bookmark the right guy:

- The Sapiosexual craves intelligence like it's a bottle of Pinot Noir.
- But he also craves sculpted torsos and bubble butts.
- His profile name on Grindr is a succinct 'Sapiosexual'. No other details are given.
- The Sapiosexual finds online porn boring, because the 'dialogues aren't stimulating enough'. He jerks off on mute.
- He has an OkCupid profile, but he hardly uses it. He feels that it's not *ready* for the Indian dating pool.

- The Sapiosexual only ever wants emotional maturity and open-mindedness. He also wants you to stop asking him silly questions.
- He'll also tell you that he prefers 'a great conversation over a make-out session'. He will then proceed to invite you over for a nightcap.
- He feels a Schrodinger's cat meme is better than a regular cat meme.
- The Sapiosexual eats quotes by Rumi for breakfast. He washes it down with a no-foam soymilk latte and sarcasm.
- He lists Haruki Murakami as his favourite author, but his bookcase is stacked with Chetan Bhagat whodunits.
- The Sapiosexual will tell you that punctuation turns him on. He'll conveniently forget to end his sentences with full stops. When further prodded, he tells you that he hates the punctuation mark because 'it is a curt symbol of passive aggression'.
- A great debate on post-structuralism gets his theoretical juices flowing. His words.
- He'll tell you that he doesn't identify with any particular group, unless you count Facebook communities with a lot of grammar memes.
- He gets excited by Charles Bukowski quotes, and loves whitewashing them on Instagram with the Valencia filter. He gets upset when no one likes them.
- He uses words like 'cultural capital'. He'll scoff at you when you ask him what it means, but will show a sudden interest in the weather when you prod him to explain.
- He's a self-proclaimed Grammar Nazi.
- But he won't tell you that he gets confused between 'your' and 'you're'. Whenever he needs to use 'either' in an email, he'll do a quick Google search for the correct option.
- He likes smart men like he likes Paulo Coelho's *The Alchemist*.

- He gets irritated when Tumblr doesn't acknowledge his sexual preferences or orientation. He writes a lengthy post about this ordeal. It doesn't get any reblogs, and he deletes it soon after.
- He'll pester you to read his button poetry. It's actually just a badly written haiku. You'll lie to him and tell him it's the best thing you've ever read, just so he buys you gluten-free beer after.
- He just wants someone for whom 'philosophical discussion is foreplay'.
- He claims his sexual kink is having a conversation where he can use a semicolon and a colon in the same sentence.
- The Sapiosexual confuses Stephen Fry with Stephen Hawking. He wonders why anybody would want to watch a theoretical physicist perform a live comedy act, but doesn't ask anyone.
- He has a strict no-sex-on-the-first-date policy because he feels that you 'only get more attracted to someone the longer you know them'.

But that's the thing: the Sapiosexual will end a conversation on every dating app by asking for you for a dick pic. And he won't send one back.

2.4 What Does Your Favourite Dating App Say about You?

Like a man's scent and his shoes, his preferred dating app can speak volumes about him (and his data usage). Does he like to swipe right or send a spark? Does he send texts or thirst traps? Are his location settings enabled? What about his notifications?

While you don't have an option of playing favourites with children, pets or cast members from *The Good Place*, you do get to be biased when it comes to online dating. The truth is every gay man has a go-to dating app, which he likes to cuddle up with (or use to *find* men to cuddle with) after a day wrapped in loneliness and long-forgotten email threads.

Which brings us to you, reader. Have you ever wondered what the dating app you're on says about you? Swipe right through this list to find out:

Tinder

Who is it for: Men who can't afford a fairy godmother to find the One.
What does it say about you: 'If I have to kiss a few frogs to find my Prince Charming, so be it.'

Grindr

Who is it for: Men looking for something *beyond* companionship and compatibility, unless it's the sort of compatibility you seek in bed.
What does it say about you: 'What? Of course I don't take this seriously. Do you stay alone btw?'

Scruff

Who is it for: Men looking for men with hair on their chests and dirt on their nails.

What does it say about you: 'Why is #NoShaveNovember not an year-round thing?'

Planet Romeo

Who is it for: Men looking for pure, uninhibited, unadulterated sex.

What does it say about you: 'I like to believe I am sex positive.'

Hinge

Who is it for: Disney princes looking for friends of friends who are also Disney princes.

What does it say about you: 'I have so many friends, why can't they set me up with someone they know?'

Happn

Who is it for: Men who believe in second chances. Just make sure you have a friend on SOS and the neighbourhood's criminal offenders list on standby.

What does it say about you: 'Maybe I should go out more …'

Hornet

Who is it for: Men who like to catch flights, but also feelings.

What does it say about you: 'What if the love of my life is halfway around the globe?'

Jack'd

Who is it for: Same as the people who use Hornet, but they also prefer being called sapiosexuals.

What does it say about you: 'Don't even get me started on what I think about the current government's administration …'

Bro

Who is it for: Men who don't want to commit – to labels, relationships or sexual orientation.

What does it say about you: 'So buddy, I'm really not gay … but you want to get a beer or two and give me a blowjob later?'

OkCupid

Who is it for: Men who trust algorithms more than they trust themselves.

What does it say about you: 'Do you think I can find love through a Buzzfeed quiz?'

Bumble

Who is it for: Men who don't really have the time (or the space on their phone) to shift between LinkedIn, Facebook and the dating app of their choice.

What does it say about you: 'All my friends are women.'

Blued

Who is it for: Men who are sick of texting, and want to sext instead.

What does it say about you: 'Sometimes I feel like I should start my own vlog …'

Recon

Who is it for: Men who prefer fisting to fist bumps.

What does it say about you: 'I am extremely aware of what I like in bed. Now be a darling, and pass me those nipple clamps?'

DaddyHunt

Who is it for: Men looking for father figures. Strictly for roleplay purposes.

What does it say about you: 'My therapist thinks I might have daddy issues.'

Number Ten: The Therapist
What's in a Name?

October 2013

It's a sweaty Friday afternoon, so we are indoors, wolfing down second helpings of Chicken Schezwan Noodles and trying to get the waiter to bring our drinks over.

The air is heavy and humid. It smells like oiled hair and halitosis and people packed together too close. I want to ask him whether he would like to share a smoke … but first, there's something more important we have to address.

'What's your name?' I ask.

Squish. Time to break the fourth wall. That's the sound of your disappointment in me, isn't it?

In the long list of questions that one wishes to never have to ask on a date, this one wins by a landslide. (Side note: When you are meeting someone through Grindr, not knowing their [real] name is almost as common as not knowing their favourite flavour of ice cream. Most men hide behind fake names and blank profiles, occasionally reaching out from the confines of their hardwood-lined closets to send you a non-committal hello, or a grainy picture of their torso.)

'Why does that matter?' he asks. I squint my eyes to see (and double-check) whether he's joking. It's dark and dinghy – an ideal spot to meet a stranger who won't tell you his name (read: an ideal spot to be killed by a stranger who won't tell you his name).

I'm sorry. How does it *not* matter?

Maybe I want to open a joint account. Maybe he has a cardiac arrest, and I have to take him to the hospital. Maybe it's the last clue to a treasure hunt. Maybe I want to introduce him to my friends. Maybe I want to know what our wedding hashtag would sound like. Maybe this, maybe that – there are so many maybes that I can sell them by the dozen.

What should I do? We've not even finished our first drink yet. I make an exception to the rule; I decide to call him John Doe. But to everyone else, he's **Ten**.

It adds mystery to the setting, he suggests. He's a therapist – intrigue is second nature, he warns me as I shake my head in disapproval.

I laugh and ask him whether I should watch everything I say lest he make mental notes. It's a silly question to ask, because what is a date if not a series of mental notes we make about each other anyway?

'Relax, this is a date. Why don't I ask you questions instead?'

I tell him I'll think about it. Where are the inkblot diagrams? The Rorschach test? The leather couch?

For now, we've got two-quarters of rum; a plate of noodles and a bedbug-ridden booth … but it's cheaper than what he usually charges for a session at his clinic.

What more could I ask for?

He tells me that he's on Grindr 'as a social experiment' – he's bicurious. Has he ever had a girlfriend? Yes. Does he still have a girlfriend? As of two weeks ago, not any more. I am only mildly annoyed. Who does he think I am … a mere lab rat in this experiment?

He evades my question.

Ten grew up in the city but always found it 'the wrong kind of exciting' – something seemed amiss, like the aftermath of a drunken night. Was it the fact that he was the first of seven children at home? The first to make all the sacrifices growing up? The first to want to break free? Or was it the fact that he thought he would be the last person to ever question his sexuality?

Six days after his Break-up, he created a profile on Grindr as a social experiment. He knew he had to begin somewhere, because every journey of self-introspection needs a starting point. That's Psychology 101. It seemed like an alternate universe – so many torsos, so many handsome bodies, and then …

… and then I popped up!

For the undiscerning eye, this might sound like a meet-cute from a rom-com, except that it's not and it happened online. He wanted a hookup; I wanted Hakka Noodles. What are we doing here again?

You don't get to ask questions, he tells me. Am I the hiccup in this social experiment? Does that make me the … problem?

Someday, I shall win an award for my self-doubt. But today is not the day. Would it be wrong if I get him to diagnose me? I don't think so.

'Ask away,' I sigh.

Am I a cat person or a dog person? What is my favourite colour? What is my idea of happiness? If given a chance, would I want to be in a relationship? When was the last time I kissed someone? Have I ever been in love? We play along to a carousel of questions.

He makes mental notes as I tell him all my answers. I love cats. Purple. Yearlong clearance sales and gluten-free cakes. Only so that someone throws me a surprise birthday party every year. Two weeks ago. Twice in my life. And so on.

So can he tell me what is wrong with me?

'You might have a drinking problem.'

He's eyeing my third glass. I take a swig and finish what's left, and we call for the cheque. An hour and a half, and what do we have?

Some undefined fears and a mild buzz from all the rum.

'Your place?' he asks. I smile and shake my head.

'We could be friends?' I bargain.

He looks unconvinced, which makes me want him more – nothing turns me on like indifference. I laugh aloud and politely brush his advances away, knowing very well I will never see him again.

Why?

I've spent the last hour and a half thinking that this date might be half-full.

It turns out that it was half-empty.

2.5 Ready, Player One: Kick-starting Your Online Dating Game

Twenty-seven-year-old Aneesh isn't fond of many things. He isn't fond of liars. He isn't fond of menthol cigarettes. He isn't fond of pigeons. He isn't fond of relationships that move too fast.

And up until last weekend, he wasn't very fond of online dating. For reasons unbeknownst to anyone else but him, Aneesh had been laying low for the past two years – a sabbatical from online dating, he likes to call it.

I try prodding him for a valid reason as to why he would just decide to give up on ~~the greatest pleasure there is~~ online dating like that, but he only has the odd hours at business school to blame (there have been multiple rumours of a secret treatment plan for genital crabs, but he makes no mention of it). An MBA programme at one of the country's top reputed business schools is tough. In fact, he barely had time for anything else.

Not that he gave up on dating entirely. He tried scrounging for dates the old-fashioned way, yes – the perks of having friends who *also* happened to be friends with other gay men. But that got exhausting after a point: meeting the many acquaintances of your classmates, ending up in bed together, and not being able to make eye contact with the common friend the morning after. Or maybe, he just got bored of the chase.

Now he wants a way back in.

Only, online dating isn't what he remembers it to be back from early 2018. Tinder has twenty-three new gender selections, Scruff has a platform for gay-friendly BnB's, Planet Romeo has an extensive portal for STI Education, and Grindr has … GIFs. Whatever happened to the good ol' fashioned dating app from yore (circa 2017)?

Darwin's theory happened. The internet is evolving, and apps update frequently based on the reviews (and ratings) left behind by erstwhile gay men (such as myself). New features mean new customers mean more ratings mean more money. Everybody loves a good payday, and your average gay dating app is no different. Didn't they teach him that at business school?

They did (he ignores my jab), but for now, he just wants to get back in the game. This is one itch he can't scratch away (that confirms the genital crabs theory). What should he do?

He should do what apps do. Evolve.

There are a whole new bunch of rules that you need to keep in mind when you are creating a profile in 2022. Your 2017 version just doesn't cut it any more. Can I help?

I thought he'd never ask.

How Do We Begin?

As you might have realized, your dating profile is your window to the world. It's your 4 x 6 advertisement in the personals section of the newspaper. So it's only natural that you'd spend more time on it, being your witty, charming and fun self; it's where you get your right swipe, your woof or your clandestine tryst for Wednesday night.

It's the least you could do.

Instead, we only look at profiles through a filter. While pictures gain priority, our bios get rehashed in the same thirty-odd stencils; and they are all as pointless as trying to get the barista at Starbucks to spell your name correctly. Here are a few template (but very real) dating bios, decoded just for you:

Translate This: Decoding Dating Bios on Every App in the World

What People Say vs What They Really Mean

What he says: 'Sane and sorted.'
What he means: 'I am not looking for drama, but I will BLOCK you if you as much as make one joke about me.'

What he says: 'No hookups please.'
What he really means: '... but can I see your shirtless photos?'

What he says: 'I am open for options.'
What he really means: 'I am looking for a hookup, but I don't want to explicitly spell it out because I don't want to seem desperate.'

What he says: 'Looking for Mr Right.'
What he really means: '... but I'm also not averse to finding Mr Right Now.'

What he says: 'Looking for a reason to delete this app.'
What he really means: '... but it's probably not you.'

What he says: 'Looking for a gym buddy.'
What he really means: 'I have a boyfriend, but I don't mind having sex on the bench press.'

What he says: 'Only faces can start a conversation.'
What he really means: '... because I don't want you to be as ugly as you sound on text.'

What he says: 'Please don't waste my time.' Or, 'No timewasters plz.'
What he really means: 'I don't want to waste my time text-flirting with you over a week. I am a muscular top looking for NSA. Call me over?'

What he says: 'No pic. No plc.'
What he really means: 'Don't catfish me, please?'

What he says: 'Video calls must.'
What he really means: 'Don't catfish me, please?'

What he says: 'NP = NR = NI/ No Picture = No Reply = Not Interested'

What he really means: 'I only talk to hot men with abs.'

What he says: 'Looking for NOW.'
What he really means: 'I need NSA sex right away.'

What he says: 'Now?'
What he really means: 'I am lazy, but I need NSA sex right away.'

What he says: 'Now wid plc.'
What he really means: 'I am lazy and looking for NSA sex right away. I can also host.'

What he says: 'I'm bored.'
What he really means: 'I'm horny.'

What he says: 'I'm busy.'
What he really means: 'I'm not interested.'

What he says: 'Looking for a man.'
What he really means: 'I still won't let you fuck me.'

What he says: 'I get HIGH on life.'
What he really means: 'I'll come over right away if you let me snort MDMA off your ass cheeks.'

What he says: 'Are you on Instagram?'
What he really means: 'I want to see more pictures of you because I can't decide whether I want to sleep with you on the basis of that *one* grainy picture you have up on your profile.'

What he says: 'Committed.'
What he really means: 'My boyfriend and I are looking to spice up our sex life with a threesome.'

What he says: 'I don't really know what to say here. Haha.'
What he really means: 'I really don't know what to say when all they need is *only* 250 characters about myself. I try not to come across as boring, but I really am. Do you want to have sex with me lol?'

What he says: 'I am discreet and looking for the same.'
What he really means: 'I am married and don't mind something on the side, as long as you don't take pictures and send them to my wife.'

What he says: 'I am discrete and looking for the same.'
What he really means: 'I am married and I also don't know how to spell.'

What he says: 'I prefer men over boys.'
What he really means: 'Only tops, please.'

What he says: 'Versatile only.'
What he really means: 'Only tops, please.'

What he says: 'Versatile top.'
What he really means: 'I am too shy to admit that I am a bottom.'

What he says: 'Bottoms only.'
What he really means: 'I will tell you that I'm a top every chance I get.'

What he says: 'Not into fats/femmes. Uncles and aunties please stay away!'
What he really means: 'I am a douchebag, and I expect you to be one too.'

What he says: 'No garlish, aunties, fatties pls.'
What he really means: 'I am a douchebag who can't spell.'

What he says: 'Classy people only.'
What he really means: 'I want to do unimaginably dirty things to you, but I will not pay you money for any of it.'

What he says: 'Wru?'
What he really means: 'I am trying to figure out how far you are to decide whether it's worth the effort to travel there to get laid.'

What he says: 'Visiting.'
What he really means: 'I have a hotel room to myself. Come over.'

Number Eleven and Twelve: The Bores
What Do Profiles Say When They Say Nothing at All?

October 2013/2016

In two Octobers of different timelines, I meet **Eleven** and **Twelve**. They are different men leading different lives. Their paths have never crossed, and to my knowledge, never will.

Eleven is a tall, strapping photographer who lives by himself in the heart of the city. **Twelve** is a burly, barrel-chested marketing manager who lives in a suburb far away, strapping himself to a local train to work his heart out every day. They have no common interest or friends; not one physical feature (one's a grower, another's a shower) or a single quirk that binds their sets together to create a Venn diagram. For the rest of the world, their chakras are never destined to align.

And yet, they are the same person.

Eleven/Twelve lacks the basic ability to ~~excite you with his words~~ sustain a conversation. On two separate dates, I hear the bore talk about his life as if he were reading from the instruction manual for an electric stove. But there's no spark.

Why did I agree to this? I scream internally, as I listen to **Eleven/ Twelve** drone about his many career choices, with the dullness of Mumbai's weather.

I look at him.

Oh yes. He *is* beautiful. But any witticism or compliment I throw his way hits a dead wall. It's like playing a game of squash. I forfeit.

'Hi.' The bores text me two days after our date.

I never reply.

Finding the Perfect Profile Picture

It's simple – sometimes he won't have time to read your profile bio … and we all know that your picture is all you've got to get him to say hello. You don't need to be a rocket scientist to know that your display picture needs to be clear and recent (unless you still look like your charming 2012 self). Just make sure it's not a mugshot or a scan of your passport picture, and you are ready to go. Remember, the focus of the picture should always be on the star attraction: **You**.

They say that everything you need to know, you can learn from a person's picture. Here's what different pictures say about you:

Profile picture: A shirtless selfie

What it says about you: When was the last time you bonded with someone over how well proportioned your abs are?

Never. Unfortunate as it may seem, it's very difficult to be taken seriously when you think the most endearing part about you is your sexy, sculpted chest.

Profile picture: A smiling selfie

What it says about you: Smiles are sexy. You might want to come across as a brooding yet beautiful 'I-am-too-good-for-you' man, but smiles always gather the most attention on dating apps. Plus it's tough to resist a full set of pearly whites.

Profile picture: A blurred scan of a photo from 2012

What it says about you: It's 2022, so the only reason to have an out-of-focus photo as your profile picture is that you used an artsy Instagram filter. Otherwise, you need to delete those scanned pictures from your phone as soon as possible.

Profile picture: A gym selfie

What it says about you: Yes, you care about fitness, love to exercise and spend about ten hours every week working on the various muscles of your lithe, supple body, but there's a catch.

Generations of (less fit, more sour) gay men have unanimously looked down at their gym-going counterparts in their quest for love, simply because they presume that the latter would give precedence to high-intensity interval training over matters of the heart.

Profile picture: A photo of you wearing sunglasses

What it says about you: When you've got monster sunglasses that cover more than half of your pretty face, people will assume that you are wearing them because you are ugly.

Yes, even if they are from Calvin Klein.

Profile picture: A photo of you with a baby

What it says about you: You probably Googled, 'What's the easiest way to get men to think I'm irresistible?'

Profile picture: A photo of you with a dog

What it says about you: You probably Googled, 'What's the easiest way to get men to think I'm irresistible?' + had a pet dog to spare.

Profile picture: A group photo of you with all your gay friends

What it says about you: 'Here are my three friends I'm stuck in the friendzone with, looking for someone that won't be added to my profile.'

Profile picture: A group photo of you with all your straight friends

What it says about you: 'Look at me, all my friends are straight'.

Profile picture: A photo of you at the beach

What it says about you: The shirtless beach picture is the ultimate way to show off. How so?

It shows that you work out (your banana hammock leaves little room for the imagination), are confident (because anybody with body issues would have a problem with being half-naked in public) and travel a lot (who else would be at a beach in the middle of the year?). Do you want to amp up those little red notifications of love on your favourite dating app?

It's time to find the nearest exotic beach and spread yourself on a bath towel.

Profile picture: None

What it says about you: 'I am discreet.'

Profile picture: A photo of you in a suit

What it says about you: Maybe you are a professional. Maybe you are a model. Maybe you are a tycoon. Maybe you are an out-of-towner in the city for work and looking for a friend to 'show you around'. Maybe you are none of the above and just trying too hard.

Remember that this is Grindr, not your LinkedIn profile.

Are We Good to Go?

Well, that was easy. You've got your best picture up on your profile: it could be at the gym or the beach, or shows you sipping cocktails against the backdrop of the Gateway of India. Maybe you are even showing off your washboard abs. Maybe you are smiling. Maybe you are smiling as you show off your washboard abs.

Is it *still* not working?

So you're still getting all the unsolicited dick pics in the world, with no genuine hellos coming your way (unless you like your hellos flapping away in your face). I'll tell you something. Sometimes, choosing an interesting, well-thought-out profile name is the only thing that determines whether you get a ping or a pass, because pretty pictures of your dimples just *don't* cut it any more. When all you want is a nice boy to go have a beer with, what's left for you to do?

Finding the Perfect Profile Handle

It's easy-peasy. You start right from scratch. Now hurry up and use this guide to find yourself an appropriate online-dating handle, because your six-pack clearly isn't doing it for you.

Q. Can I use my real name?

The obvious thing to do when you are trying to come up with your Grindr handle is to use your actual name – but it's easier said than done, because then we'd have half a dozen torsos who are all called Karan or Rahul or Akshay. What's the next best thing? You add a number or two – but then, you are just characters away from using your first-ever email address, which makes you a sitting duck for spam. Keep it simple; keep it easy – but not *so* easy that you use your ATM pin. Cashing out emotions might be fine, but you don't want someone to cash out your savings.

2. What about a reference to my location?

Too lazy to tell someone where you stay?

It's simple: squeeze in your location into those twenty-five characters, and you'll have more than one express delivery coming your way that night. Think of yourself as the friendly neighbourhood GPS tracker, because with a name like 'BandraBoy81' or 'Conn8Place_Cutie', you'll *only* get asked for directions to your bachelor pad every night.

3. Is it okay to be #NSFW?

Know that a #NSFW handle will put you in a classic Catch 22 situation: your easiest way to get noticed is also, ironically, the easiest way to get dismissed. Whether you choose to go as 'HolePlugger', 'A$$KweenForIt' or 'SluttyBtm4U', your inbox is going to be full of messages that will get you your fair share of action, but if you expect to find your future soulmate with a reference to your size, sexual preference or fetish, you probably need to change your approach.

... and When's the Perfect Time to Be Online?

While there's no *right time* to be online, it's advisable that you keep your phone away at bedtime; that is, if you are hoping to find the One – because any man who pings you post midnight, wanting to 'get to know you a little bit better', is only interested in getting to know your sexual fetishes.

On the other hand, if you are looking for something on the side, here's when to reach out to all the Romeos in your neighbourhood …

6 a.m. to 9 a.m.:

Looking for someone to work out with? Hit him up when his morning motivation is up and flaring, and he's ready to hit the bench press (or the sheets, if you are looking for a different type of cardio).

Noon to 3 p.m.:

Interested in a quickie? Afternoons are perfect for a post-lunch liaison: it is when your will to work is at its lowest and your need to find a distraction at its highest. Plus, you've got to work off those greasy rotis from lunch.

5 p.m. to 8 p.m.:

Are you thirsty for a quick drink at the local pub? Ring up a boy for a spontaneous date in the evening, because it always beats going back home to an empty apartment.

And if things go well, you won't have to.

8 p.m. to 11 p.m.:

Congratulations! You have now entered 'let's ask him out on a date' territory.

11 p.m. and beyond:

Four words. No strings attached sex.

A First Timer's Guide to First Texts

You'd think that communicating with a stranger wouldn't be a problem. We do it all the time. For a generation obsessed with their phones, just saying hello couldn't be that tough, right?

WRONG. The next time you hit up (or on) a man on a dating app, refrain from using these classic (but awful) openers:

1. 'Hey/Hi/Ssup?'

While there's nothing wrong with starting with an introductory hello, there's a high chance it'll get lost due to its lack of originality. Because here's the harsh truth. Your unimaginative introduction will *most certainly* be fighting it out with three-dozen other unopened hellos rotting away in the recipient's Grindr messages.

2.'Pic?'

The worst possible way to introduce yourself, especially in these two situations: a) When you don't have a picture up yourself, and b) when the person you are chatting with already has one on display. This is your one-way ticket to get blocked. Instead, why don't you send a headshot as a surprise?

3. A dick pic

... but not *that* headshot.

4.'You're close.'

No shit, Sherlock. This is also as close as you are going to get.

5. 'What are you looking for?'

What do you *think* I'm looking for? Read my bio already.

5. 'I'm not here too often. Care to chat on WhatsApp?'

Asking for a person's number too soon is uncomfortable, but asking for it as an opener is a new low. No one wants to be put on the spot before customary hellos are even exchanged. Refusing to comply only means that you are sane and apprehensive, which are two great qualities.

Don't fool yourself. You are going to be left on seen.

2.6 The Rookie's Rulebook for Online Dating: What Works vs What Doesn't

Three sleepless nights, a PowerPoint deck, and seventeen iterations later, Aneesh is finally ready. He's created the (perfect) online dating profile.

'Do you want to have a look?' his eyes look tired, but the last time I saw him so excited was when he found out that Katy Perry was going to be performing live in Mumbai.

The ~~remarkable dating expert~~ good friend that I am, I take his phone for a quick assessment. There's a carousel of recent photos (including one where he's smiling right into the camera); a smart and witty profile description that brings out his prime personality traits (but not too smart to seem intimidating to the unassuming user); and enough personal details for a prospective employer to do a thorough background check (and hire him on the spot). I must say, I am rather impressed.

'Does this mean that I am ready to jump right in?'

Hold your horses, mister. We are just getting started. Online dating is a lot like playing chess – there are long gaps between chats, and every move is calculated. To top it all off, you are simultaneously playing different games of chess with different people. So it's a given that there are rules to be followed, chats to be segregated, decorum to be maintained.

For those of you who don't know, here's the short version of basic online etiquette:

1. Make an effort with your profile. Your vital stats and sexual preferences might get you sex in thirty minutes or less, but a soulmate? Not so much.
2. Stop using the app only after midnight. You are not fooling anyone when you want to meet for a date in the middle of the night. In your bedroom.
3. Be nice, be charming, be yourself – but most importantly, be kind.

But **spoiler alert**: basic just doesn't cut it any more.

Online dating requires consistency, (a little bit of) persistence and some amount of hard work.

Online dating is … time consuming.

As a gay man, you spend as much time charting the dregs of a dating app as you do deciding between a glass of wine and a whisky shot at the bar – only here, there are no empty calories; just empty feelings. (And no, there are no happy hours on dating apps.) So how do you get that gold-star rating the next time you are chatting with someone online?

Follow these online dating dos and don'ts, and you'll never have to hit the bar to drown your loneliness again.

Do: Update your profile frequently.

Unless you still look like your 'gorgeous, toned self from 2015 who still bops to Wiz Khalifa's *See You Again*', update your profile as frequently as you can. You aren't the same person you were back in 2015 (or like the same things), and you need people to know that. If an app can come up with a new update every few weeks – and that's a lot more hard work – so can you.

Don't: Lie on your profile.

We know how exhilarating it can be to lie about your age, height, weight and the fact that you won 'Entrepreneur of the Year' back in 2010, but remember – you are only one Google search (or date) away from never seeing the boy of your dreams ever again.

Do: Be ready to take chances.

Does your date seem slightly more boring than he did on text? Is his nose off-centre? Do you find him a bit pudgy around the waist? You can pass him off, and wait and wait and keep waiting, but perfection will never show up knocking on your door.

While online dating can seem superficial (profile after profile of gorgeous men with pectoral muscles and PhDs can be quite anxiety-inducing), you might need to step out of your comfort zone occasionally. Who knows? Maybe the One is a freelance graphic designer who lives with his parents.

Don't: Ask for a picture if you don't have one.

If you do, you are a certified A-level douchebag.

Do: Be consistent.

A great story – just like your houseplant – needs ~~fertilizer and water~~ sustenance. Yes, a casual 'hello' might be a good way to start a chat, but for it to flourish into something substantial, you need to be more consistent when it comes to exchanging texts. Try to find the right balance – not too often, not too far between – because unlike your houseplant, you can't water an emotional connection back to life.

Don't: Be presumptuous.

Don't assume that someone wants to sleep with you just because they sent you a picture, or worse, were polite to you on chat. Never mistake manners for making a move. Want to know what someone is really looking for online?

Ask them.

Do: Understand the importance of saying no.

The beauty of getting to know a man virtually is that if someone asks you to do something that makes you uncomfortable, you can be firm and politely say no.

You don't even need to come up with excuses.

Don't: Be too persistent.

Unless you are applying for your dream job, persistence is not a sexy trait. If someone doesn't reply to three of your texts in a row, understand that they are not interested and ~~move on to fresher meat~~ give up.

Do: Understand rejection.

… And move on. There's always going to be more profiles.

Number Thirteen: The HR Manager
Can I Give You Some Feedback on This Date?

For all of three hours and forty-two minutes, **Thirteen,** an HR manager with an education startup, briefs me on his life with a not-so-brief monologue. He tells me about his loves, his successes, his dreams (and even manages to steer into a ten-minute rant about what his colleagues ate for lunch two days ago), pausing only to ask me if I want popcorn with my coke. He goes on and on and on, switching between stories about an ex who moved on too fast and a job that that's moving too slow.

I snack on my popcorn silently.

We've watched a movie, grabbed coffee, walked around the mall *twice* and even driven all the way across town, but he hasn't asked me a single question about myself. In fact, he hasn't stopped talking. On the other hand, I know enough about him to set up his LinkedIn account. I never thought I'd miss the boring introductory first date questions till they disappeared altogether.

'Should we drive back?' he asks. I cough out a single yes, my throat dry from lack of use. Another hour of anecdotes later, we finally pull into my building.

'Can I give you some feedback?' he asks, looking at me with an expression one usually reserves for funerals and financial reports. I frown. Is he going to give me an assessment review?

I nod again.

'You need to talk more,' he says gingerly, as if he is talking to a badly behaved pet. 'It almost looked like you weren't invested in our date,' he adds, looking hurt. I open my mouth, because I have a lot to say. But I don't say any of it.

Instead, I say good night and never see him again.

Number Fourteen: The Snoot: Can I Give You Some Feedback Two?

January 2018

Friday nights usually feature high on a list of my favourite things. But this is not one of them. For one, **Fourteen** isn't the 'delightful little imp' his online profile promised.

We've spent the last forty-five minutes at a crowded bar where we can hardly hear each other, even though I can barely stand his company. My date works at a finance company in the UAE (which is not the same as working *in* finance, he tells me when I joke about his hefty paychecks), and is currently skipping a friend's engagement so 'I can show him a good time instead'.

Ouch.

'So you call yourself a writer?' he asks. Each question seems like a challenge, and while I love the occasional jab, a series of exhausting exchanges aren't my idea of a fun Friday night.

'Yeah, I am', I reply, sticking to monosyllables. Talking about work isn't my idea of a first date conversation. Talking to him isn't either.

'Sounds fun. What do you write about?' he prods. I hope my blank face dissuades him from asking more questions, but he won't give up. I roll my eyes and begin to tell him about how unglamorous the life of a writer really is (but I skip the part where I write about first dates anonymously). He's barely listening.

I take offence, and open up a link to my blog.

'I think I might have read some of your work,' he lights up, and I smile. There's the compliment I've been waiting for. 'Don't take this the wrong way, but you do have the tendency to be slightly dramatic with your writing. Maybe you should tone down the clichés?'

I stare at him. He looks jokingly apologetic, but I left my sense of humour at the entrance. 'So … will you ever write about me?' he asks sardonically.

Another challenge. Sigh.

Well, challenge accepted.

2.7 Calculate Your Grindr Gay Index

Take this special edition quiz to find out whether or not you're addicted to Grindr!

Most gay men have a … complicated history with Grindr.

Like the lead pair of every popular sitcom, they'll dance through a decade-long on-again, off-again relationship, vowing to periodically cleanse off the toxicity every few months, only to find their way back to the App/Play store (and each other) a weekend later. When prodded, they'll shrug you off with a non-committal, 'We were on a break.'

Listen, mister. YOU WERE NOT ON A BREAK.

'But I am not most men,' you reason. 'I am not addicted to Grindr like the others …'

Spoiler alert, friend. Men who 'aren't-like-other-men' don't go around saying that they 'aren't-like-other-men'. Is that reason enough to prove that you could be one of them?

If you took a break from reading to go reply to an unread message on the app, the answer is probably yes. There's no denying that you've heard the faint 'buh-dupe' sound everywhere you've gone – the club, the gym, at Starbucks, your favourite restaurant, and this one weird time, from the pockets of your local general practitioner.

But is your love affair with Grindr just a mild fondness or is it borderline obsession?

Don't bother yourself with an epiphany, because there's only one way to find out. Every point you rack up on this special edition quiz brings you one step closer to finding out exactly how addicted you are to the world's most infamous 'gay networking' app. How do you play?

Simply add a point for every time you answer with a 'yes' and tally your final score to find out. Are you ready?

You have ...

- ❒ Checked your Grindr as soon as you reach a new location.
- ❒ Checked your Grindr on a pee break.
- ❒ Or a lunch break at work.
- ❒ Cursed the bad network when Grindr doesn't load.
- ❒ Got upset over not having any messages when you log in.
- ❒ Got excited because you have more than twenty when you do.
- ❒ Had a blank profile.
- ❒ Laughed at someone with a blank profile.
- ❒ Messaged someone with a blank profile just because you are horny.
- ❒ Lied about your height.
- ❒ Lied about your weight.
- ❒ Lied about both.
- ❒ Spent hours coming up with the perfect profile.
- ❒ Ended up being asked for sex right after coming up with the perfect profile.
- ❒ Said you were 'only looking for friends' but didn't really mean it.
- ❒ Mentioned you were 'straight-acting'.
- ❒ Ditched a date midway because they are ugly.
- ❒ Been ditched.
- ❒ Asked if someone's into 'high fun'.
- ❒ Been asked if you are into 'high fun'.
- ❒ Said you are 'sane and sorted' on your profile.
- ❒ Blocked someone for saying they are 'sane and sorted' on their profile.
- ❒ Been approached for a threesome.
- ❒ Approached someone for a threesome.
- ❒ Been approached for an 'orgy' or 'group fun'.
- ❒ Approached someone for an 'orgy' or 'group fun'.
- ❒ Been approached by a masseur.
- ❒ Been approached by an escort.

- ❒ Felt bad about not being approached by either.
- ❒ Just met someone for sex.
- ❒ Dated someone off Grindr.
- ❒ Made a friend through Grindr.
- ❒ Had a torso picture up.
- ❒ Objectified a torso picture.
- ❒ Had a catchphrase for Grindr.
- ❒ Used the catchphrase on the same person twice (and not even apologized.)
- ❒ Told someone you were 'home alone'.
- ❒ Asked someone if they were.
- ❒ Said you were looking for 'right now'.
- ❒ Said you were looking for 'nothing.'
- ❒ Just said you were 'looking.'
- ❒ Been asked whether 'you got plc'.
- ❒ Been asked whether 'you got pics'.
- ❒ Replied to both.
- ❒ Replied to neither.
- ❒ Not looked anything like your Grindr picture.
- ❒ Scoffed at someone for not looking anything like his Grindr picture.
- ❒ Known all the men in your neighbourhood by heart.
- ❒ Blocked ten men every day religiously.
- ❒ Cursed when you can't block the eleventh person for the day.
- ❒ Wished you had Grindr Xtra so you could block more.
- ❒ Downloaded Grindr Xtra to do so.
- ❒ Hooked up with a Grindr date during work hours.
- ❒ Hooked up with a Grindr date *before* work hours.
- ❒ Hooked up with a Grindr date *at* work.
- ❒ Not replied to a polite message on Grindr.
- ❒ Been angry when someone doesn't reply to yours.
- ❒ Been catfished.
- ❒ Catfished someone.
- ❒ Been asked whether you are a 'top or bottom' after saying hello.

- ❐ Asked someone the same question after saying hello.
- ❐ Dreamt of marrying someone you've met off Grindr.
- ❐ Cried in the shower when that didn't work out.
- ❐ Found someone new on Grindr the very next day.
- ❐ Had a holiday hookup in a foreign location through Grindr.
- ❐ Searched for a café with free Wi-Fi in said foreign location to check your Grindr messages.
- ❐ Sent a dick pic.
- ❐ Asked for a dick pic.
- ❐ Had a shirtless picture.
- ❐ Asked for a shirtless picture.
- ❐ Blocked someone for doing the above.
- ❐ Had a collection of pictures to send.
- ❐ Lied about not having any pictures to send.
- ❐ Looked for birthday sex.
- ❐ Looked for break-up sex.
- ❐ Looked for 'I am bored' sex.
- ❐ Had a conversation that went nowhere.
- ❐ Had a conversation that went straight to bed.
- ❐ Gone straight to bed but had a conversation instead.
- ❐ Used Grindr while at a meeting.
- ❐ Used Grindr while on a night out with friends.
- ❐ Got out of a night out early for a Grindr hook-up.
- ❐ Had an exasperating conversation on Grindr.
- ❐ Taken a screenshot of said conversation and tweeted it.
- ❐ Stalked an ex using a fake profile.
- ❐ Pranked a friend using a fake profile.
- ❐ Blocked someone midway through a conversation.
- ❐ Been blocked by someone midway through a conversation.
- ❐ Sexted someone on Grindr.
- ❐ Blocked them after finishing your business.
- ❐ Lied about being single on Grindr.
- ❐ Lied to your boyfriend about being on Grindr.

- ❒ Had your boyfriend lie to you about being on Grindr.
- ❒ Looked for someone on Grindr with your boyfriend.
- ❒ Saved multiple contacts under their Grindr pseudonym.
- ❒ Got confused and saved two people under the same name.
- ❒ Deleted a contact in a moment of disgust.
- ❒ Deleted Grindr in a moment of disgust.
- ❒ Facebooked about leaving Grindr.
- ❒ Reinstalled it in a moment of exasperation a couple of months later.

Excited to know what your final score means?
Read on to uncover what your Grindr Gay Index says about you:

Your score: 1–25 Grindr points
What it says about you: Congratulations! You seem to be doing great (not letting Grindr get to you). In fact, if you weren't reading this book, I would have thought you were a born-again virgin. But beware – Grindr is the deep, dark end of the web that sucks you in before you know it. Turn those notifications off and you'll do just fine, sweetie.

Your score: 26–50 Grindr points
What it says about you: Oh peaches! While you are used to the occasional lunch-break tryst, you seem to have everything under control. But I still see you using the eggplant emoji, mister – and we both know for a fact that you aren't planning on making baingan bharta for lunch.

Your score: 51–75 Grindr points
What it says about you: While you might check the app every couple of hours, remember that you are one sex tape and two threesomes away from becoming Grindr's resident poster boy for the month. Keep your phone away, and read this book instead.

Your score: 76–100 Grindr points
What it says about you: Step away from your phone as slowly as you can, and put your hands in the air, sir. You're being taken in for Grindr addiction. Now, would you prefer a pat-down or a full-body cavity search?

Number Fifteen: The Celebrity Stylist
Wait … but Is This a Date?

November 2011

4:02 p.m.

It's a busy Thursday evening, and I am waiting at a busy intersection. I dawdle on my phone as I wait. He's two minutes late. I was told a place and a time, nothing else. His messages have always been crisp and to the point. Nonchalant, some would describe his texts.

A car pulls over, and a man waves me in. It's **Fifteen**, a busy celebrity stylist, who, as he assures me, seldom kidnaps boys to whisk them off to mysterious faraway places. He studied at a textile school in Canada and lived there for half a decade, but ultimately left behind a dozen acquaintances, a startup job and a live-in girlfriend to move back home. I nod without batting an eyelid. I could ask him why he came back. I could ask him what happened to the girlfriend. I could ask him whether he's sure about his sexuality. I could ask him if we are on a date.

'Where are we off to?' I ask him instead.

You can't blame me for being suspicious. He had been strangely cryptic when he had called to ask me out. It was all done very nonchalantly. **Fifteen** laughs and tells me he's got a fun evening planned. His favourite band is performing in town, and he's been dying to watch them play live ever since he came back home.

'Do you want to get a drink first?' he asks.

'Sure, where do I sign up?'

He laughs again.

But before we get to our drinks, we have to make a *slight* detour.

4:40 p.m.

Fifteen is assisting the celebrity wife of a celebrity director in styling their latest celebrity blockbuster, and needs to drop a parcel at their home before 5 p.m. I glance at my watch: we have only twenty minutes. The parcel looks non-descript, unlike the task at hand. I am intrigued … what is in it?

It's a package; there's nothing more to it. I ask no further questions. He disappears into a palatial apartment complex for a couple of minutes as I try beating my score on Temple Run. Two diamonds and three lives later, he's back.

'I know it's too late, but you don't mind *another* detour, do you?'

'What is a date without a detour?' I ask him (right answer: it's a proper date).

5:50 p.m.

'Which one should I buy?' he asks, holding up a bottle green thong and a pair of classic white briefs. We are ~~sourcing costumes~~ buying underwear at a luxury-clothing store, sifting through essentials that sell at the price of gold. I cheekily point out that both will be covered with at least one layer of clothing in the final shot, so would it really matter? He doesn't look very amused.

The underwear in question is for an A-grade superstar. The actor in question is a perfectionist and pays a lot of attention to detail. Did I mention that he's also a strapping six feet of solid muscle? If we are going to be stuck running errands, I might as well make the most of it. He says something (witty, because my stylist friend is chuckling) but I am momentarily distracted, daydreaming about the actor in said underwear.

'Are you listening to me?' he asks me, agitated. What was he saying again?

He's really hungry. Underwear shopping does that to gay men. So, where do we go next?

'I know just the place,' he grins.

6:40 p.m.

'Are you sure you don't want to eat anything?' he asks, digging into his salad. I tell him I am good. **Fifteen** seems more relaxed as he listens to me drone on about my writing. Is this the same boy from two hours ago? I decide I prefer the 6 o'clock version of him. I *almost* forget about the multiple detours we took to get to our actual date. But wait, is this how dates work?

'Do you like your drink?' he asks me, interrupting my rant about being a career waiter. It's a watermelon cooler; there's nothing more to it. His eyes dart to the wall clock, and I notice the familiar flutter of panic on his face. Once more, and he could patent it. 'Listen, I think it's too late …' he starts.

This time, I am prepared. I pick the lint off my sweater as he picks up the tab. He leaves his salad and our conversation unfinished.

10:32 p.m.

We buy ourselves a glass of Shiraz each and slide into a pod near the stage. He sings along to songs that I've never heard before. Do I like them? Yes. Do I like him? I can't say. This day has felt like a to-do list; there's nothing more to it.

An hour later, he leans closer. It feels momentous. Three, two, one …

'I think it's getting late. Do you think we should leave?'

Abort mission. It's time to take off.

11:40 p.m.

We are home.

He hugs me goodbye. We keep it PG-13. At least one of us decides to.

'Do you want to come up for some coffee?' I ask him as I get out of the cab. There's no one home, and I forget to tell him that there's no coffee either.

'I would have loved to, but I think it's too late,' he grins apologetically. It's not even midnight. As his cab vanishes into the night, I realize that he reminds me of Mr Rabbit from Lewis Carroll's *Alice In Wonderland* – always worried that he shall be *too late*.

But I am no Alice, and this date was no Wonderland.

3

Men Are from Mars, and Some Are from Venus Too

Number Sixteen: The Horticulturist
What Do I Want to Be When I Grow Up?

May 2013

What do gay men want to be when they grow up? Proprietors of exotic vacation homes? Owners of washboard abs? Possessors of fat bank accounts? Creators of beautiful Instagram grids? Recipients of best-dressed titles, beauty pageants, and other such stereotypical hogwash?

Or do we just want to … grow up first?

Not **Sixteen**. He's already an adult.

On a cheerful Wednesday afternoon, we find ourselves at a fun pub in Bangalore, and neither of us feels out of place. Like most gay men I know, he's witty and enigmatic. Unlike most gay men I know, he's also extremely kind and optimistic. I laugh loudly at one of his many anecdotes and am surprised at how genuine my laughter really feels. He could be an advertisement for antidepressants. I make a mental note to ask my therapist if she can prescribe him to me daily.

Sixteen might be a man of many jokes, but he's also a horticulturist who bakes for his residential community. As he charms me with stories of his grandmother's cooking skills (and how she inspired him to start his own home kitchen), he seems to remind me of someone.

When I get back home after three pitchers of beer (and a promise to get his homemade brownies express-delivered to my home address), I realize that he reminds me of who I want to be five years from now.

3.1 The Twenty Kinds of Douchebags, Twits, Jerks and Dickheads You Can Avoid

'What do you look for in a man?' is a question I've asked all my friends.

Bright eyes? Irresistible wit? A smile that reaches his eyes? Billboard-style white teeth? An Instagrammable face? The ability to make you laugh and swoon at the same time? A closet full of expensive Italian shoes that are fortunately your size? A man with a trust fund?

Aneesh, Kartik and Urvaksh are all different people, and they all have different answers. The consultant wants a jigsaw puzzle and the copywriter wants a fairy tale … and the corporate banker? He wants a Pinterest board.

Let's face it, everyone has a type and there's no single tried-and-tested template for the One. Sure, there will always be personality traits/redeeming qualities that this book will nudge you towards, but when it comes to finding a single definition for the One, sadly there's none.

'Did I just buy this book for no reason?' you ask.

Not so fast, reader. This ~~dark cloud of dating~~ chapter comes with a silver lining. The One might be a ~~lie we've been fed all our lives~~ myth, but it makes every other kind of man as real as possible. My friends might disagree on what makes the(ir) perfect Prince Charming, but they all vote unanimously on one thing: they know exactly the kind of man they would *never* want to date.

And that's the whole purpose of this book.

It's not here to help you find the One (but more on that later); it's here to tell you what kind of assholes to avoid, what kind of shitheads to send to the spam folder, and what kind of douchebags to ditch. Once you know what kind of men not to settle for, you are only left with the crème de la crème. The only way to find a meaningful connection is by a simple process of elimination. This might be slightly tricky, yes, because the list of qualities that (do not) maketh a man is infinitely long – enough to fill another book – but we need to start somewhere.

So how do you separate the junk from the jackpot of your life?

It's simple – for now, you just have to make sure to be cautious of the guy who …

1. **… texts you like he's live-tweeting.**

'Hello!'
'Good morning!'
'What are you doing?'
'How's lunch?'
'Are you back home from work?'
'Hello?'
'Good night!'
'Hello?'

2. **… thinks that two glasses of sangria is enough to get you into bed.**

Try five glasses, two pints of beer, a shot of jaeger and a bucket of consent.

3. **… starts a sentence with the words, 'But I know what's good for you …'**

Fact: he's not good for you.

4. **… snds yu msgs lyk dis.**

Think about it this way – every time you misspell a word on purpose, a baby seal dies.

5. **… litters on the road like it's no big deal.**

Throw him out of your life. But use a dustbin, please.

6. **… asks you for your Facebook password.**

… and would he give you his in return?

7. **… says something like, 'My ex is the reason I haven't been able to emotionally connect with anyone else.'**

Said every red flag ever.

8. **… uses the hashtag #NotAllMen.**

And still claims to be a feminist. Ugh.

9. **… 'assumes' that the two of you are in an open relationship.**

There's a more common word for that; it's called 'cheating'.

10. **… shows up for dates half an hour late and doesn't even apologize.**

11. **… substitutes his abs for a personality.**

And while these abs (all six of them) might be dashing and full of manners in bed, they'd have a really tough time having a conversation with your friends.

12. … tags his picture with #UglyAF even though he looks like he just did a photoshoot with GQ.

You can probably count his abs as he complains about how unattractive he feels.

13. … corrects people's grammar on Grindr.

He's not at a book club; he's only here to be sexually objectified like everyone else. If he wants to look more uppity, he can have his college degree up as his profile picture.

14. … does not want to use a condom, because 'raw sex feels intimate'.

Do you know what is not intimate? Living with an STD for the rest of your life.

15. … casually asks you for your credit card details.

It's time to casually call the cops.

16. … thinks that shopping at clearance sales is beneath him.

Do you know what will never be beneath him any more? You.

17. … talks rudely to the waitstaff.

If he thinks talking politely to the bartender who's serving him his fifth drink is *not* worth his time, he's probably not worth yours.

18. … only texts you post 2 a.m.

When he wants to meet you post 2 a.m., the chances of wanting to 'get you some Chinese takeout' being the reason are pretty low.

19. … sulks when you don't compliment him for still fitting into his designer jeans from five years ago.

Because his waist is clearly not as large as his ego.

20. **… decides the kinds of boys he wants to date based on lists he read in a book.**

Unless the list has been written by a really good-looking author who's also a great kisser.

Number Seventeen: The TV Producer
Will I Catch a Case of the Douchebag from You?

October 2011

I grate my fingers on the underside of the Sunmica table, as **Seventeen** guffaws at his joke. It's unfunny in an 'I-would-laugh-if-I-could-but-I-really-don't-want-to' kind of way, especially since he's fifteen minutes late and the joke is at my expense. I look at him closely.

<u>*Why* am I doing this again?</u>

He looks thinner in his pictures. He's short, but not *too* short. He's plump, but not *too* plump. I am here, but not *too* here. He's fun, but not *too* …

No, wait. He's not fun at all.

I yawn through a particularly 'gripping' tale of his time spent working as an executive producer on a reality show, but he doesn't seem to notice. He coughs instead. He's telling me about how television rating points work. Halfway through his monologue, I realize I never asked him.

<u>*What* are we doing again?</u>

We are meeting for a post-work pick-me-up at a coffee shop, trying to see whether the spark we shared online is real. But why coffee?

Seventeen has an important meeting the following morning that he *simply* can't afford to look puffy-eyed for. His eyes dart to the wall clock. I lie and say that he can never look puffy-eyed, but it's mostly out of sheer force of habit. Did he notice? Do I see the spark? Why am I asking myself so many questions?

Because I'm *that* bored. (As for that spark? It's as scripted as the show that he works on.)

Also, most dates are a template of such questions. Isn't the weather horrid today? Did you get any traffic? Is that shirt from Zara? What do you do in life? Is writing a real job? Does it keep you busy? Where do you stay? What are you looking for? Do you stay alone? Do you like me? Do I like you? Do I think I like you? Do I like the *idea* of liking you? And so on. They should have a questionnaire for such things.

How did he decide to work for TV? I ask him. I decide to make the most of my turn. Is it the money? Is it the glamour? Is it the fame? Is it the …

'Do you know how many television shows I get to watch before the rest of the world?' He leers. Cocky is only sexy when the person's cute. Otherwise, it just seems out of place. I still laugh my fake laugh. He doesn't seem to buy it this time.

The conversation only goes downhill from there on (much like the ratings of his show), and we struggle to find common ground.

'What is that smell?' **Seventeen** furrows his eyebrows, after twenty more minutes of awkward small talk.

I secretly hope it's the smell of his mediocrity. He coughs again. (Well, what do you know? Maybe it is.) His eyes seem red. This is becoming a pattern. Hoping that he's not allergic to me, I ask him whether he's okay.

'I think I am catching something,' he says. He should catch a cab instead, but I don't say it out loud. I usually stock the snarkiest of my zingers right where they belong – the inner recesses of my mind.

And then, right on cue, he wheezes into a paper napkin and places it on the table. My hands slide away, and I make a mental note to chug half a bottle of cough syrup as soon as I get home. I can *hear* the phlegm. Pretending like it's normal to pass phlegm at the table, he beckons for the cheque.

'What do you want to do now?' I ask him half-heartedly, as the waiter gets the cheque and takes the dirty napkin away. I leave him a hefty tip, just in case.

He sniffles as he looks at his watch. It's only 8 p.m. I swear it felt a lot longer. I give him a feeble smile. He has plans for dinner and needs to leave early, he tells me, responding to my smile with one of his own. 'Would it be okay if we cut this short?' he asks. I cough and tell him I'll survive. I realize we both want the same thing, and it's not a cough drop.

When do we do this again?

We don't, because that's the last we ever hear from each other.

I catch the flu the next day.

3.2 But Where Are All the Good Men?

All the Signs That Say You've Hit the Jackpot and Found the One (for You)

We've already established that the world is littered with boys that you should never date. (If you don't know what I am talking about, you've probably just started reading this book.) It's full of deplorable narcissists, self-obsessed gym freaks, dubious know-it-alls and the select few who never call back (without a reason). But hidden between the poor taste and bad manners are a few good men. The diamonds in the rough. The needles in the haystack. The gemstones on the beach. The One in a million.

When Aneesh finally got back in the game last year, he only had one thumb rule: he'd never agree to go out on a bad date. He hadn't spent three days creating the perfect online dating ~~persona~~ profile to sink in a vortex of what he liked to call 'would-rather-not-meet-them' men.

Maybe it was the fact that he was ~~fresh meat~~ a new thumbnail in a rotation of the same faces online; maybe it was his witty profile handle (he called himself 'SherlockHomos', and apart from that one idiot who asked 'if he could be the *key* to his ass?' everyone else thought it was a great conversation starter); or maybe Aneesh just had one of those handsome faces that everyone took an instant liking to, because it worked out better than what he could have hoped for.

Over the next few weeks, he went on a series of first dates with men who had only one thumb rule: to show Aneesh 'a good time'. Writers who took him out on movie marathons, picnics in the park with yoga instructors, bar crawls that lasted weekends, and that one memorable joyride with a supermodel, that left him bowlegged for days.

Aneesh had entered – what he liked to call it – the golden age of dating.

And then, he met Vir, a twenty-five-year-old marketing strategist, two months into his new (and improved) dating life. Vir's profile wasn't all that interesting – he didn't have a bike and didn't practise yoga – but he was polite and charming on text, so Aneesh decided to ditch his template and go with his gut instinct.

They met at a bar of Aneesh's preference, but unfortunately, Vir wasn't the bouquet of wit that he seemed online. In fact, the date was anything but Aneesh's idea of textbook perfection. Their beers (and Vir's jokes) were flat, their booth was cramped, and the music wasn't loud enough to mask all the awkward pauses. So you can imagine why he was so disappointed.

When they finally split the bill two hours later, Aneesh was partly relieved. He went back home to binge-watch the latest season of *RuPaul's Drag Race* without a goodbye kiss or any hopes of seeing him ever again.

But Vir surprisingly messaged the very next morning, asking to meet Aneesh again.

'Thanks for being such a fantastic date!' he had texted, and something inside Aneesh clicked. He felt special. In fact, no man had ever made him feel so special before (not even the supermodel with the Royal Enfield).

They met for lunch the next afternoon, switched the beers with rum and avoided sitting in a booth. Only when they paid the bill did they realize that the music system was out of order. They hadn't even noticed.

Aneesh tells me that date was *game-changing*.

All his life, he had been working on this giant jigsaw puzzle of perfection. A cushy two-bedroomed flat. A well-paying consultant job. A great support system of friends. A loving family. Every milestone was a part of the puzzle, and they all fit. There was just one tiny problem.

The puzzle was a giant work-in-progress, because there were always some pieces missing. 'Great things take time', Aneesh would console himself, and continue trying to finish the impossible. That afternoon, after his second date, he realized that he was looking at the puzzle all wrong. It wasn't incomplete: he had just used up all the pieces he had.

He then looked into his pockets and found a piece he'd never seen before.

And it fit.

I chortle as Aneesh tells me this, and he rolls his eyes. 'It's supposed to be *meta*,' he scolds me. I apologize and offer to buy his next drink. 'But what happened next?' I ask as he beckons the waiter to get him a (rather expensive) glass of single malt.

They met again. And again. And again. And again. And every single time, Vir added a piece of his own jigsaw puzzle.

That was four months ago. They've been together ever since.

Aneesh had clearly hit the Jackpot.

So … Who Is the Jackpot™?

The Jackpot, also known as the One (surprise, surprise), is the one you end up with. For a more in-depth analysis on the One, head to chapter 4. When you *do* come across that person, pull up your socks and woo them (and make some space for their toothbrush in your shower cabinet, if you can) before someone else can. Because they *will.* You'll know a person is the Jackpot when he …

1. **… knows that if there's no condom, there's no sex.**
Even if you insist that it's better when there's nothing between you (which you shouldn't). Always cover those troopers, kids.

2. **… insists on splitting the cheque instead of letting you pay.**
The men who don't feel entitled to free drinks and a meal just because you asked them out are the best kind of men in the world. Now split your life with him, as you split that cheque.

3. **… tells you his Netflix password.**
Without expecting you to 'chill'.

4. **… might be passive in a fight, but is not passive-aggressive.**
Leave the passive aggression for the parents, not the pretty boy sitting across from you at the dinner table.

5. **… isn't scared of double messaging.**
The world would have a lot more romances if men weren't afraid of messaging twice in a row.

6. **… is honest about the way he feels.**
But not in the way that'd make you cry … so you can continue eating your double scoop of chocolate-chip ice cream without worrying about him telling you it's going to make you fat.

7. **... thinks that the only glass that is half empty is your glass of gin-and-tonic, and orders you another.**

He's a glass full of amazing.

8. **... finishes your sentences every once in a while ...**

... but will not finish your food (unless you really want him to).

9. **... is willing to share his French fries with you.**

Why order for the table when you can order a salad for yourself and guiltlessly share *his* fries?

10. **... doesn't think twice before telling you how he feels about you.**

You shouldn't think twice about dating him either.

11. **... believes that the only games people should play are board games.**

Mind games are for morons. Repeat after me.

12. **... is on a first-name basis with all your close friends.**

But knows that they will always be *your* friends first.

13. **... messages you right after a date to tell you he had a fantastic time.**

Because if someone waits for three days to tell you they had a great time, they'd wait all their life to tell you that *you* are the One (for them).

14. **... understands the importance of always being on time.**

Punctuality is sexy, around the clock.

15. **... respects your virtual relationship with Ranveer Singh.**

Even though Ranveer Singh has no clue that he's in one.

16. **… knows that being protective and jealous are two different things.**
But doesn't tell you their dictionary meanings every day at breakfast.

17. **… can make a baby giggle.**
The only thing more attractive than a man who can make a baby giggle is a baby who can make a man giggle.

18. **… calls you out for being an asshole when you are being one.**
As he rightfully should, you douchebag.

Number Eighteen, Nineteen, Twenty: The Visitors
Can I Have a One-way Ticket to Love, Please?

October 2012, April 2016, November 2018

A raging club in midtown New York City. A quiet speakeasy in the boroughs of Paris. A sleepy pub in central San Jose. I meet **Eighteen**, **Nineteen** and **Twenty** at three different gay bars at three different points in my life.

'What brings you here, so far away from Bombay?' the surgeon asks me, in 2012. I sip on my mojito and take in the crisp Chelsea air. It's full of cigarette smoke and concrete dreams.

'I am visiting friends,' I tell the producer, in 2014, as a French couple makes out noisily in the next booth. We both reach for the same tartine.

'Do you visit often?' asks the software engineer, in 2018. He sounds hopeful. The bartender rings for the last call. No one stirs, but I feel something stir inside me. It's the spark of a vacation fling.

Three different timelines that mesh into one. They are all nice, wholesome men. Men who had left the country long ago and have been away long enough for it to have affected their accents, but not their attitudes.

'Do I get to see you again?' they all ask when it's time for me to leave. There's only one glitch in this plan.

They also happen to live far away. I know that distance is just a test of how far love can travel, but this adds a few extra thousand miles to long-distance, and flight ticket prices are at an all-time high.

So I never buy a return ticket.

3.3 The Gentleman's Guide to the Wet Dream: The Bonus Feature That Keeps Giving

Over drinks one night, Kartik tells me about his love-hate relationship with Type A gay men. He loves the fact that they exist in the most NSFW parts of his dreams. He hates the fact that he can never be one of them.

'Why not?' I ask.

The city is dotted with queer men, and if I switch on Grindr, I'd find a dozen of (each of) them within a hundred-metre radius – Type A, Type B, Type C and so on. Our world is an alphabet soup of available men and their corresponding abs.

'He's not your standard on-the-shelf gay. He's the upgrade,' Kartik scoffs. I am confused. If we could find queer men available on shelves, would we be getting drinks at a singles bar on a Tuesday night? I don't think so.

'Where do you find these desirable boys?' I ask. If there's an Amazon-like service for attractive guys, I want to sign up right away.

'I am not talking about boys,' Kartik scoffs at me. 'I am talking about the Man™.'

I am confused again. Aren't we all men?

Kartik gulps down his drink and orders another one.

'It's not that easy. This isn't just any man, he's the Wet Dream.'

Oh well, the Wet Dream sounds like a dreamboat. So we dive right in.

Who's the Wet Dream?

Everyone knows the Wet Dream: he's spoken about at wine soirees, intimate house parties and exclusive bars, or cooed over at Sunday sundowners, gallery openings and garden bistros (invite only). The society wives call him the most eligible bachelor in town, and although their husbands don't like him, they all drink single malt together every second Sunday of the month. The Wet Dream is – no surprises here – the stereotypical gay man's wet dream. They all want to be him; but more importantly, they all want to be *with* him. Some call him unattainable, some call him the benchmark. A select few call him the ruler of the (gay) social pyramid.

In short, he's everything I've ever wanted to be.

But *who is* the Wet Dream? Where does he come from (and where does he go)? Do *you* know the Wet Dream? Could you *be* the Wet Dream?

There's only one way to find out.

Where Do You Find the Wet Dream?

If you don't have a clue, here's a checklist that might help:

- He has an important-sounding job at an important-sounding firm, but no one really knows what he does. He uses words like 'transcendental' and 'synergy' on his LinkedIn profile and has a picture that was once used in *GQ*'s 'Best Dressed Men' list.
- He has a live-in maid who dotes on him: she likes to believe that he treats her like his own mother. He doesn't know her last name.
- With his *GQ* hair and movie-star looks, he has blemish-free skin that would put a face cream commercial to shame. He has scars, but he wears those as accessories. A slight cut on his left eyebrow and a mole just under his chin – they add layers to his character,

or at least that's what everyone says about him. He has dimples that he uses to his advantage.

- He has an intense twelve-step exfoliating ritual.
- He gets upgraded from Economy to Business class, but doesn't post about it on Instagram because he thinks it's tacky.
- On his birthday, he has a gathering with his closest friends at home – an intimate affair of around sixty people – with free-flowing champagne and catered hors d'oeuvres, after which they rage all night at the newest (and most exclusive) club in town. Cocaine in the bathroom may or may not be involved.
- He has a sea-facing apartment that reeks of old money. It's done up in the post-modernist way that he absolutely adores (and will tell you all about over canapés and wine). He'd insist that he give you a house tour.
- The house is littered with curios and knick-knacks from around the world, and he has anecdotes about all of them. You don't need to ask. He'll tell you.
- His mother stays a few swanky high-rises away, but they are estranged. He still visits her once every few weeks and sends her dahlias (her favourite) on her birthday. He hopes to inherit the beachside holiday home in Goa once she passes away.
- He plans to write an informal memoir one day, but it will most certainly be ghostwritten. The author will never get the credit, and will instead be sent off on an all-expenses-paid trip to Morocco.
- He has a bevvy of close friends (but they are all acquaintances) – lawyers, designers and entrepreneurs who sell hipster furniture or/and artisanal produce. They are all slightly less attractive, slightly less rich and slightly less important. But they've never been less available.
- He doesn't go to the gym, but has a CrossFit trainer who applauds him for being his most motivated client. On alternate weekends,

he does Pilates with the girls, after which they gossip over brunch with bottomless mimosas. He only has two glasses.

- He's left behind a train wreck of broken hearts, and, on more than one occasion, has been the source of inspiration for a poem, a song or the standalone painting. He bought the painting for his curated art collection. It hangs proudly in his living room.
- At least three supermodels call him their best friend and swear that they'd die to see him in a fulfilling relationship. They wouldn't try setting him up with any of their other (read: obviously less close) gay friends though.
- His daily diet is littered with steamed vegetables, cold-pressed juices and free-range meat that he sources from the gourmet supermarket right around the corner. He doesn't do cheat days, but instead binges on a cookie sandwich as a cheat meal. He feels guilty after, and tweets about how fat he feels, which results in a string of compliments from all his friends saying it isn't so. He does an extra twenty minutes on the spinning cycle to compensate.
- He's popular, but discreet. Boys stay the night (but never for breakfast) and go home happy and smiling (without a number to call back). They still compliment him on his post-modernist decor as he lazily shuts the door in their faces. He reads Haruki Murakami after.
- He has sex and knows all his moves, but isn't sexy. He bites the pillows when he comes (and he'd want you to bite him too).

But here's the thing:

He farts in his bed when no one's around. Which makes him just like you and me.

Also, the Wet Dream™ is most probably really bad in bed, so he's really not the One for you.

You are welcome.

Number Twenty-one: The Leg Up
Why Does Every Boy Come with a Number?

November 2017

My phone buzzes loudly with an unknown number. It's 4 p.m. on a Monday.

Wary of letting yet another telemarketer down, I swipe it shut. A full five seconds later, it rings again. This time I pick it up, ready to reject yet another holiday package.

'Hi!' says a familiar voice. It's not a telemarketer. It's **Twenty-one**.

'Hello!' I say with mock enthusiasm.

The founder of a laundry-delivery startup, **Twenty-one** is a lot of things, but I mostly remember him as a man who doesn't believe in himself a lot. We met a year and a half ago, eventually drifting apart because we lived in different cities, and more importantly because we wanted different things in life. He wanted a content life with a companion, and I wanted a content-writing gig with his company.

That isn't happening any time soon, because he's already lost hopes of making his venture a full-time business. You'd think that he gives up too easily, but he's also only recently stopped pining for his co-founder – a man he's been in love with for the past seven years. A man who's also unfortunately straight.

So I decide to cut him some slack.

'I wanted to ask you for a favour,' he says to me after five minutes of polite chitchat. There it is – the entire point of the phone call.

The past eighteen months have been peppered with many frantic calls such as this one. 'Isn't that strange?' you'd ask. 'Why do we seek men with whom we have no common interests?'

But then again, we've already levelled up to complaining about our love lives to each other as most men with no common interests do, so I don't question his motives.

Twenty-one comes with a pattern. He has a habit of building men up in his head and treating them with the reverence that is only worthy of the Wet Dream. 'It's not about an illustrious career or Greek god looks', he once told me, 'it's about the little things.'

All he needs is a man who'll love him with the same vigour. That's not asking for a lot, is it? There have been a string of (one-sided) romances: there was the (alleged) prince of a remote district in Rajasthan, the writer who wanted to whisk him off to Goa and, more recently, the struggling BPO executive two cities away.

Each story ended before it could begin, because two out of these three times, he hadn't even met the man he fell in love with. It was all in his head, built over weeks of cute texts and heartwarming voice notes. Why are we habituated to fall in love with figments of our imagination – men we've only seen (and heard) on our phone screens?

Well, if we didn't, the Wet Dream would cease to exist.

"So … about that favour?'

'Shoot,' I say, preparing myself for yet another story about heartbreak and betrayal.

'Thank you! So tell me, how do you know …' he asks, namedropping an upcoming entrepreneur that I only follow on Instagram.

I sigh. Here we go again.

Our mutual acquaintance is the founder of his own digital startup, well in his thirties, and earns his capital from being handsome *and* humble – a combination that **Twenty-one** couldn't resist.

They met each other on Instagram a few weeks ago. It started small. A strategic like here, a premeditated comment there, and before they could even follow each other, they were texting like crazy.

'It felt so effortless', **Twenty-one** moans over the phone, 'and I felt like I was sharing a part of my life with him. I thought he felt the same way.'

People *never* feel the same way. Not over Instagram DMs.

'And then … he suddenly stopped replying.'

They always do.

'So, I needed your help. I was wondering if …'

This is where he asks me for advice. This is where I help him get closure. This is where I laud him for finally standing up.

'… you can pass along his number to me?'

3.4 What's Your Gay Tribe?

Kartik is having an existential crisis. It's a regular Friday night.

What could it be? The inevitability of death? The crushing loneliness of realizing all humans will eventually die alone? The meaninglessness of his dead-end job? The purpose of life? The realization that the Wet Dream is a farce? The sudden dawning of the fact that the One is a myth? I've clearly thought this through.

Kartik shrugs. It's worse. He doesn't know his gay tribe.

What Is a Gay Tribe?

You would want to believe that a gay tribe is a group of self-foraging, nomadic queer men, if not a posse of privileged gays who make plans to meet for Sunday brunch every week. But don't be surprised if you can't find any teepees or tapas when you go looking. In fact, men belonging to the same tribe don't necessarily have to hang out with each other; remember that this isn't a clique, it's a category.

A tribe is a social grouping of gay men based solely on their key physical characteristics. Long story short, tribes exist to help you find men you are attracted to based on the quantity of hair on their bodies and/or muscle on their frame. It's not exactly rocket science.

You start off with some pretty basic stereotypes: twinks, femmes, geeks, jocks and daddies. And then in (con)descending order of size, hair (yes, hair) and kink, you've got Bears, Wolves, Cubs and Otters. Is this marginalizing the gay community or moulding a human zoo?

Kartik is of the opinion that queer men shouldn't be sorted into tribes based on their looks: this isn't gay Hogwarts, and not everyone is hairy. He also finds it hard to relate to any one particular tribe.

Kartik is lanky and clean-shaven, so he's not a Bear; but he's also got tufts of hair on his chest, so he's not one of those clean-cut men either. At thirty-two, he's too old to be a Twink but also too young to be a Daddy. He works out regularly, but you can't see his abs in HD, so that rules out him being a Jock or a Gym Bunny. At best, he's a cross between a Twink and an Otter. Does that make him a Twotter? Or worse, an Oink?

Sadly, that only makes him sound like a swine. (Side note: My romantically inclined friend wants me to tell you that he's no pig.) So where does Kartik find his true calling?

The Twinks think he's too scruffy, the Otters think he's not scruffy enough, the Bears won't accept him because he's fit, and the Jocks shut him out because he's not lets-spot-each-other-at-the-gym fit. It's exasperating. For years now, Kartik has been shunted from tribe to tribe, trying to find his identity. Is there a tribe for gay men who feel like they *don't* belong?

That's all of us, I tell him.

So How Can You Identify Your Gay Tribe?

It's safe to say that Grindr is very likely to help you find your next hookup and less likely to find your soulmate, but it certainly won't help you find yourself. Until then, answer these ten questions to find out which tribe you'd best fit in with:

1. **On a Saturday night, you'd rather be**
   - a. Doing shots at a bar
   - b. Watching a movie
   - c. Attending a gallery opening
   - d. Hitting the gym
   - e. Spending a quiet night in

2. **You'd describe your body hair situation as**
   a. Smooth
   b. Average
   c. Scruffy
   d. Waxed
   e. Hairy

3. **Your favourite shade of red is**
   a. Fuchsia
   b. Blue
   c. Magenta
   d) Red
   e. Maroon

4. **You heard about this book through**
   a. Social media
   b. An internet pop up
   c. A flyer at your local bookstore
   d. Wait. This is a book?
   e. Your friends

5. **At a house party, your friends describe you as**
   a. Spunky
   b. Mysterious
   c. Witty
   d. Good looking
   e. Distinguished

6. **If you were a famous Tom, you would be**
   a. Tom Holland
   b. Tom Cruise
   c. Tom Hiddleston
   d. Tom Hardy
   e. Tom Selleck

7. **The word 'stan' means**
   a. An obsessive fan
   b. Is it short for 'understand'?
   c. I really don't know, but I'm sure it's a part of pop culture
   d. This is a trick question
   e. Is that a name?

8. **In a relationship, you see yourself as**
   a. The feisty one
   b. What relationship?
   c. The funny one
   d. The fitter one
   e. The older one

9. **Choose your favourite sex prop**
   a. Handcuffs
   b. Blindfold
   c. Dildo
   d. Jockstrap
   e. Whipped cream

10. **A song that you'd sing at karaoke**
   a. A love ballad
   b. An '80s pop song
   c. The catchiest Bollywood number
   d. A mash-up of Queen's hits
   e. A Stevie Wonder classic

Mostly As: You are a TWINK!

In gay terminology, a twink is a slim, young man with minimal body hair, a clean-shaven face and the hopelessness of a doe-eyed ingénue. He's feisty and fresh-faced, making him an easy target for stereotype jokes and mature gay men. Somebody buy the boy an appletini already. He's waiting.

A celebrity twink you can relate to: Tom Holland or Shawn Mendes

But you might also be: a TWUNK!

A twunk is a twink on a protein-rich diet. Characteristically more muscular, twunks can be identified by their raging levels of self-confidence, only made possible by their dedication to the gym and allotting two chest days every week. Fit in all the right areas, he'll meet you for an iced Americano after his workout.

A celebrity twunk you can relate to: Justin Bieber or Nick Jonas

Mostly Bs: You are DISCREET!

Hiding behind stock imagery and bathroom selfies that are strategically cropped right around the Adam's apple, the discreet gay man is the most commonly found gay subculture in the country. He's on the roads. He's in cyber cafes. He's on your phones. He's even in his closet.

A discreet celebrity you can relate to: No one, because that's the point.

But you might also be: MARRIED WITH KIDS!

In which case, you should probably get the Kindle version of this book.

Mostly Cs: You are an OTTER!

The otter is the antithesis to the twink. With a lean build and a sweater of scruff, he is laid-back and lanky, and loves things '*ironically*'. The correlation between the man and the animal has never been clear, but who cares, because both are cute.

A celebrity Otter you can relate to: Aditya Roy Kapur

But you might also be: a GEEK!

One would imagine the geek to be a cute, smart guy with glasses, but you'd be surprised. Deeply passionate and a man with many hobbies, the geek can't decide what irritates him more: meat-eaters who swear by soy milk lattes or Grindr profiles of sapiosexuals.

A celebrity geek you can relate to: Ayushmann Khurana

Mostly Ds: You are a JOCK!

Conventionally attractive, jocks are poster boys for queer fantasies in the mainstream media. Brawny and broad-shouldered, they can be identified by their low body fat (or low IQs, as jealous and cynical gay men would suggest) and their affinity for gym selfies.

A celebrity jock you can relate to: Varun Dhawan

But you might also be: a BULL!

A bull is a jock (also known as a gym rat on steroids). When he's not lifting heavy weights at the gym, he's lifting heavy weights at home. Built like a sixteen-axle truck, our heavyweight champion only sees red when he hears ignorant people go on and on about the benefits of the keto diet.

A celebrity bull you can relate to: Aamir Khan, in his post-*Dangal* avatar.

Side note: A gym rat is not to be confused with a gym bunny. Although both are obsessed with the gym, the latter works out because he cares about how he looks, and the former looks (so sweaty) because he cares about how he works out.

Mostly Es: You are a BEAR!

Bears are found at sports bars, their natural habitat, breaking queer stereotypes by drinking their own body weight in beer. Typically stockier and older than most gay men, Bears are known to be aggressively hairy and alarmingly cheerful – their jovial personalities directly proportional to the amount of hair on their chests.

A celebrity bear you can relate to: Sunny Deol and John Travolta

But you might also be: a DADDY!

Many will argue that the Daddy is not a queer tribe at all. Any gay man can be a daddy (if he finds a woman who'd donate an egg). But the Daddy is special. He's dapper, he's debonair and he's dominating. The Daddy is not a parental figure in the conventional sense, because the only things he will ever father are the wet dreams of naive gay men.

A celebrity Daddy you can relate to: Anil Kapoor and Hugh Jackman

Number Twenty-two: The Struggler
Am I a Type or a Template?

January 2015

60 minutes to target

I ring the doorbell and wait.

I am nervous. I am very nervous.

You would think that I've long banished my first date jitters to the trashcan; so vast is my experience of dating. I've walked into dozens of bars, homes and restaurants (and a car, that one time), and met so many men that I could be a veteran. Some might call me an expert. A few might call me a seasoned professional. I call myself 'someone with a lot of time'. But irrespective of lad or location, the anxiety never goes away.

Which brings me back to my nervousness at the door.

Twenty-two is the scion of a family of watchmakers from Jaipur. He moved to the city to meet merchants and other important men to further their family business and his personal dreams. Personal dreams?

Yes, he's also a model. A *struggling* model. We've never met, but his photos on Grindr look like they've been stripped out of a fashion shoot. (He tells me later that they are just behind-the-scenes shoots from his portfolio, and I tell him to shut up.) In fact, all his photos speak so highly of him, they could be his mother (even the last one where he is shirtless and appears to be taking a bathroom selfie). At least I can see his face, which is all too rare in a world where your pecs are enough to gain somebody's attention.

It all started when I'd been scrolling through Grindr a couple of weeks ago, the eager torsos melding into a patchwork quilt of faultless pecs. And then he sent me a tap. He was cute, so I sent a tap right back. That's when the deluge of photos followed. And I was hooked.

He seemed too perfect, too good looking and too eager, which is why I find this strange. He sent *me* a ping. Why on earth was he interested in me? Maybe he liked out-of-shape men who worry too much about doors that won't open.

58 minutes to target

Back to the door. I wait with bated breath as it finally opens. He's beautiful, and wearing a purple t-shirt with a wide neck that grazes his defined clavicles. Ridiculously, I pull myself up straight. There's a momentary pause where we both stare at each other. Am I not what he's looking for? Don't I look like my pictures? The seconds seem to stretch into minutes.

He finally smiles and ushers me in with a tight hug. I feel my body tense up. What is his agenda here? You have to be careful with men whose bodies have been varnished with perfection. Their washboard abs and bulging pecs may hide many a red flag. But I am still at the stage in my life where someone being interested is an attractive trait. Especially when they are so easy on the eyes.

'Would you like to drink something?' he asks me excitedly.

'Sure, surprise me,' I beam, and he rushes to the kitchen, all six feet and two inches of him. His behind is pert and sculpted, and it shows off the hours he's spent in the gym. Maybe I should keep on sending him back to the kitchen.

He comes back with a tall glass filled with protein shake. 'It's homemade,' he says.

I stare at him. I was expecting a drink. He tells me he's a teetotaler now. In fact, he hasn't touched alcohol in over two years. I am even more intrigued: most gay men I know (including myself) have a long-standing, unhealthy relationship with alcohol. Some call it overcompensation. Some call it therapy. I call it 'having a lot of time'.

45 minutes to target

I take a sip. It tastes unsurprisingly … *healthy*. He's also carrying a plate of oatmeal digestives. I take one and bite into it, though I'd rather bite him. Why doesn't he drink any more, I ask?

He grins and his dimples stretch over his scruffy face. He's neither an Otter nor a Bear, and he's definitely not a cub. My very attractive friend here is a Pup.

The model life is difficult. He has to spend every waking minute working out and eating in. He covers up to five auditions a day. Sometimes, even seven. There's no time for alcohol. For now, he's struggling with independent shoots for independent magazines. Eventually, he hopes to find himself on a billboard. Until then, he's right here in front of me.

'Is it really that difficult when a man is so attractive?' I flirt.

30 minutes to target

But he wasn't *always* this attractive, **Twenty-two** tells me, completely missing the point (and my compliment). He came to the city three years ago, forty pounds heavier and two suitcases lighter.

Back home, he was always bullied for being 'the rich kid who ate too much' or 'the rich kid who only hung out with girls', and sometimes, when they ran out of fat jokes, they would bully him for being 'the rich kid who only ate out with girls'.

He was tired of being the rich kid who didn't do anything about all the bullying. So he took a loan from his rich father and moved cities (and eventually, careers). Once here, he joined a gym, dumped his junk food habits and decided to turn his life around. That was three years ago.

Ah. The case of the former-fat-kid-turned-fabulous gay man is a tale as old as time. It's a trope we all love, because so many of us have been there. Every single gay man I know has pumped years of emotional turmoil at the gym. Only, my friend here did a better job than most of us.

'What has it been like?' I ask him.

He cut contact with all his friends back home, save for the one friend who stuck by him through thick and thin. He grins at the pun, and I grin at his ingenuity.

'She's a writer too!' he exclaims. 'Works for a publishing house back home.'

Does he have a type then? While few men are so clichéd as to lust after typically tall, dark and *GQ*-handsome men, most of us have a type. Some things will always attract us, and if you line all your ex-lovers in a row, you'll see a common thread – and no, it isn't their mutual hate for you. Sometimes it's eyes that sparkle, and sometimes it's the dimples that dig deep into your soul. Sometimes it's their passion for the arts, and occasionally, it's their pin code. What's *my* type?

Emotionally unavailable men.

20 minutes to target

'What's with you and writers?' I blush.

He laughs. 'Rajveer used to say the same thing!'

'Who's Rajveer?' I ask. Is he a brother? An uncle? A forgotten friend? A school bully? A man that I hope **Twenty-two** has no prior romantic entanglements with.

'He's my ex-boyfriend.'

Guess who spoke too soon?

12 minutes to target

Talking about the ex is one of many classic rookie mistakes, but I choose to overlook this too. The old rules that suggest you mustn't talk about politics and religion are out, but you should still avoid talking about sex (or the ex). This is because it will only remind your date that there have been lovers before them, which feels inappropriate for a first impression. But then again, this might not be a date, and I am clearly not writing a dating guide.

'He was a writer like you,' he says, and before I know it, the man brandishes his phone and pops out a photo. Rajveer looks familiar. Those narrow eyes. That lopsided grin. A crinkling dimple. Where have I seen all of it before?

'He's working on a novel, my friends tell me …' the model tells me, suggesting that he's still keeping tabs on his ex-lover. But I am not paying attention. Rajveer's face is disconcertingly familiar.

'He's not the cutest, but he was really smart, and that's always been a turn on …'

It takes me a few minutes, but it finally hits me where I've seen this man.

In the mirror. Rajveer looks exactly like … *me*.

As we flip through Rajveer's photos, I realize I could be living that life. A picnic along the Seine. Snuggled up in bed with a book. Downing an entire flagon of beer. Laughing while at a musical festival. Grinning away at my laptop. Digging into a slice of double-chocolate fudge cake. These are all the things I would do. These are all the things I have done. We don't just share a face, we also share a life. Is this what an out-of-body experience feels like?

And then I suddenly realize why I am here.

Twenty-two has a type. It's Rajveer.

<u>2 minutes to target</u>

He's talking about his ex animatedly. I still can't quite work him out. And I'm not sure I want to. If I don't do something soon, I might actually have to meet Rajveer. I'll have to meet me. I clear my throat and interrupt him.

20 seconds to target

'Wait,' I say seriously.

'What?'

'Can I kiss you?'

Twenty-two blushes and grins.

I take that as a yes and go straight for the kill.

4

The First Timer's Guide to Flirting

Number Twenty-three: The Influencer
Is #FollowForFollow the New Way to Flirt with a Fellow Gay Man?

It's a myth that all gay men are creative geniuses; that way all our LinkedIn profiles would be a potpourri of art installations, fashion soirees and writing retreats. But it isn't so. Some of us are chartered accountants, many of us are bankers, and a select few spend hours building up PowerPoint decks, cursing their consultant careers. When I am not doing this, I write copy for insurance companies. It's not a glamorous life.

So when **Twenty-three** tells me that he's a famous fashion blogger, I am intrigued. You'd assume the quintessential fashion blogger would have the aesthetic of a prepubescent tween – androgynous and wearing clothes that are too large for him, eating full acai bowls and leading half-lives on luxurious yachts – but our friend here is … *different.*

He's thirty-four, bearded and built like a bull. **Twenty-three** is visiting from Delhi and is here to collaborate with a fashion chain. The word 'collaborate' pops up five times in our chat: is he an SEO search engine?

'Would you like to get drinks?'

He's staying at a hotel nearby. I picture plush satin sheets and room service. Maybe we can get truffle fries?

I am in his room nineteen minutes later; I clean up fast. He opens the door in a shirt that is two sizes too small with two buttons undone. I like what I see. But the room?

It's modest, and there are no plush satin sheets. The menu card is frayed and his bag (like my life) is in disarray. T-shirts stumbling out, rolled up underwear lobbying for your attention and what looks like half a strip of size L condoms not even attempting to shy away. Our friend has been busy. As he hastily pushes everything into his open suitcase, I spot three other products from his recent collaborations on Instagram.

'Is this what the influencer life looks like?' I casually prod, sliding onto the bed. This is only a natural state of progression, since he slid into my DMs.

Apparently, it's not all gift bags and freebies. There are no acai bowls and no lavish yacht rides. He gets the occasional free t-shirt (I see that his bag is littered with them), but it's a lot of hard work. Gruelling hours spent in front of the camera, trying to find the perfect angle and the perfect sponsor. And then, there's the added stress of retaining his 50k followers.

Oh, well. Are there any perks?

'I know how to get the best pictures ...' he shoots. Gay men won't know how to do their taxes, but we'll swiftly tell you the right time to upload a thirst trap to get maximum views. This isn't surprising; since we are a generation of men that use Instagram likes as social currency. Which makes our influencer here adequately rich.

'... and I also get hotel rooms with queen-size beds,' he tells me. I smile, because I don't need to be asked twice.

'Why have you not followed me yet?' he asks me two hours later, as I snuggle against his chest. His shirt is missing, and so are the buttons. Under his stern gaze, I promptly send him a follow request. We never make it to drinks.

He only sends me a follow request five days later.

4.1 Making a Move: Flirting with Dudes in Virtual and Real Life

When it comes to making a move, nature has a fascinating spread of flirting rituals. There's no Tinder in the animal kingdom, so our furry and feathered friends have to stick to old-fashioned methods.

Survival of the ~~fittest~~ flirtiest – Charles Darwin

Take the red-capped manakin, for example, which does the bird equivalent of the moonwalk to bedazzle a potential partner. The Australian green tree frog, on the other hand, serenades suitors by breaking into song. Hooded seals take it a step further; inflating a giant red balloon-like sac out of their left nostril and waving it around, in the hopes of attracting a female companion. It's all about pushing your limits. Male scorpionflies risk their lives in swiping dead insects from a spider's web to woo potential mates. In insect speak, that's like getting someone a box of chocolates.

In human speak, that's a *lot* of effort.

Humans are ... *funny creatures*. You might think we have it easy, since we don't have to build an impressive skillset, blow up our body parts, or worse, worry about life-threatening situations, but men *really* don't know how to flirt. We are so used to getting applauded for doing just enough to graze past the bare minimum, we don't even try any more. What do we do instead?

We use cheesy pick-up lines. We buy rounds of cheap drinks. We tell jokes that fall flat. We ask for numbers too soon. We reply to texts too late. We send bouquets of old roses. The weak-hearted slide into DMs. The worst kinds of men send dick pics. For most of us, the bar is set really low.

Men have had it so easy for so long, we've forgotten how to make a great first impression.

Is Flirting Really That Difficult?

Not really. We all have tricks that make us more desirable. Kartik has a routine where he lightly grazes his fingers over a man's arm as he giggles at their jokes. Aneesh buys the boys a drink but acts dismissive after, his aloofness leaving them begging for more. Urvaksh flexes his muscles and goes in for a spontaneous kiss. The boys all have their signature moves.

And it's time you find one of your own.

A Quick Note on Flirting in Person

Imagine you are at a bar. It's a quiet night, and you are getting a drink. Single malt, on the rocks. And there, as the music reaches a crescendo and the closing lights shine your face up with a spotlight, you spot someone who catches your eye. He's cute, you think. He's sophisticated and strapping, and all the things you like in a man. Should I make a move, you ask yourself. You want to come across as enigmatic, but not suspicious. You want to appear larger than life, but not intimidating. You want to look dapper, but not desperate. That's a lot of self-worth issues to feel in such a short span of time.

Making a move in person is a lot about courage. But before you muster up the mettle to go make a first impression, you need to begin with the following steps.

Make eye contact.

The first rule of Fight Club is you don't talk about Fight Club. Similarly, the first rule of flirting is to not make it obvious that you are flirting. Make eye contact, yes, but don't linger. Just enough to get their attention before you approach. It's all about timing. (Side note: Anything longer than six seconds is a sign of borderline 'obsessive stalker behaviour' and is an indication for you to abort mission.)

Break eye contact only to give them a chance to check you out and to show off your side profile. But remember, your pièce de résistance is your …

Smile.

Statistics say that smiling faces are more approachable. There are 43 muscles in your face; you need to know when to use them. When the internet tells you that a smile is your most attractive feature, it's the one time it's not lying. Smiles belong to honest men. Smiles belong to charming men. Smiles belong to endearing men. Smiles belong to men we want to kiss. Smiles belong to men with Big Dick Energy.™ Smiles belong to men we need, but don't deserve.

Now, go be that man and walk right over.

Break the ice.

… but make sure you go in with a game plan. You don't want to walk over to someone all debonair and suave and just … clam up. Shadow tagging the object of your affection (i.e. like a stalker) works in a sum total of zero situations (not including Akshay Kumar's blockbusters). You don't need awful pick-up lines or simpering small talk to let someone know you are interested. Sometimes, a quick 'hi' will do.

Listen more.

The only thing more attractive than a man with a smiling face is a man with a smiling face who listens. Half the world's problems would be solved if we stopped talking, and the other half, if we just listened.

Just listen. It's really not that difficult. Hear what they say, and follow it up with questions (or a joke). It's remarkable what keeping your ears open can do for you.

Throw in a compliment.

... but make sure you mean it. Vague compliments have the success rate of buying someone a flat beer. Men love feeling special, so choose wisely. Kartik likes being told he has a beautiful laugh. Aneesh blushes when people tell him he has great hair. Urvaksh has been known to let his guard down when people compliment his biceps. Pick something you think is unique to them, and voice your feelings. Clothes, hair, eyes and smiles? Yes. Pimple on their nose? No.

... and just ask.

If you thought that leaning in for a spontaneous kiss was enigmatic, try asking for their permission first. Take things forward by asking them if they'd like to hang out sometime. If you pay attention to what they say, you'll pick up on their interests. Use it to suggest a plan.

If they say yes, ask them for their Instagram handle, or even better, their phone number. If they say no, respect it. The best way to show someone what they are missing out on is by being a gentleman. Wish them a great evening, smile and walk away.

There'll always be a next time.

A Quick Note on Flirting through Social Media

Everyone knows that social media was invented for flirting. You can *heart* someone's pictures on Instagram, *like* their posts on Facebook, send them a quick *nudge* on Hike, or *poke* them if you find them cute … social media *wants* you to tell people that you are interested.

Social media is thus the quintessential wingman that eggs you on to say hello to the cute guy at the bar – only, it can't physically nudge you towards a man or tell you off the morning after all your bad decisions.

How Do I Make a Move Online?

Say hello only if you know them.

That's short for, 'don't slide into their DMs if you don't know them'.

Especially with a dick pic. A dick pic is the universal shorthand for a dick move.

The chances of coming off as creepy are so high (even if you look like Chris Hemsworth in *Thor*) that you'll kill all chances of forging a real connection. Instead, slide in with a reference to their work (only if it's available in the public domain), a mention of a common acquaintance (only if the mutual is a close friend), or an allusion of how the two of you might know each other (only if you've met in person before). If none of these are applicable, announce your entry into their DMs with a (well-timed) compliment or a (well-intentioned) meme.

Men can't resist either. What if they still don't reply?

DO. NOT. COMMENT. ON. THEIR. PHOTOS. TO. TELL. THEM. YOU. SENT. THEM. A. DM.

They know, because they obviously saw it. They also chose to ignore it.

Skip the sleaze.

Keep the dirty jokes and sexual innuendoes to yourself: this means you can't ask them for 'sexy pics' or answer their 'ssup?' with a succinct 'my dick'. (Word from the expert: That will *never* work.)

Keep it light and exciting. There's nothing wrong with sending a thirst trap or two as long as it's not X-rated or #NSFW. If they don't react or respond, you should probably get the hint and stop.

Be patient about meeting in person. A lot of us like to hide behind our Instagram grids and Facebook walls because it's comforting. Almost everyone thinks they are more boring in person. If it helps, try convincing them that they are not. Keep the banter going till you know each other a bit more. Once you've gauged the scene and think that things are going well, ask them for their number.

A Few Guidelines for Flirting on Your Favourite Social Media Platforms

<u>Facebook/Instagram</u>

A few dos:

- Send him a friend/follow request if things are going well.
- View *all* his stories.
- Like a few of his pictures. Anything less than three is advisable.

And a few don'ts:

- Ask him to follow you back.
- Send a friend/follow request to his friends.
- Like *all* his pictures, including his first post from 2007.
- Like any of his friends' pictures.
- Tag him in any of your pictures.
- … or Facebook check-ins.

Snapchat

A few dos:

- Add him (if he's already added you or told you to add him).
- Send a couple of photos a day. Stick to pictures of what you are doing, like working out at the gym or drinking with your friends.
- Stick to *only* a couple of photos a day.
- Send him photos of something that is obviously an inside joke between the two of you.

And a few don'ts:

- Send him unsolicited pictures of your naked body.
- Ask for pictures of his naked body.
- Spam him with pictures every half-hour ...
- ... Including one of you pooping.

Clubhouse

A few dos:

- Follow him
- Join rooms that he's moderating/a part of.
- Ask to speak only if you have something intelligent to say.

And a few don'ts:

- Start a closed room with him without his permission.
- Make him a moderator for one of your rooms.
- Ask to speak in a room he's in, and try flirting with him in front of everyone.
- Cut him when he's speaking.

A Quick Note on Flirting through Text

Imagine you are playing a video game. Flirting via text is a level up from flirting in person, but it doesn't mean you've won the game. In fact, this is where it gets harder. There's a new Big Bad™ in the picture.

You aren't just competing with strangers at the bar any more, you are competing with strangers in the message inbox. You might have moved past first impressions and formal introductions, but you've also entered sacred ground – a space that is only reserved for close friends, family and push notifications from food delivery apps and online shopping services.

But beware, multiple love stories get nipped in the bud when the attraction fizzles out over a meandering conversation or gets lost in a sea of thirsty messages. What if in person you get along like a house on fire but on text have the chemistry of two sedimentary rocks?

Hold on to your energy reserves and unleash your superpowers with this quick guide:

Keep the conversation flowing.

Getting someone's number is easy; sustaining the spark is not. Nothing kills the adrenaline rush of flirting with someone like small talk. Stay away from polite conversations about what their day looks like (or worse, the weather). Pepper up your chat with questions and fun facts. Statistics say that 88 per cent of men prefer partners with a sense of humour. (Fun fact: I made those statistics up.)

Don't text too much.

You might be excited, but a barrage of good morning forwards will never be sexy. If someone doesn't reply to you immediately, cut them some slack; they might be stuck in a work meeting, a family emergency or just really busy. It doesn't mean that you can't double text, but remember that a persistent string of hellos will only lead to a 'last seen at 7:53 p.m.'.

In times of distress, breathe and keep your phone away. Go for a run. Read a book. Binge-watch a show. Read another book. Do anything, but make sure you keep your phone away. Message the next day. Keep it simple and sporadic.

… or too little.

But not so sporadic that you reply to their texts a full three weeks later.

Don't correct their grammar.

'I love it when someone points out my mistakes,' said no one ever. No one likes being told they are wrong (unless they think that the Earth is flat, in which case you should stop texting). Their inability to differentiate between 'your' and 'you're' might be disconcerting, but checking for that doesn't make you a gentleman, it makes you a ~~sapiosexual~~ Grammar Nazi. Don't be surprised if things fade out soon after, because ~~your~~ you're the problem here.

Number Twenty-four: The Newbie
The Guide to Coming Out and Going Out

October 2018

'So … what did you want to tell me?' I ask **Twenty-four**, sitting in his passenger's seat.

The young architect reached out to me forty-five minutes ago, announcing that he has 'big news to share'. As a gay man, big news can mean anything – broadcasting that you have a new boyfriend *or* revealing that you have chlamydia. It can go either way.

'But it has to happen in person,' he said, alleviating my fears. The last time someone had big news to share, I found out that a friend's new boyfriend had chlamydia.

Twenty-four is fresh out of college, which means that he's more than half a decade my junior. He's spontaneous and loves taking risks, so I can't rule out either. I wait with bated breath.

The young man's face is impassive, but I can see that he's bursting at the seams with information. It doesn't look like the face of a man who's going to announce that he has an STI. My little friend is usually full of optimism, hope and protein powder – that's a strange combination for a gay man his age. But today, he's full of adrenaline.

'I came out to my parents!' he squeals, and the car fills up with all his pent up excitement. 'Oh my god! How did it go?' I ask, genuinely happy for him.

'It was good … they were really happy …' he says, but he doesn't sound really happy. 'They could have asked me more questions though …'

I've spent more than a decade struggling inside the closet – masking my grunts with giggles and pushing my (rather) excitable hands into my back pockets every time someone as much as cocked an eyebrow during a conversation. Coming out wasn't a spontaneous whim; it was a twelve-step programme. It wasn't so … *easy*.

And yet, I see that **Twenty-four** isn't relieved. My friend here is what they would call a 'new gay', a man who's only recently come into discovering his sexuality. 'He's only twenty-four,' you'd frown, but his expectations from life are like those of a forty-something man.

'Well … what did you expect?'

'They didn't even ask if I was seeing someone …'

'Are you?'

Interesting question to ask a man who's already put you in the friend zone.

Twenty-four comes with a life chart, a five-year plan, and goals that he updates on his phone every week (and he's known to be too hard on himself when they don't work out). You can fast track through your career, but can you fast track through your sexual coming-of-age?

'That's not the point … anyway, this wouldn't have been possible without your help and …'

I only told him to come out when *he* was ready, but if he thinks that's life-changing advice, I am not going to argue. Go on, man.

'… and I realized you've been around whenever I needed a sounding board. I feel like you know me better than anyone else does. So …'

Is this when he asks me out? Do we finally go on that date I've been hinting about? Am I going to be the man his family eventually asks him about?

'… I was wondering if you could help me find a boyfriend too.'

4.2 How to Say No … and Handle Rejection like a Gentleman

Kartik has always been a 'yes' man.

Second helpings at dinner? Sure. An airport pick-up for a friend? Always. Overtime at work? Obviously. A kidney to spare? He's getting his vitals checked, but it seems like a match. Kartik might say that agreeing to plans (or avoidable commitments, like donating spare organs) gives him an adrenaline rush, but I know he's lying. The truth is that he just doesn't know how to say no.

Over the years, he has dragged himself to countless parties and pointless dates, just because he can't let down a friend or a party invitation.

What if he misses out on the love of his life just because he skipped his roommate's birthday party? What if he lucks out on a job offer simply because he skipped happy hour at work? Kartik's whole life is a series of what-ifs and why-nots – he thinks that every missed opportunity could be his golden ticket to glory. As millennials would say, Kartik suffers from a serious case of FOMO.

He just can't seem to say no.

And then, the writer matched with Amrit on Tinder a few weeks ago.

As the editor of an internationally reputed magazine, Amrit ticked every possible checkbox. Distinguished. Well-settled. Eloquent. Charming. Self-aware. Funny. Sexy in a salt-and-pepper beard kind of way. Did I mention that he was also the editor of a famous magazine?

Amrit was clearly a lot of things. But he wasn't … Kartik's *type*.

For someone who spent years writing jingles for brands that sold everything from instant noodles to insurance policies, Kartik wanted to write more. He wanted to *be* more. So even though he wasn't attracted to Amrit in the *conventional sense*, he swiped right. Not one of his finest moments.

It's a networking opportunity, Kartik told anyone who would listen. Was he actually interested? Not really. Did he find Amrit attractive? Just a little bit. Was there potential for something romantic? He hoped not.

This Tinder match was *strictly* professional. So it was only obvious that he would dodge Amrit's flirtations every chance he got. The messages and memes poured in, and casual references to drinks and dinner were made multiple times over. Kartik swerved past every single one of them.

He couldn't be too rude (what if the editor didn't let him pitch a column?) or too friendly (what if he wanted to pinch his butt instead?), so he kept up the banter with a series of his and hellos and polite conversation about the weather. Everything was going really well.

Until that one fateful day, when Amrit asked him out on a date. Point blank. Kartik never saw it coming. For a man who believed in always saying yes, how could he say no?

This was a personality test. He could try one of these four options:

a. Be firm and come up with a polite version of 'sorry, but I am not interested'.

The option seemed brutal, but no one should sit through a date they aren't into. What Kartik needed to remember was that when you are saying no to a date – whether you've met them or not – you are *rejecting* them.

You don't want to seem mean, so if you want to say, 'thanks, but no thanks' to someone you've met online; you want to do so *sensitively*. You can be a good person with a kind heart and still say no. And if that doesn't sound convincing enough, you need to know that one day, you are going to be the person at the receiving end.

b. Ignore all his messages.

... but also, live life as a spineless coward. Ghosting someone is never a good idea, but it's also the easiest exit route to avoid an excruciating conversation. Kartik thought it was the fastest way to make all his problems go away, but that would also mean saying goodbye to all the unrequited pitches that he planned to send to the editor.

c. Lie and come up with an excuse.

Or multiple excuses, in this case. Over the next few weeks, Kartik tried every excuse in the manual. He made up meetings and feigned family emergencies. He faked deadlines and, on one occasion, even faked the symptoms of a life-threatening disease. Was it the best solution?

Not at all. Kartik needed to learn the art of saying no. Not lie. Not come up with excuses. Not over-explain himself. Simply decline.

d. Throw the question back at him.

An alternative to avoiding the question was to throw the question right back at Amrit. When would *he* like to go out on a date? Countless first encounters (or dates) are cut short because men are unable to commit beyond the initial text-dance of asking each other out. We have this incessant need to play a tennis match of questions till we wear each other out.

Kartik thought about it for a really long time, and finally decided to go with option **e**. He agreed to meet Amrit for drinks over the weekend. I sigh. It can be tough to say no to someone. But what's tougher?

Having someone say no to you.

'But men don't take no for an answer,' self-proclaimed men's rights activists would grunt at you as they thump their chests and drink their flat beers. But when have ~~needy~~ persistent men ever been attractive, you ask. They stare at you for a few seconds.

'One must never give up on their dreams,' they reason, but unless you are applying for your dream job or training for the dream run, rejection is a lesson that we all need to sit through.

Ask Amrit. (More on that later.)

So How Do We Handle Rejection?

1. **Don't make anyone uncomfortable.**

Someone rebuffs your advances at the bar? Smile, bid them farewell and back off. Don't get a reply on a dating app? Don't text twice. If they say you aren't their type or they aren't interested, reply with a succinct 'not a problem' and a smile emoji. Actually *mean* the smile emoji. Nothing else is acceptable.

2. **But respect yourself.**

Spurned hearts do the silliest things. As you comfort yourself in the deep recesses of your dark space, your broken heart will tell your mind not to accept it. 'He'll change his mind,' you think as you obsessively doodle his name in your notebook. 'Maybe I should just text him again,' you soothe your soul. Your heart tells you to plead and whimper, to beg and simper. It will work. It *has* to work. It works in the movies, doesn't it?

You owe it to yourself to not be that person. No one wants to be that person. No one wants to be *with* that person. Respect yourself; because that's the only way everyone else will respect you.

3. **Be polite.**

You might think that flooding someone with texts and calls will force them to reconsider, but they will only feel sorry for you, or worse, get scared of you. A no will *always* mean no. Even the feeble 'let me think about this over a drink' ones. Back off and be a gentleman about it. No questions asked.

4. **But don't write yourself off.**

Rejection stings so hard it could be an incensed bee. But fortunately, no one is allergic to failure, so you don't need to make a quick trip to the emergency ward. It might feel personal, but sometimes it really isn't about you at all. Like the weather (or a swarm of angry bees), there will always be elements that you can't control.

5. **Use it to change.**

Make it a point to learn from every 'no' that's thrown your way. Polish it and wear it like armour. Do you seem needy? Do you seem desperate? Do you seem to care too much? Or care too little? Understand that a 'yes' is not an automatic right. Applaud yourself for this epiphany as you move on to point no. 6.

6. **And move on.**

Possibly to the next boy, or even better, to the next chapter.

Number Twenty-five: The Drunk
Why Shots Will Never Be Your First Shot at Romance!

'Why haven't you asked me to come back to your place already?' are words that no one wants to hear when they are making polite conversation with a man they have absolutely no interest in.

Yet, these words have been said.

And now there are other guests waiting for the polite conversation to end. I see a few of them drumming their fingers on the railing. There are nervous chuckles. No one wants to admit they can overhear everything.

Thankfully, the moment is saved, as the host ushers us out of his balcony and back to his birthday party indoors. Getting a drink is not the best idea at the moment, but the open bar calls out to me like an old friend, so I scamper to get myself another G&T. **Twenty-five** surprisingly follows me.

The man is the associate editor at a popular gossip magazine, earning bylines and bytes hobnobbing with B-town's very best. And who am I?

I am the eponymous drunk. PLOT TWIST.

'Do you need some water?' he asks, ignoring my sleazy comment from minutes ago.

'I'm fine,' I slur. 'I've only had a few G&Ts …'

By 'few', I mean I've had seven, and by 'fine', I mean I'm really not.

Kids, we interrupt this broadcast for a quick update. Getting plastered at a work party is bad enough, but you hit an all-time low when you make an unsolicited move *while* getting plastered at a work party. Unless you are buying someone the most expensive scotch, alcohol will always be the worst wingman ever: it plays to your weaknesses and makes you a different person, and suddenly, your sense of confidence becomes inversely proportional to common sense.

Seven drinks later, I feel like I am a gift-wrapped bundle of poise and charm. Whoever said that alcohol is like Spanx for your feelings is right, because it hides your insecurities so well. I'll find out the next morning that I spent fifteen minutes fabricating a tale to convince him that his boyfriend is secretly cheating on him with an equally influential editor of a rival magazine. But for now, I feel like I am really close to getting a one-way ticket to his apartment.

'Do you want a refill?' I ask, spilling my drink all over his shoes. People are staring.

He casually takes a few steps back. 'Are you sure you'll get home safe?'

'Yours or mine?' I grin.

I never make it back to his. I know because my wingman ushers me back to mine.

Only, I have no recollection of it.

4.3 How Hard Is Your Game™?

All of thirty-three years and five feet nine inches tall, Kashyap Srivastava is the marketing head at a small-scale education startup. Kashyap works hard, but his colleagues still snigger behind his back because of his 'peculiar style of speaking'. He's good looking, but his friends say that you won't notice him in a crowd. His mother loves him, but she once confided to her sister that she didn't think her son is *extraordinary*. If they ever make a movie on Kashyap's life (although the chances appear slim), he'd play a background character – always the supporting cast, never the lead.

Kashyap Srivastava is an ordinary man, with an ordinary name and an ordinary job. You might think that a man of such (alleged) mediocrity might be paving his way to multiple sessions with a therapist and multiple bouts of rage, but Kashyap doesn't seem to begrudge his family or his friends for any of the things they say (or don't say) about him. Because as you read this sentence, his Grindr notifications are going out of control, and he really couldn't care less. Why, you ask?

It's simple. Kashyap Srivastava has a reputation for having Game™.

What's a Man with Game Like?

A man with Game is a master of words. He slides into conversations (and your DMs) with just the right things to say. It's never too much or too little, so you never question his motive, or lack thereof. The man doesn't necessarily need to be rich or attractive or stylish, but he's revered in the queer circles because he makes people feel special. It's not the kind of special that can be bought or couriered, it's the kind of special that is *felt*.

It might be his moves on the dance floor or the dais, or even in bed, but a man's Game is always effortless. It's in the little things he does. A casual joke that's a compliment. A hint of a smile when you tell a story. A chuckle when you blush. A firm handshake. The subtle graze of his fingers on your arm. He's always one step ahead of you, because he's no novice.

How can you tell if a man has Game™?

You can't. The game isn't something you play on a video game console, or as a bluff inside someone's head. There's no trick to master or formula to learn, because anybody can have Game. That includes you.

Want to know if you are playing your cards right? Answer these ten questions to find out if you are the master of the game:

1. **The Khan you most identify with**
   a. Fawad Khan
   b. Shah Rukh Khan
   c. Aamir Khan
   d. Salman Khan

2. **Your idea of the perfect way to woo someone is**
   a. Buying them a VIP ticket for a world cruise.
   b. Buying them a drink at the bar.
   c. Introducing yourself with a joke and throwing in subtle compliments as you ease into a conversation.
   d. Sending them a note full of newspaper clippings and a strand of your hair.

3. **What's the best way to start a conversation?**
   a. With a drink
   b. With a compliment
   c. With a joke
   d. How does one start a conversation?

4. **On average, how much do you stare at your crush?**
   a. You don't. He stares at you.
   b. Just a quick glance, because why should you make it obvious?
   c. Just enough to get him to notice you.
   d. Anything more than ten seconds. The last you heard, he was considering getting a restraining order against you.

5. **Your friends would describe your flirting skills as**
   a. Awe-inspiring
   b. Amazing
   c. Adorable
   d. Abysmal

6. **If your crush were a famous Chris, he would be**
   a. Chris Hemsworth
   b. Chris Evans
   c. Chris Pine
   d. Chris Pratt

7. **The last time you experienced the 'walk of shame' was**
   a. Yesterday
   b. A few weeks ago
   c. Why call it the 'walk of shame'?
   d. Never

8. **Your signature move would be**
   a. A blowjob
   b. A throwaway compliment
   c. A subtle kiss
   d. Getting him to pay the bill.

9. **Pick a food to bring to the bedroom**
   a. You are the snack
   b. Whipped cream
   c. Chocolate-coated strawberries
   d. Bhut Jolokia peppers

10. **A song that you'd sing at karaoke**
    a. A love ballad
    b. An '80s pop song
    c. The catchiest Bollywood number
    d. A mash-up of Taylor Swift's hits

Mostly As:

While we give you full credit for your ability to flirt your way out of every situation, sometimes it can be a touch … *too much*. You might believe that you have the gift of gab, but that doesn't make you a gift *from* god.

It's time to consider calming those nerves with some tonic, because no man with real Game ever eased himself into a conversation with the not-so-subtle, 'Hello! I am the best thing that will ever happen to you.'

Mostly Bs:

There's no denying your charm … when it comes to finding your way into somebody's pants. But unless you are using your flirting skills to find a fuckbuddy, there's no point in ~~playing the~~ having Game – because remember, a few sexual innuendoes and one terrifying case of syphilis later, you'll only be left to play all by yourself.

Mostly Cs:

CONGRATULATIONS! You've mastered the Game. Now enjoy the feeling and bask in the glory. A free drink is coming your way the next time you are at a bar.

Mostly Ds:

Well, what can we say? Your flirting skills make Ross from *Friends* look like Prince Charming. But you don't need to let your hounds loose just yet, because we have a crash course on flirting right at the beginning of this chapter.

4.4 The Gentleman's Guide to Being the One

Eleven Ways to Get That Call Back for Date II

If you've been reading this book page by page, you'd see references to the One pop up like a fresh pimple after a rather oily meal. It's only fair when you are reading the most comprehensive dating guide ever. But unlike your case of Monday-morning acne, the One isn't a spot on your life; he needs to have a spot *in* your life.

The One is different from everyone: he's not a myth like the Wet Dream or a mistake in the making like the Heartbreaker (read full entry below.) He's not trouble like the Ghost or dubious like the Sapiosexual. More importantly, the One is not a figment of your imagination, only to be seen in daydreams, Jane Austen novels and Nicholas Sparks' adaptations. The One is not found in fables and urban legends; he's hiding in plain sight.

And he's waiting to be shown a good time.

So Where Do I Find the One?

The real question here isn't about finding the One.

It's about *becoming* him. And if you ask me, there's no formula to becoming the One – no instruction manuals, no quick fixes, no magical mantra. Anybody can do it. Our man of mystery isn't a singular person; he's a constant mood. The One is everywhere, and he's probably reading this book as we speak.

Just like you are. So this is where we ask the real question: How do you embrace the One hidden inside you? How do you get your date to fall *so* hopelessly in love with you that he calls you the very next morning?

1. **Be assertive.**

Choosing the time, date and place for the first date doesn't show that you are bossy; it shows that you have strength of character. After all, continuously discussing where to meet over two days on text can be a huge buzzkill. If he's bent on getting you to make the decision, do so within a single scroll of your conversation on chat. Dilly-dallying is unsexy. Take the lead. You'll thank yourself later.

And so will he.

2. **Split the cheque.**

Doing the tango is sexy, but doing the tango with the bill is just distressing. Want to be treated like gold on your first date? Act like it. Punch your credit card passcode on the card-swiping machine if you want him to punch your numbers on his cellphone.

3. **Be honest.**

But don't go all out and tell him that his hands are too big for his body.

4. **Do your research.**

Running a light background check on your date is always a good thing. Find out about their interests and snoop around on his Instagram to narrow down some great conversation topics. Just be smart enough to not bring it up when you meet them: it'll bring up so many red flags, he could start a museum.

5. **Turn up on time.**

You thought broad shoulders, strong arms and mid-afternoon stubble were sexy? Wait till you see what punctuality gets you.

6. **Know your table etiquette.**

You don't need to know the difference between your salad knife and your fish knife, but being courteous at the table can go a long way. After all, no love story ever started with, '... and as he saw me chew with my open mouth, he fell head-over-heels in love with me.'

7. **Be clean and smell nice**

Taking a shower before a date should be a requisite, just like carrying your wallet to one. Scrub yourself clean from head to toe (and go all the way from mouthwash to after-shave lotion) with the assumption that you will get lucky later that night – because if you look and smell nice, you actually might.

Also, while the masculine scent of sweat might turn on a lot of people, being clingfilmed with it as you stand cheek-to-cheek at a crowded bar can repel guys faster than telling them you have a really bad case of genital crabs.

8. **Dress like you own it.**

... but not like you own a designer boutique store. The secret is making your style look effortless, without looking like you spent all of two hours and thirty-seven minutes trying to put it together. It's important to know that the difference between enigmatic and embarrassing is an ill-fitting outfit.

As long as your clothes are clean (no ketchup stains), casual (no sequined prints or emblazoned skulls) and well fitting (no tight V-necks that might cause asphyxiation), you are good to go. Just make sure you feel comfortable in them, and you'll feel comfortable on your date.

9. **... but keep the conversations light.**

When you are not rushing to the bar to get drinks, waiting in line for the washroom or staring dreamily into each other's eyes, you are mostly going to be talking on a date. Be breezy, be witty, be charming – be a Shah Rukh Khan feature film.

Keep the heavier stuff – heartbreak, politics and how your family has a history of dementia – for a date further down the road, when you've already charmed the pants off him (literally) and there's no going back.

10. **Play it cool.**

Think that the date went well? Did you split your tiramisu just like you thought you would? Did he lean in and hold your hand as you told him the heartbreaking tale of how your dog died a few years ago? Is now a great time to go with something beautiful, like, 'I'll hear from you soon, right?'

WRONG. Instead, when it's time to part, thank him for a great evening and end the night with a hug or a kiss (or more if you feel like it). You've done your best, and now it's time for him to do his – call you as soon as he reaches home to set up date number two.

11. **Call him yourself.**

Wondering why he hasn't called back? Wait for a day or two and send him a text, paving the way for a nice, quick phone call. Intense relationships have fizzled out over the will they/won't they of text messages.

Feeling nervous? Remember, you are not coming across as pushy or needy. Quite the opposite, in fact – self-confidence is the greatest scent a man can wear.

And it comes cheap.

Number Twenty-six: The Doppelgänger
The Gentleman's Guide to Making a Move

August 2012

Churchgate

It's a blind date, but I'd recognize him anywhere. I've been told we look alike, but **Twenty-six**, a writer with twinkling eyes, is younger, brighter and happier. How do I know?

He's waving at me from across the station with a dopey grin, his face framed with a cornucopia of curls – not that it's his most discerning feature. I've also spent only the last two days guiltlessly stalking him on Instagram.

I laughed out loud at his status updates, sighed at his vacation pictures, mused over his captions, judged his check-ins, scrutinized every freckle on his face and every follower on his profile … you get the gist. His life is an open book. I am surprised by how minimal his privacy settings are. If there's one cardinal rule that most gay men follow, it's this – we keep our friends close and our enemies closer, but we'll always keep our Instagram followers under strict lock and key.

Gay culture is literally having a private profile on Instagram. Do we really want all the (other) gay men to know that they aren't the only one(s) we are flirting with? Our friend lists are like our little black books – full of old conquests, exes, one-night stands and those standalones whom you occasionally flirt with through DMs but have no intentions of meeting. Would I share my address book and lay it out bare? Not at all. It's an unspoken rule: hide your friends like you hide your prescription meds.

'Hi!' says the boy. He sounds breathless. How long was I breaking the fourth wall?

'Hi!' I smile back, full of hope. I've been told my smile is my best feature, and I use it instead of a cheesy pickup line. He blushes. It has a 100 per cent success rate.

What brings us here? He was in the neighbourhood, I was in the neighbourhood – we decided to make the most of it. Plus it makes for a great story. The greatest love stories begin at train stations.

'Do you want to take this one?' he asks, pointing at the train that's just pulled in. Waves of people rush past, but we don't lose each other. At least not yet.

'Lead the way,' I say, still smiling.

He grins.

Grant Road

The train fills up fast, and so does our conversation. I am not surprised. Twenty-six is handsome, knows his way around a semicolon and thinks I'm attractive too. Did I also mention that he's really cute?

As the train picks up speed, I collect a few more details from him to place on my mental clipboard: his work as an intern with a reputed tabloid helps him earn a byline every now and then. There is a lot of 'go get me some coffee' and 'did you call that celebrity?' or 'have you written the review I asked you to write?' if he's lucky, but he's always wanted to be a writer and he knows that's how writers start. I cough involuntarily. Is that what he *really* wants to do?

No.

He wants to write stories about food and talk about it the way people talk about love – all-consumingly. Taste is an emotion, he tells me. Can a bit of chocolate tart give you butterflies in your stomach? Do you whimper with pleasure when you dig into a portion of freshly made Eggs Benedict? If your answer is yes, *he* is the right question.

Wait. Has he seen *Ratatouille*?

'Everyone asks me that,' he sighs. He loves food, and even though he's only a home baker, it is, 'I had you at baker, can we just get married already?' I chuckle.

He laughs aloud and tells me I am funny. 'Aren't you a charmer?' he blushes.

Aren't I just?

<u>Mumbai Central</u>

He's telling me the perfect way to bake brownies (Let your eggs sit out of the fridge for a half-hour before baking. They ensure that the brownies are gooey and have a delicious crust), when –

'You should come over for dinner sometime. I cook really well.'

Would there be brownies? We both giggle. A horde of travellers gets off the emptying train, but we don't move apart.

<u>Lower Parel</u>

It's difficult to discern whether you've made an impression on someone when everyone around you is closely watching. A hundred pair of eyes. His are large and expressive, full of hope that I am too scared to crush.

'Can I tell you something you promise you won't tell anyone?'

Uh-oh. I don't like secrets that I can't share.

'The last time I went on a date, I almost got mauled in an auto-rickshaw.' He blushes. I laugh loudly and lean towards him just the teensiest bit. The men around us are not amused. What did he do then?

He pushed him away (the 'him' in question being a feisty television producer), jumped out of the rickshaw and never looked back. Every gay man is a collection of short stories. Snippets shared over unlimited sangria and cigarette breaks, or discussed over dinner plates and behind closed bedroom doors. He is an anthology.

The train ride ahead is full of these stories. An S&M-loving architect who designs celebrity homes. A thirty-something media mogul who has a weakness for twenty-two-year-olds. A young, fresh-faced doctor who had his first kiss at the age of twenty-one. If I weren't on a north-bound local train back home, I would have thought I was watching an episode of *Gossip Girl*. I take my chances and tell him so. He scrunches his eyebrows. Did I say something wrong? Did I lose my chance?

'Are you team Blair or team Serena?' he asks. I sigh. I think I should just go buy him a ring.

Mahim

He's heading off to London in two months. Is he now?

Yes, for a writing programme, and then he can kiss the internship goodbye. I listen on with rapt attention: it's the simplest way to make a move. 'It's going to be so exciting,' he says. 'The pubs, the food, the clothes, the English life, the "awws" instead of the "aahs" – can you believe all the tea and scones I will have?'

I obviously can.

'It's going to be difficult to leave Bombay behind,' he says to me. I continue looking at him intently. The pores on his nose, the brown irises of his extremely expressive eyes, the way his eyelashes flutter as he talks –

'Is everything okay?' he asks me. Am I staring too much?

'I'm sorry, I got distracted by your eyes,' I lie. He blushes again. 'You should come visit if you are in that part of the world,'

The train screeches to a halt. I've never appreciated a signal so much.

It might be too soon to tell him that I'm broke, but I know that he's going to go places. Over the next few years, he will finish his master's degree, work with a popular food magazine, start his own blog, run a YouTube Channel, become an Instagram influencer *and* have his heart broken multiple times. But where does it all start?

With me.

On cue, a disembodied voice tells us that Bandra is next. Are we there already?

<u>Bandra</u>

It's time. One of us has to go.

'Do I see you again?' one of us asks. It's a pity that the two of us have different destinations. The other one nods. I squeeze his hand gently as he leans in for a handshake. Our fingers linger for just a moment longer, writing love notes that will never be read.

He beams as he gets off the train and waves at me through the sea of faces that separate us. I wave over the faceless men and women as the train pulls at my heartstrings. The others fade away, he doesn't.

He texts me later saying that I had him at hello. Should I text him once I get back home? Should I wait till the next morning? Should I wait for the designated three days? I do the only thing that makes sense.

I text him back right away.

5

Fixing up the First Date and Other Stories

5.1 Where Do You Meet?

Your Guide to Ten First Date Ideas and What They Say About You

Ram, a project manager at an MNC, met his boyfriend, Sohail, a SAP consultant, eight months ago.

Their first date was at a coffee shop, but they didn't meet at Starbucks, like most rom-coms would like us to believe. Ram realized it was special when a twenty-minute walk turned into a two-hour-long heart to heart. Things picked up soon after, and the men have been in their honeymoon phase ever since.

The couple might have played it safe, but what about you?

A Quick Note on Safe Spaces

Queer spaces are a myth – especially in a country such as India, where we have all kinds of repulsively homophobic legislation in place – no same-sex marriage, no adoption laws, not even basic civil partnership. So you can imagine that LGBTQIA+ safety doesn't feature very high on the government's to-do list.

That is precisely why it matters that YOU choose a safe activity when you are planning a first date. A place where you (or your date) don't feel threatened or even bullied by other patrons, staff or the authorities. Avoid walks in back alleys and drives past midnight when you are meeting someone for the very first time. The ideal situation would demand that you meet them at home – it's the safest haven there is – but when was the last time anyone ever lived alone in a country where the rent is higher than our mortality rate?

Unlike Ram and Sohail's straight-to-order coffee date, deciding where to meet your date for the first time can be a tricky affair: you might have never met him and, in all probability, haven't even spoken to him on the phone yet, which raises a lot of questions with a lot of unresolved answers. What if the place is too busy? What if it's not busy at all? What if the weather turns sour? What if *he* turns sour?

Sure, asking someone 'Where do you want to go?' might seem duller than the weather report in March, but planning ahead can help you in the long run. Are you still confused about whether you should grab burgers at the new pub or seats for the latest film?

Here are eleven first date ideas that could potentially lead to a sequel.

1. The late-night movie

Success rate of the date: 7/10

Spending two hours in close proximity to a guy in complete silence is a great measure of how he is as a person. Does he breathe too loudly? Does he have good posture? What is he doing with his hands? Does he talk too much? Does he talk too little? Is he sleeping? Does he snore if he does? How does he eat his popcorn? Does he slurp while he drinks his soda? Does he *drink* soda?

These two hours (three, if it's a period drama) can tell you more than years of living together can. While men will disagree, a movie date has the potential for its very own climatic happy ending. (Sixty minutes of lights out can lead to an interlude of opportunities and back-row trysts.)

Just make sure it's a prelude to dinner, drinks or dessert. The last thing you want after a hundred minutes of HD-level intensity is an awkward hug that leads you nowhere (apart from your cold, single bed). Also, irrespective of whether you are watching a dark comedy or a breezy chick flick, pick a movie that excites you. That way, if your date isn't turning out to be the blockbuster you expected it to be, at least you get to watch one on the big screen.

What to wear: Keep it casual – a Henley and jeans – and you won't be surprised to find more than one happy ending when the curtains close.

2. After-work drinks

Success rate of the date: 8/10

If you are a corporate slave who prefers the streetlights to the sun, after-work drinks are the perfect way to end your night in high spirits (exclusive of taxes). It's breezy, it's unpretentious, it's so casual – it could be the lead actress of any Satyajit Ray movie.

Many men will frown at getting drunk on a first date with their future plus-one; some will even say it's the kryptonite to any budding romance. What if you are one shot away from shooting terrible zingers his way? What if that measure of single malt is stronger than your self-resolve not to sleep with him? What if the pitcher of sangria becomes the prologue to that messy story about your ex?

Sure, one man's drink can be another man's poison. But if you can find your drinks to match your tolerance, pretty soon, you'll be matching bath towels. Who knows? Maybe after five rounds, you'll have more happy hours to look forward to.

What to wear: Change out of your suit, unless you want to look like you are attending a sales convention in a city far away from home (and your wardrobe). Trade-in your work blazer for a fun shirt; one that says 'Hey, I made the effort of going home and changing for you. That counts, doesn't it? Do you want to buy me my first drink?'

3. The casual dinner

Success rate of the date: 8.5/10

The casual dinner is the easiest, because planning ahead isn't necessary. All you have to do is show up, and you've already met your date halfway (unless it's closer to where you stay, which is a strict no-no in first date etiquette; it shows you are lazy and not willing to make an effort).

Here, the key to a no-stress dinner date is to be your enigmatic self. Joke over a mint julep, charm your way through some charcuterie, be endearing as you eat enchiladas and finally win him over with a slice of white chocolate gateau cake – it can't get any easier than that.

But remember, while dinner might be the easiest way to 'doggy bag' a date (i.e. go home and finish it because the restaurant just isn't doing it for you), don't forget one thing – you don't want to be more into your Greek salad than you are into your dinner companion. Because if the most interesting thing on the date is the appetizers list on your menu card, there's a high chance you won't make it to dessert, both in and out of the restaurant.

What to wear: Skip t-shirts with a message (yes, even your Homer Simpson tee) and go classic with jeans and a collared polo that's not too loose (or at least not as loose as you were in your raging single days). It lessens your chances of looking like someone straight out of an Ed Hardy catalogue. Go casual, go clean and go crisp.

4. A fancy restaurant

Success rate of the date: 5/10

It's always risky to meet someone at a fancy restaurant for your very first date. What if he's not worth getting your dinner jacket dry-cleaned? What if you can't make an exit halfway through your expensive entrée? What if a bottle of champagne later, you realize that the only thing you have in common with him is your love for overpriced alcohol? The entire decision is based on an embossed menu card full of what-ifs.

Stick to the upscale eatery only if you've been on a couple of phone calls with the guy. Plan ahead and make a reservation so that your date doesn't have any. Know his tastes at the dining table, as well as in life: you don't want a lasagna-loving lad to pick at his wasabi at a sushi bar, because the only thing worse than being stuck with a bad date is a bad date that will refuse to pay his half of the bill because he thought the filet mignon was going to be fish.

What to wear: You are eating a fancy meal; you don't want to look like one. Go easy on your style, just like you would go easy on your wallet. Keep the garnishing to a bare minimum.

5. Sunday brunch

Success rate of the date: 5/10

Unlimited alcohol, breakfast items and the only plausible excuse to wear sunglasses when you are out with someone you are romantically interested in – sounds like brunch is the king of great first dates, right?

WRONG.

Sure, brunch sounds fun, it's not as serious as trudging through a five-course tasting menu or as low-key as getting a coffee at Starbucks. Most importantly, it combines three of our favourite things – preppy clothes, artisanal food and endless alcohol. It might as well be the single-most important meal of the gay. But signing up for Sunday brunch means signing up for upwards of four hours of unsupervised drinking with a person you've just met. That's upwards of four hours of awkward conversations if things don't go as well as you planned.

What to wear: Want to disregard all my reservations about Sunday brunch, and still reserve a slot for the weekend? Skip the layers and stick to something loose-fitting, because bottomless buffets don't pair well with body-hugging outfits.

6. A walk in the park

Success rate of the date: 8/10

Snotty kids, disapproving old people and pigeons aside, a walk in the park is perfect when you are nursing an empty wallet and a head full of questions – it's cheap, but romantically so. Here your conversation skills need to be on point, because unlike a movie theatre or drinks at the neighbourhood bar, you won't find sources of entertainment other than occasional people (or pet) watching. A walking date is the best way to get to know someone about whom you know nothing.

Think of it this way: a walk in the park is an anthology of multiple mini first dates. Enjoy an evening stroll, pack up *kathi* rolls and enjoy them as you walk around, feed the stray dogs, go on a nature trail, share an ice-cream cone and explore your inner child (but not the one in the sandbox), giving way to a playground (pun intended) of possibilities.

What to wear: See, you can't show up for a hike in haute couture, because mud stains will never look good on your Italian Moschinos. Wear clothes that you can sweat in (but don't show up in sweatpants) and stick to colours that are light (just like your conversations). Just make sure you wear a really good pair of sneakers so that you can sprint away should things get awkward.[6]

7. A coffee shop
Success rate of the date: 9/10

The coffee date is the equivalent of a quickie in bed. Because can you really get to know somebody in the time it takes to consume a single cappuccino?

Not really. But it gives you enough time to fork a quick opinion about your date, so that before the scalding murky brown contents of your cup reach the base of your throat, you can be out of the coffee shop and never see him again.

What to wear: Three words – keep it casual ... just like your cup of coffee (unless you are one of those horrid souls whose coffee order is more complicated than my college thesis).

8. An art gallery
Success rate of the date: 4/10

A museum date sounds great – countless movie meet-cutes have been staged at an art gallery – so why can't it happen for you?

But that's what movie meet-cutes are: staged. In real life, you are going to be jostling with school kids and tourists to get a sneak peek at the 'masterpiece you read about in the papers', only to realize that your date is yawning away into his phone. Yes, a date at the art gallery

---

6 And there's a high chance they will. What kind of weirdo suggests a walking date? Oops, sorry. That would be me.

is a red carpet full of conversation starters. What do you think this painting *really* means? Does that sculpture *speak* to you? Do you think I could have painted that better? Is it just me or does that fruit bowl look #NSFW? Is that fire bucket a part of the exhibition? Can we just go get coffee instead? But that's where the good times (and sometimes the conversations) end.

Book yourself a tour only when you know your interests align, because there's a high chance your stars won't. If you spend more time looking at the art than talking to your date, you are clearly doing it wrong.

What to wear: Like fancy restaurants, art gallery dates are tricky: you want to look like a piece of work, but you don't want to look like a piece of work that's being displayed *at* the gallery. Leave the bow tie at home with your boring ideas on postmodern surrealism.

9. Running

Success rate of the date: 1/10

This was a trick that was supposed to test you. Never agree to go on a running date.

What to wear: Just make sure your joggers aren't too tight; all that bending isn't going to be a good look when you are trying to look like someone who ~~doesn't make squats a part of their personality~~ wants to make a good first impression.

10. A quick drive

Success rate of the date: 9/10

Indians spend more time in traffic than people in most countries in the world, with more than two hours on the road every day. You might as well use the downtime for some date time. A long drive is a great (read: free) way to get to know someone, mostly because how a man behaves behind the steering wheel can speak volumes about how he is as a person.

Does he speed through signals? Does he hurl expletives when someone cuts him? Does he hurl expletives as he cuts someone else? Drive in a zig-zag as if he were in an arcade game? Is he a honker? (That was another trick question: no one should be a honker!) It's time to zip off in your own car.

What to wear: Those air-conditioning vents are going to be blasting cold air right at you. Dress wisely.

11. Bonus Feature: Online

Success rate of the date: 10/10

Pandemic-proof your date and meet them without actually *physically* meeting them: take things to the next level by jumping back to the basics. If 2020 taught[7] us anything, going virtual could lead to just as strong emotional bonds. In fact, we've been preparing for this our entire lives. We're evolving into a race that's meant to live off our (smart)phones.

Binge-watch a show together, share a virtual (drink), or trade (and make) your favourite recipes on FaceTime – the world is your oyster. Your chemistry is only as choppy as your internet connection. And the biggest perk of taking your date online?

You don't even need to change your underwear.

What to wear: Whatever you want. It's been a tough year, and you've earned it.

---

7 Or any of Netflix's three reality shows with the same premise.

Who Pays on a (Gay) Date?

Up until the Cretaceous era of courting (circa 2000s), men were expected to pay on dates just to prove they weren't total scumbags. But it's 2021, and the world isn't heteronormative any more. So what happens when two guys (or girls) go on a date?

The rules of patriarchy have officially left the building (and no, they didn't offer to pay the bill either). Now, kindness is an alluring trait to have, so one must at least offer to pay the bill. Your date will probably say (some variation of), 'Stop being so silly, we should split this instead'. The cheque dance has forever been a mating ritual exhibited by gay men on first dates, and that's how it is.

If you had a great time and want a sequel, insist on paying by saying 'Well, I'll get this and you can get the next one ...' That'll mostly force him to see you again.

If he insists on splitting the bill based on what each of you ate/drank, dump him right away.

Number Twenty-seven: The General Manager Does This Relationship Come with the Club Membership?

September 2014

I sip on my sweet lime soda as I try summing up **Twenty-seven**. He's averagely dressed and has a face I would remember for a week, but doesn't seem to have anything else going for him.

I only half-listen as he switches between two equally exasperating stories, one is the saga of how he came out at twenty-eight, and the other is a mundane narration of his struggles during a six-month HR stint in rural India. The stories have no connection, and neither do we. I react at the right intervals and feign the right amount so as to not to seem suspicious. **Twenty-seven's** eyes are sad and grey, like a dull July afternoon. As he leans across his chair, his shirt pulls at his sinewy arms, and I can tell that he works out; but his physique is hidden behind an ill-fitting shirt, just like his personality. My friend has an earnest face, but does he have any redeeming qualities? For now, he's doing a dreadful PR job on himself.

'Are you getting bored?' he asks me, like a concerned second cousin hovering over the ventilator, trying to extract the details of my last and final will. I sink back comfortably into the lounge armchair, enjoying the privileges of his exclusive club membership, and suddenly remember why I am here.

'We should do this again,' I lie.

The Gentleman's Guide to Wardrobe Essentials

A.k.a What to Wear When You Plan to Get Laid

Clean underwear

If the date goes well and you get lucky, you don't want to be caught wearing greying (or worse, stained) underpants. Always wear underwear with the assumption that you are going to take a chiselled underwear model back home. Briefs? Good. Banana hammocks? Even better.

An undershirt

Nervous sweats aren't sexy. You won't be able to exchange sweet nothings with your date when all he can think of are the giant pit stains under your arms. Invest in an undershirt, so that your flirting doesn't get underplayed. Keep it white; keep it simple.

A white shirt

The white shirt is a golden ticket: it's so versatile, it could be the Meryl Streep of clothing. Pair it with khakis, pair it with jeans, pair it with a leather jacket, pair it with beach shorts if you want to – you've got a winner every single time. Now, about your comic timing …

Well-fitting trousers

There's no point doing those free squats at the gym if you are going to wear pants that sit lower than your mother's expectations. Buy a pair of fitted trousers that accentuate your butt, since it is likely the second-most important thing that any man you are interested in will look at.

Shoes

Manners don't make a great man, good shoes do. Dates trust men with unpolished shoes much less than men without wallets. Always have five pairs of shoes with you – black dress shoes, brown dress shoes, a pair of brogues, one set of canvas sneakers and cute moccasins that you can fall in love with (on the off chance you never find anyone else).

Socks

Something with a slight dab of colour, so that you don't look like an overgrown schoolboy (or an overworked banker) when you are standing butt naked in a stranger's bedroom.

A watch

Unless you are a school student who can't tell time, there's no other reason you shouldn't be wearing a watch on your date.

Number Twenty-eight: The Sob
Does a Sympathetic Face Make a Sartorial Statement?

January 2016

Is there an instruction manual that tells you how honest you can be on a first date? Can you tell someone you don't like dogs? That you live with an estranged ex? That you aren't looking for a relationship, but 'will you be a darling and still pay for my drink'? That you *might* have gonorrhoea?

Twenty-eight seems to have missed a few chapters from the manual. A data scientist for one of the biggest global tech giants, he's only recently moved back to the country.

'Why did you move back?'

And then, the curtains drop. **Twenty-eight's** had a tough life. In the last few years, he's been deported from the United States because of an immigration glitch, lost his mother to a terminal disease and seen his ex-girlfriend get married to someone else.

And all I did was ask him what made him leave his cushy job in the United States. This makes me feel horrible because I spent the first five minutes complaining about how beer makes me feel bloated. I am *only* on my second one.

'Are you okay?' I ask.

He tells me he's getting by, but I know a broken man when I see one. I resist the urge to hug him and tell him everything is going to be fine. At this stage in the date, we should be exchanging pleasantries and subtle compliments. Instead, I am sympathetically patting him on his back, hoping that he doesn't break down. Is that a tear?

He notices me shift uncomfortably in my seat.

'Is this not something you signed up for?'

Some would say that **Twenty-eight** is emotionally slutty. He reveals too much too soon. Men will forever look at vulnerability as a weakness – the kryptonite to their egos. It's the bane of our existence. We all think we are Superman.

'But how can I tell anyone how I feel?' the casual gay man would ask, as he sips on his organic chai latte. 'Therapy is for the rich and the famous,' he would add, as he asks for an extra pump of almond milk.

I know because I am the casual gay man. I've swiftly avoided seeing a therapist for three years and counting.

'Are you there?' he asks me. Maybe we should have just stuck to polite conversation about the weather.

I break into a smile and tell him to go on. That's what the instruction manual would want me to do.

Turns out I missed a few chapters too.

5.2 The Gentleman's Guide to Every Gipster in the World: Yet Another Bonus Feature

Is the Loch Ness monster real? How do you deal with brackets in maths equations? What came first, the gay man or the hipster?

There will always be some mysteries that will remain unsolved. BODMAS jokes notwithstanding, there's no definite equation when it comes to gay men and hipsterdom. Sure, hipsters may have a certain air of smugness about them, but this legendary ire is directed toward popular culture, and not towards the people who practise it. ~~Gay men~~ Hipsters like discovering 'new things' and taking credits for trends that will become mainstream five months too late. The hipster likes, no, *loves* everything 'genuine'.

Which also describes the gay man of the new millennium.

Introducing, the Gipster™.

Who's a Gipster?

The age of the hipster might have finally come to an end, but when have gay men ever let a good thing go?

We are still here, writing in moleskin notebooks, riding twelve-gear bikes, using organic moustache wax and stocking up on ironic print t-shirts. It's safe to say that gay hipsters aren't disappearing just yet.

Jahangir, twenty-four, and Subhashish, twenty-six, would agree. The creative designer and casting director share an apartment in one of the quieter back alleys of Bombay – a home that is littered with curios, knick-knacks and pop-culture references (and often, their ex-boyfriends).

But how did these two iconic men meet?

It all happened five and a half years ago, in a city not so far away. A common friend couldn't have boys over in her building, and she asked the young casting director if her friend could crash at his house. A few glasses of rum later, they realized they shared a spark.

The rest is meet-cute history. Subhashish and Jahangir aren't your conventional boys; their ideas of love are more Wes Anderson, less Shakespeare. They don't believe in grand declarations of love – bottles of Old Monk suffice. Sometimes, something as subtle as a post-coital smoke will do.

'There was this one time we went out to a restaurant, and Jahangir took a picture of me with a banana. I thought it was cute.'

'How is that romantic?' I ask, confused.

'It said, "I am bananas for you", he says.

I look at it. It really is cute.

I leave the Gipsters in their natural habitat, craving my own picture.

Do you want to know what makes a Gipster, apart from his love for beer, bowties and his beard? Here are a few helpful hints.

How Do You Find a Gipster?

- The Gipster doesn't own a television. He'll also make sure he tells that to everyone he knows. While on a date. At a casual lunch. During a work meeting. At a birthday party. On the bus. At the grocery store. While at a funeral.
- He has his own complicated order at the coffee shop: a grande iced sugar-free vanilla latté with soymilk. It's his standard go-to drink every morning on his way to work (as a graphic designer at an independent media house).
- But if the barista can't make it, he has a large decaf instead.
- His best friend makes organic hemp t-shirts, which he freely wears and advertises. He's always handy with a card for her Instagram page.
- It doesn't list any numbers, but has a QR code.
- The Gipster owns a coffee table book with vaguely pornographic pictures. It's usually on top of his bedside drawer, because he doesn't have the money to invest in a coffee table.
- He talks about how he hates Forever 21, yet it looks like all his clothes came from there.
- Especially when they have their clearance sales.
- He has five sets of bow ties: casual, semi-casual, formal, party and 'street chic that shows I don't try too hard'.
- He doesn't watch *Game Of Thrones* because 'it's become *so mainstream*'. He won't think twice before telling you that he's read the entire series though.
- Right down to all the companion books.
- Sometimes, he bicycles to work.
- He'll complain about how the city just doesn't have the space or the infrastructure for cyclists. He'll still use UberGo.
- He rolls his eyes when people tell him they listen to EDM.
- He rolls his eyes even more when they tell him they haven't heard of his favourite indie (and also very obscure) band.

- He gives up when they say that they think Alt-J is cool.
- He'll pester you to try out amaranth, which is the new kale, which was the new quinoa.
- The Gipster doesn't love flannel. He *lives* it.
- For your birthday, he'll gift you a mixed tape of all his favourite indie music. He'll make you play it at the party. If not that, he'll gift you a potted miniature cactus. It's a little sapling from the terrarium he's working on.
- He has an Instamax camera that he takes pictures *of.*
- The camera is in mint condition. It's hidden away in his closet and only makes an appearance when his friends are over or when he's packing a suitcase for a holiday.
- Which would most definitely be a backpacking trip across Vietnam and Cambodia.
- He'll deny it, but he got excited when he heard IKEA was coming to India. When he realized that it wasn't opening a warehouse in the city, he commiserated by drinking an entire bottle of Coca Cola. It's a secret he'll take to the grave.
- He'll swear that *The Royal Tenenbaums* is his favourite film by Wes Anderson, whom he *adores*. He scoffs at you when you tell him you thought *Fantastic Mr. Fox* was cute.
- He's not heard of *Moonrise Kingdom*.
- He has a typewriter that he used to type out quotes by Charles Bukowski. They are all framed and hung in his living room. The typewriter hasn't been used ever since.
- He covers it up with fairy lights.
- The Gipster constantly bums cigarettes off people at gigs and pubs, claiming he doesn't smoke regularly and doesn't want to 'invest in a whole carton'. He looks bummed if you don't have a Davidoff. He'll have a Marlboro in that case, because 'Classic Milds just don't do it for me'.
- He has a manicured beard that looks like a permanent five o'clock shadow. He pays extra so that it looks just the right amount of

messy. The stylist is given a free pass to NH7 so that she won't tell anyone.

- When he *does* run into the stylist at a music festival, he'll pretend she's a friend he has 'collaborated' with.
- He drinks only artisanal beer, and likes to tell people about how 'beer is the new wine'.
- He absolutely despises brands. But he's *still* counting the days till the next big iPhone launch.
- It's marked as a reminder on his current (read: the latest) iPhone.
- The Gipster doesn't believe in credit cards.
- He'll always be short on cash while splitting the cheque with his date.
- And that'll probably be you.

5.3 How to Smell Good: A Quick Tutorial on Smelling Like a Man

Of the five senses, smell has the best memory, Urvaksh tells me. On his eternal quest to find true love, the corporate banker has met many suitable men. There have been stylists and models, lawyers and writers, and on that one drunken occasion, even a trapeze artist.

But none left an impression like Faraz Qureshi did.

He met Mr Qureshi at a common friend's farewell party. He found the (rather buff) academician huddled between a gaggle of chartered accountants spouting Ghalib's poetry, as he casually sipped on a glass of dry vermouth. Urvaksh was intrigued. For a professor of physics (he later found out), Faraz was both well read and well dressed. But it wasn't his intellect or his looks that drew Urvaksh to the suave gentleman in the corner. It was something else.

In a sea of men who all smelt like Davidoff's *Cool Water* or Bvlgari's *Aqua*, Faraz smelt of cinnamon and roses, of nutmeg and peppermint. He smelt of hope. He smelt refreshing.

It was love at first ~~sight~~ scent.

Urvaksh saw patches of darkness in Faraz's soul. But was Faraz, with his freshly mown beard and swept-back hair, all brand and brawn? The man of science smelt expensive, all *Hugo Boss*, or wait, was it *Armani*? Or *Calvin Klein*? No, it's *Gucci*. Or *Davidoff*? Could it be *Ralph Lauren*? Or maybe *Tom Ford*? The truth is that Faraz lingered, just like his aftershave.

Urvaksh was besotted. Was this what True Love™ smelt like?

Faraz later told him it was Paco Rabanne's *One Million*. They dated for all of three months and twenty-two days, and neither thought it was a coincidence that their relationship ended when Faraz's bottle of perfume did.

What Does This Have to Do with Me?

To be told you smell nice is probably the single best compliment there is. It means they've seen (and sniffed) you closely, so it's a rather brave compliment to make. Looks fade away, scents don't.

That is precisely why more men should smell (but only, smell) like Faraz. In fact, they should smell *better* than Faraz. It's really not that difficult.

How Do I Smell Good?

Sniff those worries away, because here's how you can always smell like the Wet Dream:

1. **Ease out to find your scent.**

Scents, like shoes, are only better (and last longer) when they are expensive. Which means you can avoid the deodorants that you find at your neighbourhood supermarket. Instead, opt for a luxury brand that you love. This doesn't necessarily mean you have to sell your kidney to smell nice. Most brands have special collections that are as easy on your pockets as they are on other people's olfactory nerves. After all, simple can also be suave.

2. **Learn to experiment.**

Pick a scent that you can flirt with. One that you want to take out for drinks. Find a scent that makes you feel sexy. In fact, court as many scents as you can till you eventually find the One that makes you feel confident. Ask it to marry you. But remember, there will also be a Two, a Three and a Four, because who wants to smell the same every day?

3. **Know how much to use.**

Love, avocadoes and perfumes always work best when consumed in small doses. So be cautious of the amount you use, because you don't want to end up smelling like the men's perfumery at Duty Free. When in doubt, use the following thumb rule: four sprays to be split over your chest, your lower biceps, your collarbone and the back of your neck. Steer clear of everything under the belt – eau de cologne does NOT taste (or burn) nice.

4. **Find a signature.**

There's nothing more attractive than recollection. It's the familiarity that makes it your signature scent. Find something that lingers on a sweater or a bed sheet; something you leave behind on every boy you love (or even better, who loves you). Own it, and then sign off with a flourish.

5. **Make it one that matches your personality.**

Do remember that things won't help if it's a shitty one.

6. **Shower twice a day.**

Because you really don't smell like the bouquet of roses you feel like at the end of the day.

7. **Change out of those gym clothes.**

There's no point looking gorgeous while you do your lateral curls if you smell like the insides of a public latrine.

Number Twenty-nine: The Yogi
Zen and the Art of Conversation Maintenance

December 2012

I apologize profusely as I turn up twenty minutes late for a movie date with **Twenty-nine**, but he seems unperturbed. On some men, a general air of nonchalance can be quite attractive. But he has other problems with me, clearly.

My face, for instance. He looks let down, almost immediately. Do I not look like the pictures that I sent him? But now is not the time to sink into my insecurities.

We've already missed *Silver Linings Playbook*, and he tells me that we should get coffee instead. Do I want to get coffee with a man who's lost all interest?

I shouldn't. But then again, I am not in a position to tell him there are things I don't want to do. Dating is a ~~continuous struggle~~ journey that's worth all the effort in the end, and you have to appear like you are up for anything. So I shrug and agree. To be honest, he looked great on paper; well, he looked great on my phone screen. He seemed to find my jokes funny and said he couldn't wait to meet up. Sometimes that is enough.

As we sip on our coffees, he tells me that he likes to practise guided yoga and take time off work to do his bit for the world: he gives a fifteen-minute monologue about the time he volunteered to teach underprivileged kids in Thailand.

What he doesn't like is paying the bill, or even a part of it.

My dreams die an early death, and there are no silver linings to this playbook.

5.4 What Not to Talk About When You Finally Get Talking

Five Conversation Topics to Avoid on the Big Date and Beyond

CONGRATULATIONS!

You've done it. You've booked yourself a date (and a dinner table), spruced up your clothes (and your attitude) and showed up right on time.

Now comes the difficult bit. You are faced with around two-to-four hours of unsupervised meandering, where you can either giggle nervously, nibble at your food or make light conversation about a collection of topics ranging from your pet cat, Ranbir Kapoor's failed romances, all the way to the political unrest in Russia (because let's face it – there's always going to be political unrest in Russia).

Everyone knows the basics of first date chit chat: you shouldn't be sleazy ('when was the last time you had sex?') or make references to your dating life ('oh yes, please do tell me more about all the other dates you have lined up for this week!'), but to make real progress, you need to better understand the art of making small talk.

Every Guy's Small-Talk Starter Pack for First Dates

Based on what you say (or don't), you can either charm or harm your chances of getting another chance to woo your date. Do you want to keep it suave and simple (with the right smidgeon of sexy) so that you get a call back the very next morning?

It's time to steer clear of the following extremely avoidable topics.

Politics

While witty banter is always a great way to make a good impression, you must know that awkward is just one opinion away from appealing. One minute you are exchanging ribald jokes about the government, and before you know it, you are tearing at each other's political ideologies (and hair) rather than tearing at each other's clothes. Whether you are team Left or raise a candle to the Alt-Right, vent out your anger on the comments thread of Arnab Goswami's Republic TV.

What you should do instead: Stick to topics that you both feel positively about, such as Ariana Grande's Instagram feed or the benefits of intermittent fasting.

The weather

Talking about the weather is so obvious, it would be a cliché to call it a cliché. But what do we do? Every once in a while, you'll reach that dead end where you'll try peppering up pauses with comments about how it's too sunny for a Sunday.

Don't.

What you should do instead: Cherish those awkward silences instead, and think of a flirty compliment that can win you a free drink the next time. After all, no great love story ever began with the line, 'Isn't the weather great today?'

Your exes

This shouldn't even be a point, but if it were not, we'd continue sabotaging any chances we have of true love, talking about failed relationships and giving out red flags as if they were red roses. Talking about your ex on the first date is a one-way ticket to never seeing a boy again. It speaks of insecurities and unresolved issues, and reeks of feelings that might not have necessarily ebbed away. Want yellow tape all around any mentions of your ex?

Then make sure you don't bring up any of the following:

1. Your ex's name and other information
2. A thirty-page letter on why it didn't work out with him
3. A two-hundred-and-fifty-page book on why you still might be in love with him
4. His parents' bank account details

However, if your date mentions one of his own exes out of turn (or reason), get your nearest friend on speed dial and fake heartburn. It's going to save you from the heartache later.

What you should do instead: Stick to anecdotes about your family and friends, but keep it light and non-controversial. The idea of a family man is endearing, but no one is signing up to hear about your older brother's marriage problems.

Your problems

Want to impress that gorgeous boy sitting across from you at the bar? Keep your problems (work and otherwise) right where they belong: away.

While your turbulent relationship with the colleague who shares your cubicle might seem exceptionally relevant to you, it doesn't make for such a great story to share over a bottle of Pinot Noir. That includes the heartwarming tale of how your irritable bowel syndrome might finally be improving, or how you might have to give up your house on a mortgage because you haven't paid your loans since last April.

What you should do instead: Save these stories for just before you are buying wedding bands for each other. There's no going back after.

You

As riveting as your life story can be, remember you aren't on *Ellen*.[8] Selling yourself on a date is not necessarily bad, but if you do it enough to warrant movie rights and a three-book deal, you should probably stop. You might think you are irresistibly interesting, but do remember that *everyone* is interesting after they've had four large whisky sours.

What you should do instead: Listen. Find out what *he's* into. Ask him about *his* family or his favourite book. Talk about movies. Talk about art. Talk about him. Keep the self-loving to a bare minimum, and your movie just might get a sequel.

Number Thirty: The Glow Up
Will Karma Give Me a Second Chance ... or Bite Me in the Car?

Thirty is the kind of man who hits me up on Grindr with a gym selfie.

Thirty is also the kind of man who spontaneously decides to take me out for a drive because he's bored.

'Are you ready?' he asks as I get into his car, and I end up doing a double-take.

Thirty is the kind of man whose face is so angular it would feel right at home in a math textbook. **Thirty** is also the kind of man who looks like he bench-presses his own body weight.

'So … where do you want to go?' he asks as both his biceps greet me with a flex.

'Wherever the road takes us …' I blush. And so we drive on.

8 Or the Kapil Sharma Show.

Thirty is the kind of man who has a postgrad degree from the States, but moved back home to help his father set up a design factory. **Thirty** is also the kind of man who has no regrets about making the move.

As he drives through a boulevard, I sneeze involuntarily. Am I allergic to gorgeous men? 'Bless you,' he says, whipping a paper napkin out of his dashboard.

'How is a pretty man like you so polite?' I giggle after he apologizes for making the conversation all about himself. What has he been talking about? In the last forty minutes, he's neither cut a signal nor any of my monologues about my life.

Maybe it's a myth that a gay man's sexual appeal is inversely proportional to his personality. But **Thirty** doesn't think he's an exception.

Because he hasn't *always* been so pretty. He feels like he started the decade in a different body, but also in a different headspace.

'I don't need to have a great body to feel loved,' he remembers telling his friends. I sigh empathetically.

We both know how that turns out. The next half of the decade was cathartic, he tells me. Maybe it was the constant rejection or maybe it was the fact that he couldn't run around an entire block without feeling like he was experiencing a cardiac arrest, but he realized that *maybe* he had it all wrong. It was the *classic* gay man's curse. Our life is a trail of maybes.

For the last three years now, he's been loading up on protein bars, but he's also been loading up on positivity. There are days when he wants to give up and go back to a happier (and less healthy) life, but what is life but a constant work in progress?

It's so heartbreaking, I want to hug him. Instead, I say, 'Can I find you on Instagram?

With one eye on the road, he turns and smiles. 'Sure, why don't you send me a DM?'

Grinning to myself, I hit up his handle and message him. My smile freezes.

He's already in my archives. In fact, he's been there since 2013. I scroll through miles of messages (mostly him) and monosyllables (mostly me). **Thirty** seems like the kind of man who hit on me before his glow up. And me?

I look like the kind of man who rejected him. I shift uncomfortably in my seat and think of the right words to say. There's a strong sense of déjà vu from that time I ran into **Four** back in 2014, but only this time, I am on the other side of the table. Now I am the douche who rejects people based on their looks. I must say it isn't a very attractive look on me.

'It's okay.'

'So … maybe this is a chance for a do-over?' I ask bleakly, as he pulls into my society.

He smiles, but doesn't kiss me goodbye.

5.5 All the Reasons You Might Not Get a Second Date

A.k.a All the Dating Mistakes You Might Be Making

Urvaksh is in a fix. He feels that the city has run out of suitable men.

That's surprising, considering he has a track record of dating the city's most eligible queer men. I count them down on my fingers. There was the architect who designed all the celebrity homes; the dashing entrepreneur who made it to Forbes' esteemed '30 Under 30' list; the entertainment lawyer with the drug problem; and my personal favourite, an ageing superstar's closeted B-lister son, who was teeming with daddy issues and debt. I feel like I am missing a thumb. What happened to all of them?

All the dates were fabulous, but not *one* called back.

'Have you tried …' I begin, but Urvaksh shushes me right away.

He's done it all. He's never lied on his profile. He's always on time. He's assertive, but also understanding. Basically, he's the compatible version of every character Ranbir Kapoor has ever played. And yet, he suffers from the First Date Jinx™.

'Maybe you haven't been taking chances,' I suggest, but he dismisses me instantly. He's taken *so many* chances he could give guest lectures in Probability 101. I am disappointed. There goes my carpe diem spiel.

'So why aren't things working out?' Urvaksh finds it confusing. 'I've *perfected* the perfect date. I have all these beautiful lines and all these suave moves. I even have this perfect little rooftop bar that I take them all to. It overlooks the sea, and all the waiters know my name, so ...'

I sigh. Unlike Kartik, who is a hopeless romantic, and Aneesh, who is a hopeless flirt, Urvaksh is just ... *hopeless*. There's no such thing as a template date.

Does That Mean There Are Other Dating Mistakes We Could Be Making?

Most certainly. You might have the Ten Commandments of Online Dating™ (from chapter 3) down to a tee, but if you are guilty of these common dating malpractices, there's a reason you aren't getting those text replies.

1. **Being a douchebag on dating apps**

You might be hiding behind the façade of a pretty photo and a witty bio, but your shitty attitude isn't helping you rake up those right swipes.

2. **Being too picky**

Sushant is too short. Tanveer is too tall. Jhala jokes too much. Jasmeet doesn't joke at all. Rishabh drives too rashly. Dushyant lacks self-drive. These are just a few of the reasons Urvaksh has given for dumping men. There might be plenty of fish, but if you throw them all back into the sea, there's a fat chance you are going to go back home with a catch. Save your cynicism for the freshness of the fish you buy at the supermarket, not the boys you date.

3. Not texting back

Urvaksh has a three-day strategy when it comes to texting boys that he likes. 'I don't want to look needy,' he drawls when I ask him why he would want to wait for seventy-two hours to send a quick 'hello'. For someone who's constantly glued to his phone, it really isn't that difficult.

The 'three-day rule' is a myth. Like someone enough? Text them back right away. Don't like them enough? Text them back to (politely) tell them that you don't think it will work out.

Repeat till you no longer feel the need to pick up your phone.

4. Going all out with grand gestures

As long as you don't overdo it, sweet nothings and small gestures can take you a long way. Sending a heartwarming text to a man will never be the end of the world, I tell Urvaksh. It's when you go overboard that you have a problem.

Grand declarations of love only work in rom-coms and romance novels, not in real life. Go easy on the weekend getaways and round-trip tickets to Bali for your second-month anniversary (in the case of the celebrity architect mentioned above), unless you want them to wonder what you are trying to hide.

5. But also being cheap

Half-priced cocktails are as effective as half-hearted compliments, which means that boasting about how your Zomato Gold membership is getting you a free dish is probably not a good idea. When in doubt, remember the golden rule: cheap is *never* charming.

6. Having a dating pattern

There's no set formula for making a date (or relationship) work. Just because your words worked on Ravi, the radiologist, doesn't mean they'd work on Tarun, the tax accountant (unless they are the same person, in which case you have a bigger problem at hand). Every boy is a unique story, which means he has to be read differently. Keep your patterns right where they belong: on your shirts and in the closet. Switch them with bookmarks instead.

7. And going to the same places all the time

Some boys like sushi, some boys like sandwiches and some boys even like sev puri. 'But they *know* me there!' Urvaksh insists, speaking fondly of his favourite bar. He's had all his first dates there. It's a tradition, he tells me.

See, the booths might feel like home and the waiters might seem like family, but it's time to create new memories with new menu cards. Step out of your comfort zone and step into a new bar instead.

8. ... but also, going out with different boys all the time

Stop with the serial dating. This isn't an episode of *The Bachelor*, and there are no final roses.

9. Being too presumptuous

Don't expect your date to reach for any of these three things through the course of the night: the door at the restaurant, their wallet or you.

10. And ultimately, not taking rejection well

No really means no, and no amount of begging and reasoning (or worse, blackmailing) is going to get someone to change their mind. Take rejection like a gentleman and wear it proud. Use it as a lesson on self-improvement.

Just like this book.

5.6 But Do You Deserve a Second Date?

Hello again, quiz-taker and reader of dating guides. Would you rather deal with first-date jitters than be cursed with the First-Date Jinx?

Answer these ten questions to find out if you get a sequel to what you thought was the Best Date of Your Life™:

1. **Your template first date setting would be**
   a. Your favourite bar, where the wait staff knows your name
   b. A ridiculously fancy restaurant that you can't afford
   c. It depends on where your date wants to go
   d. His house

2. **The first thing you compliment someone about is**
   a. Their smile
   b. Compliments are tacky
   c. Their best feature
   d. Generic muscles that catch your eye

3. **You usually end your first date with**
   a. A quickie in the car
   b. Obviously in the bedroom
   c. A quick peck on the cheek, with a warm hug
   d. A goodbye

4. **The conversation topic to avoid at all costs would be**
   a. Politics
   b. His Instagram profile
   c. Exes
   d. His life

5. **At the end of the evening, your date offers to pay for the meal, you …**
   a. Let him, but also tell him that 'the next one's on me'.
   b. Argue a bit and pretend to do the cheque dance, but let him pay in the end
   c. Suggest splitting the cheque, because it's the only fair thing to do
   d. Aren't carrying your wallet, because you *expected* him to pay

6. **Your date insists on a round of drinks, so you decide to get**
   a. Whatever he's having
   b. Vodka shots
   c. Gin & Tonic
   d. Water: you have abs to maintain

7. **Your date is a few minutes late, but he apologizes as soon as he walks in. You …**
   a. Brush it off and tell him it's not a big deal
   b. Yell at him
   c. Joke about it and tell him that the first round of drinks is on him
   d. This doesn't work, because you walk in after he does

8. **First kiss at the end of a date?**
   a. Obviously, because every date is spectacular
   b. Not unless he makes the first move
   c. With consent, of course
   d. Never

9. **A line you'd use on a first date.**
   a. 'So, tell me more about yourself.'
   b. 'Do you want to just skip the small talk and head back to mine?'
   c. 'Aren't you a delight!'
   d. 'I really need to leave right now.'

10. **Your favourite comfort food:**
    a. French fries
    b. Onion rings
    c. Popcorn
    d. Kale chips

Mostly As:

With your template answers and near-perfect reactions, you aren't just looking at a sequel, but *a full series* order for your dating life (unlike Urvaksh). But would people want to watch this thrilling saga that is a culmination of all your romantic escapades?

Nope. See, this is a date and not a beauty pageant; so stock answers will only get you through a dinner reservation for next week. But soon, your compliments will fall flat, your jokes will sound boring, and you'll be left with a sequel that *everyone* complains about. Instead, try something new and think outside the box, and you might just end up going back home with the crown prize. Prince Charming himself.

Mostly Bs:

Unless you are trying to sabotage your date (or worse, this quiz), there's no reason to choose the answers that you did. Life might not give you a second chance, but this quiz definitely will. How about you try again later?

Mostly Cs:

CONGRATULATIONS! You've played your cards so perfectly the first time around, there's a high chance you'll be asked out for a repeat before you finish reading this sentence.

Mostly Ds:

Judging by your train wreck of answers, it's a surprise your dating life hasn't derailed already. But don't worry; I've got you covered. Head back to Chapter 2 for a quick discourse on how NOT to be a douchebag on the first date.

You are welcome.

Number Thirty-one: The Lawyer
The Beginner's Guide to Blind Dates

I am here and I am waiting. It's ten minutes to nine, and I feel anxious. I light up a cigarette just as my phone chimes with a warning. 'He's waiting for you inside,' it reads mysteriously, '... and he's wearing a white shirt'.

A white shirt? Everybody owns a white shirt. How original. I take a deep puff and keep my phone away. Well, I did sign up for this.

It all started a few days ago. I met an acquaintance at a friend's house party, and it took her all of two drinks and five minutes to needle me about my relationship status.

No 'Hi! How are you?', no 'It's been so long!' Straight to the point.

Oh, to be the lone gay man at a party full of women.

'Why?' I asked – a question that was fair because I'd only met this woman twice before. 'Because I met this guy last night, and I think he's perfect for you. Do you want me to set you up?' she had giggled.

I sigh. Give a straight woman a drink and a gay man for company, and she'll make it her life's mission to find him a partner. If I had a list of all the men that would be 'perfect for me', I'd be running a cabal of eligible bachelors who are as attractive as they are accomplished. But there's no cabal, and not a single eligible bachelor on the horizon.

The 'he' in question is a man she wouldn't tell me anything about.

'But that's the point of a blind date!' she reasoned, when I tried to interject.

Blind dates are always tricky. How can you show interest in someone when you know *nothing* about them – no name, no face, no red flags to unfurl. Social media has ruined us all. We are so used to looking up our dates before we meet them that the thought of the unknown is terrifying. A blind date is all about starting at ground zero. What if we have nothing in common? What if we have family in common? What if he raises multiple red flags? What if he shows up wearing an actual red flag? What if he's not my type? Or worse, what if I am not his type?

But I still said yes, because that's what men do when the only thing they have to look forward to is an empty horizon.

Which is why I am currently standing in front of my favourite bar, drenched in nervous sweats. How does one not get blindsided by a blind date?

It's easy. You take it step by step and just dive in.

1. Pick and wear something you are comfortable with.

I'm already dreading the thought of damaging my liver with drinks that are too expensive, on the off chance that the stranger sitting awkwardly in front of me may end up being the One. What if he turns out to be a troll or, worse, a serial killer? Or a serial killer who looks like a troll?

In any case, I might as well dress the part. I pick my favourite first date shirt and pair it with straight-fitting jeans. It's seen (and been disappointed by) dozens of boys before tonight, but one machine wash and we are back as new. I give myself a final check in the bathroom mirror, and then I am off to meet a man I know nothing about. So where do we go?

You need to choose an activity that let's you relax, but also allows you to make a clean exit if things aren't going too well. Casual drinks at the bar? Yes. A five-course tasting menu and/or a three-hour-long biopic at the theatre? No.

I've said it before – the location you select says a lot more about you than pages worth of electronic small talk. A poor choice can reveal the worst of your personality flaws. I skip my own advice and pick my favourite bar: the wait staff is polite and chatty, and I know the menu like the back of my hand. If things go south and we find no common ground, the chances of running into someone I know (and finding a way out) are ridiculously high.

There's no way this can go wrong. Plus, they know me well enough to put more wine in my sangria.

2. Throw out expectations.

I stub my expectations out with my cigarette, and walk in. It's a quiet night at the bar. It's empty. My gut tells me I am moments away from being disappointed, and I even wore my favourite shirt, so I can't imagine why this would …

Oh. Who's that waving at me?

It's **Thirty-one**. I breathe a sigh of relief. He doesn't look like a troll *or* a serial killer. In fact, my not-so-blind date is textbook pretty: twinkling eyes, a beautiful nose and long eyelashes. And a smile so wide I can see it all the way from the other end of the bar.

I smile back.

As I walk towards him, I notice that he's tall, but also mousy – and I am scared that if I don't keep him in check, he might scuttle away back to our common friend (who I am secretly thanking at the moment). But now is not the time to worry about that, because …

'Hi!'

'Hello!'

'Are you …?'

'Yes, I am!' We introduce ourselves. I can't read his expression. It doesn't look like disgust, but his eyes don't widen with wonder either. That's okay, I'm no Adonis.

'You look great,' I say to him.

'You do too.'

Well, that went well. What are we waiting for? Let the interview begin.

3. Learn to go with the flow.

'So ... what do you do?'

Thirty-one works in the legal department of a high-profile music label (read: he's rich). 'Does that make you an entertainment lawyer?' I ask him, my eyes widening to twice their size. I imagine cocktail soirees, sneaker launches and (but I don't tell him) underground raves, and my eyes mist over. I've seen too much television.

It's mostly boring paperwork and lots of board meetings, he insists, but they have casual Fridays at work, which are fun (read: he's not a wild child). I am only slightly let down. And then I notice his tattoos. He has four of them (read: he's not boring). And suddenly, the night pulls ahead.

Sometimes, on dates, you become someone else for a while. You become someone your date wants you to be. You smile at gaps in conversation that would usually result in an eye roll, you nod silently instead of voicing your disagreement, and you blush. You always blush.

But with **Thirty-one**, I feel like I am wearing only one skin tonight. My own. The pretences have been shed and the veil has been pulled off. Here I am, peeling thirty-four years (read: he looks only twenty-seven) of his life like a red onion.

It turns out we've had the same childhood, six years apart. We both grew up with overachieving sisters and overbearing bullies in school, only to pull through it all and still become the people we were born to be.

Out and proud gay men. We've broken hearts and had our hearts broken, loved and lost, shed and shaded. Our ideas of a typical Friday night involve alcohol, and for Sunday morning it's brunch. We could be the same person.

Only he rakes an eight-figure salary and has homes in three different cities. And I can't even afford rent.

4. Keep your mind open.

We are three drinks down and things are looking up. My SOS contacts have long been abandoned and are currently screaming silent nothings into my notifications. I will only see them tomorrow morning. He leans over his bar stool and kisses me lightly on my lips (read: he's spontaneous). I am taken aback, but I don't pull back.

'Do you want to ditch this bar and go somewhere else?'

(Read: he's decisive.)

5. Watch the alcohol.

Bar two, scene two. One of the key rules of any date (blind or otherwise) is to never let the alcohol get to you, because …

Shots. Shots. Shots. We are doing shots. Exactly seven hours from now, I am going to wake up next to this man with a massive hangover that's going to make me swear off sangria for months. It will last all of two days (till I eventually meet him next) … but wait, I digress. This is not THAT story.

The night is blurring fast, and eventually, I'll only remember the shots we chugged one after the other, but for now …

'You are so much fun!' I squeal, and he hugs me tight. I can smell the aftershave on the nape of his neck. It smells of joy.

'What do you want to do next?' I scream over the speakers. My heart is thumping, and it's only partly because of the alcohol.

'Karaoke?' he yells back.

My eyes widen again.

6. Try something new.

It's our third bar of the night. He's singing Vanilla Ice's 'Ice Ice Baby'. He's on a table. He's dancing. He's asking me to join him.

And in that moment, I lose myself.

7. Get up and do something.

It's morning. The sunlight streaming through his window nudges me awake.

He's already up and sipping on his coffee. There's a mug waiting for me on the bedside drawer. I smile at him apologetically, because conventional morning-after situations involve me picking up my clothes and leaving.

But nothing about last night was conventional. There's no awkwardness, and I don't feel the need to pull up my pants and make a hasty (but also, clean) exit.

'What are you doing tomorrow night?' he asks me.

Wow. Isn't it too soon? What if I already have other plans? Or another date? What if I don't want to see him again? What if I want to wait before round two? I can come up with a lot of excuses and never see the man again. Instead, I say:

'You, I guess?'

6

Wait … Are We Halfway Through This Rom-com?

Number Thirty-two: The Flake
Is It a Date If It Doesn't Happen?

August 2018

Thirty-two is a product designer who also runs his own art studio in Pune. **Thirty-two** likes to think of himself as a struggling artist, but makes it a point to conveniently namedrop all his awards in every conversation. Sometimes, he also moonlights as a model. **Thirty-two** is visiting, and asks if I'd like to get some coffee on Friday. **Thirty-two** looks slightly familiar. If I haven't met him before, he's definitely popped up on my grid. What can I say? The queer community just shrank another kilometre.

Thirty-two never shows up. I hail a cab back home, hurling expletives by the dozen.

6.1 A Guide to Worst-Case Scenarios and How to Deal with Them Like an Adult

Kartik found the German on Grindr two weekends ago. He was a 6'2", 205-pound blue-eyed socialist with a passion for coffee-table art books, genetics and iced tea. Those cherub-like eyes made Kartik send the first ping. Over the course of the night, my friend found out that the German also had a bachelor's degree in anthropology, a master's degree in fine arts *and* a love-hate relationship with his own beard. He wasn't *just* a pretty sight.

The German told Kartik that his name was Fynn, and my friend immediately fell in love with the name. After two weeks of tumultuous text-dancing, they decided to meet for drinks on a Friday night.

Kartik gets there early (who shows up late on a first date?), excited to make a good first impression. He's wearing his favourite first date shirt and smells of anxiety. It's 8:55 p.m. Kartik lights up a cigarette and runs through all the questions he has lined up about Darwin's theory. At 9:00 pm, he stubs his smoke and walks right in.

At 9:02 p.m., he finds himself a table right by the bar.

At 9:04 p.m., he sends a quick text to Fynn telling him that he's here.

At 9:09 p.m., he orders a whisky sour.

At 9:12 p.m., he checks his phone to see if Fynn replied. He hasn't seen his text.

At 9:18 p.m., the waiter comes over with his drink and a complimentary breadbasket.

At 9:21 p.m., he checks his phone again. No response. Maybe he's stuck in traffic, Kartik sighs. He keeps his phone away and digs into the breadbasket.

The minutes crawl by, and after what feels like an hour (and three bread rolls), Kartik picks up his phone. It's only 9:24 p.m. The double grey ticks of his delivered text stare right back at him. What could be wrong? Is he stuck in a never-ending tunnel of no network connection? Have aliens abducted him? Did they have questions about anthropology?

He waits and waits and waits. He waits till the waiter politely comes over to tell him that they'll have to charge him for the extra bread.

It's 9:43 p.m.

Kartik looks down at the crumbs of sourdough trailing the empty basket. Fynn isn't going to show up. He quietly gulps the last of his whisky sour, clears the cheque and leaves. *Fin* indeed.

So what does one do when their date pulls a no-show?

Unless he's been kidnapped or stuck in an emergency, there's no valid reason to not show up for a date. While being stood up can be extremely bruising to one's ego, know that you've dodged a bullet (and a split cheque) with this one. Pat yourself on the back and order a drink as you guiltlessly dig into the breadbasket. Make it a double.

A first date can go wrong in multiple ways. Your date might not show up, but he might also show up with friends, or worse, drunk. How do *you* deal with these worst-case scenarios?

Here's a quick guide to follow when …

1. **… he shows up without his wallet.**

Three courses and four rounds of drinks later, he realizes he forgot his wallet back home. (It could also be a ploy to get you to pay, in which case goodbye hard-earned money.) Don't make a scene, and offer to clear the bill. Chances are he'll get so overwhelmed by your nonchalance, he'll buy you a meal the next time. Because there *will* be a next time.

2. **… he shows up drunk.**

First dates can be pretty nerve-racking, so a quick shot (or two) can calm your anxiety. But if your date shows up four beers and seven tequila shooters down, we might have a problem. Drunken personas might be a great way to gauge someone's true personality, but you know they need to stop when they start throwing up all over your tapas. If he's apologetic, be polite and ask if he wants to reschedule. If he's not, call yourself a cab. But make sure you call him one before you leave.

3. **… your ex shows up.**

Midway through your date, just as you are about to make a breakthrough and 'accidentally' brush his arm, your ex shows up. Having to explain to your date that you are ducking under the table to avoid your ~~past from haunting you~~ ex seeing you is not a good look. If you'd really like to see him again, come clean and tell him the truth. If things work between the two of you, he'll find out anyway. Just make sure you stick to the basics and don't go into the details of your relationship. You don't want him to think you still harbour residual feelings for your ex-boyfriend.

Because you obviously don't.

4. **… his ex shows up.**

Midway through your date, just as you are about to make a breakthrough and 'accidentally' brush his arm, *his* ex shows up. If he introduces the two of you, don't blink an eye because you think that the ex looks like a better version of you. Just smile politely and say, 'Nice to meet you!' Then blend into the background till they finish their conversation.

Once the ex walks away, ask your date if he's okay/feels weird. These questions stick within the realm of polite concern. Leave the intrusive ones for your six-month anniversary.

5. **… he doesn't look like his picture.**

There are two kinds of people in this world. The ones who look like their online dating profile pictures, and the ones who don't. If your date is the latter, don't skip town. Smile and stick around, because you are obviously not a bad person.

6. … you don't know what he looks like.

Maybe you matched with him when you were drunk-texting an ex. Maybe you deleted his photo when you were clearing your phone cache. Maybe he never sent a picture. Maybe you wanted him to be a mystery. Maybe you suffer from amnesia. There are a lot of maybes when it comes to first dates. If you show up second to a date and can't find your prospective playmate, here's what you should do:

- Cross your fingers that you are not being catfished, and text him, 'Are you here yet?'
- Scout the restaurant for other lost souls who are *also* constantly looking up from their phones.
- Seat yourself right at the bar and hope they find you first.

7. … leans in for a kiss.

There's a time and place to be nice, but sadly this is not it. If you don't want to kiss them back, you don't have to feel pressured into puckering up those lips. Just pull back, smile, and tell them you aren't ready.

You don't even need to apologize, because you don't owe them anything.

8. … it's not a date.

You know because he also invited his friends. Don't sulk in a corner because the night isn't panning out the way you had imagined. Enjoy the company and make the most of the situation. Mingle with new people. Have a refreshing debate over politics with people you'll never see again. Get that large slice of cake for dessert. Let your hair down. Relish every moment of spontaneity. Great dates (with men who are actually interested) can always happen later.

Number Thirty-three: The Namesake: Wasn't This Supposed to Be a Party for Two?

October 2012

I open my inbox. It's a simple text from **Thirty-three**, entrepreneur and eligible bachelor, calling me home for a party he's throwing for close friends.

It's true that we've never *actually* met, and it's truer that our text dance is not as frequent as I would like it to be, but maybe he *finally* realized what a catch I am. 'Should you be going to a complete stranger's house party?' you'd ask. As a gay man, I've met strangers in stranger locations.

I build us up on the way to ~~his~~ our sea-facing apartment downtown, wine bottle in hand and filled with newfound optimism.

I reach there to find at least ten other cookie-cutter boys like me holding similar bottles of wine. 'Add your bottle to the table over there,' he hugs me like an old friend, pointing at a countertop that's already bursting at its seams with bottles of expensive spirits and (even more) exotic liquor.

I smile and excuse myself to go strangle my optimism in the bathroom.

Number Thirty-four: The Marketing Guru Is This a Lunch Date or a LinkedIn Request?

August 2013

'Are you free on Friday?'

It's **Thirty-four**, the square-jawed sales guru from Grindr. It's also Thursday morning. How late is too late to set up a date?

But the man is beautiful and has eyes so tan they could be on a month-long beach vacation. But my principles are my principles, so …

I reply with an affirmative. Meh, I've never been very principled.

'My company might have some work for you too,' he texts back, crisp like the shirt he's wearing in his profile picture. Should I be mixing business *and* pleasure?

I'll make an exception this one time. Over Mexican food and mojitos, I rush through his company profile and read about luxury homes in the eastern suburbs, while he runs me through brochures and menu cards simultaneously.

When I go back home, I delete him from Grindr and add him on LinkedIn.

6.2 The Fifty-Five Lies You Tell Yourself while You Are on a Bad First Date

As adults, we lie to ourselves about a lot of things. We lie about happiness, we lie about failure, we lie about how we did not deserve an 80 in our board exams, we lie about how we can pull off neon green, and we lie about how our parents love us as much as they love our overachieving siblings.

We lie so much that we can put it up on our LinkedIn profiles as a skill. Hence, it is only natural that we lie to ourselves when it comes to finding love.

Here are fifty-five lies we've all told ourselves as we sit across a man who's so wrong he could be a Honey Singh song:

1. I'm so done with all of this.
2. Online dating is not exhausting at all.
3. I'm not going to get drunk tonight.
4. I'm so glad I decided to starve myself before coming here.
5. I'm not drunk right now.

6. He's so wrong if he thinks I am going to get another drink.
7. I'm sure my breath doesn't smell.
8. That's definitely not a wedding ring on his finger.
9. I have a really good feeling about this.
10. He's right; I really don't look anything like my profile picture.
11. It's so sweet that he can talk about his ex so openly, and so often. It can only mean he's definitely over him!
12. My friends are going to love him so much!
13. His friends are going to love me so much!
14. When he says my cheeks look full, he doesn't mean that I am fat.
15. It's exciting how he's going through all the songs in my playlist and telling me how he really feels about them.
16. I think he confused my drink for his. It's no big deal.
17. I am going to laugh at his joke about Syria because I think it's really funny.
18. Who cares if he's checking out the guy sitting at the other table? He only had eyes for me when I asked for my fifth glass of wine.
19. If he says he's looking for a long-term relationship, it must be true.
20. That little boil on his lip is definitely not herpes.
21. He's just really quiet because he's so adorably shy. Look at him checking his phone every other minute? He's so awkward he can't make eye contact!
22. I love the way he looks away when I ask him about his family.
23. If this doesn't work out, I won't let it affect me.
24. His style is … so unique.
25. Look at him! Updating his Facebook status between courses. SO CUTE!
26. It's totally okay that he asked to borrow my credit card …
27. I am sure he'll understand if I tell him that I don't want to kiss him goodnight at the end of the date.
28. But it's just one kiss. It really doesn't mean anything, does it?

29. He went through an entire packet of cigarettes in the last two hours that we've been here. Wow, that's so sexy.
30. This silence is not awkward at all.
31. Can he smell my desperation?
32. I am sure he's never used that line before.
33. Or that one.
34. I feel like now is the right time to tell him all the problems I had with my ex.
35. He didn't say nigger. He said bigger.
36. When he said he hates dogs, he probably didn't mean he *hates* dogs.
37. He's right. I should have just called and confirmed the date before leaving.
38. I like how he jokes about having a boyfriend at home. This boy is hilarious!
39. It's so endearing that he calls himself a nomad.
40. Who knew that chewing with your mouth open can be so … attractive.
41. Look at him typing away on his phone! Maybe he's texting his friends, telling them how cute I am.
42. I probably shouldn't ask him why he said he has to get back home in thirty minutes.
43. Well, there's no such thing as a bad first date.
44. This is a one-off. I am going to delete his number the instant we are done.
45. When he says he thinks we'd make great bros, he means it in a romantic way.
46. He's going to love how I can snort my shots up my nose.
47. I'm sure he's thinking about getting matching wedding bands too.
48. He's just asking me if my flatmate is out of town because he's really concerned about me being alone at home. Such a sweet guy!

49. It's completely fine that he didn't offer to split the bill. I'm sure he'll pay next time.
50. I am not going to sleep with him tonight.
51. If I do sleep with him tonight, I'm going to make sure I don't develop feelings and wait for him to call me back. That would be pathetic.
52. Oh yes, I'm crazy about unprotected sex too!
53. I'm really looking forward to my walk of shame tomorrow morning!
54. I have a feeling he's going to ask me out this weekend.
55. Oh yes! I'm definitely going to see him again.

Number Thirty-five: The Socialite: Has Price Charming Been a Lie All This While?

October 2011

As we wait outside a dingy watering hole, **Thirty-five** and I bond over our Instagram feeds. I'm simpering over his Bengali ancestry and his imminent PhD in something I don't remember, but the boy is barely listening. He's besotted by the watering hole.

'I've never been to a place like this before,' he states. I think of saying something clichéd, like 'There's a first time for everything,' but I don't want to *sound* clichéd.

'Well, there's a first time for everything,' I say as I usher him inside. At least I can say I tried.

He peers around the dirty hallways of the bar. The air is heavy with the smell of cheap hair oil, cigarette smoke and urinal cakes. But my date is clearly intrigued. The waiter walks over with a menu card, laminated and stained with yesterday's chilly chicken.

His eyes open wider than our melamine dinner plates. **Thirty-five** inspects the menu with great interest. He thinks it's kitsch; I think it's the cheapest date money can buy.

I attempt small talk till our drinks arrive because it's too dark to scroll through our Instagram feeds. Plus, I've already asked him everything there is to ask about the PhD that I don't remember anything about. Is this going anywhere?

Fifteen minutes later, our first round of drinks are down and we are best friends. He talks fondly of a rich aunt involved in a famous property dispute (fondly, because she also gives him weekly golf lessons after lunch at the club), as I sip my rum in wide-eyed wonder. Just recently, he was at a friend's gallery opening and got an offer to work on the prime minister's socio-economic committee as an advisor; the stories seem larger than life for this little tavern, and I can feel our booth bursting at its seams. With all these art soirees, luncheons and consulate meetings, how does he get time to unwind?

He laughs like they do on television. 'Why don't you have another drink?' he slurs romantically. I can tell when someone's avoiding a question, but if he's buying, why not?

'I shouldn't have more of these.' He stifles a giggle. 'I'll become fat.' You can ask a gay man how much he earns, but you can never ask him how much he weighs. This is my cue to fawn over him. My glass is empty, and I wouldn't mind a refill. He beckons the waiter over with his fingers as I sycophantically gush over his lean, athletic frame. The rum pours freely, and I hear three new cubes of ice clink in my glass. That's three reasons I need to down this glass sooner.

It hasn't all been child's play, the boy says to me. He's been a cancer survivor thrice over, but hasn't looked back ever since. Somehow, downing my drink doesn't seem like a very good idea any more. It's not deterred him, and now he takes life more seriously (luncheons and art soirees aside). Spending months in chemotherapy makes you appreciate the smaller things in life. So what happens next?

He'll be moving to Delhi in a month, and is considering taking up the job on the advisory board while he studies three times a week. For an average twenty-seven-year-old, that sounds like a lot to handle. But he's not your average twenty-seven-year-old.

So how is he feeling now?

He's feeling feisty. He leans over and kisses me on my nose, and then gawks at his own foolhardy behaviour.

'What if someone saw us?' 'Will they throw us out?' 'Do you think the man at the next table is looking at us?' 'Do you think the man at the next table is cute?' 'Do you think I am drunk?' 'Do you think I ask too many questions?'

I giggle, and tell him he doesn't. Seven rounds later, he tells me he has something else to tell me. My heart skips a beat, and I almost pull my feet away. What can it be this time?

Is he a CBI spy? Did aliens abduct him as a child? Has he been lying this whole time? Does he have to go back home? Am I too fat? Did I say something wrong? Is there something stuck in my teeth? I'm sure there's something stuck in my teeth.

As I feel around my mouth with my tongue, he tells me he has royal blood. I give him the once-over once again. He might not be the conventional Disney prince, but he will do. I smile at him. He smiles back.

I pay the bill, because he's forgotten his wallet back home.

6.3 All the Lies They Tell You about Dating IRL

Some of the Worst Dating Advice You'll Ever Hear

For decades now, well-meaning couples, wide-eyed dating experts in fashion magazines and die-hard romance columnists (such as myself) have provided singles with life hacks to find lifelong relationships. There are rules to follow, lists to read and guides to go over – things NOT to do on a date. Five ways to snare a man? Fifteen outfits to wow away that wonderful guy? Seventeen ideas for a great date that lead right up to the bedroom.

Still single? Feel like none of the hack-your-way-to-his-heart articles are helping you? You can't always live life based on a listicle (unless it's this one), people.

So bust these common dating myths before you bust a move on your date:

1. 'You need to relax and just be yourself.'

You see this one in dating columns and glossy magazines, telling you to be only one person every time you meet someone new: You!

No one wants a compulsive liar sitting across them at a pub, but most often, our daily selves are not really-first date material. Does anyone really want to know how your day was at your desk job? Do they care about what dressing you had your salad with? Or that cockroach you whacked right out of the window?

There's nothing wrong with sprucing yourself up after a drink or two. That poetry jam you won in college? Bring it up, and make it the highlight of your conversation. After all, what is one's true self anyway?

2. 'Opposites always attract, don't they?'

~~Karan Johar's films~~ Mainstream movies would like us to believe that stark opposites are drawn to each other, like moths to a flame. But in real life, they would burn just as bad.

'Look at them fight their way through the interval, only to sort their differences and eventually fall in love in the second half,' pop culture goads you, as the romantic leads get pushed into holy matrimony by the time the end credits roll.

This is a myth. Opposites only work out in films, because it makes for a great story. Think about it this way: can a cleanliness freak ever get along with a slob?

If they stay in different rooms, yes.

In reality, chances are you'll plan your wedding with someone you have a lot in common with. You love brunch, drinking cocktails by the beach and reading Margaret Atwood? Let's set up a family Netflix account.

3. 'An awkward silence means it's time to say goodbye.'

If you ever reach a point during your date when neither of you has anything to say, don't say anything stupid. Relish the silence.

But don't let it make you uncomfortable. Savour every bit of the quiet. Let it flow through your veins. Punctuate the long pauses with long sips of your cappuccino and break the tension with a joke about the awkward silence. Sometimes, honesty is the best icebreaker.

4. 'If you have sex on the first date, they won't take you seriously.'

There is a general idea that withholding sex from a date, even when you really want to do it, will lead to date number two. 'Don't put out on the first date; they'll only think you want to keep it casual. Make them wait for it. The wait is what makes it beautiful,' says every friend and every other well-wisher in the world.

Sex isn't a bad thing, and whether you decide to put out after the first date, the third or the twenty-seventh, it's completely your choice. This way you at least know if it's going to work out with someone or not – bad sex with the dog-loving IIM graduate who loves internet cat memes *and* Amy Winehouse? Let's just say goodbye with words.

Keeping your legs closed is no measure of how nice a person you are, especially when you are out on a date with someone. If you are a horrible human being who casually engages in animal cruelty but still won't have sex after the first date, you're still a horrible human being. If you are having a good time and you can feel that certain pull, head to the bedroom.

Go to bed thinking about this one, but preferably not alone.

5. 'Maybe if you just tried more dating apps, you'd have more chances of finding the one ...'

Nope. The only thing you'll have more chances of getting is disappointed.

Number Thirty-six: The Foreigner
The Gentleman's Guide on How Not to Greet People

June 2014

It's a busy Saturday night at the pub. The one night of the month when a certain suburban bar becomes LGBTQIA+ only, which means Grindr's entire database has been packed like sardines on a dance floor that can usually accommodate just fifty.

I push my way through a crowd of men in sequined tops, sidestep a boy I ghosted three months, sneak around a man who never called back and finally find myself at the bar. It's busier than the dance floor. As I gesticulate to get the bartender's attention, someone taps me on my shoulder.

It's **Thirty-six**, and he's grinning. He's the dean of admissions at an elite school, and we've never officially met, even though we found each other on Grindr years ago. It took twenty lines of text for him to realize I was not his type. He preferred young, enterprising twinks, and since I was neither young nor enterprising, we relegated each other to our respective Facebook friend lists.

'Funny that I finally run into you here ...' he yells over the stereo, and I respectfully feign surprise. As the only white man in this sea of sardines, he sticks out like a sore thumb.

We politely make small talk for a few minutes, like two Facebook friends would do. 'You look a lot different than I expected ...' he says, cutting short my monologue about feeling claustrophobic. The sweat glistens on his forehead.

'Really?' I bat my eyelids, expecting a compliment. He might not be my type, but that doesn't mean I won't take any affirmation that pops up my way.

'Yeah, you are really good at editing your pictures, aren't you?'

6.4 The Potential Boyfriend Test: Is He the One You Were Looking for?

Things are going well, and you've finally managed to sink your claws (and your teeth, if you are lucky) into that perfect guy, and you can't stop gushing about him to your friends. You've had half a dozen great dates, with half a dozen happier endings. He's clean behind the ears, dresses well and can even sustain a conversation (and more) well until the wee hours of the morning.

But hold on, you have to test drive the goods before you get on to the boyfriend bandwagon. So how do you know he has long-term potential?

Wind up your paramour through these ten tests before you seal the deal, and decide to change your Grindr status to 'Committed':

1. **Ask him to eat a submarine sandwich in front of you.**

Is he fast, sloppy and unaware that the mustard relish is dripping down his front? Choose wisely: this is an exclusive preview of what it's going to be like when he *goes down* on you.

2. **Switch off the Wi-Fi when he's working.**

His level of irritation is inversely proportional to how essential it is for you to date him in the long run (unless of course, he's in the middle of a very important presentation, in which case, you are the one no one should commit to).

3. **Tell him to joke about your best friend.**

This is a trick question: no one makes a joke about your best friend.

No one.

4. **Ask him to make a cup of coffee.**

Pours the milk last? Doesn't beat the coffee? Makes it that dull milky brown that you'll never touch? No, no and an extra no. Plus, if he can't make a simple cup of coffee, he's not ready to be in a relationship yet.

5. **Go on a weekend trip.**

There are a thousand things that can go wrong when you spend forty-eight (or more) hours in each other's company away from home. From flat tires, delayed flights to overbooked hotels – you have the potential to fight about anything from who sleeps on the right side of the bed to which one of you takes the cheap shampoo bottles back home. Well, think of it this way, if it doesn't work out, you can always leave him behind.

6. **Get him to try on and buy a suit.**

Nothing too loose for the shoulders, nothing that struggles at the waist – if he buys a suit that fits like a glove, you've found yourself your Goldilocks, oh wise bear.

7. **Press all the buttons when you are in the elevator with him.**

Bonus points if it doesn't press his buttons.

8. **Take him to a restaurant with really bad service.**

If he doesn't roll his eyes, talk rudely to the wait staff, make faces at the food or tut loudly whenever the manager passes by, he's a keeper.

9. **Ask him what he thinks about feminism.**

If he goes on a rant about how women *already* have equal rights and how *he* could do with a seat on the bus instead, I'll go on a longer rant about why you shouldn't pursue him any further.

10. **Call him.**

Don't judge him if he doesn't pick up your call – he could be driving, at work, in a meeting, using the washroom, saving a baby from a burning building or, even worse, dead. Reserve the judgement for when he doesn't call back.

But then again, it probably means he doesn't want to date you either.

Number Thirty-seven: The Litigator
Can Mr Right in Reel Life be Mr Wrong in Real Life?

October 2016

It's a lazy Sunday afternoon when **Thirty-seven** waltzes into my DMs.

Most men open with a simple 'hello'. A few use the less elaborate 'how are you?' Some make the effort and ask about my day, and some even ask about my bearings. A majority simply sends a dick pic. But not **Thirty-seven**. He's not one to prance or do the tango; he just gracefully waltzes in with a little pun on my profile name. That's a double bonus.

Twenty minutes into texting, and I'm already interested. He sends pun after pun, joke after joke, and signal after signal. There's been no reference to sexual preferences or space availability, and our man here has not once asked to see my showreel. I haven't either.

Thirty-seven is a litigator with a corporate law firm downtown, but ten texts in, he confides in me that he'd rather be doing something else with his life.

'What would you rather do?' I ask, expecting to hear about a five-year plan that takes him around the world.

'You,' he replies promptly.

And just like that, I know we are in this for the long haul. How could this go wrong?

I'm going to break the fourth wall and be brutally honest here: a lot of men are going to seem charming only because they want to get inside your pants. But a select few (such as myself) are nice, and actually online just ~~for research purposes~~ to meet new and interesting people. You can usually weed out the former because they will send you a picture of their dick (or their disproportionate torsos) within two minutes of sending you a text. So you can imagine my apprehension when …

'I'm going to send you a picture,' the litigator says after a rapid-fire round of jokes at his own expense. We were so close.

Oh, wait. There it is. It's not a dick pic. It's not a pic of his torso. It's a beaming selfie. A very attractive selfie – one that's so unedited, it could be from a Scorsese film. For someone who hates his job, he looks very content in life.

Do you want to get a drink sometime?

I thought he'd never ask.

<u>The first date</u>

'You don't need to use those chopsticks just because you want to impress me,' **Thirty-seven** laughs as he watches me struggle with my sushi. 'You've made a great first impression anyway.'

I'm too busy trying to master my chopsticks to notice, but I promptly blush. As he deliberates whether he'd like a whisky sour or single malt, I deliberate whether I'd like him in a shirt or without one. In fact, his pictures don't do him justice at all. His face is prettier without the pixels of a phone camera.

'Would you also like something to drink?' **Thirty-seven** asks, with the politeness of a steward. He's full of such courtesies in person, which is a huge disparity from his cheeky sense of humour on text. It's surprising that a man so strapping can be so meek – but it doesn't ring any warning bells. People will always be larger than life online. We hide our real personalities behind our phone screens on a daily basis.

Am I being the real me?

At which point, he stares very intently into my eyes and compliments my smile, which is rather new for me. I'm usually the last person in the room to realize when someone is attracted to me, but this one is a lighthouse for lost signals.

Over the course of dinner, he tells me stories about his family that stays far away ('but there's no love lost between us'), friends from law school ('they'd love to meet you sometime') and the lone gay best friend who stays a few blocks away ('but no, we don't love each other *that* way').

'Can I drop you home?' he asks, three hours later. We've shared bento boxes, guzzled a few drinks and even split a pot of tea. That's three different dates, all for the price of one. He lives all by himself on the opposite side of town and this is an hour-long detour, so I don't see the point …

'Sure!' I beam.

We make small talk on our way, and I notice that he's unusually jumpy. It's the kind of nervous energy that drives a romance forward.

'Is this it?' he asks after we pull into my building complex.

'Yeah, right there in that corner …' I steer him to where he needs to be. He looks conflicted but finally moves in for a kiss. I taste a hint of soy and sake, and it feels like we are at the restaurant again.

'Do you have to go?' he moans. If this were a movie, it would make an excellent scene.

'But I must …' I sigh.

'I wish I could tie you up and take you back home.'

I giggle nervously. That's a weird thing to say to someone you barely know, but I let it pass. He's charming, and movie scripts aren't drafted in a day.

'Promise that you'll see me soon?'

Oh, indeed.

<u>The third date</u>

'Do you want a bite of my sandwich?' I cautiously push my plate across the hardwood table. He looks mulish but accepts my peace treaty without a beat. And suddenly, he's grinning again.

'It's just that I want to spend more time with you,' he tells me, apologizing for his hissy fit from moments ago. 'This isn't enough!'

I chuckle, but don't say anything. I've only just turned down an invitation for a nightcap; I wouldn't want to jeopardize what we have.

'So … what are your plans for the rest of the night?'

He's already rung up his best friend for drinks. It's always nice to have a gay man in the neighbourhood to try out new things, he says. They'll probably watch a movie at home after. Is this a ruse to make me jealous?

'What does your friend do?' I ask in what I think is a that's-cool-I'm-not-insecure-at-all tone. He's a doctor who's launching his own skincare label. He promptly pulls out his phone and shows me a picture. The doctor is *also* ruggedly handsome. This is a complication I hadn't thought about. Can two attractive gay men *just* be friends?

'There's nothing for you to worry about. He's not even my type …'

What's his type then?

'You are.'

And *there's* the lighthouse of lost signals.

'Shall we leave?' He flickers in approval.

He becomes a different person in his car. Suddenly, he's the delightfully quick-witted guy who slid into my DMs more than a fortnight ago. As he fills me in on his plans to quit his job and apply to the environmental law firm of his dreams, I realize that maybe he just needs time to settle in. Maybe I had it all wrong. Maybe I should have just agreed to the nightcap. Maybe I …

'Why do you have to leave already?' he frowns as I lean forward to kiss him goodbye. He turns his head away.

'But I must …' I repeat. I expect another grand gesture, another romantic interlude. Our scripts can become a thing.

'Fine. I'll text you later.' Now *that's* a plot twist.

And with a thud on the passenger seat, he's gone.

The fifth date

'Sorry for being late,' I apologize as I walk into the bar ten minutes late.

'It's okay. I got us a table,' **Thirty-seven** mutters, swatting away my excuses like a fly. There are no polite affirmations, no backhanded compliments. The lighthouse seems to be officially out of business.

Dinner is a subdued affair. He seems distracted throughout drinks and only half-listens as I tell him about my day. We both ignore his constantly buzzing phone; this constant ignoring has become a part of the deal. Is this what being an old married couple feels like?

Over the past month and a half, I've picked him up at the airport and got him a housewarming present (hint: me). In exchange, he's driven me to all our dates and made an exception on his no-sugar diet. In gay terms, we are only two dates away from making it 'Instagram official'.

'Do you want to go for a drive?' he cuts off my social media soliloquy, and I gladly agree. Dinner wasn't a good idea. Maybe we need to go back to our comfort zone in his car.

'Where are we headed?' I ask.

'Let's see.'

A full five minutes into the car ride, I see a vast expanse of silence stretch ahead of us. Should I say something? Should I start a dialogue before we hit a dead end?

'I think we should be friends,' he tells me, and I wait for him to go on. This can go anywhere. Friends who bang every other day? Friends who see each other exclusively? Friends who send memes all day? Friends who only flirt through Instagram DMs?

'I don't think I have the bandwidth to see anyone at the moment.'

There it is. He's sliding out, and he's taking all his puns with him. Maybe I can ask for joint custody? Maybe I can ask to visit them over the weekends? Maybe I can see them twice a year at Diwali parties and Christmas dinners? Maybe I need to … leave already?

'You can stop right here,' I say as he pulls in closer to my gates.

'Well, if you want to ever …'

And with a thud on the passenger seat, I'm gone.

7

Deal or No Deal?

❋❋

Number Thirty-eight: The Medic
Is It a Deal-Breaker if This Is My First Time Ever?

June 2018

'Wait, you are half Indian?' I ask **Thirty-eight**, a fresh-faced medic in his early twenties, at a storybook-styled café a few streets away from the sea. It turns out that he's also half Italian, which makes me fully interested.

'But you look so … white.'

I'd urge the casual reader not to judge me, because I've had worse conversation openers in the past. The boy laughs, and then, over a shared plate of nachos of questionable origin, shares his life story. Born to an Italian mother, he grew up in the United States and went through medical school to live his Indian father's dreams. He's currently in the city visiting his grandmother to explore his paternal ancestry, but is also exploring an internship at a health-based NGO. Oh hello, Disney called – they want their Prince Charming back.

'So, I've read a few of your pieces. I think they are lovely, and …'

Well, well, looks like he's also been exploring my Google search results. This might seem like my date with **Fourteen** all over again, but **Thirty-eight** is the gift that just keeps giving. It's not every day that I match with a crisp Italian who speaks crisp Hindi. I cut him some slack and give him a rehearsed speech about how writing is not glamorous and how I spend most of my days in boxers, trying to reach my word count for the day while chasing clients to pay my dues. As I am in the middle of an extremely gripping tale about my invoicing system, he cuts me off.

'… I have a confession to make. I've never done this before …'

I am confused. Never eaten soggy nachos? Never heard about how badly writers are paid? Never heard a ten-minute monologue? Never been on a date with a writer? He needs to be more specific. What is it?

'Well, I am bicurious, and …'

In the last eight years of my dating career, I've met all sorts of men. I've met gay men who've never had sex, I've met bisexual men who've never had sex with a woman, and I've met married men who've only had sex with men. I've met so many guys across the spectrum, I can start a convenience store that stocks men who are confused about their identity. Bicuriosity is an aisle between the dairy and produce section.

I kindly tell him so, but avoid making the convenience store analogy. He grins.

'So when did you know? How long has it been?'

'Well, three days ago.'

Three days ago? I've have had leftover rice in my refrigerator for longer. Why are we even here? What does he want from me? Where's the Disney prince that I need but don't deserve?

The short version involves him kissing his best friend of ten years. The long version involves him *drunkenly* kissing his best friend of ten years.

'… and I just wanted to ask you a few questions that could help.'

This is the moment. I can grow a spine, wish him luck and walk away without looking back. I can fling my glass of coke at him for having wasted my time. I can delete his number and never see him again. Instead, I look him straight in his eye, and say:

'Sure. How can I help you?'

7.1. How Do You Deal with Deal-Breakers?

Everybody raises red flags. Yes, *everybody*.

That includes you, reader.

Kartik hears warning bells when a man never invites him home. For Aneesh, his brain goes on high alert when a guy only texts past midnight. For Urvaksh, it's men who wear crocs. But *what* is a red flag, and why have you seen it pop up so many times throughout this book?

As a gay man, dealing with red flags is second nature. Because we have a lot of them.

So What's a Red Flag?

A red flag is a warning sign for you to slow down and question where your relationship is headed. But remember, if someone's behaviour makes you nervous; trust your instincts and GTFO.

If your relationship was a long drive, a red flag is a speed bump on the road. You hit one and automatically feel a tingling sense of panic sweep over your body. The hair at the nape of your neck prickles, and your brain goes into fight-or-flight mode. Your senses are suddenly on high alert, screaming at you to hit the brakes before it is too late.

And what's a Deal-Breaker?

There are some red flags you can deal with and some that are too jarring to avoid. When a red flag becomes a dead end, it's a deal-breaker.

He talks about how hot Varun Dhawan is? Red flag. He talks about how hot every other guy is? Deal-breaker. Avoids introducing you to his friends? Red flag. Avoids being introduced to your friends? Deal-breaker. Dating someone with a lot of red flags? Red flag. Dating someone with even one deal-breaker? Deal-breaker.

So what's the Difference between a Red Flag and a Deal-Breaker?

Urvaksh thinks it's really simple – a red flag is when you weigh in your partner's emotional baggage, and a deal-breaker is when you pack up your suitcases and leave. The banker might think it's that easy, but he's also been conditioned to have a black-and-white approach to relationships.

Knowing the difference between the two is what helps you decide whether you need to save or say goodbye to a prospective relationship. The truth is, all deal-breakers are also red flags. But not all red flags are deal-breakers.

How can you tell? Use this table to find out:

It's a red flag if: he checks out the waiter on a date.
It's a deal-breaker if: he hits on the waiter on a date.

Why is this a problem?
Because it's not going to end with *this* waiter.

It's a red flag if: he won't stop talking about himself.
It's a deal-breaker if: he won't stop talking about his ex-boyfriend.

Why is this a problem?
There's only one place for excess baggage, and it's the check-in kiosk at the airport.

It's a red flag if: he introduces you to his friends on the first date.
It's a deal-breaker if: he never introduces you to his friends.

Why is this a problem?
If he's always talking about his friends but you've never met them, it's a red flag. Not a red flag like his friends might be imaginary (which is possible) but one that says, 'Yeah, I have a life besides you, and I don't want you to be a part of it.' Get out now.

It's a red flag if: he blacks out after a night of drinking.
It's a deal-breaker if: he blacks out and gets in a shouting match with you after a night of drinking.

Why is this a problem?
The only thing worse than being a drunk is being an aggressive drunk.

It's a red flag if: he admits to having cheated on an ex.
It's a deal-breaker if: he admits to having cheated on you.

Why is this a problem?
Is cheating ever excusable in a monogamous relationship? The simple answer is no.

It's a red flag if: his roommate is his mom.
It's a deal-breaker if: his roommate is his ex.

Why is this a problem?
This is more common than you would think. Men who live under the same roof as their exes will give all sorts of excuses: their finances,

the housing market, the commute to work, their sexual drive, etc. But *none* of them will ever be valid.

It's a red flag if: you don't agree on things.
It's a deal breaker if: you don't agree on monogamy.

Why is this a problem?
There's a word for one-sided monogamous relationships. It's called cheating.

It's a red flag if: there's zero chemistry in bed.
It's a deal-breaker if: there's zero chemistry in life.

Why is this a problem?
Does he give you butterflies in your stomach? Does the thought of him make you blush? Do you look forward to the witty, award-winning banter? If the answer to all these questions is no, then you have zero chances of making this work.

It's a red flag if: he's discreet about his sexuality.
It's a deal-breaker if: he's discreet about his sexuality because he's married.

Why is this a problem?
Having a wife, two kids and a pet dog has never been an endearing quality among queer men.

It's a red flag if: he's jealous of your cat.
It's a deal-breaker if: he's jealous of everyone in your life.

Why is this a problem?
A twinge of jealousy is cute, but if your partner regularly goes through your phone, keeps a tab on your chats and pulls the strings on your social calendar, we have a giant green-eyed problem.

It's a red flag if: he lied about having a gym membership.
It's a deal-breaker if: he lied about having a job.

Why is this a problem?
We've all told our fair share of white lies ('Yeah, I called your best friend to wish her a happy birthday'), but when it becomes pathological lying, especially about the big stuff, it corrodes trust. If you can't trust your partner, it's a lost cause – even if he *does* have a gym membership.

It's a red flag if: you have different views.
It's a deal-breaker if: you have differing values.

Why is this a problem?
There's no wrong or right set of values, but if you are on contrasting sides of the moral spectrum, you might need to question your relationship (or your values).

Number Thirty-nine: The Addict
I Huff and I Puff and I Blow Your Guard Down

October 2013

'A reformed Delhi brat who runs his own production house.' **Thirty-nine** introduces himself as we trudge through traffic to a multiplex a few stations away. That's an odd term to use to describe oneself, but it's been a slow month, and I really want to watch the latest *Star Trek* before message boards post spoilers all over the internet.

The man casually rolls up a spiff and offers me a puff. I do a quick double take. We are stuck at the busiest intersection in Mumbai. A tenth of the city's population is within a 200-metre radius away from us.

'In broad daylight?'

'Why not?'

I am apprehensive, but I don't deny myself a quick drag.

'What are you afraid of?' he sniggers, as I slide down the cab's vinyl upholstery.

The cops? The law? The government? Him? My mother?

Our taxi is moving at a glacial pace, but I still feel the thrill of a joyride. It's true that everybody loves a bad boy. Being an honest, law-abiding citizen never got anybody laid.

He hands the joint back to me after a long drag. 'I don't want to turn into an addict,' I joke weakly, but I take it anyway.

'You don't understand addiction like I do,' he says, and I giggle.

'Is being addicted to bad boys a thing?' I flirt, and he laughs, screeching like nails on a blackboard. I should say something before he laughs like that again.

'What brings you to Mumbai?' I ask, steering the conversation as our cab steers into the mall. We are holding hands, and I run my fingers through the fine creases of his palms when he tells me that he's in the city for rehab because of his 'drug problem'.

'For this?' I frown, pointing to the joint as he ashes it out of the window. How is that a big thing? Most gay men I know then would have a drug problem.

It was cocaine. And meth. And heroin. My mind slips away, but my hands don't.

7.2 The Gentleman's Guide to Every Fuckboy in the World: Do These Bonus Features Ever Stop?

Kartik matched with Atul, a senior associate at a top legal firm, about two years ago. They bonded over their love for bad puns, great gin and the fact that they were both self-proclaimed Ravenclaws. What could I say?

Wit beyond measure led them down each other's treasure trails.

For Kartik, it was love at first swipe. Like most love stories, it had its highs (mostly) and lows (many). But something seemed wrong

– the dates were always at home, friends were never involved and future plans were never made. Their trysts started late, but Kartik was never invited to stay the night (including that one time he puked all over the bathroom floor). It seemed strange, but Kartik (being Kartik) decided not to second-guess things. He continued making bad puns and drinking great gin. Why wouldn't he?

Atul was a great many things. He was smart. He was handsome. He was successful. He was charming.

Atul was also a Fuckboy.

What Is a Fuckboy?

The quintessential Fuckboy (just like Atul) is not very easy to spot, given his adaptive nature and ability to blend in. Fuckboys don't come wearing warning t-shirts; otherwise, you wouldn't need this book. The Fuckboy is everywhere. Smiling at you in the checkout aisle at the supermarket. Making googly eyes in your yoga class. At the library. In your poetry class. On the bus. At the local pub. In your untouched list of Tinder matches. Anyone who's traversed the giant desert of dating knows that finding a Fuckboy is like finding a wild Rattata on Pokemon Go – it's that common, which makes avoiding them that much more difficult.

How Do I Spot a Fuckboy in the Wild?

Want to know how to bypass the boys that most bad decisions are made of? Look no further, kids. Here are some telltale signs the guy you are hopelessly crushing on only plans to crush your heart after:

- The Fuckboy only messages you post midnight.
- He'll never disappoint.
- The only time he messages you at 8 p.m. is when his flatmates are away.

- He drinks his cold-pressed juice straight out of the carton.
- Just like he drinks his pre-mixed cocktails straight out of plastic bottles.
- The Fuckboy is an amalgamation of bad pick-up lines, expensive perfume and template text messages that he broadcasts to his little black book of men.
- All three have high success rates.
- He hoards all his used condom wrappers, because how else will he know that he's the supreme sex god that he claims to be?
- He addresses you as his bro. Even when he meets you in person.
- And he doesn't mean it in the endearing I'm-so-comfortable-around-you-I-can-call-you-anything kind of way.
- He's always vague about his Friday night plans.
- But he already has advance tickets for Tomorrowland.
- The Fuckboy doesn't snuggle. He prefers the post-coital smoke to the post-coital cuddle.
- His idea of the perfect date includes drinks at a dive bar and dessert back at his place. Dinner is usually not part of the deal, unless you offer to eat it off him.
- He wears his charm like he wears his signature perfume.
- In excess.
- The Fuckboy is looking for 'friends with benefits', but he also doesn't want to be friends.
- He introduces you to his friends as a 'friend from work that he bumped into'.
- Eight months into knowing you. You never see them again.
- All his friends know exactly who you are, but their behaviour shows they know something that you obviously don't: that he's seeing other people.
- He's always busy when it's time to meet your friends.
- Once, it was his dog's funeral. Twice, it was a late night at the office.
- And thrice, it was his mother's birthday.

- In the same year.
- The Fuckboy rolls up his shirtsleeves to just below his elbows, because he likes to live on the edge.
- He likes to drive with his windows down, and uses styling mousse so that his hair doesn't look 'too windswept.' Sometimes he doubles it up as lubricant.
- He never lets you stay, and has an excuse ready every time you suggest pulling out your jammies. Sometimes it's an early morning gym session at 5 a.m. Sometimes it's an over-inquisitive maid who can't mind her own business. Sometimes it's an Uber he booked for you when you were cleaning up in the bathroom.
- He likes his boys just like he likes his chardonnay.
- Free flowing and out of his system the next morning.
- He doesn't see the point of crossword puzzles, middle-school trigonometry or commitment.
- He downloads Grindr Xtra just so he can get unlimited blocks.
- And an unlimited pass into everyone's pants.
- At some point in your relationship, he'll tell you that you are the One.
- He'll also say the same thing to Rizwan. To Sam. To Kabir. To Nikhil. To Rahul. To Kiran. To Sameer. To Zishaan.
- He breaks up with you eventually because 'he's not good enough for you, and you deserve better'. He then stops replying to your texts, phone calls and that one long drunken email.

The Fuckboy will only lead you to another one. And another one. And another one. He'll lead you through a string of bad decisions, heartbreak and life-altering mistakes.

You'll sigh every time, but you'll never learn.

Number Forty: The Analyst
Is It a Deal-Breaker If I Am Only Here Because of His Dealer?

March 2014

I stare closely at **Forty** as he smokes his joint. He has a traveller's face – his features boast of a deep tan and a glow that only comes with not having wasted your life at an office desk for months. Is he an analyst with a tech giant or an IT junkie? Is he a writer? Is he a travel journalist? What does he really do? I've always been an unreliable narrator. However, we have more important things to think about. Is he going to pass? Is he not? It's such an exciting game!

There it is. I take it in my hand, and burst out into giggles.

He stares.

'Take it all the way in, and then blow it out *deep and slow*.'

So infested is that line with innuendoes, it needs an exterminator. He grins.

What am I doing here?

He passes the spliff back to me.

Yes, *that*.

We are at **Forty**'s house – a modest one-bedroom flat in the depths of Andheri. Any closer, and he would be a next-door neighbour; any further, and I'd never make the effort to meet him again. His house is bare, and it looks like it belongs to a nomad. You could pack up and leave in an instant. There are bulging bookcases, but no wardrobe. Where does he keep his clothes?

He practically lives out of a suitcase unless his parents are visiting, he says. That's when all his clothes go under the kitchen counter.

I spot William Dalrymple's *City of Djinns* on his bookstand by the bed.

'It's my favourite book,' he tells me. I lie that I love it too. I don't have a clue what it's about. I've not really read it. But that's the rest of his bookshelf – full of books I'll never have the patience to read, but I'll never admit it. I take a closer look. There are some titles on sexuality and homoerotica.

'Are you out to your parents?' I ask. Visiting parents would hardly notice a copy of *Queer Science*. He laughs. They found out a year ago – stumbled upon his diary.

He has a *diary*?

Not in the conventional sense – it was a journal of his most lucid dating encounters.

It's my time to have a laugh now. Where have we heard that before?

'How did your parents take it?'

The same way most Indian parents do – there was some crying and some cajoling, but they came out stronger as a family, and he came out stronger as a gay man. It's been a good year.

Where does he see himself a year later?

Travelling, he replies almost instantaneously. I cough. He thinks it's the joint.

I've heard this one so many times. I have it tattooed on my brain from one of those cheap parlours at the mall. It's a classic answer. A gay man lusting after the idea of travel is like gay men lusting after, well, other gay men.

'Where then?' I ask him.

He spent the last two months in the hills up north (that explains the tan) searching for substance or spirit, and sometimes even both. But one thing that's constant – he's always searching for himself. Gay men often find themselves in the strangest of places – the hills, the beach, the theatre, a fashion show, the runway and sometimes even in abandoned restrooms a little after midnight.

I usually head to the bookstore.

'Sometimes I wish I could just pack up and leave.' He's excited about quitting his job and leaving with a suitcase and an open ticket. The man wants to live his dreams through his travels – scuba diving by the Andaman Islands, building bonfires in Rishikesh and attending rave parties in Kasol. Instead, in exactly a year, he'll go on to work for a major political campaign and then find himself at business school. But that's all in the future. For now, his dreams and aspirations are as pure as the Malana cream we are smoking.

'Have you been to Parvati Valley? I spent a month there last year,' he tells me, taking a long peaceful drag. 'Can you imagine sleeping under the stars and waking up to the morning sun?'

Yes, I almost say – like the mornings after every night of drunken debauchery. Sometimes I even forget where my pants are.

'I'd want to go there again and never come back,' he says wistfully. I realize what else isn't coming back.

The joint.

He takes a long drag and blows out the fumes in concentric circles.

'You know what I was thinking?'

What can it be? Why is the sky blue? How does touchscreen work? Where does life come from? Am I eyeing the joint too much?

He exhales. I can be at peace. He hands it over. Another dose of peace.

'What?' I ask. If this were a B-grade softcore thriller, now would be the point where he pulls out his machete and hacks me into pieces. Instead …

'Want to see me hula hoop?'

Why not?

He heads inside and comes out with hula rings and a pair of clackers. Soon, the speakers are playing EDM on loop, the strobe lights are on and we are behaving like kids on a mad sugar rush. The hula hoop lies unnoticed.

'Wait, we need just one more thing,' he quips and darts back inside.

Ten minutes (or forty) pass, but he's been inside the kitchen for too long. My paranoia could be the third wheel on this date. Maybe he *does* have a machete. If I end up dying tonight, I won't be surprised. I've had a good life, seen great love, understood joy …

He comes out right on cue. There's no gleaming knife; only a pack of chips and some salsa dip. Fifteen minutes and two packets of chips later, we are satiated. Well, almost.

'So what do we do now?' he asks expectantly. We fade to black.

'Let me know if you ever want to come over again?' he asks as I ~~pull my pants back on~~ prepare to leave half an hour later. I smile but hesitate at the same time. It's a now-or-never situation.

'I will … but I had a question. Where do you buy your stuff from?' I ask, tying my shoelaces. He gives me a peck on my cheek.

He has a supplier who stays close; she's twenty minutes away. Any closer and she could be my mother. I take down her number, and *accidentally* delete his.

Number Forty-one: The Fashion Designer
What is Love If Not a Loan of the Heart?

May 2015

'Can I ask you a question?' **Forty-one** asks me at the end of a film; the fourth we've watched together that week.

I look at him and smile. We watched a marathon of back-to-back horror movies on Monday, snuggled through a thriller on Thursday and finished a sci-fi flick just ten minutes ago. It's Saturday, and he's cuddled up in my arms. There's been no drama, on the screen or otherwise.

He looks up expectantly and I pore deep into his hazelnut eyes. He's perfect, I sigh. A stubbled square jaw with a nose that gradually curves downwards over full lips. Lips that I lean in and kiss.

Forty-one is a fashion designer who's *just* at the brink of putting together his own label. He's a hustler, he told me during our first movie date. His grit has always been a turn on, but the fact that he doesn't conform to the fashion stereotype is a bigger one.

What does he want to ask me? Out on another date? (I'd say yes.) Am I bored of all his movie choices? (I'd say no.) To go steady? (I'd say I'll have to think about it.)

'Ask away,' I say instead.

'I urgently need some cash to bootstrap my collection … do you think you can loan me 20,000 bucks? I promise I'll pay it back really soon.'

And that's how my blockbuster never makes it past its opening week.

7.3. The Gentleman's Guide to the Dick Pic

Over dinner one Thursday night, Urvaksh excitedly tells me that he has big news. He's decided to become a curator.

Urvaksh is a high-flying investment banker with money to spare, so I'm not surprised. In 2015, he went on a rampage collecting fridge magnets from around the world. The following year, he ~~stole~~ picked up coasters from all the restaurants he dined at. And then, during the market boom of 2017, he even collected paintings.

I've only ever collected red flags.

So what's the new obsession?

He flips out his phone and hands it to me. My jaw drops. It's a close up of a penis. In fact, when I look closely, it's a grid of all kinds of penises. Long ones. Short ones. Thick ones. Thin ones. Questionable ones. Ones that look like they *could* be quests. Pixelated ones. And one that even looks like it has genital herpes. They all look really lonely.

Why would anyone collect dick pics?

Urvaksh laughs, flashing dimples that can light up the whole city. It wasn't always this funny, he confides in me. In the beginning, he was repulsed, and then he was angry. He felt disillusioned for a while, but that slowly turned into amusement. It is remarkable – the number of men who feel that sending you a dick pic in lieu of an introductory hello is going to land you straight in their arms (and in their pants). As the pictures poured in, he decided to just embrace them all.

Now he thinks it's art. Like the average female reader, Urvaksh gets sent nudes on the daily. Unlike the average female reader, he doesn't mind them any more.

'I can start a museum,' he says, now that he has a gallery full of dick pics to boast. A hundred and seventeen, to be precise (not counting the screen grabs he sneakily stole from Snapchat). When you count them all, that's a *lot* of penises.

'Do you want to see some more?' he grins. I'm hungry, but the idea of graphic male genitalia isn't particularly appetizing. The waiter arrives with our order just in time.

It's a platter of grilled sausages. Touché.

Hasn't anyone accidentally seen his stash of photos?

Urvaksh is a smart man, so he's got that covered too. He has a secret folder stashed in an album full of screenshots of bill receipts. A job in corporate banking does that to you.

'Do you want another sneak peek?' he grins as the sauce dribbles down his sharp, stubbled jaw. I bite back a snide remark about his table etiquette, but the only thing worse than an unsolicited dick pic is unsolicited advice. I politely decline, but it does get me thinking. Why do men feel inclined to send dick pics anyway?

IMPORTANT: Do People Really Want to See Your Dick Pic?

Ask yourself this question before you send one. Would you want a stranger's dick pic in your DMs?

If you answered no, then don't send one.

If you answered yes, ask yourself: 'What if it was unsolicited?'

If you answered no, then don't send one.

If you answered yes again, you need to question your priorities. If you think that using a picture of your genitalia as an introduction is the right way to start a conversation, you've got it all wrong.

A Quick Note on Nudes: Should You Be Sending Them?

The short answer is no. The long answer is … still no. Don't send it, regardless of how much he pleads or pressurizes you. If you absolutely must send one, ask for consent first, and never, I repeat, NEVER include your face in it. Nudes get passed around faster than chlamydia, and before you know it, all his friends have seen a picture of you in your birthday suit. And they aren't getting you any presents.

Sure, your relationship might seem like a romance novel right now, but there's no guarantee it's going to end that way. What does he do with your #NSFW photos once things go south?

If you think he's going to send it to the recycle bin, here's some mental manure: he won't. The last thing you want is to end up on the Google image search result for 'Hot Boys XXX', and we all know that the internet has the memory of an elephant.

So how does one really send a nude?

With permission. Follow the golden rule: ask, before you send one.

Q. What if I really want to send a dick pic?

A. If you want to dismiss everything you read above and *really* want to send a dick pic, think about how you are going to send it. Your work email? Never a good idea. Twitter? Not unless you can describe your manhood in 280 characters or less. Stick to channels you can control, like Snapchat or Instagram, where spur-of-the-moment decisions can be deleted and photos can be unsent. Avoid Whatsapping pictures of your schlong unless you want to be confronted by pictures of it as you scroll through your messages.

It's not going to be a pretty sight.

Q. Should I trim?

A. A quick trim is recommended, because it makes your knob appear larger and also shows that you care about personal grooming.

Q. What about the composition?

A. You might think that your pecker is the reflection of perfection, but that doesn't mean it will photograph well. When people are asked to list the 100 prettiest things on earth, there's a reason the human penis doesn't feature in most lists. It's not very … *pretty*. See, the penis isn't conventionally beautiful, and it needs all hands on deck (no pun intended) to get a standing ovation. Plus, it helps with scale and perspective.

No one's expecting you to roll out the red carpet and demand an entire portfolio. Your penis is no movie star (although having a collection of your best shots is recommended), but that doesn't mean you can make do with that one grainy photo you took in the bathroom five months ago.

If you want your dick to look like a piece of art, frame it well. Otherwise, it'll look like any other rolled up piece of junk. Experiment with the kind of lighting that suits you (and your skin tone). Find a clean mirror to snap yourself in, and go full-frontal only if you want to skip showing your protruding potbelly. Just by itself, the penis sticks out like a sore thumb, so avoid close-ups. You don't want your dick to look bland and grumpy; it's not John Abraham. Skip the sepia mode; it's not a John Abraham film.

Include a bit of your torso if you can; otherwise, a sneak peek at the side of your arse should do the trick (unless your butt is hairier than the Himalayan bear). The goal here is to tease; not traumatize someone into never wanting to have sex ever again.

Under NO circumstances should you put your face in the picture. You want to send your paramour an appetizer before the final act, not ammo for blackmail. Everything leaves a digital footprint, and a dick pic is no exception.

Q. And what about the background?

A. Tidy up your room and remove anything that you don't want to be seen – old socks, open packs of condoms, vacation pictures, or worse, a portrait of your mom. Also, your dick might be god's gift to mankind, but that pair of dirty underwear right next to it is not earning you any points.

Q. Can I ask for one in return?
A. Yes, but don't act surprised when they don't send one back. No one is under any obligation to return the favour.

So don't be *that* dick.

Number Forty-two: The Performer
Some Dick (Pics) Have Dreams Too!

June 2016

'So what do you do?' I ask **Forty-two** as he buttons up his shirt after a brisk ~~romp~~ date at home. He turns around and frowns, 'Wait, you're only just asking me that?'

Forty-two doesn't look too surprised, but his abs look disappointed. All six of them.

How would I know? Sure, I do the odd background check before I meet someone, but do I send requests on LinkedIn? Not for the kind of jobs I am looking for on Grindr. When a man is looking for a potential bedmate, one's proficiency at work features rather low on the list. His sexual prowess on the other hand …

Forty-two rolls his eyes but continues combing his hair in my bathroom mirror. It's remarkable how tousled it looks after an hour and a half's worth of tossing and turning.

Forty-two tells me that he's an established screenwriter, but his abs tell me that he also goes to the gym in his free time. Clearly, this man writes and works out with more dedication than I do. He's spent the half of last decade living in a tiny apartment sublet by his uncle, working on jingles by day and long-form scripts by night. When does he get time to bench-press, I stop myself from asking.

'Working on your body is hard,' he says, reading my mind (and I blush a deep magenta), 'but working on a script is harder.'

It turns out that my friend here comes with so much substance that I could snort him off the kitchen counter. Have I been doing it all wrong? As gay men, do we forget to humanize our sexual conquests?

Maybe I can start afresh. 'So what *else* do you do?' I ask, hoping I get back in his good graces with some polite conversation. I don't want to say goodbye to his abs yet. All six of them.

He chuckles. He's just finished telling me his life story, with minute details that include everything from his favourite book (Arundhati Roy's *God Of Small Things*) to his favourite drink (classic rum and coke).

'Well, funny you should ask, because I've recently been dabbling in a new passion project ...'

Here we go. Men will forever glorify their hobbies as their second jobs. So what does he do? Travel? Cook in his free time? Go on long hikes? Post home workout videos online? Teach salsa online? I brace myself for the worst ...

He's an amateur pornstar.

Oh, that's sweet ... WAIT. Did he just say *pornstar*?

He beams again and flips out his phone. A few deft clicks and there's his profile on an amateur porn website. I see row after row of thumbnails starring his abs in pixels. They're blurred, but I'd recognize them anywhere. All six of them starring in various home videos. A few even stare right back at me.

'So,' he continues, as if announcing you have a listing on a popular adult website is commonplace, 'what's *your* favourite book?'

7.4 How to Survive Ghosting in this Grindr World

Arvind, an aspiring playwright in his mid-twenties, met Aarav less than a year ago.

Aarav, a successful lawyer, was slightly older (and thus, slightly more attractive), slightly aloof (and thus, slightly more interesting) and knew his 'writs from his wrongs'. Once Arvind heard the pun, there was no going back. It was love in Act 1 Scene 1, straight out of one of Arvind's unfinished plays.

Aarav was the right measure of roguishly charming and endearingly enigmatic, and each time they'd met had been a flurry of interesting conversations, stolen kisses and rapid heartbeats.

And multiple lawyer jokes.

As he made his way home from their last date (they split the bill and dessert before they split ways for the night), Arvind had a strong feeling that Aarav just might be the One. It happens to the best of us. People stare, but you don't care. You smile and can't wait to see him again.

But you don't, and Arvind didn't either.

The phone wouldn't ring. Messages lay bare and unanswered. Emails came with automated replies. Was it real? Was he in trouble? Had he lost his phone? Was he dead?

It was worse than Arvind could ever imagine.

He had been ghosted, and the future father of his adopted twins had vanished without a trace. No explanations; only regrets. Arvind had a funeral for the broken pieces of his heart soon after.

They never rose from the dead.

But Hey, What's Ghosting?

For the uninitiated and the ignorant, **Ghosting** refers to the highly pervasive act where someone ends a relationship by simply disappearing. The Ghost does not give any explanations, leaving the ghosted to wonder where he went wrong. And then, three dates in, Mr Wonderful suddenly finds himself to be a cold case in a long list of failed romances.

That's the thing about being ghosted – the accused often disappears without a memo, which makes switching from 'Honey! I'm home!' to three unanswered calls as effortless as riding a bicycle, and equally daunting.

How Do You Know You Are Being Ghosted?

While it can be quite the rude shock (especially when you've already started planning the beachside proposal in your head) when the object of your affections disappears in a puff of smoke, here are a few hints that show he might have been planning the greatest heist of them all for a while.

1. **He's always busy.**

He's always occupied with something slightly more important. A friend's birthday. An office conference. His sister's new baby. His dog's vet appointment. His sister's newer baby. But at the end of the day, when you check his daily planner (and don't even deny that you will), you'll see that it's been emptier than his soul.

2. **And if he is not 'busy', he cancels plans.**

Cancelling plans is the first chapter in the beginner's guide to ghosting. Sure, he'll make plans with you, but he'll seem less excited than someone who's just about to get their root-canal surgery done. And then one fine day, just when you are about to give up hope, he'll text and ask you to meet him for a beer. He'll cancel three hours later, when you are already half a cab ride away.

3. **He's dropped hints that he isn't looking for something serious.**

He'll say something along the lines of: 'Hey, so I am not looking for anything serious.'

4. **You've never met any of his friends**

Does he have any? Who does he have those brunches with? Which school did he go to? Where have all those fridge magnets come from? Who are all those people in his pictures? Who got him those fridge magnets? If he feigns deafness at all of these questions, you are signing up for trouble. After all, the number of friends you know is directly proportional to how difficult it is for a guy to ghost you. Don't want to be ghosted?

Keep your friends close, but keep his friends closer.

5. **You have a gut feeling.**

And it's probably right. Follow it and end things before he ends your will to ever date again.

6. **He has more excuses than the government.**

And they are equally dubious.

7. **His texts are short, really short.**

This is how it goes – his texts go from being giant anecdotes to monosyllables to singular grunts till they reach the classic 'Use only in case of emergency'.

I am not saying that each text has to be a short story, but if you feel like you've had longer conversations with your pet dog, then you are clearly texting yourself towards doom.

8. **He takes forever to respond to your texts.**

Apart from the following reasons, there is no other plausible excuse for a person to not reply to a text within the hour:

- He's driving.
- He's sleeping.
- He's working.
- He's dying.

If he still takes forever too long, it's time to forever say goodbye.

9. **He doesn't respond to your texts.**

Well, if he isn't responding to your texts, he isn't just thinking of ghosting you, he's *already* ghosted you.

The fact is that being ghosted can be the death of you: it can leave you sad, depressed, broke (the retail therapy won't pay for itself, will it?) and terribly insecure. What do you do then?

Do you swear off men? Swear off romance? Swear off scary movies because your recent heartbreak was such a horror flick?

Like Arvind, being left in the lurch can be quite stressful. One minute, Aarav was muttering sweet nothings into his ear, and the very next, he had disappeared into nothingness.

Poof. It was that simple. Just like that, he was gone, having retreated into the ones and zeros to haunt another corner of the digital universe (or as per Arvind's worst fears, another boy).

Which brings us to the single-most important question (after you've asked yourself how many bottles of wine you'll need to get over that messy break-up). Are you scared that someone will *spirit away* your feelings? Keep your phone back in your pocket; you don't need the Ghostbusters on speed dial just yet. What *do* you do then?

It's easy. Just read on and follow this five-step process to make sure you survive what I call the 'Houdini Hijinks of Heartbreak':

1. **Recognize you can feel angry.**

Go break that glass. Tear that book up. Punch that bag. Write that scathing email (but don't send it). Watch a rom-com. Watch a dozen rom-coms. Watch rom-coms till you get sick of watching rom-coms. Shatter that vase. Scream out loud. Go for a run. Cry. Get sad. Feel angry. You need to.

Repeat till you make peace with yourself and are whole-heartedly happy, because you deserve every bit of it.

2. **Don't blame yourself.**

Unless you killed his pet dog, had sex with the twin brother or set fire to his house, it's not your fault, so don't even go there. Now, write out a list of reasons you hate him and learn it till you can recite it in your sleep. You dodged a bullet with this one, so go celebrate with some beer (and a few boys).

3. **Call him out.**

Everybody needs answers, and so do you. Remember that it's better to reach out for answers than reaching for that large bottle of wine.

Make sure that you are okay, and if you can get yourself to do it, ask him for the reason(s). If he replies, hear him out and make peace with it, because that will only save you countless hours (and bills) at the therapist's. But stop at that *one* time.

He doesn't want to get back, and neither should you.

4. **Cut him out completely.**

Delete his texts. Erase his pictures. Unfollow him on Instagram, Twitter and Snapchat, and unfriend him on Facebook. Remove every trace of him (virtual and otherwise) so that no bits or bytes of him survive – make it full and final so that you can never get back in touch with him.

PS: Sending him a sloppy text message (or forty) at a quarter past three in the morning will not earn you any callbacks.

5. **Know that there's still some hope left in the world**

Will it happen again? Should you ever fall in love? Why don't you just delete Grindr? Remove Tinder off your phone, maybe? How about going on a dating detox? Who needs the right guy when you have your right hand? Don't think about it. Just because it happened to you once (or twice), doesn't mean that it will happen every single time. Sure, the graphic designer with the soft, wavy hair and twinkling eyes might have *seemed* like the One, but there are plenty more fish in the sea (and too many graphic designers with soft, wavy hair and twinkling eyes).

But Is Cutting Him Out Enough?

Cutting something out of your life only works when it involves one of these four broad categories – complex carbohydrates, processed sugar, cheap vodka and bad vibes … but that's about it.

I'll let you in on a secret. It's not the same when it involves people.

Arvind learnt the hard way that being shut out can be a truly haunting experience. People like to see death and destruction in horror films, but not in their relationships. While dealing with it can be a terrifying ordeal, it's fair to say that it's a whole new ball game when you are sitting on the other side of the table.

An Important Note from the Author's Desk

I've ghosted a fair number of men. I've left calls unanswered, texts unseen, hellos unacknowledged and emails unopened. This one (dreadful) time, I even left midway through a date (RIP half-eaten sirloin steak and grilled vegetables). One by one, all the boys vanished into oblivion (just like all the unread messages in the 'Other' folder of my Facebook inbox), disappearing forever into the darkest and deepest recesses of my mind. I continued living my life (with other boys that suffered a similar fate).

Here's the sad thing about ghosting – it's easy when you're the one doing it. One minute you are romantically entangled with a cute boy you met online (either in the middle of a date, or worse, a relationship), and then POP! – you disappear quicker than Bobby Deol's dwindling career.

Can it get any better than that?

Yes. (Side note: But not for Bobby Deol.) Just because the relationship lacks chemistry doesn't mean you should lack manners. Don't be the asshole here.

How Then Do I Tell Someone I Am Not Interested?

Don't like someone enough to see them again?

Here are a few alternatives to ~~pretending they don't exist any more~~ ghosting them:

1. The slow fade

This is probably the longest way to end things that aren't going well, but it's ideal if you have all the time in the world and don't want to get your hands dirty.

All you have to do is play along till the relationship fizzles out – just like a bottle of Coca Cola that's been left open too long. You keep up the banter with increasingly opaque replies till things die a slow painful death, because the only thing worse than giving him an STI is giving him false hope that this relationship is headed somewhere.

2. The long text

If you have the makings of a writer, send him a heartfelt text telling him why it's not going to work out – the longer the text, the higher the chances of making it seem right. Just make sure that you are kind (or as kind as you can be to someone you never plan to see again) and honest:

'Hey! Thanks for asking me out again, but I feel like we are in different places right now. I had a great time, and you seem like a nice guy, but unfortunately, I don't see a romantic connection. I hope you understand?'

Copy and paste this template if you feel like it.

3. The great big lie

Don't have the courage to come clean and tell him that you aren't interested? There's something that's only slightly less bad – lie to them. Say that you got back together with the ex. Tell him you are moving to Yemen. Say that you are a born-again virgin. Tell him that you might be going to prison. Tell him that you've been selected for a space-exploration programme.

Just make sure your story is believable and try not running into him at the bar next weekend.

4. The doggy bag

Your date might not necessarily be the object of your affection, but he could be someone else's – perhaps one of your friends?

If soy-latte-loving Sam likes Jhumpa Lahiri and tacos just like your friend Dev, why don't you set them up? That way, if things work out between them, there's a higher chance of you being the best man at their wedding as opposed to being the douchebag who preferred matcha green tea and Zadie Smith (and never called back).

Now that you've done all of these (or haven't), just go find someone better to date.

Number Forty-three: The Marketing Whizz
The Devil Replies Nada?

October 2011

Over two large pitchers of beer and chicken burgers, **Forty-three** tells me about his orthodox south Indian family and his hectic job at Kemps Corner. He's a marketing executive at a leading fashion label run by two successful gay men, who are bosses that he adores but is equally terrified of. I joke about how he could star in an Indian adaptation of *Devil Wears Prada*. 'But wasn't that a fashion magazine?' he asks, his smile stretching across his manicured face (and my heart).

This devil knows all his details.

And that's exactly what I tell him.

Forty-three laughs loudly, without a care in the world. We say goodbye two hours later, with promises to meet again the very next weekend.

I text him on my way back to tell him I had a great first date.

It's been 2,794 days. He still hasn't replied.

Number Forty-four: The Associate
Notice Those Red Flags – Decoding the Ultimate Deal-Breakers in Life

March 2016

After a long string of left swipes, **Forty-four** skydives – quite literally, because his display picture has him diving over the Dubai skyline – into my matches, and eventually, into my social calendar all through the month of March 2016.

At twenty-nine the man is already a senior associate with a reputed corporate law firm, but he also hates his job. At twenty-nine he lives in a sprawling midtown flat with a roommate, but he's always away. At twenty-nine, he's only had one serious relationship, but that only means our dating histories haven't overlapped. At twenty-nine, he doesn't want to put a label on his sexuality, but he's also not out of the closet yet.

At twenty-nine, he comes with a lot of red flags, but I can't tell if they are deal-breakers yet. For the uninitiated, **Forty-four** shows classic signs of having buoy-friend potential.

What Is a Buoyfriend?

The buoyfriend (or *buoy-friend)* is the complete opposite of the Ghoster (see page xxx), this is a man who floats around your life for months, giving you the bare minimum to make you hope that he'll materialize into relationship material.

But he never does. So once you recognize that our man friend here has no intentions of fully committing, it is your responsibility to ditch the (non) sinking ship and move on.

There's technically nothing wrong with a man who doesn't necessarily want to settle down – but he'll say just the right amount of nice things and treat you *almost* like a boyfriend, which means you'll get your hopes up and start planning your joint Instagram grid for the rest of your life.

'But I don't see any red flag ...' you start, eager to start an argument. See, that's the problem. Gay men (and most straight women) have conditioned themselves to always settle for less. We'll prefer coming up with excuses for our romantic prospects rather than face the hard truth in life: he's just not that invested in you.

Like our friend here.

Forty-four is a man with a game plan. In the next six months, he needs to shift to a bigger pad in the suburbs. By next year, he wants to make partner at his law firm. In two years, he hopes to retire and move to Amsterdam.

Unsurprisingly, I find no mention in his checklist of things to accomplish. Out of the half a dozen times we've met over the past month, we've spent a majority of our time locked in his apartment. Now, there's nothing wrong with a date that's homebound. In fact, some of my most liberating romantic escapades have had less-than-stellar openings (including that one time I courted someone over Instagram DMs). This isn't a book that date-shames, thank you very much.

Men are at complete liberty to be homebodies, but I can't help but notice that the two times I met **Forty-four** at a restaurant, he spent most of it with his eyes darting all over the place, looking at me with the nervousness one usually reserves for toddlers handling expensive bone china. He's had an excuse ready to stay at home every other time.

My roommate is out for the weekend. I feel slightly feverish. I am expecting an important courier. I feel feverish again. My maid needs to do the dishes tonight. Am I sick again?

Which brings us to tonight. We are currently cross-legged across his sofa set, watching a Netflix special on mute. A joint lies extinguished in a crumbling ashtray. It's a little after 11 p.m.

This is our ninth date.

But wait … is this a date? Sure, if it walked up to me at a bar and introduced itself as a date, I'd have no reason not to believe it. I'd even let it buy me a drink. We'd make small talk, before eventually parting ways for the night.

But something seems amiss. There are dates, and then are situations that *feel* like dates – they even have the basic ingredients of a date in place – but are definitely not dates. This is one of them.

The sensible thing to do would be to just ask him where we are headed, but that would be too easy. Instead, I devise a game to decide which side we'd tip over on the relationship scale.

The rules are simple. Points are added for ~~endearing declarations of love~~ bare minimum displays of affection and docked for grievances. The seriousness of said action decides how many points are deducted or awarded. Going out in public? +20 points. Making our relationship public? + 50 points. Texting me *only* after 10 p.m.? -20 points. Sexting me *only* after 10 p.m.? -50 points.

'Do you want a drink?' he asks, pointing towards a well-stocked home bar (+10 points).

'Why don't you surprise me?'

He grins and pours me a generous measure of gin (+10 points).

'… You are so easy to read,' he tells me, as he plonks down right next to me. That's another 30 points credited to his system.

The lawyer is currently at a tally of 65 points. While he gained major credentials for knowing (and freely supplying) my choice of drink, he's lost a handful of points for 1) making this a last-minute invitation (-25 points) and 2) switching off to attend a few work calls (-30 points) in the past hour. There's a platter of restaurant-ordered food going cold on his coffee table (+20 points), but then again, we aren't at an actual restaurant (-25 points).

Maybe it's the … thought that counts?

'Your drink's almost done,' he says, pouring me another gin and tonic (+10 points). Find someone who plies you with attention the same way **Forty-four** plies me with gin.

Twenty minutes later, we are both sprawled lazily on his couch. Maybe it's the excess of gin or I am just feeling foolhardy, because I ask him if he wants to get cosier. His ears turn pink, but he leans in and I go in for a swift kiss.

Thirty seconds in, he pulls back nervously, 'I want to tell you something ...'

This is it. This is the moment when I finally find out why we haven't gone out on an actual date in weeks. Is he allergic to people? Maybe he's a vampire? Is there a secret girlfriend? Or worse, is he being sent on a one-way trip to Yemen for work?

'You ... aren't really a good kisser.'

MINUS HUNDRED POINTS. Telling someone that they are a bad kisser is the social equivalent of telling a close friend that they have terrible breath. Sometimes, they might even be correlated.

But not this time. This isn't just criticism; it's straight-up cruelty. Anyone who shames their partner over intimacy should be kissed goodbye. No pun intended.

'It's just ... your technique,' he offers, but it's not very helpful. 'Maybe you should try opening your mouth more?'

Almost on cue, I gape like a fish. Is he insinuating that I haven't read my instruction manual from cover to cover? Do I tell him that he kisses with the enthusiasm of a blow-up doll (-25 points)? Should I point out that he's never made the first move (-15 points)? Or the last one (-15 points)?

I do no such thing.

Forty-four's phone rings for the fourth time (-20 points), and he grins apologetically.

'Sorry, I have to take this,' he darts off, and I am fully aware that he's secretly thanking his stars for this opportune exit strategy (-20 points). Somehow, I feel less guilty about docking those points.

Forty-four has always been a connoisseur of handing out mixed signals. He'll only text post dinner, but drive me down to get ice cream. We'll get matching ice-cream flavours, but he'll forget his wallet at home. He'll always end up inviting me for a post-dinner nightcap, but only when his flatmate is travelling.

It's always the bare minimum with gay men.

'Be right back,' he mouths, simultaneously rolling his eyes at whoever's on the other end of the line. I say a silent prayer for the miserable ~~minion~~ intern who's had to make this extremely difficult call to his boss on a Saturday night. 'You aren't supposed to treat them as equals,' I remember him joking once, 'they are here to do their job.' Should I deduct marks for that?

And he's back.

'Sorry about that. I deal with the most exasperating bunch of buffoons at work.' He rolls his eyes once again, losing 20 more points. Looks like my lawyer friend isn't concerned about getting on a loyalty programme for my reward points.

'So, what do you think about going away on a weekend trip?' he asks, pretending he didn't just shame my kissing skills fifteen minutes ago. I can tell that he's been practising asking this question all night. He looks nervous.

And just like that, we are back in the game: +50 points.

'What did you have in mind?' I ask. I don't want to get my hopes up, but I am suddenly imagining cocktails by the beach. An invitation to a weekend getaway is a big deal, so I award him an extra 20 points.

'A cousin is performing at a club in a Pune. What do you think? Do you want to come with?

Okay, that works too. Maybe we can have cocktails by the infinity pool instead.

'But, how will you introduce me?' I ask. I've only just realized that being introduced to a cousin will invite a lot of questions. Who am I? Where did we meet? How did we meet? When did we meet? How he chooses to answer these can make or break my entire game. His choices are easy. He could say we are 'boyfriends' (+100 points), but that would be taking it too far. Maybe he could say that 'we are dating' (+50 points), but he's discreet, so that's not happening either.

What are we left with? In decreasing order of relevance: there's 'close friends' (+25 points), 'friends' (+15 points) or my least favourite, 'acquaintances '(0 points).

'I was going to say that you are a buddy that I am crashing with.'

I laugh loudly, but stop when I realize that he's not joking. 'It's just that … I am not out to anyone, and I don't want to answer any awkward questions.'

Well, that answers my question on where we stand. When he says, 'I am not looking for a defined relationship', he's really saying, 'I am not looking for a defined relationship with you'. No amount of points will matter. The silence spreads thin, staining our conversation with a new level of awkwardness, until –

'Okay, listen …'

There it is. Another flimsy excuse, another point reduction.

'My maid gets here at nine in the morning …' he starts. 'Do you think it's possible for you to sneak out before that?' (-50 points)

We've found the final nail in our coffin. On my way out, I dump all his points in the trashcan by the door.

Unsurprisingly, there aren't any left.

8

Love, Sex and (Other) Drugs

8.1 The Single Man's Guide to Self-Pleasure

Gay men have a very (un)complicated relationship with sex.

Over the past few centuries, we've devised new methods to (seek out and) satiate our most primal urges. Some of us flirt on dating apps, some of us aggressively hit on strangers at the bar, and some of us cruise into the depths of the night. Some of us are charming, some of us are honest, and some of us are extremely dodgy when it comes to our eternal quest of finding a bedmate.

It's time to address the elephant in the room. You can't write a guide for gay men and not talk about our relationship with sex; that's like writing a cookbook and skipping the dessert section. It's just not done. Sex is natural, and ~~contrary to what prudes the world over would tell you,~~ there's no reason to be ashamed about it.

REMEMBER THIS HARD TRUTH: As long as it's safe and consensual, you can have as much sex as you want. There are no limits.

BUT … WHAT COUNTS AS SEX?

Sex cannot be defined. It doesn't have one single definition. If you think you are having sex, then you are probably having sex. Sex varies from man to man, experience to experience. We live in a heteronormative world, where penetration – sex between a man and a woman – is seen as the only real kind of intercourse there is. This is utter bullshit. Bigots assume that all gay men have anal sex, but that's 100% inaccurate. A lot of gay men enjoy great sex lives even though they've never had anal sex. A lot of gay men have anal sex but also don't enjoy their sex lives.

Sex isn't about positions and other such useless parameters; sex is about giving (and receiving) pleasure. But news flash, guys: can you really pleasure another man without knowing how to pleasure yourself?

Self-~~love~~ pleasure is the best kind of ~~love~~ pleasure there is.

The only way you can actually understand another man's body is by understanding your body first. Which means, before you get down and dirty with someone else, you need to get down and dirty with the single-most important person in your life.

YOU. Remember the elephant from before?

It's time to address it.

Say hello to the P-spot.

What's a P-spot?

For decades, men have been ~~perplexed~~ intrigued by the female G-spot.

Where is it? *What* is it? And most importantly, *how* does one get there?

These are questions you won't find the answers to in this book. That's unfortunate because the female G-spot *still* holds a very important role in the history of men's sexual liberation. Ever since the G-spot was written about in the early 1940s, most men *only* had one question on their minds.

What about *us*? Why don't *we* have a G-spot? But then again, when have men ever let women have a good thing to themselves?

The female G-spot has always been elusive, and like basic dinner table etiquette, it's an endeavour that men spend a lifetime trying to find. After all, it's not *just* a spot – more like a cluster of nerves that create powerful orgasms of catastrophic proportions. Some men try their best. Some don't give up till they do. A few pretend like it doesn't exist. Most men lie about having found it.

The male G-spot (or the P-spot), on the other hand, is … *as real.* And contrary to its female counterpart, it's a *lot* easier to find.[9] So why can't we see it?

That's because it's literally *behind* us.

Casually tucked away between the bladder and the penis is the prostate gland, a.k.a the McDonald's of male pleasure. The prostate is in uncharted territory, and it takes a little bit of effort to get to – but it's an absolute haven when reached. It's a bit like Mount Everest. With zero snowcapped peaks. And definitely no snow leopards.

Now for many men, the idea of someone touching their prostate is a thought that's as appealing as getting a colonoscopy. That's fair enough, because both involve penetrating your butt. Men have forever associated their posterior with rectal examinations, vaccine shots and anxiety-inducing WebMD searches.

'Wouldn't having a finger up my butt hurt?' the average heterosexual man would ask. On the other hand, the average homosexual man would just chuckle.

---

9 We know because generations of well-meaning men have tried and failed.

Relax, ~~boys~~ men. It's not as far in as you would think. The prostate is a wonder gland *just* inside your asshole, and it's packed with enough nerve endings to fire up a power plant.

Did you know?

A prostate massage is 33 per cent more intense than a penile massage by itself. We really do have the math in our favour, men. Statistics can never be wrong.

So how does one find their P-spot without (cough) challenging their 'alpha male status'? The key is to not be an asshole, but to explore one. Yours, to begin with. Thankfully, we have a quick five-step guide that will help you find ~~yourself~~ your pleasure point right here.

The Man's Guide to the P-Spot

A.k.a the One Where You Learn How to Finger Yourself

1. Prepare yourself.
Before you start, make sure your hands are clean. No long fingernails. No dirty tips. No ketchup smears, and definitely no sudden movements.

2. Never underestimate the power of lube.
There are two things the casual reader must remember: 1) the ass does not self-lubricate and 2) there's no such thing as too much lube.

3. Take small, baby steps …
This is a marathon, not a sprint. Imagine you are taking your body on a date. Get to know it better. Relax, and start slow. You can't buy it flowers, but you can begin with a massage right around your perineum.

4. And nudge in with a quick technique.
This might not work as a flirting technique, but a curved (at this point, lubed up) finger can do things that no pointed fingers can. You'll know when you hit the spot, because it's about two inches in and it's *also* walnut sized (only this one's not rich in Omega 3 fatty acids).

5. But make sure to experiment.
And surprise yourself. Find the right way you like it. Try different positions. Open your minds, and dive deep in. Go wild (but not *so* wild that you need to see yourself to the ICU). Put all your worries behind you.

Pun intended. You are welcome.

The Handy Guide for Giving Yourself a Handy

Men have been masturbating since the dawn of civilization. It seems like the only possible explanation as to why we haven't all killed each other to extinction (yet).

But that's not important. This is not a sociology textbook; it's a guide to self-love. See, masturbation is not for 'single men who have too much time on their hands'; masturbation is not a sin or the 'last resort for losers who didn't luck at the bar last night.' Masturbation is one of nature's most wonderful gifts. You know it, because you've probably been jacking off all your life (no point denying it); in fact, you are so good at it that can do it in your sleep.

While jerking off before bedtime is a ~~substitute for therapy~~ giant stress buster; what makes it so interesting is that we all know exactly how we like it. That's what makes all of us so unique (that, and our DNA.)

TRUTH TIME.

No one knows what pleases you like you do, so the entire point of having a guide to help you masturbate can seem a little extravagant.

But what if there were ways to prolong your orgasm, and thus, create stronger sensations of self-pleasure?

It's easy. Just keep these helpful tips handy the next time you are playing for one.

Create the mood.

And no, that doesn't mean dimming the lights as you fap in the confines of your natural habitat, a.k.a your messy room. Pour yourself a glass of wine. Play some soft, sensual music (or soft, sensual porn). Masturbation is an act of self-care. Relish it.

Spice it up with sex toys.

A fleshlight can do things that no man can ever do. Plus, a fleshlight will never cheat on you (or ghost your texts).

Change positions frequently.

Sex is fun when you are frequently changing positions. Sometimes you are flat on your back, sometimes you are pressed against a wall; the possibilities are infinite. So why limit yourself when masturbation is on the menu card?

Give the other hand a go.

If you've been masturbating a lot (we know you do), you might have noticed that it's hard to come unless you do it a particular way – an art no other man can replicate. To ~~beat those blue balls~~ overcome this, mix things up a bit. Swap your dominant arm with the other one: left to right, right to left. Left, to right, right to left. Look at that, you also learnt a new manoeuvring trick to dole out those handies.

Moisturize.

Dry dicks burn harder than the idea of your ex hooking up with a hot supermodel. Use lube every time you are lending a helpful hand to your joystick.

No, not lotion. Not Vaseline. Not your mum's aloe vera night cream. Definitely not the groundnut oil you find in the kitchen. Lube, always.

There's more to your body than your privates.

You might be used to treating your shaft like a movie star every time you are masturbating, but why not roll out that red carpet for the rest of your body?

Anthony Bourdain had it all wrong. Your body is a temple *and* an amusement park. Focus your attention on other (oft-forgotten) parts of your body – your nipples, the insides of your thighs, and even your new friend, the prostate gland. Find that breakout character and give it a starring role. You deserve it.

Know how to use porn.

... As a window to create a mental picture that is your fantasy, not as a means to end.

A Quick Note on Porn

Spoiler alert, guys: porn isn't how real sex works. Real sex is messy and sweaty, and it involves a lot of heaving and grunting you'd be mortified to hear on playback.

But that's what makes sex ... real. It's the sweating and the grunting and the (occasional) muscle pulling. Much like mermaids and unicorns, porn is an idea of fantasy (but that doesn't mean you tell your seven-

year-old nephew about it). Porn stars are actors who are paid to do their job – have sex aesthetically, and that's only after the final reel has spent hundreds of hours on the edit table. Even the pixellated amateur porn that looks like it was filmed on phone. No one expects you to be able to do the things they do (or climax on command). They have been specifically selected because they have fantastic bodies (or ginormous penises). Regular people don't look like that – not when they have a day job.

Gay porn doesn't reflect real life. If doctors, plumbers, firemen and pizza delivery guys were having as much sex as gay porn suggests, the entire service industry would go kaput. The economy would collapse.

Also, that bit where all the actors are ~~having unprotected sex~~ barebacking and moisturizing each other's lithe, supple bodies with their love juices? They all get tested for STIs regularly. So use a condom.

Number Forty-five: The Art Director
What Do First Kisses Taste Like?

July 2014

A friend once told me that a kiss is an appetizer to intimacy. It's supposed to be a prelude to all the good things that follow. A taste of chocolate-covered strawberries. The relish of salted caramel ice cream. The tang of orange zest. A smack of hot buttered popcorn. It's supposed to taste like happiness and hope, like lust and liberation.

An art director for an important fashion magazine, **Forty-five** clearly missed the memo. We've reached our final destination at the end of a long drive: the door to my home.

He turns to face me, and I look into his auburn eyes – giant pools of deep, dark brown that I can take a dip in. This is it. The Moment™ is here. He leans in, and I expect to taste pure joy.

Instead, **Forty-five** tastes of … onions. I've always hated raw onions. I pull back.

'Sorry, I had biryani for dinner. Can you taste it?' he grins sheepishly.

I decide to skip the main course.

8.2. How to Kiss a Man (As a Man)

Girish Singh Sherawat is a man with refined taste. The strapping litigator rakes a seven-figure paycheck and lives all by himself in a swanky four-bedroomed penthouse right off the Sea Link. He takes jiu-jitsu classes thrice a week, and spends his Sundays walking his two golden retrievers at the beach. His lovers describe him as 'generous' and his friends praise him on being 'the life of every party'. His exes remember him for being 'well endowed'. People say that Girish Singh Sherawat is the Jackpot that we all crave.

But he's also … a terrible kisser.

The boys have all been scarred by their experiences with his Jaws of Death™.

'It's the way he just jumps right in and *eats* your face,' Kartik tells me in strict confidence. 'There's no foreplay. Kissing is *all* about foreplay.'

Aneesh agrees. He thinks Girish uses too much tongue. 'I thought we were tongue wrestling that one time. It felt like a workout. My mouth ached for days …'

Urvaksh thought it was like kissing a toilet plunger.

Is Girish aware of the trail of sore lips he's left behind? Apparently not. Why hasn't anyone told him yet?

He's so sweet and gentle and charming (and rich, Urvaksh adds), the boys say. Nobody wants to break his heart. Instead, they come up with white lies. Some tell him they can't match his expectations in bed. A few tell him his extravagant lifestyle is intimidating. Urvaksh broke up with him citing indefinite abstinence as his new calling. They all left him feeling confused and clueless.

The kiss is the universal shorthand for intimacy. One minute you are smiling and stumbling your way into each other's arms, and just like that, you are there – even before you can stop and ask for directions. It hits your core, and tingles all the way down to your Vitamin D deficient toes. See, a great first kiss can feel like a rocket launch of serotonin, but what does a bad first kiss compare with?

Snail mail.

And it probably gets lost at the post office.

'I'm an excellent kisser. Nobody's ever had any bad things to say ...' the ignorant man would boast. He'd pause for effect, and (like **Forty-five** from a few pages ago) pick at the raw onions in his biryani.

People don't usually complain about the way someone kisses. It just isn't done. But I know the truth – nobody wants to bell the cat. Telling a person that he's a bad kisser is just bad manners. What if someone does it to *you*? Once you break the glass, you can't put it back together. Future kissers will just have to bear the brunt of Girish's bad kissing.

If a man is a bad kisser, it doesn't matter how he measures elsewhere. Those seven-digit paychecks, geometrically aligned jawlines and four bedroomed penthouses can kiss themselves goodbye.

So How Do You Kiss a Man (As a Man)?

A kiss is like a handshake. You can tell a lot about the person by the way they kiss. If you want the kiss equivalent of a firm handshake, you have to make sure you do it right. The first kiss is a relationship milestone that usually makes its way to long-forgotten journals and recycled rom-coms, so make sure it counts. How?

Use these five steps to master your technique and make out like a magician.

1. **Ask first.**

If you thought that leaning in for an impulsive kiss was charismatic, try asking for their permission first. Rom-coms will have us believe that we need to seize the day, because carpe diem, but there's something sexier than spontaneity.

It's called consent.

Before you ask him, ask yourself this question first. Does he really want to be kissed? Or are you heading towards their lips because the conversation is headed towards a dead end?

Kiss someone because it feels right, not because you want a distraction since you obviously forgot your wallet back home. It'll be just as magical.

2. **Don't make it too wet.**

When people advise you to 'switch on the waterworks', they don't intend it as a kissing strategy. You don't need to hold back like the Bakhra Dam, but it doesn't give you the right to pour in like the Sutlej River. Saliva might have a lot of uses, but slobbering all over your partner's face is not one of them. Remember, an off-putting wet kiss is the sign of someone who's rather inexperienced. You are a human being, not a golden retriever.

If you are on the receiving end of a bad kiss, take long pauses between the deep kissing to exaggeratedly wipe off all that excessive drool. That'll send the right 'making out' memo.

3. **... or too aggressive.**

Aneesh thinks that a little aggression is always good – no one wants to date a doormat – but that doesn't mean you have permission to turn someone's mouth into a crime scene. Stay away from bites and bruises, because scars might heal but memories don't.

A bad kiss will always leave a mark. Start gentle, and tease your way into a full-on snog (and yes, that's when you bring in the waterworks), instead of going from zero to sixty like a Ferrari.

4. **Work on a routine.**

Start slow. Make him want it. Kiss him on his cheeks (but not for too long, because you aren't his mother), his neck (but not for too long, because you aren't creepy) and the tip of his nose (but not for too long, because you don't aren't his pet dog). Kiss him anywhere else but his mouth. Make him crave for it till he locks lips first.

Kissing is a lot like dancing. Someone has to take the lead. If he follows and reciprocates your feelings by mirroring your technique, you are doing it right.

Now waltz into the glorious sunset.

5. **Use your tongue.**

Sure, a quick peck on the lips might work well for wine soirees and whiny babies, but if you want to play tonsil hockey, you need to make sure you don't roll out the red carpet as soon as you start. Is there such a thing as too much tongue? Definitely. When you are kissing someone using your tongue, you need the right technique. Gently folding eggs till the whites create fluffy peaks? Yes. Hastily rummaging in your underwear drawer for your favourite pair? NEVER.

But that doesn't mean your tongue can just lie there like dead weight. It's not your dusty gym membership. Dead tongues relate to lazy kissing. Say no to the dead tongue. Enthusiasm is vital.

If you feel resistance, take a break and ask them if they are enjoying it. Ask them if you are doing it wrong. Ask them if they want it a certain way. Ask, ask, and ask. Asking is the first step in honing your skills as a kisser.

The key to being a great kisser is self-confidence. Actions speak louder than words. So just go ahead and kiss them already.

8.3 The Dude's Guide to Doing It Right

Aneesh and Vir's relationship has been a fairy tale.

The same can't be said about how they fare in the bedroom.

'What's the problem?' I ask Aneesh, but I hope he doesn't answer. I'm halfway through a large steak, and I have no room for other people's (bedroom) problems on my plate.

These aren't intimacy issues, he clarifies. In fact, they are still living the rom-com that they both signed up for. I frown. If this is some long, convoluted plan to make me feel bad about the lack of love in my own life, it's clearly working.

'So what is it?' I reiterate.

I have a steak to finish, and his problems are getting in the way.

It's penetration.

Like his aversion to badly written profiles, Aneesh is clearly averse to full-blown intercourse. I sigh with empathy. This is a tale as old as time.

For most gay men, anal sex isn't the first thing that comes to mind when you think of *mutually pleasing* things to do together. Baking pot brownies and eating them all at once? Yes. Sharing a plate of spaghetti? Always. Going camping? Maybe. Watching Ryan Reynolds half-naked in a movie? Definitely.

For a man who spends his days immersed in excel sheets and PowerPoint slides, this is a problem no colour-coded pie chart can solve. I am surprised he hasn't made a SWOT analysis sheet for the same. But then again, there's no template presentation on penetration. Aneesh hates feeling so inadequate, but it doesn't mean that it stems from a lack of trying.

He's tried every possible remedy he could find online. Special lubricants from Germany. Space cakes from Amsterdam. Douching kits from the United States. Breathing techniques from Japan. As a last effort, even the Ayurvedic pills from his hometown back in Punjab weren't spared. They've all been terribly expensive, but also terribly useless.

Aneesh has been contemplating taking an enema.

I would tell him to just relax, but then I would sound like every (well-meaning) top-identifying gay man I know. Instead, I pat him on his back and ask him to buy a copy of the illustrated *Kama Sutra*.

He already has. In fact, he's tried every possible position from the coffee table book (including that one time when he *actually* used the book as a lever to support his back), but they've all been extremely unhelpful.

This is a conundrum. For Aneesh, who likes to think of his love story as a giant jigsaw puzzle, it's a pity that these pieces don't fit. I resume the periodic patting of his back and push my half-eaten steak away. I am suddenly not hungry any more.

That's the thing about penetrative sex. Tops have always had it easy. All they need to do is point and shoot. Bottoming on the other hand ... is tough. Unless you are trying to use it as a bargain, a birthday present or a lost bet, penetration is always slightly less pleasurable for one half of the team (no surprises as to which one).

But not any more, because we have an expert in the house.

It's Urvaksh.

After years of ~~wild sex~~ extensive research, my friend seems to have found his hacks to bring the backdoor experience to the forefront. Here's him presenting six of his it's-time-to-maximize-your-pleasure tips.

Eat light, eat right

What Urvaksh has to say: 'Eating a large cheesy burrito with a side order of nachos and soda will have you raring to go – but not to the bedroom. In the moments that precede sex, even a single potato chip can make you feel bloated. Keep your meals light and hydrate as often as you can.

Feeling gassy is natural when it comes to sex, but you don't want to be excusing yourself every ten minutes to go relieve yourself.

Consult a nutritionist if you want to, and consume a lot of fibre. Here's a quick guide of foods to eat (and avoid) if you plan to bottom anytime within the next eight hours:

Bottom-friendly snacks: raw nuts, berries, lentils, chickpeas, popcorn and brown rice.

Bottom-adverse snacks: red meat, dairy, sugary snacks and anything greasy.'

Stay clean

What Urvaksh has to say: 'If you think skid marks aren't sexy in your underwear, they are definitely not sexy on your partner's condom. Use a shower spray or a baby wipe if you are feeling lazy, but go all out with a douche if you are feeling queasy about ~~being~~ staying clean.

If you really want to up your game, you can use the shower time as foreplay. Some light fingering in the bath will go a long way. Most importantly, use the loo beforehand. A little mess is always okay. It's a part of life.'

Just breathe

What Urvaksh has to say: 'Self-help guides (and Oprah Winfrey) are of the opinion that deep breathing will always be an effective technique for stress management. Here's the thing – it helps with ~~sphincter stress management~~ relaxing too.

Count till ten as you prepare yourself to do the deed. Breathing helps as a tool for relaxation, which in turn helps relax your anal sphincter muscles. Write a haiku in your head. Recite the multiplication tables. Make a five-year plan. Practise pranayam. Ponder over life. But breathe, because relaxing is more than half the battle won, in life and otherwise.'

Lubricate, lubricate, lubricate

What Urvaksh has to say: 'There are three things gay men can never have enough of: lube, inspiring divas from the '80s, and more lube. Whenever you plan to get busy between the sheets, use lube like you would use spinach in your organic salads – freely.

Your sphincter muscles might relax during stimulation, but they don't self-lubricate. Trust me, a little more will always help. Good lube, like undeniable chemistry between two people, is a catalyst for great sex. Your sphincter muscles would agree.

For the guys swearing by how saliva feels more natural, I have one thing to say. Sorry, dudes. This isn't *Brokeback Mountain*. Saliva might help ease the experience, but you need to keep in mind that it also dries faster than wet concrete.

… And eventually, so will your romantic pursuits.'

Know what works for you

What Urvaksh has to say: 'Every ~~person~~ bottom has a sexual position they feel most confident in. Like zodiac signs, everyone has a sexual position they feel compatible with. Some prefer the easy access of doggy style, some love the sheer brilliance of the reverse cowgirl and some step up to the elevated pirate's booty; others simply choose missionary for flexibility. Find the position that works best for you and stick to it, so that you can even do it blindfolded.'

… And be cool!

What Urvaksh has to say: 'As much as you prepare your body to be up for penetration, the only way you will get to *fifth base* is by preparing your mind. Have a conversation with your partner about your threshold. Have a safe word if it helps.

Take it slow. Remember that it's not a marathon, and the only finish line you have in sight is reaching an orgasm. You need to know that only *you* can make yourself comfortable enough to go all the way.

Or not. Because if you really feel that anal sex isn't your thing, it doesn't *need* to be.'

Number Forty-six: The Gifted
Tales of the Towering Penis and Other Not-so-short Stories

May 2017

When **Forty-six**, a visiting sales associate from a neighbouring city, hits me up on Grindr for the very first time, I find it *odd*. He's shirtless and wearing gym shorts that leave little to the imagination. **Forty-six** looks like he counts his calories. He also calls himself 'MonsterTopXL'.

In short, he looks exactly like the kind of man who hit me up by accident. But **Forty-six** is also witty and can construct grammatically correct sentences – a first for men of his breed. So I decide to forgive him for his temporary lapse of judgement.

'Why do you call yourself MonsterTopXL?' I can't help but ask. Men have an innate need to exaggerate. Some call it overcompensating.

We obsess over our bodies just like women do. Am I fat? Am I skinny? Why do I have love handles? Do my bulging biceps show? What is my gut doing popping out like that? And we are particularly sensitive about how we measure up between our legs. In fact, when it comes to size and aesthetics, there will be very few dudes who would want a ~~seathing~~ honest assessment of their private stats.

Which is why 'What do you think of my penis?' is not a question most gay men like to hear. What should you do? Lie through your teeth? Be honest and tell the truth? The most divulging fact about the question is not in the obvious egomania, but the naked vulnerability it reveals; it's the male equivalent of 'Do you think I look fat in this outfit?'

'Would you like to see a picture?' **Forty-six** asks politely; too politely for a man asking to send nudes.

This is the moment of reckoning. For all the reassurances from sex therapists, urologists and lovers that it's not the size of the tool but the skill of the craftsman that matters, guys will still wonder: 'Am I big enough?'

Just like Mr MonsterTopXL here.

'Why not?' I shoot back. Asking to send nudes on a gay dating app is like asking about the weather: it's mostly used as a conversation starter. And here we are, four scrolls worth of texts in.

My jaw drops.

It's massive. Not 'Wow, you have really great genes' massive, but more like 'Wow, did you grow that in a lab?' massive. If the Incas made their way to modern times, they would worship it. I know I would.

Yet, it's not the first thing that grabs my attention. It also looks angry. I won't pick a fight with it at the bar. In fact, if it sends me a cheap beer at the bar, I'd meekly accept it. The cultural perception is that bigger is always better, but that's not always the case. It's also scarier.

I suddenly have a lot of questions.

How long is it? Eleven inches. Has he ever measured it? Yes, with a foot ruler. That's no penis, it's a Subway sandwich, I joke. He doesn't find it amusing.

Does it hurt? Yes, when he has a boner. Do they make condoms that size? Only in the United States. Isn't sex painful? Not for him. Do his partners complain? Almost all the time. Has he ever wished it were smaller? Yes, but only so more people would sleep with him.

His answers are short and crisp (unlike his crown jewels), but I am still curious. How many questions are too many questions? Even if I laid out my questions end to end, they wouldn't match the length of his …

'Your pic?' he interjects. I jump, apologizing for not having the basic courtesy of sending him the choicest of my mug shots. He seems to like what he sees, because barely seconds later …

'Would you like to come over for a coffee?' he asks innocently. I smile and tell him that my dog has an appointment with the vet later in the evening.

I don't have a dog.

8.4 A Field Guide to Pleasure

When You Don't Want to Get Anal About Sex

As gay men, we know that anal sex can quite literally be a pain in the butt.

If you don't believe me, ask Aneesh.

Whether you are repressing old memories, are sensitive to pain or are just particular about hygiene, it turns out that some guys just don't enjoy the act. But there's more to a fulfilling sex life than ~~damaging your backside~~ switching over to fourth base – it's not your only means to end, boys. Sexuality is a spectrum, and as it turns out, so is sexual pleasure.

But(t) … What Else Have We Got?

'But isn't gay sex all about penetration?' the uniformed heterosexual-identifying reader would ask.

Well, the uninformed heterosexual-identifying reader is also an idiot. Turns out there are a lot of things that gay men can do that doesn't involve ~~a carnal colonoscopy~~ anal sex. If you thought that your sexual crescendo is the rim of your ass, you are wrong. So what do you do if you don't like penetration?

Luckily for us, Aneesh found alternatives. Ever the solution-oriented strategist, he toiled for hours scouring page after page on the internet, till he found the light.

Aneesh had done it. He had finally found the Holy Grail of 'How to go all the way when you didn't really feel like going all the way'. The consultant's aversion to anal sex no longer needed to be a deal breaker, because he could still break the bed with these NSFW acts instead. Here are seven such substitutes straight from the horse's mouth.

Nipple Play

What is it: Second only to the appendix, most men grow up thinking that nipples play no major role in our bodies (like the typical heroine in Bollywood movies) and exist only because the chest would look too bare without them. Can you picture the Giza without the pyramids? Paris without the Eiffel Tower? Or the Windows XP desktop without Stonehenge? So wait … are they really there just for the aesthetic?

Nothing ever is. Not even the pyramids.

How does it work: Think of it this way: nipples are the pleasure centres for your sexual liberation, the anode and cathode to your sexual electrolysis, the soft peaks of icing on your erotic cake, the dialling knobs to toe-curling sex. You get the point.

Use your partner's nipples correctly, and you'll find yourself with a flash-lit GPS to a mind-blowing orgasm. And yes, it will be the quickest route possible.

Aneesh's bonus tip: 'Just make sure you don't go overboard. Nipples hurt more than broken hearts.'

Frotting

What is it: You don't need to be a boy scout to know that rubbing two flint stones together is the key to your survival out in the wild. Frotting is just like that, only you are rubbing your penises together, and the fire you are starting is of the sexual kind.

How does it work: Since both partners are gaining sexual pleasure from rubbing their genitals *against* each other, some call frotting (or dry humping) the male equivalent of scissoring.

This also makes it the most 'woke' form of sexual ~~intercourse~~ outercourse there is: it completely eliminates the dominating/submissive interplay that is often a byproduct of anal sex, as both partners are operating on an equal and communal platform of seeking pleasure. There are no tops or bottoms or versatiles when it comes to dry humping. Everyone stands on common ground. Who knew equality could be so sexy?

Aneesh's bonus tip: 'Moisturize. Any physics expert will be quick to tell you that a little amount of lubrication always helps with the friction. After all, hell hath no fury like a penis ~~scorned~~ chaffed.'

Handjob

What is it: Remember all those formative years you spent jerking off before you discovered your sexual identity? Well, now it's time to return the favour.

How does it work: The good news is that you've been practising for this moment all your life. The bad news is, everyone has their unique style of getting themselves off. It might take days, or (sometimes) even weeks, to find what your partner likes, but once you do, it's going to be worth every single bit of it.

Or you can just save yourself all that trouble and ask them to show you.

Mutual Masturbation

What is it: Mutual masturbation – no rocket science here – is exactly what it sounds like: two men watching each other masturbate, without *actually* touching each other.

How does it work: From an STI point of view (as long as you aren't sharing sex toys), it's pretty safe, as far as sex goes. Which makes mutual masturbation the quickest (and also the least anxiety-inducing) way to reach an orgasm. Distance isn't a construct here; so it doesn't matter whether you are in the same room, or connected by webcams halfway across the world, because pleasure is a sure thing when it comes to mutual masturbation. After all, no one knows what turns *you* on like you do.

In this case, the joystick is in your hand. And you (and your partner) are putting on a puppet show for an audience of one.

Each other.

Aneesh's bonus tip: 'Sexual ~~newbies~~ deductionists can use this as a visual tutorial to learn what turns their partner on sexually. Because as long as your eyes aren't rolling into the back of your head in pleasure, you get to see *exactly* how your partner likes to be touched in bed. Think of him as the mayor of his very own pleasureville.

And you are getting a personal tour.'

Tea-bagging

What is it: Tea-bagging actually gets its name due to the many similarities it shares with dipping a tea bag into a hot mug of water. Only in this case, the tea bags are your partner's testicles.

How does it work: Tea-bagging is the first course of fellatio. Tread carefully though, because a man's gonads are more fragile than the bone china in your kitchen cabinet.

Aneesh's bonus tip: 'Warm water. That's it. That's the tip.'

Rimming

What is it: If giving a blowjob were the equivalent of housesitting someone's beachside shack, people assume that giving a rim job would be like doing their taxes for free.

How does it work: A rim job is ~~nature's~~ your way of telling your partner that you want to help ease them into anal sex. Although many might frown at the idea of going down on someone's backside, butt play is not as gross as you think it is, because there's a very small chance of tasting last night's *rajma chawal* when you are licking someone's derriere.

Aneesh's bonus tip: 'Take a nice hot shower before you open the buffet to your partner. Have a discussion about health and hygiene before diving in. The cleaner you feel, the easier it is to get down and dirty.'

Edging

What is it: You know how they say that life is all about the journey, and not the destination? Edging is the act of almost reaching your sexual climax and deliberately delaying it so as to make the next wave even more delightful. In plain speak, that's like driving into the sunset.

Only the horizon here is the height of your sexual crescendo.

How does it work: Do your sessions in the sack not last longer than the average commercial break? Unless you have a meeting in the next fifteen minutes or need to escape a burning building, a satisfying sexual experience should last for at least twenty minutes. So then how do you make it last as long as Shah Rukh and Gauri Khan's relationship?

Why hello, edging. Say goodbye to all your problems of ~~premature ejaculation~~ reaching an orgasm too soon, because the art of edging is ideal for men who come within five minutes (only to roll across the bed to watch the latest episode of Family Man for the next forty). Who knew that (temporarily) denying yourself an orgasm could be more exciting than the orgasm itself?

Aneesh's bonus tip: 'Get your partner hot and heavy with foreplay, and just when they're about to climax, stop and start all over again. It's like a tape of mutual masturbation stuck in a loop. Play the mixtape for as long as you like.'

8.5 The Gentleman's Guide to Going Down

For First-Time Fellatio or Otherwise

'How does one give perfect head?' I ask the boys.

'No teeth,' suggests Kartik.

'No hands,' says Aneesh. He's always been the odd one.

'I don't give head,' Urvaksh mutters over his drink.

Is there a story here?

I prod to ask about his *fellatio faux pas*, but he doesn't want to talk about it.

But then, three drinks later …

Urvaksh found Kunaal on Grindr a few months ago. The man, a painter with bright brown eyes, described himself as an 'explorer struggling to find his muse'. It helped that he had shoulders that looked like they could carry the weight of the world. It took Urvaksh forty minutes of flirting to convince Kunaal to go on a date with him the same night. It took him another forty minutes to pretend like he cared about the artist's 'fascination with the abstract expressionist movement and the impact that Jackson Pollock had on artists everywhere'. It took him two hours (and three tequila shots) to persuade him to come over for a nightcap. More drinks were consumed, and a steady flow of flirtation led them right where they needed to be.

The bedroom.

The night is a blur. But at some point, their clothes came off and my friend snaked his way down the painter's treasure trail. Urvaksh had found *his* muse.

'I'd been at it for about ten minutes when *it* happened,' he shudders.

He had *felt* Kunaal convulse. It had pleased him to know that he still had that effect on his conquests. But the painter had another surprise in store for him.

It was vomit.

Maybe it was the three shots of tequila. Maybe it was the platter of nachos. Maybe it was a hot day. Maybe it was just a bad day. Maybe it was all of those things. Maybe it was none of those things.

Urvaksh remembers the retching, and the three long showers he had to take after, but he's blanked out the rest of the night in his mind. He couldn't get himself to touch tequila for weeks after, and he's not had a nacho chip since. He shampoos twice daily. But most importantly, he hates Jackson Pollock's work.

Does It Always End This Way?

Well, no. Urvaksh just had really bad luck. Giving head is, in fact, an art form that you can only perfect with time. Rest assured, it's no Jackson Pollock painting.

See, you don't need to use your head while giving head. Learning to give the perfect BJ is a lot like learning to tie your shoelaces – once you've got the basics right, you can even do it with your eyes closed (but if you are Urvaksh, you shouldn't).

Get comfortable.

Before you get down to business, make sure you are *both* comfortable. The average Indian man takes only about four minutes to orgasm, so make it count.

Do: Find a position that makes both of you feel at home, and ease yourself into it. Give your knees a much-needed break. God knows they deserve it. Opt for a bed or get a pillow if you must, because you are in for the long haul. Make sure that you can move around and explore.

Don't: Force yourself to explore uncharted positions. Limit the body contortion to a game of *Twister* with your friends, and give it a wide berth in the bedroom.

It's important to start slow.

As children's fables will tell you, slow and steady wins the race.

Do: Start slowly and gently. Make it an event. Tease him. Liberate all his erogenous zones. Touch him everywhere else but his shaft. Pretend you can't see it. Pretend it's that friend you've been trying to avoid. Avoid it like the plague. Look him in the eyes every now and then to see how much longer you can play the game. And when he can't take it any more – when he's *literally* begging and making false promises to share his Instagram password with you – you begin.

Don't: Start right off the bat. Remember that only fools rush in. After all, great fellatio needs foreplay too. Make it a game of 'connect the dots'. Conquer each body part before you level up to the next one.

Don't use your teeth.

Everyone knows that a penis is extremely sensitive and that it bruises faster than a man's fragile ego.

Do: Let your teeth make a minor blink-and-you-miss-it cameo – just a slight graze to shock those nerve endings. You want him to know that you are still around. Your tongue, on the other hand? Give it the importance Salman Khan gets in all his movies.

Don't: Bite. The only thing worse than a messy blowjob is a messy blowjob that ends in the hospital.

Treat his crown jewels with respect.

If fellatio is the main course, foreplay is the appetizer that gets you salivating. Start with the basics before you shift your attention to the shaft. Treat the boys with respect, because they are the ones who are putting in a good word for you.

Do: Be gentle. But always have a conversation with your partner about the ratios of pressure to pleasure; they aren't always directly proportional.

Don't: Squeeze too hard. A guy's balls are his kryptonite. Bruise them too hard, and you'll see a grown man crying out for his mother, which does not make for a very attractive trait in a sexual partner.

Know that gagging is never sexy.

Know your limits, boys. If it doesn't fit, don't try to shove it in – gagging is a one-way ticket to limp land, and there's no happily ever after when the curtain drops.

Do: Ease your gag reflex by positioning yourself so your mouth and throat are aligned horizontally. Breathe openly through your nose. It'll help relax your airways.

Don't: Force yourself to take up a challenge. If it *looks* too big to take in, it *definitely* is too big to take in. You've grown up with your body, and you know its limits. Respect it.

Get handsy.

Not a lot of men know that their hands are the breakout stars in a blowjob. Don't just keep them hanging. Use them to your advantage.

Do: Start by gently stroking him all over. Trace out the entire alphabet all over his body. Play the piano if you want to. Keep it slow and sensuous, but stop when he gets more excited.

Don't: Scratch too hard, even if it is in the heat of the moment. You aren't a cat.

Find a rhythm.

Remember that enthusiasm goes a long way. Show him that you *really* want it. Make sure that you really do want it. Gauge your limits. Get the saliva flowing before you start your magic. Keep on switching positions.

Everyone has a different technique. Some men like long strokes. Some men like soft kisses. Some men like to tease. Some men like to dive right in. It could be anything. Find out what works best for you. Enjoy it.

Do: Keep making eye contact to see how he's responding to your techniques. If his eyes are closed or he's gone quiet, it's not a sign that he's fallen asleep (or stressing over that passive-aggressive work email); it probably means he's enjoying it.

Don't: Pull all your tricks from the hat at once. Make him earn it.

Make it a dialogue.

… But know that you'll always be in control. Talk about what he likes. Talk about what you like. Talk about how you want it to end. Do you want to spit it out? Do you want to swallow? Do you want him to spray it on the (washable) walls of your bedroom? You are in charge of this plotline, so you get to decide whether the story gets a happy ending, not him.

Do: Talk about what you are comfortable with. Have a safe word for if he comes on too strong. 'Stop' is usually a great one to begin with.

Don't: Get pressurized into doing anything. Sure, you might feel helpless when you are down on your knees, but with such close access to his most vulnerable spots, know that the ball is in *your* court. No pun intended.

How do I behave when I am getting head?

There are plenty of guides out there that teach you how to give the perfect blowjob, but when it comes to receiving one, most men are clueless.

'What should I do?' the self-aware man would ask. Should I have my hands at the back of my head or use them to push my partner's head down? Is pushing their head down even cool? Should I pat them on their back? Should I have my eyes wide open or tightly shut? Should I be quiet? Should I be moaning? What sounds are okay? Can I sing a song? Can I tell a joke? What if they don't find my joke funny? What if they insist on a condom? What if they insist on not swallowing? And in the case of the self-aware gay man from above, what if they insist on one in *return*?

But hey, a blowjob isn't only about *you*. So put those hands to better use. Use them for anything other than grabbing heads. Caress their faces, tousle their hair or hold their hands to show how much it means to you. Moan if you are enjoying yourself, but try not singing a song.

Once you've registered all these lessons in your head, here are a few more to remember when you are getting some.

1. **Stay clean.**

A few men might argue that the musky, masculine scent of a man is a big turn-on, but know that smelly privates are as desirable as a garbage truck.

So make sure you don't smell like one. Think of all the horrible things about oral sex – poor hygiene, ball sweat, stray pubic hairs and dirty, old underwear – and make sure you cross them all off your checklist. Trim off the excess, take a long shower and wear underwear that's fresh out of the laundry. Use a fabric softener if you can. You'll be ready for business.

2. **Do talk.**

Moan if you have to. Dirty talk. Tell them how much you like it. Make minor (but convenient) suggestions. Lighten the mood with a joke. Literally any noise you make is better than sitting in awkward silence, leaving the squelching sex noises resonating in your (and worse, your partner's) ears.

3. **But don't say 'go down on me'.**

The only thing that's worse than a man with stinky privates is a man with a stinky attitude. Seduction is an art. Don't blow it.

4. **Eat and drink right.**

Let's face it – a man's private parts are never going to taste like chocolate cake. Your natural smell is a part of your sexuality, and as long as you are healthy, there's nothing wrong with how the universe made you. But there are a few things you can eat that can make you *taste* better (but unfortunately, you're still not going to taste like chocolate cake).

Things to eat: Fruit (citrus, bananas and papayas), spices (cinnamon, nutmeg and peppermint, among others) and wheatgrass.

Things to avoid: Cigarettes, onions, garlic and red meat – basically anything that your mother warned you about.

5. **Don't be pushy…**

… or you'll seriously be pushing your luck. Acting like you are entitled to a BJ is a one-way ticket to ensuring you *never* get one in the first place. After all, there's no space for bad behaviour when it comes to blowjob etiquette. Don't make the experience suck for your partner, no pun intended.

Thrusting into their mouth? Only if they want it that way (otherwise, leave the gyrating of your pelvis to the disco floor). Pushing their head down? Ask for permission first. Gagging? No one really likes it, guys.

6. **… Or stare …**
Your orgasm face isn't as attractive as you think it is.

7. **Instead, ask them what they want.**
More importantly, warn them when you are about to climax. Semen doesn't *always* taste bad, but it doesn't exactly taste like a vanilla Frappuccino either. When people say they like surprises, they are talking about birthday parties, not the gift of spunk trailing down their chin.

You don't need to set a reminder on their phone, but a quick heads-up always helps. Let *them* decide what they want to do. Make it a conversation. They can choose to spit. They can choose to swallow. They can choose to paint with it if they want to. Respect it. And make sure you buy the artwork, because it's obviously going to be a masterpiece.

Just like Jackson Pollock's work.

8. **Be prepared to return the favour.**
Because honestly, it's the least you can do.

Number Forty-seven: The Admissions Counsellor The Gentleman's Guide on How Not to Receive a Blowjob

December 2018

'Do you want to get a drink later tonight?'

Well, this is a tight one. The first (of many a) rule is to have the basic courtesy of giving a person enough notice before you set up a date. What if they have a calendar full of commitments, or worse, a day planned with nothing on the horizon?

So, when **Forty-seven** asks me out a little after noon, I find myself in a conundrum. My new friend here is an admission counsellor for an Ivy League school back in the United States, but he's also only visiting Bombay for the wedding. I see that **Forty-seven's** Instagram grid is well curated; his photos colour-coded and stacked like the contents of a Microsoft Excel sheet. But ever since men became adept at using photo-editing apps – hiding red flags and the occasional deal-breaker behind the right filter – can one really judge a person's worth based on ~~face~~ grid value?

Not really. What if he's a douchebag in real life? Or worse, someone who says he 'does it for the gram'? But since the admissions counsellor is 'only here for two more days', I decide to make him the exception to this rule.

'Sure', I shoot right back, setting up a date at my favourite bar for later that night.

It takes me one look at **Forty-seven** to realize that his Instagram is a curation of lies. His face isn't pretty like in his pictures … it's *perfect.*

He smiles as he sees me, revealing a set of perfectly aligned white teeth. The last time I saw something so symmetrical, it was the Taj Mahal on a school trip to Agra. **Forty-seven** seems to know how to play to his strengths, because he bats his eyelashes right on cue: they are so long and fluttery, I realize they can sweep my room clean.

Over our first round of drinks, **Forty-seven** tells me that he plans to quit his job so that he can relocate to Singapore for a more prestigious position. After our second round, he coyly asks me if I would visit him next summer. After a quick third, we share a quick kiss. Four rounds in, and I am already making false promises to look up tickets to Singapore.

It's after the fifth and final round that **Forty-seven** realizes that he's had too much to drink and needs to use the washroom.

'Are you sure you don't want to use it too?' he slurs on his way, lingering. His giddiness is exciting, because I realize my bladder is rather full. There they are again, those long fluttering eyelashes, only this time I'm actually swept off my feet ...

... straight into the bathroom. Are there people waiting outside? We don't even care any more. One of us latches the door shut. The other one pulls down his pants. I giggle as I move down his treasure trail, toying with the elastic strap of his briefs ... at which point, I suddenly stop.

There's funky, and then there's ... *this*. It smells like something died and reanimated in there. Fighting back the urge to retch, I turn around before its undead hands can strangle me with its stench.

'Are you okay?'

I lie, telling him that I might have had a bit too much to drink. 'I'll see you outside?' I pretend to dry-heave.

He doesn't need to be asked twice. He's out before I hit the pot.

Only this time, I flush down those tickets to Singapore instead.

8.6 Condoms and Coitus: What We Talk about When We Talk about Barebacking

Urvaksh has never had it easy.

On his lifelong quest of finding love, the banker has jumped headlong into many relationships.[10] There was the fitness expert who forced him to sign up for Krav Maga classes. The graphic designer who dragged him to rave parties. The lawyer who guilt-tripped him into attending his cousin's wedding. And the painter who puked all over his ... well, you get the point. Every man was an oversight, every decision was a compromise.

And then, along came Surya. Like his name, he was the light at the end of a really long, dreary tunnel. There were no aching bones

---

10 And many more mistakes.

(because no Krav Maga classes). No splitting migraines (because no rave parties). No nosy second cousins (because no family weddings). Most importantly, there was no vomit.

With Surya the surgeon, everything seemed exponentially easy. It was a carousel of happy memories; a joyride that didn't make Urvaksh feel dizzy. So when it was finally time to cover up his troops and make it exclusive, Urvaksh raced to the springboard and dived right in.

Over the next few weeks, the happy couple found themselves at many exciting places – art galleries, music recitals, jazz bars and on that one occasion, even the circus – until they found themselves in the bedroom.

'Are you ready?' Surya asked after forty minutes of fantastic foreplay.

Urvaksh had never felt *more* ready in his life.

But something didn't feel right. Something was missing.

It was a condom.

Urvaksh hesitated as he saw his carousel come to a screeching halt. Was barebacking the first step in baring his soul?

The Author's Note on Barebacking

A term for the act of having anal sex without a condom, i.e. unprotected (but not uncharted) sex. Usually a staple for monogamous couples that haven't touched another man for months (if not years), the practice is also considered a fad for the frivolous and the foolhardy.

'Why do we need a condom?' Surya had argued, as Urvaksh pulled his pants back on.

Urvaksh didn't want to take a chance.

The surgeon had tried to reason. He blamed (and gaslit) Urvaksh for being paranoid ('isn't this a true test of our trust?') and a prude (all my friends are doing it).

'Why don't you just learn to live a little?' soft-spoken Surya had yelled.

But that's exactly what Urvaksh planned to do. Live a little (longer). In a fit of anger, Surya stormed out of the room.[11] For a man who was such a joyride, the surgeon had swooped in without a safety helmet.

So when did barebacking become so … *common*?

Urvaksh thinks it happened when he was ~~regretting~~ attending those rave parties. Or it happened when he was signing up for Krav Maga classes. Maybe it happened when he was attending his ex's family wedding.

Or maybe he's got it all wrong.

In fact, it all started when treatments for HIV/AIDS made the disease more manageable and convinced many gay men not to think of semen as potentially life-threatening poison. Suddenly, barebacking wasn't a 'novelty for LTR-oriented couples'; it was a trend for the masses.' Unprotected sex was no longer a luxury; it was a commodity.

Sometimes, Urvaksh has the most succinct things to say.

With the advent of PrEP – a pill that makes it difficult (but not impossible) to contract HIV – it's no surprise that more queer men are now exploring going unprotected. PrEP is definitely pushing the boundaries of what is forbidden and what is not.

Kush Trivedi,[12] a headhunter for a big pharmaceutical company, has rather polarizing views on safe sex. After clocking long hours in a windowless cubicle, it is his one chance to stop thinking and just go with the flow. Barebacking helps him feel *unshackled* and *unrestrained*. It helps him feel *alive*.

Are those seventeen minutes worth of pleasure worth contracting syphilis?

---

11 And eventually, out of Urvaksh's life.

12 Name changed to protect identity.

It all boils down to trust, Kush explains. 'You can't just bareback with anyone: even though most men are on PrEP, you have to find a guy who gives you the *right* vibe.'

But since when have men been truthful about the STIs they may (or may not) have?

Kush has been on PrEP since 2017. He's always believed in personal accountability and responsibility for his own health. Over the last decade, he's learnt to become more open and upfront with his (multiple) sexual partners, from everything regarding his sexual status to his dislike for condoms.

So what about syphilis? Or gonorrhoea? Or worse … genital herpes?

Last I checked, the average STI didn't need a memo to come knocking on your door. Having unprotected sex is your choice, yes, but you need to make sure you have all your facts in place. Yes, most diseases are commonly passed through penetration (or the exchange of bodily fluids such as semen, blood and anal fluid), but certain infections can also be passed through kissing, touching or dry humping. See, information regarding sexual health in the country has always been a sore spot (to put it mildly), quite like the symptoms of many of these infections themselves.

You can never tell if someone is carrying an STI (or not) *just* by looking at them: Men seldom come wearing tags that say they have a venereal disease. There's no slogan t-shirt either. Just remember, every time you have sex with someone, you are having sex with everyone they've had sex with. And everybody has a random person they won't tell you about. Having said that, it's okay to say no if you see something that makes you unsure. It's okay to be ~~paranoid~~ conscious of the sores, boils and warts around the genital area of someone you plan to have sex with.

When is barebacking okay …

- When you are in a monogamous relationship
- When you know each other's latest STI status

When is it not okay …

- When you have multiple sexual partners
- When you don't know your partner's STI status
- When you plan on having NSA sex
- Literally every situation in which you feel pressured

Until then, use a condom.

The Timid Man's Manual on Getting Tested

Knock knock?

Who's there?

A sexually transmitted disease.

A sexually transmitted disease who?

A sexually transmitted disease you didn't know you were carrying.

'But I always use protection,' you squeal. 'How could this happen to me?'

Well, it happens to the best of us. One in four people in the world has had an STI at some point in their life. Another half will get one at some point in the future. If you are having unprotected sex, chances are that an STI (like the quintessential unwanted houseguest) *will* come knocking when you least expect it.

And it won't ring the bell before it barges into your body.

Men will always be evasive when you ask about their STI status. It's not that we *don't* want to know that we are clean, but that we don't want to find out that we are *not*. Unlike women, we can't have our tests done as a part of our annual checkup: it's a decision that needs to be made with a purpose, and doing so makes us feel like dirty, mite-infested drug addicts.

But getting tested is a rite of passage if you are a ~~raging~~ sexually active gay man. Of course, this is easier said than done. This is not North America, where you can just waltz into a public health clinic and fill out a few forms. In India, you will not be able to do it so easily, especially if you have no symptoms.

However, proper preventive healthcare is essential for your physical and mental health. You need to make sure that you don't self-diagnose, because WebMD *will* tell you that you are dying of severe bronchitis (or worse, testicular cancer). A precise diagnosis and treatment plan will get rid of *most* infections and you'll be back to your healthy, happy self in days.[13]

DO. NOT. FREAK. OUT. BOYS.

It's never the ideal scenario to find out that you may have contracted an STI, but it's worse not to tell the people you could have passed it on to. This *isn't* the common cold, and (usually) over-the-counter prescriptions won't help.

How Do I Tell Someone I Might Have Passed Them an STI?

Here's a quick five-step guide that will help make the burn less painful.

Find the right facts to tell them.

The first thing to do is to get tested yourself. Having an STI might not be that big a deal in 2021, but it doesn't mean that people won't freak out when you tell them. You need to get your facts right, before you pass on the stress (because you are already passing on something that's equally bad). Arm yourself with all the necessary info, lest they harm you with all the necessary blows.

Find the right way to tell them.

For a one-night stand or a casual hookup, a cursory text message is fine. Make sure your message sounds apologetic. Someone you

13 If not weeks.

spent the weekend with deserves a phone call. Make sure *you* sound apologetic. But for anyone you've met more than twice, a face-to-face explanation is as mandatory as getting tested every three months.

Refrain from meeting in coffee shops and/or restaurants where sharp objects and/or the scalding contents of their mugs can be thrown at you. You don't want to increase those hospital bills. The prescriptions are going to bruise your wallets anyway.

Find the right time to tell them.

Break the news first thing in the morning, so they can get tested the same day. Which poor, unsuspecting soul deserves to spend the night racking up several worst-case scenarios in his head, the best of which involve your death at his hands?

Be the right person and tell them.

You don't want them to find out through a common friend (or worse, a common sexual partner). Open up with unadulterated honesty, just like you opened up your legs all those months ago.

Have the right things to tell them.

Some of us feign ignorance when it comes to telling someone you might have passed them a STI. Some of us play the blame game. Don't be either of those two. Instead, state the facts and hash out how quickly/easily it can be treated. Be matter-of-fact: it might seem cold, but beating around the bush will only distract you both from the objectives here.

Get tested. Be honest about your needs and safe-sex measures to practise in the future. After all, getting an STI might not be the end of the world, but it doesn't need to be a replacement for a relationship. Now go wild.

Just make sure you always use a condom.

A Gentleman's Guide to Condom Etiquette

Wearing a condom is a lot like going on a vacation. You have to go through airport security and deal with long layovers – these are the not-so-great parts. But eventually, you reach your destination and it's still fulfilling. These are the parts you look forward to. Without baggage claim and long check-in lines, there would be no vacation. Similarly, without condoms, there ~~wouldn't~~ shouldn't be any sex.

Even though it's not as adventurous as 'going for sex' spontaneously, protection is just a necessary part of the fun. If you've never worn a condom before (or had sex), it's highly recommended that you try one out yourself so you understand how they work. Keep practising till it feels like your second skin. Want to know the details of slipping on the sheath?

Here's a step-by-step guide to making safe sex a lot more scintillating.

1. **Take the condom out of the wrapper.**

Sounds easy, right? WRONG. You have to make sure you don't end up tearing it. Even the tiniest of tears can make a condom as useful as that time you accidentally used a fork to drink soup.

2. **Know which side is up.**

The number of people who make the mistake of wearing a condom upside down and then complaining about how 'it won't unroll' *will* surprise you. Play with the rim a bit to make sure you know which direction it goes on. No 'this side up' signs here, sorry. The only disclaimer that comes on condom packaging is that it's effective only 97% of the time.

3. **Use lube to reduce dryness.**

Just a couple of drops inside the tip to make the experience (much) better.

4. **Pinch the tip.**
… as if it were the cheeks of an extremely cherubic puppy (but don't try it on an actual one), and then gently place it over the tip of your penis …

5. **Put it on.**
… and make sure you slide it all the way down.

6. **Handle with care.**
If at any point the condom slips off or breaks, don't hyperventilate. Simply unwrap a new one. But make sure you …

7. **Throw out the used condom!**
Especially if it's still full of your love junk. When you're done, hold on to the base while you are pulling it off. Then, roll it up and tie it up in a knot. Your used condom is now ready to be dispatched to the garbage chute. Make sure you dispose of it in the trashcan, because flushing a condom down the toilet is not a good idea.

Or your plumber is going to have a lot of *awkward* questions.

Do You Have Any Other Tips?

- Condoms, like chips and chocolates, come with an expiry date. Make sure you check the date before you rip open the packet. Expired chocolates may lead to food poisoning, but expired condoms lead to potential STIs.
- The faster you cover up with a condom, the less likely you are to go limp. Minimize the 'but I was just hard a moment ago' fumbling by opening the wrapper *during* foreplay.
- Most people spend all of five seconds to ~~avoid stares~~ buy a condom at the pharmacy. But a last-minute dash to the medical store can mean a severe lack of satisfaction in the bedroom. Choose a condom that fits properly, but also *feels* right. Self-confidence is great, but whom are we kidding when we buy XL-sized condoms?

- Think of a condom as a suit (but for your penis). If it's too big, it will droop and slide off mid-intercourse, and if it's too tight, it will reduce sensation in your penis.
- Like men, condoms come in all shapes and sizes. But unlike men, they also come with a lot of character – ribbed, dotted or ultra-thin. Experiment with *all* of them!

8.7 Love, Sex and Drugs: The Growing Rise of Chem Sex in the Community

Kartik is extremely distressed.

'Is everything okay?' I ask. It's hard to see the (usually) optimistic writer all balled up in a shell. It was a little after midnight, Kartik tells me, when he got that familiar ping on Grindr a few weeks ago. I don't question the time, because Grindr pings often find comfort in the depths of the night.

Kartik opened his notifications to a bright, beaming torso – one that looked like it belonged to a good-natured man. (Side note: usually, there's no chance of knowing whether a man is good-natured or not just by looking at a photo of his well-defined pecs, but in this case, our mystery man also sent smiling photos.) The torso was also in town '*just for the night*'.

Sounds like every second profile on Grindr, I tell him.

But our beaming torso was different. He was handsome and chatty, and looked like someone 'who updated his LinkedIn bio for breakfast', a rare combination for men you'd find lurking on Grindr.

'Do you want to meet?' Mystery man had pinged.

'Right now?'

'Yes. Come right over. I'll be waiting.'

'*Now*?'

'Why aren't you here yet? Just come. I have a surprise for you ...'

Kartik tallied the odds.

Mr Torso was a mere 630 metres away. A brisk five-minute walk, and he would be right over. But the man was a complete stranger, and he also seemed eager.

In fact, he seemed *so* eager it seemed *odd*. What if he was a serial killer who preyed on witty men? Kartik found it strange, but didn't question his gut. It was his libido, he reassures me, when I cock my eyebrows. Sadly, when it comes to men, it's *always* their libido (or in this case, the sweet dangling surprise that awaited him).

With mounting apprehension, Kartik rang the bell to the hotel room. His date opened the door right away. He was beaming. That's not what serial killers look like. (Side note: Serial killers can't be profiled, so kids, please don't try this.) Kartik walked into the modest hotel suite, and his eyes almost immediately fell on the syringe.

'What's that?' he asked.

'Aren't you into high fun?' the not-so-mysterious man asked.

And just like that, Kartik's LinkedIn dreams came crashing down. My writer friend says that the next forty minutes were some of the most harrowing he has ever experienced. After spending twenty minutes convincing his date that he wasn't interested in trying out drugs with a stranger, Kartik spent the next few minutes trying to find a way out of an experience that he didn't want to be a part of. He wasn't just trying to appease a horny stranger on his home turf; he was trying to appease a horny stranger who was *also* very high.

Thankfully, it went well. No scenes were created. No boundaries were harmed. The torso was understanding. Disappointed, yes, but understanding nonetheless.

'Are you really sure?' he had pleaded at the door.

Kartik shook his head and left, and never heard from him ever again.

Kartik's heard multiple horror stories of men being abused, blackmailed and coerced (and sometimes, even drugged) into having chem sex. Each of these worst-case scenarios flashed in front of his eyes. When every fourth profile on Grindr is a not-so-silent plea that squeals for sex on drugs, it's not easy to ignore the relationship that queer men have with chem sex. It's the elephant in the room that everyone voluntarily chooses to ignore.

And yet, it exists.

Every generation finds new ways to get high, get laid and scare the authorities. The recipe varies every time, but it's usually some combination of alcohol, mephedrone, alkyl nitrates and GHB, with romps that extend to days, and occasionally, multiple partners. As countless thought pieces on the internet will tell you, gay men have been using narcotics (and sometimes even the needle) to enhance their sexual experiences for *aeons*.

It's only recently that they slammed through the shackles of secrecy and started talking about their fetishes openly. Akaash Dutt[14] is one such example. At first glance, Akaash is an ordinary man. A marketing executive for a bustling education startup, he spends his time shuttling between work and post-work drinks. He's hooked on catchy Bollywood numbers, football and the sweet taste of cheap rum.

And then, four months ago, he got hooked on chem sex. His story matches Kartik's – a mysterious stranger who pinged him in the dead of the night with the promise of bliss at an arm's reach.

Unlike Kartik, he decided to take the leap (read: slam) of faith.

He remembers it vividly. Initially, there was some hesitancy when he saw the syringe (injecting it into your bloodstream seems to be more potent than licking the drug, the man had reasoned), but seconds later, the deed had been done.

Nothing happened for a while, Akaash tells me, and he feared it was a cheap strain. Was this how his first drug-fuelled experience was going to be – a cop out?

And then suddenly, he felt ... *free*.

14 Name changed to protect identity.

'It's like every single pore on my body was alive,' he tells me, 'and every single pore of my body wanted to feel intimacy.'

The definition of intimacy is questionable here; because Akaash went on to do a lot of things he wouldn't usually talk about. But he doesn't hold back on the details. The experience was surreal, and he felt like he wanted to go on and on and on, and never stop.

And he didn't.

They went at it all over the house, and thrice in the car (including that one blissful time over the Sea Link). Akaash says they tried positions and used toys he didn't know existed. Queer men usually avoid talking about substance abuse like they avoid complex carbohydrates.

But not Akaash. At the end of his seventeen-minute monologue where he spoke at length about his out-of-body experience, I feel goosebumps on my arm. He says he fell in love that night. Akaash has fallen in love a total of seven times in the last four months. Most users will tell you that this is usual – replacing endorphins and oxytocins with mephedrones and methylenedioxymethamphetamines (popularly known as MDMA or Ecstacy) to stimulate chemically induced love. 'It's so much easier,' Akaash reminisces, 'why doesn't love come with a prescription?'

It's simple. Because prescriptions also come with multiple side effects.

Now I'm no medical expert, and this is no mental health guide (considering you're reading a memoir), but before you jump down the rabbit hole of PnP, here's what you need to know from my ~~own personal experience~~ extensive field research.

Get your facts right.

Most of the stigma attached to chem sex comes from the fear of catching an STI from a frequent user. Newsflash: Drugs don't lead to STIs or HIV transmissions. Practising unsafe sex and sharing contaminated needles do.

Remember, safety comes first.

That's code for 'condoms always'. No matter how convincing your partner is about 'trust and inhibitions'. No matter how well you know them. No matter how free you feel. No matter how high you are. No matter how low your inhibitions get. No matter how many times people tell you that 'a condom will just ruin the whole experience'.

Read up on-long term effects.

Some of the more widespread effects of using chemicals include anxiety, depression, fatigue and panic attacks. But of course, not every user will look worse for wear – just as not every alcoholic will be found splayed shirtless in their building's elevator.

Know that addiction is real.

It's as real as the person reading this book.

Understand that consent is everything.

You can leave whenever you feel uncomfortable. No questions asked, no explanations given. Just agreeing to meet someone through an app or stepping into a PnP party/hangout DOES NOT mean you agree to whatever anyone else wants to do. It's 2021, and consent needs to be as accessible as your bedside drawer.

It's always going to be your choice.

Just you, and no one else.

Number Forty-eight: The Junkie
If Love Is a Drug, Does It Come with a Prescription?

April 2015

Life after death is not the endorphin-laced gift card they show in the movies – it's a lot worse, because it steamrolls all over you till all that's left is a giant puddle of misery. Once this steamroller trudges on, you pick up all the flattened pieces and move on. That's how it ends. The roller marks never fade away, because there really are no happy endings after. It's a funny thing, grief.

Grief makes us behave in ways we never expected. Some write poetry, some go on world cruises and some even adopt cats. A handful publish books.

And me?

Grief finds me having coffee with **Forty-eight**, a macho make-up artist, a mere four days after my grandmother's funeral. Now is the right time to tell you that **Forty-eight** is Greek – with a last name that's too difficult to pronounce – and is originally from an island that's too obscure to remember (not all of them are called Crete or Mykonos or Santorini.)

So what's a man like him doing in a city like this?

It was supposed to be a vacation, he explains over iced Americanos and biscotti, but he never ended up leaving. A week turned into ten days into a month, and he realized something was holding him back (not the immigration officers I hope, I stop myself from saying) so he decided to stay. What held him back?

No, it wasn't a boy (that would make him too mainstream) or the rent (that would make him too cheap); it was the city itself.

'*Moombai* changed my soul,' he says, massacring the pronunciation in what I assume is a Greek accent. 'I've become so spiritual here.'

Give a white man a yoga mat, and he'll espouse the virtues of Buddhism like it were a steal at the farmer's market. I find him so endearing that I almost discount the coffee breath. So what's work like for an expat here?

The make-up industry is not an easy business to crack. He gets a lot of preferential treatment because of his skin colour (here, and on Grindr), but it's not something he's proud of. Does he like Mumbai?

'I love the *punny poori* here. It's like nothing I've ever tasted before ...'

Here we go again. We spend the next twenty minutes discussing the many perks of his foreigner status – not limited to the bevvy of international models that are on speed dial – when he notices my mind is far away.

'Is everything okay?'

He's in the middle of an extremely scandalous story that involves the tantrums of an erstwhile starlet. I am rather surprised myself. I usually take to B-lister gossip like I take to clickbait, but I am really not feeling like myself. My internal monologues have hit an all-time low. I decide to come clean and tell him about my grandmother.

His empathy is the right amount of earnest – too much and it would seem tasteless; too little and it would seem distasteful. 'Have you thought about healing?'

I try not to roll my eyes. Here it comes – the white man's curse. He's going to suggest everything from tantric sex to pranayama to Bikram yoga. Bonus points if he suggests cleansing my charkas with sage. I brace myself for a crash course on Indian Vedic rituals.

'I think I know what you need to do,' he says with the Zen of a recently converted monk. He leans in conspiringly and beckons me closer. Oh well, here comes the pyramid scheme of pranic healing.

'What is it?' I ask, giving up. I might as well as take the crash course before things come crashing down.

'I have some *blow* at home. Want to do a few lines?'

8.8 The Bedside Box Set: What Every Gay Man Needs in His Bedside Drawer

Whether you are bringing home a guy or a large stuffed pepperoni pizza, the bedside drawer is a collection of odds and ends that makes your life easier (and cleaner): it's where you keep your old receipts and your delivery menus, your long-forgotten love notes and your recently used condom wrappers. It's your den, when you can't afford to have a den. But what makes the bedside drawer your treasure chest of essentials, your personal oasis in ~~the pandemic~~ times of loneliness?

Stock up on these essentials to find out.

❒ A giant super-sized box of condoms.

Dotted, ribbed or flavoured, keep your condoms right where you need them – at arm's length. There's nothing that kills a boner more than having to tiptoe to the bathroom to find that lone condom hidden behind your antidepressants in the shower cabinet.

Another perk of having your condoms close by? There's a smaller chance of you deciding to go against basic common sense and plunging in without protection.

Quick tip: Also stock up on non-latex condoms; you never know if someone reacts negatively to the regular ones. (Let's just pretend they aren't reacting to you.)

❒ Essential oils and candles

Want to get rid of the combined smell of weeks-old underwear, leftover pizza, cigarette smoke and the faint stench of being forever lonely?

A wholesale box of aromatic candles and oils can make the dankest of rooms smell like the deluxe suite of a boutique hotel. You may thank me later.

❒ **A bottle of water-based lube**
Spent the night recreating the NSFW bits of *Call Me By Your Name*? You don't want to wake up the morning after with a bad case of haemorrhoids. Keep the lube ready to make the sex as enjoyable as it sounds in lifestyle magazines and online listicles about pleasure.

❒ **Breath mints**
You might have a full head of *GQ* hair and cheekbones that can cut through glass, but no one wants to kiss someone with morning breath, even if you look like Ryan Gosling's long-lost twin. Want a repeat romp with the delicious dude you had over last night?

Pop a mint before you pop him over again.

❒ **Tissue paper**
Unless you want to lie around in your love juice (or worse, someone else's), it's probably a good idea to invest in a giant roll of wet wipes.

Plus, tissues help in cleaning up after the leftover pizza too.

❒ **A little pocketbook and a pen**
That next big idea that lets you retire at forty-five (with daiquiris by the beach) will probably hit you just before you hit the pillow.

❒ **Your phone charger**
Sending mid-morning bedhead selfies can be more exhausting for your phone than you think. Conversations can die midway; phones shouldn't.

❒ **Lip balm**
The only thing worse than kissing someone with morning breath is kissing someone with lips that look like your morning cereal. Want him to *stay back* for cereal? Stock up on that lip balm.

❑ Baby oil
Your skincare routine could do with a revival.

❑ Sex toys
… and so could your sex life.

❑ A stash of porn on your phone
A day will come when you'll be stuck in the vast desert land that lies between being bored and being lazy. On that day, you'll need your respite – pages and pages worth of wet dreams (opened in incognito mode) at your beckoning.

You are welcome.

❑ Some empty space
Where else will you proudly display this book for all the men to see?

8.9 The Moron's Manual for Morning-After Etiquette

How to Handle Yourself after a One-Night Stand

Uh-oh.

It's 7 a.m., and you've just opened your eyes to a ceiling that doesn't look very familiar, and a bedmate you've *never* seen before. As you collect your bearings (and your belongings), you remember snippets from the previous night.

We've all been there. You've had a drink too many the night before, and are now sprawled on a bed (that isn't yours) with guilt (that most certainly is). In an ideal world, this is the meet-cute they talk about in movies. The one where you meet the right person at the right time. But ~~most often~~ every once in a while, you meet the wrong person at the wrong time. One minute (read: twelve hours ago), you are playing tonsil hockey with each other at your favourite bar, and the very next (read: now), you wake up as complete strangers in a bed that feels as awkward as the entire experience. So what do we do?

Stop making bad decisions? Stop chatting up attractive strangers? Or worse, completely stop going to bars?

Relax. Irrespective of whether this is a one-night stand, a casual hookup or the beginning of something fun, here's how to behave yourself (with or) without waking up your 'date from the previous night' the morning after.

Making the exit

Open your bleary eyes to see a room that you can't recall?

If there's something a man needs after a ~~mistake~~ messy one-night stand, it's the ability to make a quicker exit than the time it took him to get there in the first place. See, the only thing worse than waking up next to a stranger is waking up next to a stranger who *doesn't* look like the 'vision of beauty' you remember chatting up from the night before (or worse, a stranger who doesn't think *you* are the 'vision of beauty' they remember chatting up from the night before).

Don't want to be caught leaving wearing a shirt, *their* underwear and half a sock? Want to avoid the awkward small talk and pointed silences that will follow once they know how you look in broad daylight?

If your post-midnight paramour is still sleeping, and you *don't* want round two, tiptoe out of their house before you can spell regret (even backwards). Dash out of the door (and their life) before they have a chance to make you stay back for brunch.

Just make sure that you leave a quick note saying goodbye. Do not (and we repeat, *do not*) be that person who disappears without a trace. You want to be a person *with* interest, not a 'Person *of* Interest'.

Breaking in for breakfast

Woke up to the sound of the kettle whistling like a giant call of shame and a bed that is as empty as your life?

Well, it looks like you aren't going back home on an empty stomach! Chances are that the kindred soul outside still thinks you are the quick-witted charmer that they met at the bar last night, and if you plan to keep it that way, you'd better rush to the bathroom and touch up your face and your manners, while they touch up your eggs benedict (or quinoa upma, if you like it that way). Load up on (their) mouthwash; you'll only thank us later.

Make small talk as you bite into their butter cookies and sip on your lemon tea. Ask about their job (that they have to get to) and their family (that is not around) if you have to – that's the least you can do as you chomp down on complimentary breakfast service.

Cleaning up

The morning after is no Nicholas Sparks novel. As the long, hard sunlight falls unforgivingly on your body, it's no surprise that you aren't the Calvin Klein model that he thought you were. You see that look on his face?

It's not shock. It's disappointment. Feel your ears burn as his eyes give you the deprecating look down – they gaze over your bulges and bruises, and stop on your love handles just for a second longer than they should.

There's only one thing to be done. Make as little eye contact as possible, word out a quick goodbye, and plan a hurried exit before he has the chance to process that your face doesn't usually come attached with an Instagram filter.

You'll eventually wash off his disdain in a week (or ten).

Is there a sequel?

If you are the one who has to leave after what's been a night that you are going to gush about in group chats with friends in *exactly* twenty minutes, leave your number behind before you do.

Give him a warm goodbye hug. Forget everything else you read in this piece. Maybe seal the deal with a quick kiss (but make sure you've used his mouthwash from before). Ask him to call you if they want to see you again.

He most certainly will.

But Hold On ... What If It's *My* Home?

Okay, picture this.

You wake up as the first rays of sunlight hit your face.

It's a beautiful morning.

Your cat nuzzles up to your leg as you make snow angels in the sheets of your familiar bed. Pushing him away with your toes, you stifle a yawn and smile at the picture on the bedside drawer. It's from your month-long holiday across uncharted Europe. 'That was a great vacation, wasn't it?' you chuckle to yourself. It's right next to the book you'll never finish reading, but that doesn't stop you from making a mental note to get back to it soon. Your clothes are bundled up in a mysterious heap on the floor, and your laptop whirs away peacefully on your beanbag by the door. You have a vague memory of buying too many shots at the bar last night. 'Was that the bartender who booked me a cab?' you ask yourself. Well, that isn't your problem any more. Because you are right where you belong. Your room is just the way you left it last night – messy and imperfect, but it's still home. You turn around.

There he is. The ~~mistake~~ man you met last night – sprawled across your bed, drooling all over your favourite pillow (you *hope* that's drool). It's what's-his-name from what-was-I-thinking-last-night.

While making the hasty exit after a regretful night might be easy when you are at a stranger's house, things aren't all that simple when you have to say goodbye to someone who's just shared your bed(room). And as you struggle to remember his name, remember that you'll *also* have a lot of questions.

How do you wake him up (just like you woke up your conscience)? Do you offer him breakfast or break it to him that he has to leave? Should there be a parting gift (that's not necessarily your phone number)? How can you be polite and send him packing?

Relax, and follow these steps.

Making the exit (for him)

If you wake up first, pretend to be sleeping till he does (but only if you never want to see him ever again). Give him a ten-minute getaway gap where he can make a quick dash for the door; no questions asked, no judgements passed.

Once he does, keep your beer goggles where they firmly belong – in your bedside drawer – and only take them out when you need them next.

Next weekend.

Breaking out for breakfast

Offer a cup of tea, but don't make the mistake of *already* making one. The only thing worse than waking up to a surprise cup of tea by a stranger is waking up to a surprise cup of tea that has way more sugar than you usually like.

Cleaning up

Have a go at your bachelor pad with a duster and a trash bag before he wakes up, and clean up your room before he realizes you ~~have sociopathic tendencies~~ hoard old newspapers (and used condom wrappers) by the dozen.

Is there a sequel?

We've got ourselves a winner!

The fair chance that your ~~hookup~~ date from the previous night survived waking up, sharing breakfast and enjoying your relatively cleaner room, now means that you both probably want to see each other again. Accompany him to the door (when he finally feels like leaving) and say goodbye with either a kiss or your phone number.

Or both.

Some more pointers:

1. Unless you want to wake up to the happy (but also, frozen) faces of your parents, your brother, and the family dog (high up from the Eiffel Tower) staring down at your naked bodies, shove all your family pictures into a box before you have a hookup over.
2. Book a taxi at least five minutes before you've got your shoes on. Say your goodbyes (or flash those feeble smiles) only once your ~~chariot~~ cab-of-shame is on its way. After all, you don't want to be left waiting for your cab as you dawdle by the door (a.k.a the no man's land), being forced to make polite conversation with a man you have no intention of ever seeing again.
3. Don't want a flatmate to consider therapy because he/she walked in on you while you were busy trying to replicate the spread-eagle from the downloadable version of the Kama Sutra? Invest in a lock.

Number Forty-nine: The Entrepreneur
Can We Have A Conversation about (Sexual) Compatibility?

This particular story begins on a Saturday. It's a regular Saturday – no gimmicks, no grievances – and perchance if you passed it as you crossed the road, you wouldn't even look at it twice. A gratuitous head nod maybe, but nothing else. And yet, I find myself at the beginning of a new story. Any arbitrary turning in my path, and I would be elsewhere. I wouldn't be me.

I usually prefer spending my Saturdays curled up with a book (or the occasional man), daydreaming about my next trip to the refrigerator.

Instead, I find myself at a focus group for queer men. There are four of us, and we've spent the last fifteen minutes introducing ourselves, pretending as if we haven't already stalked each other on Instagram. But to understand why I am here, we need to go back in time to two nights ago.

'Can I ask you for a favour?' a friend had texted. One of his acquaintances is planning to launch a new LGBTQIA+ dating app, and wants to interview queer folx for market research. 'Would you be available the day after tomorrow?'

I frown. Do we really need another dating app in the market? Don't we already have enough ways to get routinely disappointed by other gay men? Do our lives (and phones) have space for more clutter?

'This one's different. It's going to be completely home grown. *Made in India*. The whole spiel. They are building up a team from scratch, maybe you should hit them up for content ...' He trails off, but the trap has been set. A source of income has been promised.

The damage has been done.

'Just show up, please?' he begs, and I agree when he finally promises to buy me a drink.

Give a gay man an open forum to have an opinion, and we won't waste a single moment to make it about ourselves. Do I fancy having my opinions drowned in a sea of otherwise type-A gay men?

The type-A gay man only moves around in packs, in matching outfits (bespoke shirts and khaki pants) holding matching drinks ('*waituh*, get me an old fashioned, please).

Which brings me back to the focus group.

I arrive at the bistro with ten minutes to spare. I am surprisingly nervous (and also unsurprisingly hungover). My friend is a no-show. '*Family emergency,*' he texts in a hurry, when I send him a string of question marks on Whatsapp, swiftly disappearing off the grid for the next few hours. Ugh, these are four hours I will never get back. Anticipation and disappointment seldom go without the other, do they?

Cursing my friend's (conveniently timed) family emergency, I climb up the stairs to the loft-like bistro begrudgingly, expecting to walk into a room full of pompous, overconfident men in khaki pants, but instead …

There are only three other men.

There's **Forty-nine**, dressed in a crisp white shirt and tight black denims that automatically accentuate my interest in him; a reedy-looking stylist whom I've never officially met but know through Grindr; and looking terribly out of place … **Seven**, my video editor friend from three years ago. He smiles and waves at the sight of a familiar face.

I smile and wave back.

'Thank you all for making it,' **Forty-nine** says excitedly as I grab myself a seat, but I can sense a tone of disappointment. Was he expecting more people? Other people? Better people?

So we do what any group of self-respecting gay men would do: paint ourselves as the lone survivors of the dating apocalypse. 'Why don't we all just settle in, before I start asking you all the questions?'

His eagerness is not over-the-top; it's more over-the-counter, accessible, affordable and easy. If I ask politely, he'll wrap it up in a brown paper bag and let me take it home.

'Should we order drinks?'

Now we are talking. The stylist asks for a glass of sparkling water, the editor calls for a diet coke, and I get a *Cuba Libre*.

'So … what's the Indian dating scene like?' **Forty-nine** asks, as the waiter bustles to get our drink orders. He's asking the question to three single gay men who've consciously agreed to sacrifice their social calendar and meet him at his focus group. It's a Saturday evening.

And then, we jump right down to business. **Forty-nine** wants to create the 'LGBTQIA+ dating app of tomorrow', and for that he needs … the men of tomorrow.

That's the three of us.

I can see the joke write itself. Four Cis-gay men walking into a bar … to discuss the needs of the entire queer spectrum. In straight speak, that's like four able-bodied straight white men walking into a bar … to discuss the needs of all mankind.

Jokes apart, what's the dating app upgrade that we actually need? A filter to weed out emotionally unavailable men? An upvote feature that ranks people on recommendations left behind by past lovers and ex-boyfriends? Or something that gay men have been asking for years: a system that finally sorts men by their sexual preferences?

Suddenly, we are in the middle of a war zone. Most dating apps will say that they are queer-friendly, but ask any gay man and he'll tell you that it's routine to find the occasional straight woman (or the *occasionally* straight man) accidentally pop up on the home screens of your preferred app. Some people blame the algorithm. Some people blame the audience. But code or crowd-related glitches aside, one thing's for certain.

The average dating app will never really know what gay men want. But then again, does the average gay man know what he wants?

Some men want a man they can fall in love with. Some men want a fuckbuddy. Some men want a pal who'll hit the clubs with them. Some men want a wingman. Most men are looking for basic compatibility. Most men also lie.

'Okay, let me rephrase that … what are you looking for?' **Forty-nine** asks of us, looking eagerly across the table. No one wants to go first. How do I answer this question and sound self-effacing at the same time?

'An intellectual.' That's the stylist.

'Someone chill, probably?' that's **Seven** being himself.

'Maybe someone I am compatible with?' I say, like a liar. (We are all here with roles to play, clearly I am meant to provide comic relief).

The others look highly unconvinced. One of them yawns obviously.

Forty-nine, however, looks impressed. It's surprising that not one of us is smooth enough to throw the question back at him.

Compatibility is a funny word. What makes two queer-identifying men truly compatible? Can it be reduced to a checklist of traits, or worse, a series of convenient lies that we tell each other just so we can fall hopelessly in love the instant we lock eyes?

Love at first sight is a lie. There's no such thing as flying sparks, and if at any point in your life you see sparks flying, I'd advise you to step back and call the fire department. It's the same with compatibility.

I am compatible with men who ~~like open bars~~ have an open outlook on life; I am attracted to men who leave their shirts open at the beach. Sure, we all want to end up with honest, good-natured men who fed us gluten-free pancakes every morning, but if things don't work out the night before, most of us will throw the gift horse away. Men have been conditioned to believe that fireworks in the bedroom will translate to fireworks IRL. Yet, sexual chemistry has nothing to do with compatibility, but compatibility has everything to do with sexual chemistry (and preferences). One is a subset of the other. Two negatives might make a positive, but two bottoms don't make a top.

Does that make compatibility a myth – utter hogwash we've been spoon-fed so that (the less fortunate) single men don't feel sorry for themselves? After all, there's a better ring to 'maybe you are single because you haven't found someone you are compatible with', as opposed to 'maybe you are single because you haven't managed to turn anyone on.'

No one wants a dose of *that* medicine. Which is why we lie to ourselves. Which is why we usually end up with anyone who would ~~not hate to be with us~~ have us. Which is why in the span of the last two hours, we've spent a considerable time sizing each other up, instead of addressing the main reason we are here. Is this a focus group or an audition for a boyfriend?

It's safe to say that no compatibility tests have been taken; no dating app can remedy that situation. Instead, we've all been preening our feathers; in fact, I've only casually referenced my blog thrice. We are all here to play the game, but it's obvious that there's a clear winner.

The good news? I don't know it yet, but in exactly a fortnight from now, **Forty-nine** will ask me out for drinks in the garb of a work email. I'll blush and instantly say yes.

The bad news? After four happy months of blissful togetherness, we'll decide to call things off because of one glaring problem.

We'll find out that we are *highly* incompatible in bed.

9

Maybe It's Love, Actually

9.1. The Single's Guide to Settling In

Is It Finally Time to Be Exclusive?

Nine long chapters in, you've found what (we think) you were looking for.

Stability. In fact, you've gone past the basics of being in a relationship: you find every pore on his body incredibly sexy, laugh at the silliest of his jokes, finish his half-eaten sandwich and crave a whiff of his perfume every morning when you wake up. You drool all over each other and store your love in pictures on your phone and empty condom wrappers. You go on a date. You go on two. You go on a dozen. You go on a gazillion dates.

It's going really well, you think to yourself, as you finish the sandwich from before. In fact, it can't get any better than this.

But … are you in love? More importantly, is he your (much discussed) One from chapter 4? And *even* more importantly, is it time to take the plunge and be exclusive?

If you are crazy about your ~~boyfriend~~ partner, but not sure whether you've stepped into the right end of the pool, here are ten signs that suggest that you've comfortably settled in.

1. **You know you'll survive the fight.**

It could be a scuffle over not switching the lights off when you leave the room. A rant about not flushing the toilet. A tiff over who ate the last chicken-and-coriander dumpling. A fight about why he didn't reply to your thirty-two texts. A full-blown war over why his friends don't like you.

Every time you have a row, a part of you breaks away but you don't break it off. (You'd break his favourite vase, but that's another story.)

2. **Friday nights are settling.**

You crave to unwind with Chinese takeout and binge-watch Netflix in your pyjamas until you slowly transcend to cat videos on the internet. At some point, you'll pass out with your glass of wine, but it won't leave any stains on your rug. You'll wake up on Saturday morning without a hangover, and with a man who's still in bed with you (and not sneaking out with your wallet and phone in the middle of the night).

Goodbye, nights of drug-fuelled debauchery. Hello, world of domestic bliss.

3. **You give up looking for red flags.**

Everybody comes with a red flag or two. Some even come with half a dozen. Look at it this way: every time you meet someone new, you collect a new flag. Hates children? Can't commit? Likes Kim Kardashian? Went to jail? Loves mint-flavoured Oreos? There's one for each of them. Soon, you have enough red flags to start your own souvenir shop.

When you finally find someone you love, you shut shop, sell it off to the trade union and enjoy a couple's trip to the Andaman Islands.

4. **The sex is great, but the sangria after is even better.**

You might have an alcohol problem, but if you choose to dress up after your post-coital smoke and head out for brunch with him rather than scuttle over to your house and never see each other again, you've got yourselves a winner.

Seize the moment and capture as much of this phase as you can, because you are going to need it when you are older.

5. **You don't think twice about going out of your way for him.**

Even if it means going and picking him up at the airport. At 3 a.m. in the morning. When you stay two hours away and have to change two modes of transport to get there. And it's pouring. Especially when he could have called for an Uber.

But you are there nevertheless, with a big 'welcome back' sign and a bigger smile.

6. **You get jealous.**

You get jealous of his closest friend. You get jealous of the bartender who smiles at him when he's off getting you drinks at the bar. You get jealous of his pet cat. Sometimes, you even get jealous of his phone.

You get jealous not in the 'crazy-don't-you-dare-talk-to-my-man' way, but in the endearing 'I-see-some-potential-here-so-give-me-some-space-with-him' way.

7. **You make plans to move in.**

You've made all the right moves till now, and you've officially reached move day.

Your toothbrush joins his, and your hair products find their own little sweet spot in his shower cabinet. Your socks get tangled with his, your underwear finds its own intimate drawer, and you even find your side of the bed.[15] You are just moments away from getting matching towels. As you unpack and spread your life all over his, applaud. This is where the rollercoaster begins.

8. **You see yourself with him ten years later.**

It's not surprising that you see him in your (bleak, but considerably bright) future, sitting with you in your garden-facing balcony with cups of tea and the Sunday crossword.

Or you could be talking about how great it is to finally be able to take a trip to the moon, because that's totally going to be a thing.

9. **You finally delete Grindr.**

When you finally pull the plug and delete your Grindr profile (so that there's no going back), you know you're one step closer to the endgame. There's no bigger sacrifice than saying goodbye to the neuroscientist-turned-billboard-model two rows down in your saved favourites.

10. **You make fun of this book together.**

Because you don't really need it any more. Now pass it on to someone else.

Just kidding. Read it till the very end. The best is yet to come.

Number Fifty: The Expat: Is an Open House Reason for an Open Relationship?

November 2013

Over a home-cooked meal of baked fish with parsley, **Fifty**, a French expatriate living in a mansion in a wealthy suburb, tells me about growing up in the vineyards of Bordeaux. I am really sorry, but his

15 The one that doesn't face the window.

monologue on countryside living isn't ~~worth filling up the pages of this book~~ very inspiring. I have more important things on my mind at the moment.

His mansion. It's so exquisite.

'Don't you feel alone in this big home?' I flirt dangerously, eyeing the French windows and the art-deco furnishings. I could live here, I think to myself (but I'd probably change the upholstery, because it's too … *opulent*).

'I have a boyfriend back home,' he tells me casually, and my blueprints wither away. 'We are in an open relationship.'

Newsflash, readers. An open relationship is a relationship between two people who believe that fidelity is fluid – one person does not *own* the other, and they are free to flirt, date and/or even hook up with other people should they wish to, usually with full disclosure.

But what if he falls in love with someone else? Or falls out of love with the far-away boyfriend? I ask. He laughs. An open relationship opens up so many opportunities. It's a DIY kit for adding some spice to long-term romances.

Another newsflash, readers. See, an open relationship isn't just a substitute for an open house – doors left ajar and minds left open. In fact, the doors are double-sealed, padlocked and password-protected with boundaries and mutual trust. Plus, it is all reinforced by laying down some ground rules.

Otherwise, it's just cheating. **Fifty** and his (unnamed) partner have clearly thought it through. They have clauses of course – no emotional entanglements involved.

And what about … sexual entanglements?

I feel his hand slide into mine. He looks me straight in the eyes and smiles.

A year later, he sends me a letter from his vineyard. I don't open it.

9.2. Where Does Your Partner Fall on the Boyfriend Scale?

Answer these seventeen questions to find out how high the 'love of your life' falls on the boyfriend scale.

1. **On a typical Sunday afternoon, you'd find your boyfriend:**
   a. Reading you a book.
   b. Reading a book, while beside you.
   c. Coaxing you to join him in bed.
   d. Setting up a threesome on Grindr.

2. **When you tell him that you need space, he promptly:**
   a. Buys you a first-class ticket to Paris.
   b. Makes a joke about being an astronaut, but lets you be.
   c. Leaves and waits for you to text him the all-clear.
   d. Breaks up with you.

3. **In a minor argument, he brings up:**
   a. Nothing. But he does bring out a tub of your favourite ice cream as a peace offering.
   b. The thing about you that annoys him the most.
   c. Your ex – your sore spot.
   d. His ex – your bigger sore spot.

4. **For a quick getaway, you both plan to head to:**
   a. Paris.
   b. A secluded beach that is a two-hour drive away.
   c. The neighbourhood mall.
   d. Your bedroom.

5. **When he's trying to be cute, he tells you that you look like:**
   a. Yourself. Because that's how he likes you best.
   b. Your favourite celebrity.
   c. His favourite celebrity.
   d. Your neighbour's pit bull.

6. **In his phone gallery, you'll find:**
   a. You wouldn't know, because you haven't felt the need to check it.
   b. Lots of boring photos, including some that include you.
   c. Screenshots of his conversations with you.
   d. Dick pics. That don't belong to him.

7. **His idea of a casual date for the weekend would be:**
   a. Whisking you off to the hills for a panoramic lunch by the Himalayas.
   b. Brunch at your favourite restaurant, with endless mimosas and endless hand-holding.
   c. A movie followed by two tacos and a soda to share. Dessert (among other things) at home after.
   d. Four hours of NSA sex.

8. **At 8:30 p.m., he's:**
   a. With you.
   b. Talking to you.
   c. Doing this own thing, who knows?
   d. MIA for the past week, with a 'last seen at 8:29 p.m.'

9. **The last time you had a real heartfelt conversation with him was:**
   a. Today. It felt like a Pablo Neruda poem.
   b. Two days ago, after a particularly memorable date.
   c. What's a heartfelt conversation like?
   d. Does having him send you a dick pic count?

10. **You plan a hypothetical threesome with a celebrity. Your boyfriend chooses:**
    a. No one. He can't think of anyone to share you with.
    b. Ryan Gosling. Have you seen those perfect cheekbones and those kind eyes?
    c. Ranveer Singh, in red underwear.
    d. Hypothetical? He's already in bed with two guys. Not including you.

11. **You run into his friends while out on a date, and he:**
    a. Blushes and introduces you as his boyfriend.
    b. Nonchalantly tells them that you are a friend.
    c. Says that you are a second cousin who's visiting from out of town.
    d. Pretends that you don't exist.

12. **Conversations about your future are:**
    a. What made you pick up this book.
    b. A work-in-progress novel.
    c. Almost non-existent.
    d. What future?

13. **It's your birthday, and your significant other is out of town. What does he do?**
    a. Flies down to surprise you, complete with fireworks and a seven-member jazz ensemble to serenade you all day.
    b. Calls you at midnight and couriers you a care package.
    c. Wishes you on Facebook and sends you a dick pic as a secret treat.
    d. Forgets it's your birthday.

14. **On average, he messages you:**
    a. Every few minutes. In fact, you had to pause taking this quiz because you were replying to his text.
    b. You wake up to a good morning text and put yourself to sleep to a good night ping.
    c. Once a day.
    d. Once every week, usually at midnight. Especially when he's alone. More so when he's horny.

15. **When he says he wants to 'spend the night in', he means:**
    a. He wants to spend on takeout and watch Netflix with you.
    b. He wants to not spend.
    c. He wants to spend it *in* you.
    d. He wants to spend it alone.

16. **The last time you guys hung out, he took a cute picture of the two of you. What does he do with it?**
    a. Prints it out and sends it to you through snail mail, attached with a love note.
    b. Puts it up on Instagram with a heartwarming caption. Counts the likes and tells you about it.
    c. Lets the picture rot away in his archive of spam emails, forgotten contacts and undeleted messages.
    d. Threatens to out you to your parents and the police using the photograph as evidence. Blackmails you for money, and then uses it to holiday with his actual boyfriend. Who's twice as hot as you are.

17. **A song that describes how you feel about him:**
    a. 'Home' by Edward Sharpe and the Magnetic Zeros
    b. 'Best Day of My Life' by American Authors
    c. 'Hit The Road Jack!' by Ray Charles
    d. 'Someone Like You' by Adele

Mostly As:

If there ever were Academy Award nominations for boyfriends, the Type A lover would sweep through all the categories. He's like the Meryl Streep of boyfriends – adaptable and charming – and so perfect he could be Leonardo Fibonacci's golden ratio.

But that also makes him equally intimidating, and you'd always be left wondering if this is all just one big act for him. The truth is that you'd never be able to match up to all his whims and quirks, like that one time he flew you off to Amritsar because you were craving butter chicken. A relationship with the 'Type A' will only end in resentment and receipts for gifts you could never afford.

Mostly Bs:

The Type B isn't Disney-level perfect, but he does have the credentials to star in his own Netflix original (He'll probably be played by Vikrant Massey). The Type B might be flawed and might never know the right things to say, but that's perfect because it means he'll definitely call you out on your shit when he needs to. Remember, the perfect boyfriend isn't the man who puts you up on the pedestal; it's the man who helps you climb on to it.

Mostly Cs:

We might not be there yet, but you still have to tread with caution with this one. The 'C type' is a ticking time bomb that sways dangerously between 'I am going to make this work' and 'Oh my god, how do I get out of this?'

At the end of the day, remember that Mr C (no last name) is only one petty fight away from spilling the contents of your heart all over the floor.

Mostly Ds:

There's a reason you bought this book. Now dump him, and read on.

Number Fifty-one: The Actor
Am I a Background Character in My Own Love Story?

July 2013

A stormy July night. The clouds are heavier than a Naipaul novel. It's almost 11 p.m. And he's *almost* here. I am sitting at my favourite coffee shop; only this time, I am living another day, with yet another man. Another man who is late, another man who loses a crucial brownie point. Just when I feel like I've been stood up, someone taps me on my shoulder. It's *him*.

'Did I keep you waiting?' He smiles like they do in the movies. It's shy but unsettling. I smile back at him. **Fifty-one** is impishly cute, with short hair and a trimmed stubble that looks like the reason he's so late. Who cares about brownie points anyway?

'Can we order something? I am famished,' he says to me. **Fifty-one** runs a production house by day, attends combined training classes in the evening, and sweats it out at the gym at night. Like a lot of gay men, he does not have the time (or calories) to spare for unnecessary cups of coffee. I push my emptying mug away.

Fifteen minutes later, over a second cup of cappuccino and a dry sandwich, he tells me he wants to be an actor. Should I be surprised? Should I laud him for having larger-than-life dreams? Should I walk away and cry myself to sleep?

'Why do so many attractive gay men want to try their hand at modelling?' asked no one ever.

'Sounds fascinating.' I giggle a little too loudly.

A second cup of cappuccino always makes me spritzy.

'Are you making fun of me?'

Uh-oh. Emotions run high on first dates. There's always that one thing that you say that determines whether you pick up the tab for the night, or pick up the boy instead. I try to steer the conversation away from the former. These coffees aren't buying themselves.

But *what* about his production house? Is he planning to shut it down?

'Are you mad?' he scoffs. (I don't say anything. Any man who questions my sanity rises higher in my lust list.) It's too early to decide anything, he tells me. Until he finds his big break, he's going to shuffle between the business and the auditions, just like how I'm shuffling between whether I like him or not.

The former shouldn't be too difficult: gay men are quite adept at handling double lives, and **Fifty-one** seems like a professional. The latter will take more time.

Or another cappuccino.

'I still don't know whether I am cut out to be an actor,' he says. 'There's no shortage of good-looking men in the city, do you know what I mean?'

Cue for me to feed his insecurities. It's a common dating tactic in the city. When things seem bleak, go straight for the *piece de resistance*.

'I don't think a handsome man like you should have a problem,' I half-lie. He's good looking, but he's not good looking *enough*.

'Yeah, I agree, but I still need to work on my art.' He shrugs it off, and my self-worth nosedives.

What else did I expect? A tennis game of compliments? A sudden declaration of love? This isn't a movie scene, and neither of us is a movie star. The lights change for the rest of the ~~scene~~ night. He drones on about his weekend classes at a top acting school (the second-best in the city) as I nod like a puppet. Midway through his monologue on the nuances of method acting, I realize that the curtains are closing.

'So … what do you think?'

Do I tell him that he's going to be a successful actor? He could play the hero's best friend or younger brother, but a self-made superstar with a duplex in the boroughs of Bandra? Not really. There are thousands of others like him – hopeful, fresh-faced boys, with dreams that can't be sold in cartons. Boys with handsome faces but not the good looks of a movie star, each trying to make their mark and stand out in a sea of too-pretty-to-be-true men. Nonetheless, a sea I would not mind taking a dip in.

'How about I help you practise your lines for now?'

Dreams can always be crushed later. Being ~~the best~~ a better version of yourself on the first date is a classic date move. He tells me that we can begin by reading lines for an Indian adaptation of Oedipus that's due next week.

He plays the protagonist. I play everyone else.

9.3 What Happens after 'Happily Ever After'?

Rohit, a business consultant from New York, met his husband when he was twenty-four years old. Hours into a special LGBTQIA+ Holi party on a crisp March night, they locked eyes over a jazzy Bollywood number.

'It felt simple, the spontaneity,' Rohit tells me on chat. 'Ravi asked me for dinner the very next day, and I said yes.'

When did he know it was for the long run?

'Immediately. I had hardly expected to meet someone who would understand my journey as a brown, gay and immigrant man, and here he was, someone who understood all three. We didn't have to explain ourselves to each other; we found home.'

The proposal happened years later, over a quick Euro trip (Rohit's first) during the summer. The question was popped over a bottle of Veuve Clicquot in their hotel room in the middle of Champ-Elysees. They shared half a dozen macarons after and celebrated at a gay bar with go-go dancers all night long.

'What has marriage been like?' I ask.

'When we were getting into it, it was for very practical reasons, even though we knew that we were in it for the long haul. Marriage gave us legal guarantees of [hospital] visitations, inheritance and partnership that we wanted. People treat our relationship with greater weight and respect, now that the government sanctions it. Also, there's certainly a greater degree of closeness that comes with making vows. Inviting seventy of your closest friends to come dance the night away – that is hard to describe. '

They both seem content with their lives. Ravi runs a bar in Philadelphia today, and they plan to raise puppies in a world that is both peaceful and inclusive. It's a wonderful plan for their future. I feel a dull ache in my chest as I type out my goodbyes, but I know it's only the beginning.

Marriage, children and a house with an attached terrace might not necessarily be the dream for a lot of gay men any more (I'd prefer a sea-facing studio apartment and a long-distance relationship any day), but my friends, Bikram and Wren, share a similar story across the Atlantic.

Twenty-seven-year-old Bikram is an environmental scientist based in Switzerland. Wren is a Human Rights consultant. They both save the world when they are not saving each other from all its problems.

Their first date was a disastrous dinner at home. Bikram turns a beetroot red when he thinks about it even today. 'I word-vomited through three courses of dinner. Somewhere over the entrée, I thought I would never see him again.'

Bikram found it embarrassing. Wren found it endearing.

Two years later, they moved in together.

They decided to get married while on a walk one wintery evening. There was no grand declaration of love. No rings in champagne glasses. No elevator ride on the Eiffel tower. No planetarium full of stars. No macarons, and definitely no go-go dancers.

It just made sense; it was one of those things that had to be done; the end of one journey, the beginning of another. They didn't exchange conventional rings; instead, they opted for toe rings at a traditional Indian ceremony months later. Their parents cried, hugs were exchanged and a new family was made.

'Have things changed?' I ask. His voice crackles. It's the bane of long-distance phone calls. I press the phone closer to my ear. Bad reception can be worse than a bad relationship.

'Do you know what being in a relationship is like? Being married is no different. We just have a piece of paper now that lets us address the other as a husband.' That sounds fair enough, but does that mean they do the crossword on Sundays?

'We don't *need* to do things together. We still lead our lives the way we used to.' Bikram prefers trance; Wren likes his classical music. They both like chocolate ice cream.

'Finding your happily-ever-after is not about finding someone who completes you; it's about finding someone who lets you be. Being accepted for who you are is a powerful aphrodisiac. Do you know what I mean?'

I actually don't. I've been a train wreck of bad decisions, failed relationships, and boys who never text me back. I'm this ~~long confession~~ book you're reading.

But wait; is there *no* jigsaw puzzle to be completed?

Only on Sundays, by the fireplace. Sometimes they even bake a cake.

I am only slightly disappointed, but both couples are still surprisingly happy. Their families accept their decision and speak to each other on the phone every other weekend. They shop for groceries, cook dinner, do laundry and watch repeat telecasts of *Seinfeld* on television. There's no drama, just domestic bliss.

It's happening! Men are getting married to each other, and society isn't crumbling!

The cake does though – the one that they bake on Sundays. But they genuinely seem to enjoy their delightfully boring routines.

The thing about fairy tales is that we never know what happens after 'happily ever after'. Stories end with grand weddings, but there's no epilogue to tell us what happens next. Sometimes they come up with a sequel, but they skip past the settling in and head straight to the next big bad – heroes and heroines fighting it out, rather than fighting each other. Fairy tales never have time for the everyday and the ordinary. But neither do we.

It's important not to forget that my friends also live in countries where gay men enjoy the same basic rights as other people – the option to make your vows or break them. Marriage equality in such countries hasn't just changed the reality for gay men, it has also tamed romance. It isn't as nuanced as Disney makes it out to be, they all tell me.

Gay marriage in India might be a faraway fairytale concept. (Side note: Being gay in India in 2021 is like being gay in Europe in the '70s.) We still have a long way to go before we reach our own versions of matrimonial mediocrity. It might take time to reach that point where we can bake a cake together over the weekend, but it doesn't mean it won't happen.

It might take a year. It might take a decade. It might take two. Until that day, I raise a glass to all the grooms in the world and know that if the day comes when I decide to (and more importantly, have the legal right to) get married, I'd want red velvet cake with cream cheese frosting at my wedding …

… and preferably a groom who doesn't run away before I do.

Number Fifty-two and Fifty-three: The First Couple Strangers in the Midnight – Three's Company Two?

July 2013

I meet **Fifty-two** and **Fifty-three**, both media men, at the end of a cocktail soiree. We are all waiting for our cabs, making small talk till we take our drunken selves back home. They've just finished telling me the adorable story of how they met. It involved half a quarter of rum, misplaced keys and a clueless friend's suitcase.

'Does that mean I need a friend's suitcase to find a boyfriend?' I ask, and we all giggle the way silly drunken men do at the end of cocktail soirees.

'Our cab's almost here,' the casting director tells his partner, as our giggles die down. It's a cold night, and they are huddled together. I look at them here, and yet, I feel so far away.

On cue, I look down at my phone screen. My cab is still nine minutes away.

As I loiter on my phone, **Fifty-two** grabs his boyfriend by the waist and gently kisses his cheek. There are some whispers, and they burst into another fit of giggles. I've never felt more out of place. A third wheel, perhaps. Maybe this is what I've been looking for all this while – a sense of belonging.

Their cab is here.

'Can we ask you a question?' **Fifty-three** asks, and they look at each other expectantly. Here it comes, I sigh. It's going to be yet another 'Why are you still single?' – the eternal backhanded compliment. I've heard that question so many times; the answer pops up as a suggestion whenever I am texting. But instead …

'Why don't we drop you on our way back home?'

Oh, that's sweet of them. Maybe this is the kind of kinship I need in my life. Maybe I've been looking at companionship all wrong.

'… Or maybe you could join us for a threesome?'

Oh kinship, all right.

Number Fifty-four: The Writer
Is a Long-Distance Relationship Worth the Long Shot?

My first date with **Fifty-four** does not start on a very nice note. For starters, the writer shows up ninety minutes late, and by then, I am already drunk on four long island iced teas. He mutters a dozen apologies when he eventually makes it, and I accidentally touch his crotch, misinterpreting his handshake for a hug. While I mutter a dozen apologies, he orders himself a drink. After all that, it only gets consistently worse.

The next four hours are a series of unfortunate events, the highlights of which include:

1. Having half our order spilt all over us by an extremely enthusiastic waiter.
2. Being rudely interrupted by an acquaintance who runs into us at the bar and then decides to join us for the rest of the night.
3. A misplaced credit card.
4. The grand reveal that the reason for **Fifty-four**'s delay was the fact that he was 'helping his best friend brainstorm for his new startup', a man who turns out to be **Twenty-six**, the fresh-faced food blogger I shamelessly ghosted four years ago.

To cap it all off, we end the night by being refused entry at a private bar opening, the tickets to which I forgot on my bed stand back home. In the history of bad first dates, this would top the charts. 'But one bad date doesn't mean anything, right?' you ask aloud, already regretting buying this book.

No, it doesn't. A bad first date is no measure of any hypothetical relationship's expiry date. As long as there's a second date, first impressions can always get a do-over.

But we don't have the time for a second date. **Fifty-four** is visiting from Delhi, and has a flight back home in forty-eight hours. Any hypothetical relationship we may (or may not) have is doomed right from the beginning. Which is a pity, because this is a beautiful man – the nave of his slender neck, the frescoes of his sparkling eyes, the rib vaults on his lean, muscled back and his gentle, engulfing arms, flaying like flying buttresses – and all he needs is a pigeon to roost, and he'd be complete.

'This night could have gone a lot better, right?'

I go in for a handshake – steering clear of his crotch – but he pulls me in a tight hug. His hair smells like honeysuckle. 'How do you know what honeysuckle smells like?' he asks. Sometimes, I think I break the fourth wall too often. As he walks away, I wave dejectedly at the best date I'll never have. Oh well, at least I tried.

And yet, we successfully make it to the one-month mark.

Over the past few weeks, we've furiously texted every day, forwarding and tagging each other in memes, posts and whatnots. 'Why do we need to conform?' we snigger, as we send each other naughty GIFs every night.

We create our own language of love: a slippery string of emojis and emoticons, each with their own secret origins. A clown emoji that means this, a thunderbolt emoticon that means that. An octopus emoji that means this, a shooting star emoticon that means that. This, that, this, that, unsaid words, unspoken feelings.

Him, me, me, him. It's flirting 2.0.

A long-distance relationship comes with its own set of hurdles, and the real hard work starts once the dust settles. Falling in love isn't really simple; because if it were, you'd meet and fall in love with someone who stays a stone throw's away. Instead we *choose* to make it difficult. The thing about the human heart is that it sees no parameter when it comes to love; distance is a mere social construct. Keeping the spark alive is a challenge, sure – but in this case, it also comes at the added cost of frequent flight tickets.

Fifty-four is the nice kind of nice – not boring, not dull, not 'eh', not a book that you'd keep away after twenty pages or a movie that you would speed through so that you reach the end credits. He's one of those men. A puppy dog. A panda. A koala bear. A pony. But don't worry; he's not a petting zoo.

One would expect constant sparring – with two writers on board – but this is a dance. We don't just finish each other's sentences; we also *help* finish each other's sentences.

But first, we have to finish this personality test.

Q. It's his birthday weekend! How do I prove myself as a great boyfriend?

a. Fly out to meet him and throw him a surprise birthday party.
b. Get all his friends to send video bits to create a mix-tape of feelings.
c. Send him a care package.
d. Forget about it and send him a text last minute.

The average dating guide would tell you to pull out the big guns to make a long-distance relationship work. 'Go the long distance *for* the long distance', they'd sell it with clickbait. There's no space for humdrumness. Book an impromptu flight ticket to see them. Ship sixteen dozen roses to their doorsteps (one for each day that you've known each other). Write a song and produce a music video. The works.

But this is no average dating guide. Spontaneous acts of love are tough acts to follow. You want your relationship to simmer with a slow burn, not stew over. Which means you want to be … reliable. You want to be there when it counts.

He's overjoyed with the gifts I send over (two of my favourite books express-delivered to his doorstep, and a personalized love poem express scheduled to his email inbox).

'I wish you were here,' he tells me when I call him at midnight, 'my friends would have loved to meet you.' I can hear laughter in the background.

'I wish I was there too.'

Clown emoji. Thunderbolt. Thunderbolt. Shooting star emoticon. Octopus. Exit right.

Writers. Always knowing the right things to say.

Q. But … are we boyfriends?

a. Obviously.
b. Not yet, but we are on our way.
c. We are just two dudes hanging out, no pressure.
d. What?

'Never worry about labels when you are aiming for the long run.' The average dating guide would *also* tell you. Sure, jumping the gun to define a relationship can seem slightly tacky, but when you are literally lining up your calendars to see each other, your relationship needs definite parameters. Are you dating? Are you exclusive? Are you dating but also flirting with other people on the side? It's tougher being breezy when you only get to see each once every month.

That means you need to fast-forward through all the pleasantries when you are looking to get serious with someone who stays hundreds (or thousands) of kilometres away. Decide where you stand. It can be anywhere on the spectrum of relationship definitions. Boyfriends? Sure. Casually flirting? Definitely. Two men who live far away but speak to each other every day? Yes, please. Guys looking to hang but also bang occasionally? Bring it on. Just know that you need to set boundaries now, so that your hearts don't go astray later.

Sadly, I am not one to heed my own dating advice. 'Let's not shackle ourselves with definition.' We giggle at each other over texts, deciding to play it cool. 'Who needs to label this?' We laugh as we send each other memes. 'Why do we need to conform?' We snigger as we send naughty GIFs to each other every other night.

Clown emoji. Thunderbolt. Thunderbolt. Shooting star emoticon. Exit right. It's all fun and games over the next month, up until that one fateful Wednesday afternoon, when…

Q. He's caught me right in the middle of an important deadline. What do I do?

a. Shut my laptop and get on the call right away.
b. Send him an emergency text and call him back right after.
c. Text a few hours later telling him I was busy.
d. Not return his call for a week.

Sounds like the reasonable thing to do, doesn't it? Sure, communication is key for any long-distance dalliance, but the best thing about living in the digital age is that nobody's really far away. We are all – worryingly – always in touch. Feeling bored? Send a WhatsApp. Feeling bored but don't want your read receipts on? Send a text. Feeling pretty? Send a Skype invite. Feeling horny? Send a Snapchat. As long as they're up for it, any new relationship milestone is only a text away.

Clown emoji. Thunderbolt. Shooting star emoticon. Exit right.

Yes, our texts have been sporadic these past few weeks – mostly bitmojis and emoticons – but for now, I am acing this personality test. I am just about to pat myself on my back, when…

Q. He follows up with a passive-aggressive text that goes along the lines of 'Wow. You are always busy when I text.' How should I respond?

a. Take a deep breath and ignore his tone.
b. Get passive-aggressive in turn.
c. Reply with a 'K'.
d. Don't reply at all.

No. That's his actual text: 'Wow. You are always busy when I text.' Trust a writer to never leave space for subtext. 'I am so sorry.' I text back. Clown emoji. Thunderbolt. Shooting star emoticon. Exit right.

'Yeah. I guess so.' No smiley faces. No clown emojis. Not even a single thunderbolt.

I find myself mildly annoyed. He mildly accuses me of always being busy. I mildly accuse him of not having a deadline to work on. He mildly accuses me of never having time for him. I mildly accuse him of not giving me any space. He mildly accuses me of being too pragmatic. I mildly accuse him of being too dramatic.

'K.'

'Thumbs up emoji.'

'Smiley face.'

And just like that, we get into our first fight.

Q. Three days later, and the tension levels are slowly simmering down. How do we get past this?

a. Pretend everything's okay.
b. Talk about it.
c. Pull the plug abruptly.
d. Decide to end things together.

There's been a paradigm shift in our conversation, and I can sense we are ~~walking~~ texting on eggshells around each other. For the untrained eye, we could be politely discussing the weather over tea. But each text is laced with conversational arsenic.

'When will you be free?' *clown emoji*. 'Whenever you want me to be.' *Thunderbolt*. 'Call me then.' *Smiley face*. 'Okay.' *Smiley face*. Exit right.

Q. A fortnight on, he suggests we should plan a trip to rekindle our spark. What do I say to that?

a. Jump at the idea and tell him I am coming to meet him.
b. Jump at the idea and tell him that he should come meet me.
c. Jump at the idea and decide to meet at a vacation hotspot midway.
d. Seem disinterested.

'Why don't you plan a trip? I ask him, secretly hoping that he's busy for the next few months. But here's the thing: if someone's looking forward to seeing you, and you cancel on them, it can be shattering. Maybe I should stop being so hard on him-

'Are you completely sure?' he asks. The word is italicized.

No emojis follow for a few seconds.

'Smiley face.'

I find myself mildly annoyed again.

Q. He makes a standing offer to fly down next month. Do I want him to show up?

a. Oh yes.
b. **Sound enthusiastic, but also be vague about timing.**
c. Oh no, please don't.
d. Stop replying.

'Yeah, but don't stress yourself.' I lie.

I send a thunderbolt, but he doesn't reply.

Q. A month on, things seem to have calmed down, but we might be hitting a dead-end. What do we do next?

a. **Embrace the humdrum**.
b. Get bored and end things.
c. Try my luck elsewhere.
d. Stop replying.

As things return to normalcy, we message each other with a newfound vigour – but our texts are politer; more formal. The long-standing invitation to fly down to visit me has been long forgotten. Our conversations are banal now, frequent bulletins of our daily routines. Without our constant streams of emoji-driven endearment, I realize that most of our texts lack the basic requisite. Emotional depth.

'How are you?'

'I am good, you?'

'Fine, I'll talk to you later.'

'Sure.'

A Mobius strip that we repeat day in and day out.

There are no emojis left in this conversation.

Q. How does this story end?

a. We make it work, and thankfully, are still together.
b. We have a nasty fight that ends in a toxic break-up.
c. I ghost him.
d. He ghosts him.

Surprisingly, we chose none of these options.

We should be talking about this prolonged separation and whether we can handle it. We should be talking about whether we want to take it to the next level. We should be moving forward in the same direction, if not moving to the same city together.

Instead, we text each other less and less frequently, until we fade out of each other's chat histories, and eventually, each other's lives.

No emojis survive in the end.

And neither do we.

10

The Happily Queer After

Number Fifty-five and Fifty-six: The Second Couple
Can We Be Friends with(out) Benefits?

March 2018

I am panting.

'Do you need some help for the final stretch?' **Fifty-five** asks, popping out from behind me. He's grinning, his face shining brighter than the sun.

'I can't … go … so … fast …' I pant, and he laughs. On cue, **Fifty-six** shows up. Great, now it's time to embarrass myself in front of not one, but two attractive men.

'Just a little bit more …' says one of them.

'Yeah, it'll be worth it …' says the other.

I can't tell their voices apart because I am currently clutching at the stitches on the sides of my stomach.

'Meet us at the other end of the park?' they yell in unison before sprinting into the sunset. We've just finished running a 10K, and I couldn't have been less prepared.

Why would anyone choose to go on a running date, you'd ask? Who wants a potential fling in track pants? When is sweat *ever* attractive? Can you really be your gorgeous self as you gasp for air?

But this little excursion … *isn't* a date. It's a group hang.

I met **Fifty-five**, an academic trainer for an NGO, and his partner, an IT consultant, only a fortnight ago on Grindr. They were looking for friends; I was looking for an excuse not to roll my eyes. I look at men on Grindr looking for friends the same way I look at brands on Instagram looking for a free shout out: with complete disdain.

But our couple here is different. They are actually here for friends *without* benefits. They met each other only two years ago when they randomly bumped into each other mere days after **Fifty-five** broke up with his vicious ex, but thankfully, that's been the only bump along the way.

They have a lovely apartment in which they cohabit, two sets of loving parents that coexist, and jobs that cooperate when they go on extended vacations together. They've taken four of those in the past three months.

Three of them were out of the country.

I am only *mildly* jealous. I've spent the last two hours watching them order coffees for each other, laugh at inside jokes and steal quick kisses when no one's watching. Why is their life so perfect – with their beaming faces that won't sweat buckets after running a 10K across the promenade?

Meanwhile, my face is melting down my sides into the gaps of my oversized trainers. Sometimes, life just isn't fair.

'Do you want to get a post-workout drink back at ours?' they ask.

Here it is. The sneaky invite to get me back to their pad. Just when I thought they only wanted to hang. If I had a rupee for every single time I've been disappointed by a gay couple that doesn't practise monogamy. Sue me for being judgemental. I never said I was a beacon of perfection.

'Sure,' I say, never one to pass on a free drink.

Yet, forty-five minutes later, no moves are made. They sprawl over their modest sofa, and I sit meekly by myself in the corner on an armchair. Our drinks have been chugged and complimented (is that a fennel emulsion in your gin?), and they've stretched their sore muscles for the world (mostly me) to see. It feels like I'm moments away from being asked to take a picture of them playing the perfect couple.

And then I realize they aren't looking for a threesome.

All they needed was a third wheel.

10.1 The Ten Kinds of Friends That Make Every Gay Man's Crew

Gay men are collectors. They collect right swipes on Tinder, V-necks from clearance sales, loyalty points at the bar, and sometimes, they even collect friends.

As we live our fabulous lives, we collect friends like we collect favourites on dating apps – greedily. You have friends you unwind with, friends that wind you up and even some friends who flake on you faster than the wind in a storm (that would be me). People come and people go, but some stay till the very end, or till last call, whichever is more convenient. Those are the ones that matter; the ones you make unfulfilled vacation plans with. Why so?

Because a gay man's friends (especially in the Indian context) are his family. In a country that's burdened with societal stigma and traditional values, your friend circle becomes an extension of your support system. With issues such as neglect, isolation, abuse, confinement, abuse and discrimination, queer folk from various backgrounds have had to redefine the role of their family. We can create meaningful bonds with people through one single thing.

Your personal choice. Presenting, your **chosen family** – people you choose to embrace, nurture, love and support, regardless of blood, marriage and DNA strands. Irrespective of the kind of gay man you are, you'll realize that this chosen family you've fostered is more important than anything else you've come looking for in this book.

So round up your friends in your head and place them in the following categories.

The Woman

'I don't usually adhere to stereotypes, but this is the one stereotype I approve of,' you'll speak fondly of the *Woman* to anyone who'd listen. It's a relationship you embrace with open arms. Have you dissed each other's exes as you downed shots of Ciroc? *Check*. Made fun of someone you mutually hate over several scrolls worth of Whatsapp messages? *Check*. Proclaimed your undying love for each other every alternate date? *Check*.

You'll be a great friend to a lot of people, but to her, you'll always be her everyday guy. Her crown jewel. Her 4 a.m. friend. Her little pet. Her therapist. Her punching bag. Her shopping cart. Her grocery list. And occasionally, even her prescription reminder. It won't be a problem, because she'll most certainly be all those things for you as well.

Fair warning: If you're the kind of gay man who's reading this book, you probably have more than one *Woman* in your repository. But don't feel guilty just yet.

She probably has more of you too.

The Wild Child

With the sole purpose of making sure you have a great time every night, the *Wild Child* eats, sleeps and sometimes even snorts party invitations till his eyes end up with the same glaze as your greasy breakfast doughnut – only, he's just as nourishing.

When he's not running to clearance sales for wardrobe checks, he's bustling over to the STD clinic for health check-ups. The *Wild Child* knows it's better to be safe than sorry, but he'll still want to push his limits, just like he pushes his snooze button every morning. The guy counts his minutes in vodka shots, regrets and credit card bills, and he feels that every moment he's not raging and having the time of his life is a moment wasted (on Instagram). As you can tell, the Child (first name, Wild) will most definitely be the poster boy for all the bad decisions in your life – including that one time you threw up the contents of your vodka-lined stomach on your neighbour's front door.

In broad daylight.

When the door was open.

But he'll also hold your head and make sure you don't ruin your shoes.

The Diva

In his bespoke shirts and Italian brogues, the *Diva* feels terribly out of place in your motley crew of misfits, and he makes it a point to tell you so (repeatedly). He has an important-sounding job in an important-sounding organization, which is what lets him eat at 'all the right restaurants', shop at 'all the right places' and date 'all the right boys'. He'll (repeatedly) tell you all about them over expensive drinks, but never introduce you to any of them. Apart from his raucous jokes, his high self-worth and his complete disregard for anyone's (or more importantly, your) feelings, he's a really nice guy. Plus, he is friends with 'all the right people in the world.'

Including you.

The Former Flame

Hidden behind deleted cookies, incognito browses and emptied caches, the *Former Flame* and you have a history that neither likes to bring up at the dinner table (or the bar). You've probably hooked up with him in the past, but decided to stay friends because of one major reason: the sex was bad but the subsequent fallout wasn't. Now, months later, you bond over your similar taste in alcohol and different taste in men. You overcompensate your (un)resolved feelings by slurring out compliments to each other every time you hit the bar, because you don't want to make the mistake of hitting the bed ever again.

The Lovebug

The *Lovebug* is the ditzy lead character from every feel-good romcom – he falls in love so often (every week, if you want to keep a count), he's a walking ad for Tinder. All it takes is a gorgeous, Rumi-reciting man to send him a charming 'hello' on Grindr, and he's already planning out their wedding. He's spoken about so many boys over quarters of cheap rum and soda that you've reached a point where you just nod and smile every time he starts a new story, because now you don't really care who 'Sam from Santa Cruz' is.

The Breadcrumb

The *Breadcrumb* and you have history (obviously), and although it wasn't *all* fireworks (like your sordid past with the *Former Flame*), you still hold a feeble sparkler for him in your heart. Why don't you take the leap and act on it then?

It's simple. He's not as smart as Suryaveer, not as good looking as Ravi, not as charming as Bilal, not as enigmatic as Ishaan, not as athletic as Krish, not as funny as Kabir, not as breathtaking as Ranbir and not as witty as Farhad.

He's also not as unavailable as the rest of them. Which only makes him that much less desirable. One day, you hope to find your way back to the boy through your breadcrumb trail of broken hearts.

Just make sure that someone else doesn't get there first.

The Pile On

Eager and simpering, the *Pile On* is the perfect minion for every gang of gay friends. He snakes his way to movies scenes, worms his way to soirees, crawls into cocktail plans, and squeezes into the booth while the rest of you enjoy burgers at the diner. No one really likes the *Pile On*, but also, no one really has the heart to tell him that.

The Dude

The *Dude* makes sexist jokes, generalizes about gay men and jocularly tells you not to hit on him if you as much as tap him on his shoulder in front of other people. He might not ask you questions like 'who's the man and who's the woman?' but he'll *still* get you a flamingo pink phone case for your birthday.

Just for laughs, obviously.

The *Dude* is your token straight friend. The two of you have a great how-we-met story, which you tell everyone (and anyone) over multiple pints of beer at the bar. He calls himself your 'straight best friend', your 'perennial wingman' and other such *douchey* things, at which point you grimace like a depressed clown from the circus. On cue, he guffaws and punches your shoulder, and you wince in mock pain. Everyone has fun and laughs. It's a routine you've both perfected over the years. Sometimes, you wonder why you are friends with the *Dude*.

Then you realize it's because he keeps all the other *straight bully* douchebags away.

The Husband

The *Husband* is only here because his wife/girlfriend/lover wants him to 'try a bit harder and get to know her friends as well'. You both show a mild interest in each other's lives because of that one thing you have in common: his significant other. He'll ask you questions about your boys, you'll ask him questions about his work, peppered with polite affirmations.

You finally give up trying to get to know each other because it's going to be a losing battle. Now, you stick to politely nodding at him every time you hang out, chuckling over sports jokes that you don't get while drinking mimosas that he doesn't like.

The Flake

The *Flake* is always 'away' – five minutes away, a traffic light away, a meeting away, maybe a weekend away – until he's not. And then sometimes, he's *really* away.

He ghosts on your plans more often than the hot model that lives 800 metres away (the one that never replies to any of your texts on Grindr). Only, he's more appealing, and you don't want to get inside his pants. It's not that the *Flake* doesn't love you; he does, irrevocably so. It's just that he loves cancelling plans more. He's used every excuse in the book to get out of a plan – haemorrhoids, his dog's funeral, the flu, an important exam, a boring deadline, head lice, a broken kettle, thunderstorms in the other part of town and that one time he had a doctor's appointment … with the gynaecologist.

But eventually, when you do meet him (and you obviously will), he'll pretend like nothing happened and pick up right where you left off.

And so will you.

Number Fifty-seven: The Undergrad What They Didn't Teach You about Flirting with Strangers?

December 2011

My phone buzzes rudely one sweaty afternoon. 'Hi,' texts **Fifty-seven**, a final-year architectural undergrad who stays only a suburb away. I send a quick 'hello' back. We've been at this for weeks; monosyllabic conversations that end before they even begin. I am bored, and it's time to finally take the plunge. I ask him whether he wants to meet.

He's busy with his dissertation thesis and can't step out. Can I come over?

I think about it. I've never met him, and this could be a really bad idea, like the time I decided to fry an egg in the microwave. Exchanging sweet nothings over text messages is one thing, but meeting someone new in the confines of their house for the very first time? Hello, how do I get out of this hot mess? What if he turns out to be an axe murderer? What if he robs me? What if he's an imposter?

I ring his doorbell in exactly twenty minutes.

For an undergrad who's only a month away from his final thesis, he looks surprisingly fresh (and smells of peaches). I greet him with a smile; he greets me with a tight hug.

He's the quintessential twenty-something gay boy. **Fifty-seven** likes his men older, loves his drinks neat and seems to know exactly what he wants from life even when it seems like he doesn't. Twenty-something gay men might be effortlessly cocky and a little too self-aware for my tastes, but they also have a flair for saying all the right things in life.

'You smell great,' he says to me. See, what did I tell you?

His apartment is sparse, filled with empty rolls of paper and scribbled drawings on tracing sheets. I see a stack of books that I've always wanted to read but never did, and a heap of clothes on the couch that I wish I could fit into but never would. He's telling me about moving to a more luxurious pad in town in three months. Does he have a sore point at all?

I could just ask him. But then, looking him up online is the next best option. Oh well, what do we have here? It turns out he had a nervous breakdown on a reality show a couple of years ago, where he might have come out on national television. Was it intentional? No idea. Did it change his life? Obviously. A big family intervention and two years of therapy later, he's doing better and currently trying to find himself in architectural school.

Does he tell me any of this?

No.

Why, hello Google.

Do you want brownies with some ice cream, he asks, snapping me out of my social-network-induced reverie, but he's already holding out a bowl. He inches closer, and his reality TV stint inches away. I can see the bristles of hair on the back of his neck. Is that the smell of French vanilla or light-headed nervousness?

Fifty-seven talks passionately about his undergrad thesis, and I am surprised that it's neither grating nor boring. He's making a conservatory for birds on the outskirts of the city and a rehabilitation centre for injured animals. I listen in mock earnest. Do I like hearing about dissertations in general? No. Do I like hearing him? Yes.

'Am I boring you?' he asks me sheepishly. I smile. My ice cream isn't the only thing melting away.

'Can I add you on Facebook', he asks me unexpectedly. Why not?

Friend request sent. Friend request accepted. He beams and goes back inside to get us refills. I lounge about on the sofa set and look around the room. My eyes move over the wine rack, and then head over to a large tack board by the door. It's full of pictures, postcards and post-its – schedules and lists that will not be completed, takeout menus that will be lost and numbers that will never be called.

I move closer and peer at the pictures on the wall, and a picture of a boy I know peers back at me. I frown. It's **Thirty-five**, from two months ago. The picture looks faded, but it's not *that* faded. They seem to be at a Halloween party, wearing identical school uniforms with identical smiles. Wait a minute. Are they friends? Acquaintances? Brothers? Lovers? Random strangers who accidentally got a photo taken together?

I am no Sherlock Holmes, and there's only one way to get to the end of this mystery. I pull out my phone and swipe through his Facebook profile. Happy photos, happier times from just weeks ago. More boys I know pop up, like a bad case of overnight acne. Wait a minute. What's that right there?

There's a check-in at a movie theatre with **One**, and another picture with identical smiles. And another one. And another one. There's him getting ice cream with **Seven**. A kiss on the cheek with **Twenty-two**. My heart skips multiple beats.

I am going to break the fourth wall, because it's time for a 'did you know?' fun fact.

You can sort every local gay man you know in either one of these four categories: an ex's ex, a friend's friend, a friend's ex or your ex's friend. It turns out **Fifty-seven** is all four. I sigh loudly and watch my ice cream melt away into milky nothingness.

'I'm out of ice cream,' he comes back, apologetically.

Well, so am I.

10.2 Ten Ways to Win His Friends Over … and How Not to Lose Them!

You've been seeing each other for a few weeks and have finally reached the most important milestone of them all – meeting *his* friends.

'But isn't meeting the parents the ultimate sign of approval?' the unwary reader would ask.

For the average gay man in India, friends are most often also his family. If you don't believe me, read the previous section and introspect. They've seen him drunk. They've seen him go without a shower for days. They've seen him without copious amounts of hair product. And they've also seen him wolf down three burgers and a plate of fries all by himself.

Which means they've seen him at *every* possible low, but *still* adore him to death. They complete his sentences, his shortcomings (if any, but don't tell him), and most importantly, they complete him. So you can only imagine how fiercely protective they are of him.

Thus, meeting the friends is the real litmus test. And here you are, trying your best to ~~steal their best friend away from them~~ be a part of their life.

Remember how your friends would do anything for you?

Well, so would his – even if it meant cutting you out of his life if they think you aren't worthy of him. A man's friend circle will always be the trump card that makes or breaks any budding relationship (so they can set him up with their more lovable, more attractive, more accomplished gay friend from work).

Does that sound intimidating?

Don't break into nervous sweats just yet. If you play your cards right and follow these ten steps, you'll be a part of his inner circle in no time:

1. **Start a conversation.**

Think you are nervous to meet the gang? Think again. The truth is they are equally nervous to meet you too. Get to know them as people first, and his friends later. Make eye contact (but don't stare), smile and laugh (only when someone makes a joke) and chat (but not only about yourself), and you'll do just fine. Play the field with small talk.

Throw in the compliments every once in a while – 'That's a great watch,' 'I've never seen anyone carry off a dress *so* well,' 'You have great cheekbones,' or 'Your sense of humour is out of this world' (okay, not so much). Did you know that getting to know someone is the easiest way to make friends? Well, now you do.

2. **… but don't get too personal.**

Know when to stop with the questions.

If they seem to be getting uncomfortable at any point, it's *probably* because you are asking them how they lost their virginity when they were fifteen years old. Keep it simple, keep it crisp and keep it to the point where you don't jokingly ask them about their criminal records. Because once you do, there's no going back from knowing that you are talking to someone who went to jail for tax evasion. You don't want your conversation starter to be a relationship ender, do you?

3. **Keep the PDA in check.**

It's difficult to root for a romance when it's a slobbering twenty centimetres away from your face. Sure, you want his friends to know how much you love him, but they already know – that's why you are meeting them, aren't you?

Keep the PDA to a bare minimum, including the nicknames. No one wants to know you call him your 'stud muffin'. Absolutely no one.

4. **… and the alcohol too.**

While a drink just before you meet a group of new people can calm your nerves, it's best not to win the title of the 'most drunk person in the room.' Chugging two pints of beer in twenty seconds might impress his friends, trashing the bathroom with the contents of your stomach will not.

A bad reputation is worse than a bad hangover, and five drinks down, you might just end up making vacation plans with people who probably never want to see you again.

5. **Throw in the occasional joke …**

You've had a couple of drinks and you are feeling roguishly witty. They've all been sharing in-jokes (that obviously don't include you), and you feel like now is the time you need to contribute to ~~all the jokes at your boyfriend's expense~~ the conversation. Maybe you think that the bass is building up like the humour at AIB's roast? Hold your horses – this is not network television. AIB died a fast death, and so will your relationship.

Keep the banter going at a moderate tempo, like the lyrics of a song from the *Sound Of Music*. You don't want your audience of ten to turn into a party of one.

6. **… but don't get insulting.**

In a fit of alcohol-induced euphoria, you might be tempted to follow your stand-up routine with jokes at your date's expense. High off your success from all the joking from above, but don't fall for the bait, even if everyone insists that they want to see you roast your romantic half. Save the oversharing for your therapist.

Instead, ask *them* for stories with punch lines about him. That way, you get to be a part of the gang and don't need to do damage control the next morning.

7. **Don't overanalyse his gay friends.**

No, Kaivan with the green polo shirt is *not* trying to steal your boyfriend away from you. He's not his *Yesterlove* or his *Breadcrumb*. So don't even go there, because the only place you'll be going from here is out of your boyfriend's life.

8. **Don't get too friendly.**

Natasha loves board game nights. Rajeev likes guacamole. Sam loves happy hours.

Just like you do! As the drinks add up, so will the compliments (and frequent reminders): 'You are the one he should end up with! I call dibs on being the best man at your wedding!' But hey, don't let the flattery get to you.

Sure, there's a one-off chance that you might end up liking the friends more than you should, but remember, they are *his* friends. Your future here is just as uncertain as Rajeev's guacamole recipe. At the end of the day, if this relationship doesn't work out, those promised board-game nights (with salsa and guacamole dip) *would* cease to exist, just like your presence in the gang.

Accept that you can't like all of them. There are bound to be some douchebags. Some of them may even try to jeopardize your relationship. Such is life. Ignore the occasional jab, hold your head up high and gravitate towards the friend you like best.

Because there will be a friend you like best. Now go make him/her your ally.

9. **Dress like you wanted to make an effort ...**

Put on your best dress shirt, pair it with great-fitting chinos and pepper it up with cologne and a warm smile. You are halfway there already.

10. **... but be yourself.**

While a billboard version of yourself can seem very intriguing, it's best to stick to what you know best.

Being yourself. Remember how your boyfriend fell in love with all your quirks, laughs at all your silly jokes, and adores the way your eyes crinkle when you tell stories? That's exactly why you are meeting the friends.

Now show them why.

But What If He's Meeting My Friends?

Getting your boyfriend to meet your friends is a lot easier.

Not because this is your home ground, but because these are *your* friends. While there's no magic hack to get your friends to instantly fall in love with him (just like you did), here are a few tips that might help:

1. **Decide who gets to meet him first.**

Start small. Start with your nicest, friendliest friend. Start with one-on-one dinners (drinks add too many variables), because you don't want your boyfriend to get overwhelmed by the idea of facing more than one close friend (and one opinion) at the same time. As your relationship (and his confidence) blooms, keep on adding more friends to the mix (but make sure you always include the first one, because he will need an ally to gravitate towards). Repeat till you've purged through your friends' list.

2. **Share your research.**

Giving both parties a little background information about each other before you head to the actual party would help tremendously. Make sure you don't overshare, because that would only lead to a lot of awkwardness. Your buddy Rohan likes internet cat videos? Yes. Your buddy Rohan also likes bondage porn? Obviously not.

3. **Don't try to force it.**

Yes, you obviously want to helicopter the situation and get everybody to like each other so you can all live like one giant happy family a decade down the line, but that's not how life works. This isn't the global economy, and you aren't China.

Be like Switzerland instead. Neutral and nonchalant. You'll be saying cheese when your friends beg for a group picture at the end of the night.

4. **... or let their opinions bother you.**

Don't beat yourself up too hard if your friends don't like him/get along. Everyone's entitled to an opinion. You need to respect it.

… And no, that's not a hint for you to remove them from your favourites list. If nothing else works, get him to buy a round of drinks for the table. Knowing all your friends, they'll think he's so '*am … azing*.'

Just kidding. You pay for drinks. Obviously.

Meeting your friends is an important milestone, yes, but that also means that you can't introduce *just about anyone* to the gang. You need to know that you have standards to maintain (and a reputation to keep). So whatever you do, make sure you don't introduce them to these five less-than-average dudes.

The first one

You are always excited about the first guy you ever date. After countless years of having a one-sided relationship with your right hand, you've finally met (who you think is) the One: he's decently charming, reasonably good looking and, most importantly, seems as invested in this as you. Seems like a great guy to introduce to your friends, no?

Wrong. Unless you are the luckiest person in the world, the first guy you ever date is going to be the first big mistake of your life. Don't make introducing him to your friends the second big mistake of your life.

The temp

You met Kabir while backpacking across Cambodia. He wears a sarong, bathes thrice a week and keeps quoting Buddha. As you best friend peppers his/her salad, they'll worry that Kabir's going to go away soon – or worse, take you with him.

The hand-me-down

He's been another friend's lover. Another friend's boyfriend. Another friend's *husband*. Your friends look at him the same way they look at the half-priced second-hand cane furniture at Amar Colony in Delhi.

With distrust, because they think he's probably infested with mites.

The ex

You'll want to show your best friend that you are mature enough to be friends with the ex, but they'll know that you are probably hooking up with him the very same night. They'll give you a warning look as a parting gift the night of, and a stern lecture the morning after.

The rebound

They won't tell you it's too soon, but they will roll their eyes as you gush over how perfect the rebound (and his timing) is. When you do get them to meet, your friends will be polite and warm, but won't make any efforts to remember his name or what he does. When you start talking about your best friend's wedding over drinks, an invitation will be avoided as well as eye contact with him.

He'll never be spoken about after.

Number Fifty-eight: the Intern
Will You Wine and Dine with a Friend of Mine?

Fifty-eight and I exchange quick texts and make a plan to flirt dangerously over unlimited wine on a school night.

What the reader needs to know right now is that this date is a set-up. We have mutual friends who believe that we would be 'perfect for each other'. See, being set up by straight friends is always a tricky affair; because their *only* criteria for introducing two gay men is that we are men with penises who enjoy the romantic company of other men with penises. There's no other requisite. It's the straight (wo) man's curse. Do we share common interests? '*Oh well, why don't you meet him first.*' What about our sexual preferences? '*That really doesn't sound like a criterion to find love.*' Okay … do we have the same goals and dreams for the future? '*Why don't you just shut up and trust my gut instinct this one time!*'

But then again, a recurring theme of gay culture is being constantly disappointed with your heterosexual friends for trying to set you up with the only other homosexual they know, but *still* wanting to see a picture of the aforementioned gay man, just in case.

So I ask for one, and I am pleasantly surprised. **Fifty-eight** is 'Why-don't-you-just-shut-up-and-trust-my-gut-instinct-this-one-time' cute. Which brings us back to making a plan to meet on a dreary school night. Why does it matter that it's a school night?

I teach writing classes at an architectural school, and he's a fashion intern with an early shift, which means neither of us has the time for late nights or morning afters. The man takes his job very seriously; he shows up at the date ten minutes late, in suspenders and a broach, thrown casually (he confides later) over a crisp button-down navy blue shirt that … wait; is he wearing a bow tie?

Yes. He's wearing a bow tie. That's commendable because he put more effort into choosing an outfit than I put in choosing my postgraduate college.

'You look great,' I say to him.

'You do too.'

Only one of us is lying.

He's taller and prettier than his pictures, but also mousier, and I am scared that he might scuttle away from between my feet, which would be a big waste, because we've not even started on the *Endless Stem* yet.

We belong to the same alumni, we realize over our first drink (two glasses of mildly spiced *Sangria Rosso*) but neither of us remembers the other from 2008. The man was a sophomore when I was a senior, and we never took the same courses. He left midway, he tells me, as I shift to a second glass (one glass of *Sangria Bianco*, please?) and moved to a different college, postponing our meet-cute (and our friends' plan to get us married off) by five whole years.

Fifty-eight works under the creative head of a design lab for now, but that's 'only a temp job' – so is my third glass, a flute of *Sula Brut* – 'he's going to volunteer at Fashion Week next month', scuttling between the models and the designers, before he heads to start his post-grad degree in London. One of his friends is showcasing, and he's really … hello, are you *listening*?

'I am … I am,' I apologize as I reach for my fourth glass (a delightful concoction of sparkling wine and peach) for the night. I ask him about our sum total of three mutual acquaintances (all women), and he laughs about how their group chat has been constantly buzzing ever since he got here ninety minutes ago. At least two of them have called dibs on naming our future firstborn, and all three have elaborate strategies to be that One True Friend™ who officiates our wedding in Tuscany. I am only nine hours away from swearing off wine for the next two months, so I am barely paying attention, but until then –

'Can I kiss you?' I ask. Is it me or is it the wine (glass five, a vintage Chilean *Pinot Noir*) talking?

He smiles and beckons me towards the washroom. It's definitely the wine. Swig. Wipe mouth. Smile. Follow.

We scuttle into the wide restroom, and I push him against the wall. **Fifty-eight** kisses fiercely, and I am surprised by how casually he takes control. I hear a faint buzzing somewhere in the background, and I smile. It's the clinking-of-glass sound that usually accompanies falling in love.

But we aren't falling in love. Instead, we've toppled one of the wall lamps. There's broken glass everywhere.

And an usher outside, who doesn't look very happy. He mutters something about manners, as we scuttle back to our table, our faces as red as the Rosé that I would soon drink (glass six, with slices of pears and pineapple). My friend is clearly unperturbed.

'Do I get to see you again?' he prods at my feet, as I finish off the dregs of my drink. Somewhere, three women are on the brink of an orgasm.

But does he get to see me again? He's cute. He's funny. He's surprisingly smart. But I long to reach for my wine glass more than I long to reach for him (number I-lost-count-somewhere-after-six, red wine with soaked tangerines, and a hint of thyme).

There's only one thing I want at the table, and unfortunately, it's not him. I still play footsie secretly, because I am drunk, and because that's the least I can do to stop myself from scuttling away.

Number Fifty-nine: The Screenwriter
City of Stars: Won't You Share Your Friends with Me?

November 2011

It's 2 p.m. on a Wednesday. Our cold coffee glasses leave rings on the Formica tables. **Fifty-nine**, a screenwriter for Indian soaps, is a man of many moods and even more words. He's spent the past two hours yapping about his influential friend circle and the circling state of television, and I've just found out that we share a second cousin from my mother's side. Wait. Are we *actually* related? Would this be incest? Should I alert the porn sites?

This is the stuff that makes primetime television. As he drones on about plans to buy a *third* house in the city, I realize that I am starstruck by his job. I am starstruck by his life. I am starstruck by his starry friends.

Sadly, I am not starstruck by him.

10.3 The Six Men You Should Never Take Back Home

Every relationship has a different milestone that locks it in. Sometimes it's farting in front of each other. Sometimes it's deleting Grindr. Sometimes it's introducing him to your friends. And one in a thousand times, it's introducing him to your family.

For Kartik, the game usually stops at the third option.

It's plausible. The single highlight of Kartik's coming-out story was his mother asking him what he wanted them to do with all the gold they had saved up for his wedding. Kartik loves his parents, but they can be a bit … *too much*.

Does he want his potential boyfriend to know of his mollycoddling relationship of codependence with his mother? Should he be made aware of the years of indifference Kartik's suffered at the hands of an emotionally distant father?

Kartik takes the boys he dates very seriously. He's introduced them to friends. He's introduced them to acquaintances. And on that one occasion, he even introduced one to his sister. Kartik craves validation like he craves pizza.

Which is why getting his parents (or more importantly, his overbearing mother) to approve of his life decisions has been so important for the writer, considering that a thousand other gay men are never going to be as blessed as he is when it comes to acceptance. He doesn't know whether any of his exes would have made the cut, or how his parents would react, but he does know one thing: if and when he does find the One, all he wants is to get his mother on board. Why?

Because … it's *mom*.

I am not trying to discount Indian dads (because let's face it, the quintessential Indian father [not mine] has the emotional range of a teaspoon), but there's always something more substantial about your mother's approval. After all, she's the one who quit her dreams, braved morning sickness apart from nine months of labour, and popped you out with nothing more than a nurse's hand to squeeze.

Or maybe because most Indian men are out-and-proud mumma's boys.

In all cases, getting your mom to meet your (potential) significant other – irrespective of your sexuality – is a big deal. She's made most of your big decisions in life, so she can help you make this one too.

He might be the perfect guy to bring home on a platter for the mother, or someone who isn't worth the bother (but you still want to see how it goes), just make sure you avoid taking these six men back home if you don't want your mum to give you a disapproving glare the morning after.

The sycophant

The sycophant is every mother's wet-dream-come-true. On paper.

He'll bring her a care package of *rasmalai* (and a bottle of Reisling) when he meets her and pile her with compliments when he's not piling her plate with refills of her own cooking. Does your hair always look so lovely? Can you please give me the recipe for this *aloo gobhi*? How do you get your roses to bloom so well? Where do you get your gorgeous sarees stitched? Isn't your son the handsomest? (Yeah, she knows.)

He'll eventually break your heart when two months later in the middle of a fight, he tells you that her *palak paneer* was too salty.

The Type A

The Type A is rich, successful and an encyclopedia of table manners, and like a Tupperware sale, he leaves your mother happy and flustered at the same time. She doesn't know how to react to him. What will he eat? Will he judge the throwaway rug? Or the faded sofa set? Will he love her chicken ghee roast? What do we talk about? No matter how many times you tell your mother to calm down, she won't.

And as you see your mother trying her best to impress the Duke of Delhi with her homemade samosas and chamomile tea (in her best china), you'll know that your relationship is doomed to crack, just like the bone china will one day.

The chatterbox

Your mum wants to talk at the dinner table too, thank you very much.

The loner

At the same time, don't take back a man who just sits there and lets your mum go on and on and on – about your incessant drinking, your financial woes, and lastly, your mortifying bladder problems from back when you were six.

The mess

'No shoes on the coffee table, please.'

The miser

While your mother might enjoy giving you the occasional lecture for being a spendthrift ('Did you really need those clothes?' 'Who spends half their salary on drinks at the bar?' 'Is it important to go for your friend's bachelor trip to Bangkok?' 'Who would have known lobster risotto could cost so much?'), she wouldn't like you spending the rest of your life with a miser.

From your PlayStation to those AirPods she got you for your last birthday, she's spoiled you with some of the best things in life. And she'd want your future plus one to do the same.

Number Sixty: The Son
How I Met Your Mother: A Not-So-Happy Ending

October 2012

Sixty opens the door and looks automatically apologetic. It can't be my face, because we've recently exchanged an album full of pictures.

'What's up?' I ask, looking for a way in. He won't budge. I've just climbed up three flights of stairs on a hot summer afternoon. I am *not* amused.

'I am not alone,' he confesses, and I frown.

'Oh … do you have company?'

The bank manager blushes. Who could it be? A random friend I'll have to make small talk with? A domineering boyfriend I didn't know existed? Another gay man who's expecting an a ménage à trois? I am not looking forward to any of these scenarios, but since I've come all this way, I might as well as brush up on some introductory chitchat before I get down to ~~charming my way into his pants~~ business.

He beckons me indoors and introduces me to the kink in the plan. It's his mother.

10.4 What (Not) to Do When You Are in a Relationship!

Being single can be really difficult.

Urvaksh thinks that it is a constant reminder of how woefully lonely and unloved you are. Sure, he gets to read a book on the weekends, or down shots by the dozen with his latest fling at the bar, but sometimes he just wants someone to share a ~~titillating orgasm~~ family pack of ice cream with. Urvaksh is one of many, many men who need to be reading this book (but congratulations, dear reader, you are doing just fine!)

'It's all the couples around me,' he says, ever the wistful lad who is days away from deleting Grindr from his phone for the seventeenth time. We all know exactly what he's talking about. We've all seen it.

He's talking about gay men who relentlessly post about their relationship status on social media, spamming your Instagram feed with their love. There's a whole album of them celebrating their four-month anniversary in Maldives (who has the money?), a Twitter thread about how they met each other exactly eighty-three days ago (who has the time?) and a black-and-white portrait of them entwined in bed (who has the camera?).

And if THAT doesn't bother you, it really doesn't help when they pull the following stunts to hammer in how utterly hopeless your love life can be.

Time for a Quick PSA, Boys in Beautiful Relationships!

Have you recently started seeing someone? Here are a few things you should avoid doing as a couple:

1. **Being patronizing**

… and saying things like, 'you know, you'll find someone really, really soon. He's getting here as fast as he can!' when a single friend as much as ~~complains about companionship~~ breathes. Instead, how about going with something that's more casual, like, 'Do you want to have another gin and tonic? It's on me!'

2. **Only taking photos together**

Did you think there was nothing worse than a selfie? Think again.

3. **Looking down on dating apps**

Let's have a moment of silence for the hours you've spent on Tinder, swiping right on every second profile till you found each other.

4. **Holding hands wherever you go**

Including the urinal.

5. **Pretending you don't enjoy gay bars any more because it's only for 'single boys who only want sex'**

While I'll pretend like you didn't go cruising at one just three months ago.

6. **Gushing about how happy you make each other on social media**

(But you obviously delete the post when it doesn't get the requisite likes)

7. **Never socializing separately**

Like one of those buy-one-get-one-free coupons (but not really).

8. **But if you do, you only talking about how intense your relationship is**

I'm just politely nodding when you tell me how he has a snoring problem and you might need to go see a sleep therapist tomorrow.

9. **Doing yoga together on your Instagram Live**

But you probably only have one yoga mat.

10. **Looking at someone in the disappointing way mothers do when their sons are single**

Only you didn't give birth to us.

Number Sixty-one: The French Teacher
All the Ways You Can Be the Bad Guy at the End of a Relationship

June 2012

Sixty-one is a simple man who lives a simple life. At twenty-three, he could play the lead's goofy best friend in every romantic comedy – his handsome face hidden behind spectacles too small for his face, and clothes a size too big. For context, he's the one with the occasional one-liner and the routine monologue at the end of the film. He also never ends up getting the girl (or in this case, the boy).

The second favourite of his parent's two children, **Sixty-one** might not behave like his movie archetype, but he is a man of routines. Every evening, our friend goes for a walk, shops for groceries, feeds the neighbourhood dogs, and ends his day grading papers. It's surprising how everyone wants to be a performance artist, or an actor, or sometimes even a painter, but not him.

Sixty-one is happy being a middle school teacher. He's happier being an absolute delight for his class seventh students. But he's the happiest when he's with me, he tells me after our third date – and we spend the rest of the night tracing snow angels all over his single bed.

Most people will tell you that a great love story is a lot like a bag of popcorn. Some people like it hot right as they dive in, a few enjoy how it gets warm and toasty in the middle, and a majority likes the cold, congealed mess right at the end.

'That felt really good,' they say once they are done, 'I am so happy I finished that,' and then … they throw the bag away. The empty bag is forgotten, and people move on.

My relationship with **Sixty-one** is that empty bag of popcorn.

This isn't the happy story of our two and a half months of blissful union, where we spend weekends at his home grading papers (mostly him), eating snacks (mostly me) and occasionally tracing snow angels on his single bed. As much as you would like it to be, this isn't the story of **Sixty-one** hand-feeding me a snack every time I visit, while I leave a piece of my melting heart behind. I am no bag of buttered popcorn. See, this isn't the story of what makes **Sixty-one** the *perfect* boyfriend.

This is the story of what makes me the worst one yet. When did it end? Why did it end? How did it end?

What's important here is not why he dumped me (short version: I cheated) or what made him take such a drastic step (longer version: I cheated with an ex), what's important is how I chose to handle the rejection.[16]

Everyone from Oprah Winfrey To *Cosmopolitan Magazine* has the same opinions on getting over a relationship: the practical thing to do is to behave with as much grace as possible. Carry yourself with respect. Be a constant beacon of hope. How you behave when a relationship ends can speak volumes about you. But practicality is not a trait that comes naturally to most gay men.

No two men react the same way to a break-up. Some move away. Some jump right back into the dating pool. Some plead. Some scowl. Some throw a hissy fit (or worse, things).

Or we end up becoming assholes.

Now most guides only skim through the basics of handling heartbreak: pick up the pieces of your heart, introspect, speak to a close friend (or a therapist) for closure and move on. Yada yada yada. Basic self-love spiel. But no one tells you how *not* to behave. The internet is rife with many lists, but not one tells you how not to be an absolute asshole at the end of a relationship.

'But … I've never dated an asshole,' you say. Here's a quick update for you, dear reader. If you've never encountered an asshole, there's a

---

16 Side note: At this point, the average reader would take a break from the book, frown and ask, 'Is cheating ever excusable?' The short answer is: no. The more complicated, longer answer is: Still … no.

high chance you were one. Now, being an asshole doesn't necessarily make you a villain. But it doesn't make you the romantic lead's best friend either.

How I chose to behave with **Sixty-one** is a classic example of how you shouldn't at the end of a relationship.

What you should do: **cut off all contact.** No texts, no DMs, no calls, and definitely no surprise visits to his house.

What I do: Twenty days after our rather abrupt break-up, I pay him a surprise visit. He opens the door to my beaming face, and he doesn't look happy.

'What are you doing here?'

'I needed to say sorry in person ...'

He hesitates for a few seconds, but lets me in. His house looks different than the last time I was here. Was it always so ... empty? How long has it been since we last toppled over his books and clothes scattered all over the floor? How long has it been since he hand-fed me a snack?

I see that his bed has been pushed right next to the window, and the sunlight falls directly on the snow angels in the creases. These are new snow angels. Where did they from? *Who* did they come from?

'Can we at least be friends?' I ask turning his way, all hopes of being hand-fed a snack lost, 'I miss you.'

He hears me out patiently over the next twenty minutes, punctuating my monologue with multiple 'hmms' and 'uh-huhs'.

'I don't think this is going to work out,' he tells me, when I am done listing down all the reasons why I deserve a second chance.

'But ...' I begin, ' don't you remember the good times? Doesn't the fact that we loved each other for seventy-two days and eighteen hours mean more to you than mere words?'

'You should leave,' he suggests, pointing towards the door.

'Is it someone else?' I ask, shifting gears in a heartbeat. I look accusatorily at the snow angels on his bed, making a mental note that they lack the grace I left behind.

'I don't think it's any of your business,' he points out, and just like that, a switch flips deep inside me. The rage rises up like bile as I open my mouth to argue, but he cuts my angry sermon before I can even begin.

The open door gawks in my face, and I leave with my fists clenched.

What you should do: **take the time off to introspect.** Understand that you can't look for happiness in the same place you lost it.

What I do: on a particularly bumpy ride home, I shoot him a series of vicious texts. They are bitter strings of composed vitriol, each telling him that he's incapable (read: undeserving) of love. Multiple unsavoury comments ('maybe this is why your parents never loved you'). and allegations ('I feel like your students love you for *other* reasons)' are made.

He responds by leaving my messages on read.

That night, egged on by a few glasses of Cabernet Shiraz, I write him a long email. I pour out my thoughts and feelings in three hundred and eighty-seven words, like the wine I shamelessly poured out forty-five minutes earlier.

'How about we start right over? What do you think about second chances?' I begin. This is great, I think.

It's brash but sensitive. I end with a simple 'I just wanted to own up to all my toxicity and tell you how much you meant to me. I just wanted you to know that.'

That's heartfelt, but not desperate.

'Do reply if you feel like it.'

Send.

What you should do: **Don't involve their friends.** It's important to remember that your ex's friends will *always* be his friends first, which means you will *always* (first-degree murder aside) be the bad guy.

What I do: I cc all his friends in the previous email. Ten days later, he replies with a curt text requesting me not to involve his friends in our relationship drama.

Well, at least he replied.

Not one to understand cues, I use his text as a bottleneck to engage –' I am really sorry about that, what's up with you?' – but he's already gone. You cannot hollow out a person like termites hollow out a log and then stroke the surface gently and tell him he is beautiful.

At this point, the average human being would give up. They would badmouth the ex and move on. 'He really wasn't the right guy for me,' they'd tell their friends.

Not me. This just makes me want him more. It makes me want to wake up next to him, grow old and fat together. It makes me want to solve crossword puzzles as a couple. It makes me want to trace out new snow angels on his bed.

What you should do: **Learn from your mistakes.**

What I do: I send him a series of emails over the following fortnight, ranging from needy (subject: 'Will you ever forgive me?') to downright delusional (subject: 'WHY WON'T YOU REPLY?'), just waiting for a text telling me he's taking me back. A reply finally comes on a Tuesday night, when I am in the middle of a taxing pitch presentation for a client.

'Please stop bothering me. I am seeing someone now, and we don't want to deal with you.'

My mind draws up a graphic image of him tracing out snow angels with a faceless man – he's surprisingly fitter than I am, with six-pack abs that I'll never have, making love to a boy I'll never touch.

And just like that, I am back at square one.

What you should do: Accept that this is the end of the road, and **move on**. We are all scared to put our hearts out there, but good things only happen when we let the bad things happen to us.

What I do: Not one to give up, I draft out a final email. I dole out sentence after sentence of beautifully constructed prose, creating a literal *piece de resistance* of words. Once finished, I read it over and pat myself on the back for a job well done. It's the e-mail to end all e-mails. I would call it *the* e-mail™ if I weren't sulking like a ~~baby~~ lovesick fool.

I hit send, and I wait. Days pass, and his display picture disappears into a grey silhouette. My messages jeer back with a single tick.

Not *seen*. Not *even* delivered.

Does the gut-wrenching realization that he's blocked me turn me down? I should say it does, but …

'Hey, did you read my email?'

'Hi there, I didn't want to bother you again, but …'

'So it's been a week but you haven't replied yet …'

'Hi, it's me again!'

'Hello?'

'Hello 2.0?'

'U there?'

'Fuck off …'

I wait for a whole week. He never replies.

11

Fight Or Flight?

11.1 The First-timer's Guide to First Fights

It started with something small. It always starts with something small.

'You never have time to meet my friends,' Aneesh joked at dinner. Vir had sighed and rolled his eyes. But Aneesh wouldn't let go.

'Why won't you do it?' he asked playfully. He thought he was being cute. Vir snapped back, saying he thought Aneesh's friends were silly.

I take great offence, because I am Aneesh's friend. But this is not about me.

It's always the little things. The little things pile up. And that's when it escalated. They hadn't realized it, but they had been piling up these problems like dirty dishes in the kitchen sink. And then, the dam (of dirty dishes) exploded. Suddenly, every little inconvenience felt magnified. The way Vir always forgot to turn off the tap. The way Aneesh wore his socks to bed. The way Vir was still friends with his ex. The way Aneesh still hadn't deleted Tinder. The way Vir did this. The way Aneesh did that. This. That. This. That.

And then, before they know it, the riptide of witty banter transformed into verbal blows. Why? How? What? When?

Heated words were exchanged and insults hurled. Instagram tags were deleted. Aneesh called Vir an 'emotionally absent bastard' and Vir retaliated by calling him 'a vindictive train wreck'. They both called each other an 'asshole' multiple times over. Aneesh went to bed feeling angry and deeply unsettled. He couldn't sleep for hours. It hit him later that in the ten months and seventeen days of their relationship, this was the first time they'd *actually* fought.

Aneesh seems visibly upset when he recounts the fight. Save for a few monosyllabic texts of dwindling importance, they haven't spoken at all. It's been two days.

I am surprised to see him in such a brittle state. His eyes are bloodshot, and his face is weighed down by dark circles. He looks like he hasn't showered in days. This isn't like him. The Aneesh I know cares about how he looks. The Aneesh I know jumps at the smallest of inconveniences. The Aneesh I know doesn't brood.

But in the four years that I've known him, this is also the first time I've seen him in love.

How Do You Deal with a Fight?

A relationship is like a comforter. The first time you fight, you tear a little hole in your security blanket. But what do you do: try to fix it or just buy a new comforter?

Inevitably, you will annoy each other. If you don't, either you are a doormat or you really need to raise your standards. See, men do stupid things all the time; it's in our nature. Eventually, one of you *will* snap. Maybe you'll disagree on how obnoxious his comment about your Pride outfit was (it really didn't make you look like a peacock.) Maybe he'll get irritated with how you *always* eat the last slice of pizza. Fights happen, and there's little you can do to avoid them. Sometimes it will be soul crushing. Sometimes it will be gut wrenching. Sometimes it will seem like the end of the world.

But the next time, you'll be ready.

Do: Talk about how you feel.

As people, we have the habit of holding back our feelings. Feelings are for women, misogynists say. But if you are reading this book, you probably don't care about what misogynists have to say anyway. Think of it this way – every time you hold back your feelings, they accumulate, slowly stewing inside your head. Feelings have a way of festering. If something is bothering you, bring it up right away. Talk about it. Remember, having a conversation will save you lots of bills at the therapist's.

Don't: Call each other names.

Sticks and stones may break your bones, but a poisoned jab only wounds harder. If you call someone an insufferable douchebag every day, it's not going to stop him from being an insufferable douchebag. In fact, he'll only be more of an insufferable douchebag to get back at you.

Leave the name-calling to Twitter trolls and kindergarten kids. You might not be using actual blows (more on that later), but using unsavoury affirmations can be downright aggressive. And also mean.

Stick to your pet names instead. Just make sure you don't use them around other people.

Do: Pick your battles.

He forgot to wish your best friend on her birthday, so you cancel the surprise party you were throwing him *(and break his phone accidentally)*. Sure, you often get irritated with people you care about, but no one wants to be that psychopathic boyfriend his friends warned him about. Sometimes, you *really* need to learn to let things go. Breathe. Take a time out. Cool down with a beer. Choose your battles wisely.

If you are constantly forcing someone to walk on eggshells around you because they are afraid you might explode, the faults aren't *just* limited to your relationship. Not every minor argument needs to be a full-fledged war. Use your heavy artillery for something more momentous, like when you catch him cheating on you with his best friend.

Don't: Use low blows.

Imagine you are having pizza with your boyfriend. It's chicken tikka with extra mushrooms. Just the way you like it. There are two slices in the box, and then suddenly, they are gone.

'I didn't have them!' he lies, the cheese dripping down his chin. You get into a row. Words are thrown, eyes are rolled. And then, it gets worse.

One minute you are fighting about who ate the last slice of pizza, and the next you're having a major row about how the sex was bad three days ago. Before you know it, you are bringing up exes and tearing through each other's Instagram likes. No one likes to bring up old mistakes, and bringing up something from seven months, four days and eight hours (you know because you have a reminder) ago will never help.

It's just ... *petty*.

Do: Stick to a strict no-abuse policy.

'But there's bound to be friction when there are two men in a relationship. It's all the testosterone!' you cry. Here's a gentle reminder to avoid making comments that reek of toxic masculinity.

NEVER. HIT. ANYONE. PERIOD.

Other things that are completely avoidable? Throwing phones, glasses and plates (or something heavier, like him) across the room (or at him) in a fit of rage. Much like negativity or non-alcoholic beer, violence has no place in our lives. You might be furious. You might be seething. Your blood might be boiling. But you need to control yourself and never reach that point where someone has to file a case of manhandling against you. Leave the wrestling to the bedroom.

But only if he likes it that way.

Don't: Put up with gaslighting.

Imagine you pour your heart out to your partner through an apologetic text message. He dismisses your feelings with a curt 'K'. (Side note: Never respond to a text that way, unless someone's asking you for the chemical symbol for Potassium.) When you respond angrily, he tells you to 'CTFO and just stop acting so crazy'.

This is a typical example of gaslighting.

What is Gaslighting?

When someone constantly defects their own shitty behaviour by making you feel insecure and silly, they are gaslighting you.

Playing the blame game is easy, but when someone makes you feel small all the time, they really aren't worth your time or mental space. Gaslighting is bullshit, and it's an indicator that someone doesn't respect you enough. The entire point of being in a relationship is to find someone who makes you love yourself. But if every step of your journey is filled with self-doubt, what even is the point of being in a relationship any more?

I have one word of advice for you. GTFO.

There are certain fights that are too huge to avoid and some issues that can never be truly swept under the rug. These are instances there's no turning back from, in which case, just pick up your bags and leave. Cut it off completely. Start with a clean slate. Not being in a relationship is any day better than being in a shitty one.

Because the first fight is *only* the beginning.

11.2 Dear Gay Men, When Is It Time to Call It Off?

The Warning Signs No One Ever Told You about!

So you've found the One.

He's charming, handsome and well read, and is a hit with your family and friends. He laughs at your jokes and feeds you bits of his caramel custard, but most importantly, he:

- Doesn't message you only past midnight. *Check.*
- Is not commitment-phobic. *Check.*
- Is not mysteriously secretive about his life. *Check.*
- Does not bring up his ex at all. *Check.*
- Doesn't get drunk every second night of the week. *Check.*
- Is definitely not cheating on you. *Check.*
- Is always available to talk. *Check.*
- Loves you. *Double check.*

You've personally scoured his life (and all his social media profiles) for a red flag, but you can't find any.

Red flags: 0
Romance: 1

It seems like he's perfect. But something *still* seems off. Do you give up?

How to Spot a Red Flag When There's No Red Flag

Here are nine home-tested ways to spot a red flag when you can't seem to find a red flag at all.

1. **He has a sense of humour that is cruel.**

While the occasional laugh at a stumbling child (or a man walking straight into a glass door) can be harmless, if someone finds humour in other people's misfortune more than three times a day, it's eyebrow-raising.

Because at some point in the future, *you* might end up being the joke. It could be your hyena-like laugh or the way you slurp your noodles, or that one time you *almost* peed yourself through a re-run of *The Ring* (the sequel, not the less scary prequel). Be with someone who *makes* you laugh all the time, not someone who laughs *at* you all the time.

2. **He love-bombs you.**

What do you do the next time someone uses the L word three minutes into the relationship?

When someone says they love you early in the relationship, there's a very high chance they are trying to direct it with their own terms, and if they can't – things might only take an ugly (and a more resentful) turn.

3. **You both have opposing life goals.**

You want to be an animal rights activist, but he wants to start his own barbeque restaurant? If you aren't on the same page professionally (or financially), the chances of having a happy ending are next to nil. Clashing life choices (and wage gaps) aside, the last thing you want is for someone to hold you back from where or what you need to be – even if it means freeing all the chickens.

4. **He doesn't respect your boundaries.**

Does he tickle you jokingly even when you laugh and beg for him to stop? Call incessantly when all you want is a quiet day? Prod you about your problems when you tell him you need time to think about them on your own?

If you are with someone who doesn't respect your boundaries (even innocently), you are only two steps away from not having him respect you.

5. **He says he hates conflict.**

You've heard the same sob story over and over again, over drunken fights at home or between arguments at dinner. He dodges all your accusations and ignores all your pleas to come to a peaceful conclusion. And just when you are about to prod him for a reason and put an end to your misery, he tells you he absolutely hates conflict; that it's happened before with *so many boys*, and he can't deal with it any more.

Don't fall for it. He might as well say, '*Don't* confront me about anything in life, because I will ignore you or leave you.' And somewhere down the line, he'll tell all his friends how you were '*just* like the rest of them'.

6. **He thinks all his exes are crazy.**

Ravi wanted to move in too early. Shyam would never stop calling. Rajeev decided to tell his friends why they broke up. Kunal begged to be taken back by standing outside his apartment all night. Ahmed called him a cheating scumbag. Ryan asked his mom if she knew her son was a psycho. They were *all* so crazy.

Do you see the pattern? You obviously do. If a boy spews venom about an ex or two, it's fine – we all have relationships that sour out. But if he badmouths every boy he's ever been with, chances are *he's* the problem.

7. **He gets upset when you have to go back home.**

Can't we watch the movie just ten minutes longer? Do you really have to leave after two helpings of ice cream? Can we walk around your society one more time? Must you leave right now? Can't you stay the night? The morning? The day? The week? The month?

Makes you go 'aww'? Naww, push those romantic aspirations back in your pockets, sir, because it's not long before his 'but we just met' turns into 'you're leaving so you can hook up with your ex, right?'

8. **His sex drive doesn't work for you.**

While there's no *wrong* amount of sex that two people can have in a relationship, matching libidos are important for one to work. What if one half of the couple wants to get it on every three hours and the other thinks thrice a month is fine?

There's no place for sexual chemistry when it's already brewing with resentment, hurt egos and an urge to get on Grindr and message the gorgeous man from 800 metres away. Do you think you have different libidos?

It's time you look for a different partner.

9. **He's passive-aggressive about tiny things.**

'Try making it to dinner on time?'

'Do you *really* need to go for a drink with your friends?'

'I would have loved to see you yesterday, but it's okay, I guess?'

'Can you please send it to me before I have to remind you again.'

You know that little voice at the back of your head nagging you to end things? You should probably listen to it, because it's not going to be passive-aggressive like your paramour here.

Number Sixty-two: The Protégé
Why 'You Dated My Boss' Is Never a Good Sign

January 2018

'Do you want another slice?' **Sixty-two** asks, pushing the pizza to my side of the table. Who says no to pizza?

Not me. He laughs, his dimples stretching across his full face. **Sixty-two's** teeth are so white, they could start a colony in a third-world country. I'd probably lead the revolution.

He's a junior associate at an unnamed law firm by day and runs a shelter for homeless animals by night. Some superheroes wear capes; some become lawyers because they also need to pay the bills.

'It's not really a shelter … more like a friend's farmhouse where we are allowed to let the dogs loose,' he corrects me, biting into the crust.

Only a select few can eat pizza so endearingly, and my date here is one of them. He's a beautiful boy; his smile lights up a dozen bulbs in my heart. It melts a little.

He's animatedly telling me about applying for a post-grad degree aboard (oh no), when his phone buzzes loudly. He frowns.

'Can I take this?' he asks, 'It's my boss.' It's also Saturday evening. We both roll our eyes on cue. He excuses himself, and I chomp on a slice.

'Sorry about that,' the lawyer apologizes when he's back. 'My boss had a work SOS he wanted me to take care of.' He grins again, and my heart slides down a slippery slope to my intestines.

Talking to him is easy. Our chat is punctuated with constant references to his domineering boss. Over the next twenty-odd minutes, I find out that the boss is a high flyer that treats his juniors like scum, overburdening them with odd jobs and jokes. He's only half a decade older than my friend here, but miles ahead on the career path. Karma doesn't come easy when you are a hotshot lawyer in the corporate world.

Well, back to our pizza.

'So what was I saying?' **Sixty-two** smiles again, pushing his phone to the far end of our table. I can sense that he's stressed. The boss's presence looms over our head, like a desi mother who's suspicious of her son's internet search history. I feel nervous around it … should I offer it a slice of pizza?

His phone buzzes again, and I see a familiar name pop up.

'Sorry, it's my boss again. I think I'll reply in a bit …'

My insides turn cold, and my heart stops sliding. This is too much of a coincidence. Could it be? I have to ask.

'Wait … where do you work again?'

He tells me the name of the firm. It's true, then. The domineering boss isn't just another faceless douchebag. It's **Forty-four**, the litigator from eighteen dates ago. The one with whom I played the points game.

'Is everything okay?' he asks me. 'You look a bit peaky.'

Dating an ex's friend is bad, and dating an ex's ex is worse … but what about dating an ex's protégé from work?

I smile and tell him everything is fine. Only, my heart isn't smiling any more.

Number Sixty-three: The Bottom
What Were the Roles We Were Porn to Play?

January 2019

In early 2016, I go on two separate dates with **Sixty-three**, a puppy-faced banker with deep, doleful eyes, but we (okay, me) decide to part ways because there's no spark. He's sweet, eager and adorable, but if I wanted any of those things, I would have adopted an actual puppy.

His niceness exhausts me. There are too many when-can-I-see-you-agains and too little time between texts. One minute we are holding hands, the next he's hinting at taking me along as a plus one to a wedding six months later.

His brother's wedding. Doesn't he know that first dates come with expiry dates? I gradually let him fade out of my life and my chat history, until he's a detail that gets archived to make space for vacation pictures and photo-editing apps.

And now here we are, three years later. I still don't have a puppy, and I don't have any dates either. Well, now is the time to make amends. I wipe off my ~~memories of ghosting him~~ conscience and decide to start over with a clean slate.

'How's it going, pup?' I shoot a quick non-committal text.

'Do I know you?' he texts back, almost immediately.

Oh … how rude. I might be unreasonable, but am I unforgettable? I am just about to type something scathing when he texts again.

'Can I see your pictures, please?'

I switch back to my profile, confused, and realize that my pictures have been accidentally deleted. He really doesn't know who I am. I could just be yet another blank profile shooting blanks in the online datingscape. Where does this take me?

Well, I can be anybody he wants me to be. Should I try being a nicer person? A man who shows grit? A gentleman who's against ghosting? There's always a first time.

'Did you forget me already, kid?' I type, playing the mysterious stranger card.

'How about you jog my memory with a picture?'

'So soon, son?' I joke, giggling into my knuckles.

'A little refresher will always help …'

'Are you ready to be refreshed?' I send. It might sound like an innuendo, but I am in good company.

He types, and then he deletes. As I decide between a meme and a mug shot, I see the dancing dots yet again. He's typing.

And then there's a picture of him butt naked, his hands tied with a work tie.

'Would daddy like to gag me to help me remember?'

Number Sixty-four: The Artist
Why Do We Mistake Toxicity as a Prescription Drug for True Love?

One of life's biggest tragedies is assuming you'll meet the Greatest Love Of Your Life™ through a meet-cute. 'Why can't we have it all?' the average gay man would ask, 'The pyrotechnics, the bevvy of doves, or a four-string quartet … at the very least?'

The average gay man is a tough species to please, but real life has different plans. There are no birds, no fireworks, and definitely no quartets. Not even a solo clarinet. Instead, I meet **Sixty-four** on Grindr.

This is no meet-cute. It's a meat-cute.

Sixty-four is a painter – no, an artist, he corrects my narration – 'I paint to feel alive, so it's different,' he says. That's so pretentious it might actually be true. **Sixty-four** dreams by day and paints by night, fuelled by whatever intoxicant that takes his fantasy. Sometimes he finds it packed and stacked in Ziploc pouches, sometimes he finds it hidden away in tin cases and empty cigarette boxes. And very rarely, he finds it in a man. I mostly want to be free, he tells me. It takes me eight months to realize that I am included in this elaborate list of things he wishes to be freed from.

For now, he's on a search to be many someones, but he's not worried about finding himself yet. What he's worried about finding is, in fact, some inspiration.

Have you ever thought about being a muse?

Is he serious? When has a line that flat ever worked on anyone, I can't even begin to—

'Why won't I be?' he grins a crooked smile, and the butterflies do the Congo in the deep recesses of my stomach. What are these palpitations but not a sign of fresh blooming love?

Sixty-four is not conventionally good looking. In fact, the average gay man would say that he's not even *remotely* good looking. His face is too disproportionate, and his smile seems dispassionate – only reinforced by a weak cleft chin and tiny lips – but his kohl-rimmed eyes speak more words than mine ever could.

The ~~painter~~ artist lives in a modest two-bedroomed house in the central suburbs, with a mother who doesn't ask too many questions and a sister who doesn't give too many answers. He paints cultures and mythologies, sometimes using the floor as an easel – splatters of paint on the wall, strokes of oil pastels on tile. He draws everywhere he can – scribbles on loose paper, doodles on his phone. Sometimes, he even draws on (and out of) people.

Like me, for instance. 'Why don't you consider it?' he asks, tracing a deep scrawl down my soul.

I chuckle, but he doesn't laugh. Instead, he takes a swig of his beer, and I see an old tattoo slithering down his collarbone. I long to touch it; trace it with my fingers, create lusty invisible boundaries down his lanky frame. His body is a treasure trail of such tattoos; a '*map of all the men who've left him heartbroken over the past decade*', he calls it.

That's a *lot* of tattoos, but I am here writing this book, so I can't complain. A right-wing political consultant left him with a thristle of roses, an Italian expat with the pentagram on his wrist; there's a band around his ankle from a brief fling with a Bollywood B-lister, and an embroidery of carnations from his longest relationship ever: the young, rebellious son of an erstwhile MLA. His body is an evergrowing canvas, he proudly tells me, and he wears each heartbreak like a war medal. No fallouts are explained, no answers given.

What will I leave behind? I sigh. What is this constant breathlessness if not a sign of solidifying love?

'Do you want a smoke?' he asks, offering me a cigarette. Ours is an adventure of adrenaline, excitement, spontaneity and ... cigarette butts? There are too many cigarette butts. He's already on his ninth for the night. I am only eight hundred and fifty-five cigarettes away from a severe heartbreak.

'Where do we go from here?'

We go on a whirlwind, sir.

That's exactly how it is with **Sixty-four**. Every meeting is a short burst of serotonin, dopamine, oxytocin and whatnots. He's addictive. When it's time for me to leave, I already crave to go back. I want more.

Can I have some more, please?

'I'll see you soon …' he laughs, and shuts the door on my face. I live on, sustained by the anticipation of my next endorphin rush.

Over the next six-odd months, we feed each other memories, like we feed each other lunch. That time he made me fish curry? *Can I have another bite?* That lovely long drive down to the beach? *So tasty.* That party at his friend's where he tells them we are together? *I am really liking this, can you give me some more?* His indifferent attitude towards my lack of a job? *I think you should eat some of this too.* His utter disregard for my time that one time he was supposed to meet my friends? *I don't think I can eat any more, but maybe I should have one more bite?*

'So … where are we really headed?' I ask him, at the end of it all. *He's suddenly full.*

The change doesn't happen overnight; it creeps in slowly. A cruel joke here, a casual remark there. There's a reference to a 'sex date from last Wednesday', an anecdote shared about a 'Grindr chat'. He's weaning me off – microdosing me with frequent jibs and jabs – so that it would only soften the blow later. It's like magic.

And for my next trick, I'd confuse emotional unavailability with sizzling chemistry. But for now, I only want one more hit, just one tiny hit. A drag. One whiff.

Hit me.

Hit me.

Hit me.

And then he does.

'I need some time off …' he texts me, eight months from our first meeting.

And then he's gone.

If you've never gone through withdrawal, you don't know shit about it. You think you do, because you saw a movie in the '90s with Sanjay Dutt in it, but you don't. You think you know because you went cold turkey on cigarettes, or did a 'social media detox for your mental sanity', but you still … don't. Going off Instagram is great, but it's not going to leave you with a foreboding sense of despair for the rest of your life. It's not going to leave you waking up with cold sweats. It's not going to make you want to die.

What is this trepidation but not a sign of impending heartbreak? Do I want to be left behind as a doodle on his tapestry of ink – or worse, does he even think I'm not worthy to be a part of his giant tapestry? Am I not smart enough for him? Am I not distinguished? Am I not dapper? Am I not proper? Am I not nice? Am I not good? Am I not right?

Wait. Am I not secure enough?

It's time to remove the emotional Band-Aid once and for all. Maybe someday I'll have the courage to run away from everything that makes me miserable, but today is not that day. I flip out my phone and pour it all out. Every tiny feeling, every minuscule detail. I highlight all the highs and gloss over all the lows. This email could be a prescription.

And then I wait.

He's typing, and then he's not. Typing. Not typing. Typing. Not typing.

My heart beats to those dancing dots and then it stops.

And then he disappears again. Three days later, my phone lights up to a text. It's him.

'I can't do this. We have to stop seeing each other. Please don't text me any more.'

'Why?' I get myself to ask.

The dots are dancing again.

'Sweetheart ...' he starts, and my face lights up with hope. 'I don't know how to tell you, but you aren't my type. I'll only you hurt you.'

So easy. It can't be this ... easy. I want more. I need more. Hit me. Hit me. Hit me.

'What's your type then?'

'Not you.'

'Why not?'

'You are fat. You are ugly. You are desperate.'

He decides we need to part ways because of artistic differences. He sees himself as alone, I see myself as finally awake.

12

Heartbreak Hotel

12.1 The Gentleman's Guide to Every Heartbreaker in the World: Sometimes a Bonus Feature Is All You Need

Sumit, an illustrator, met Zishaan, an interior designer, at a friend's bring-a-single mixer.

It was a classic meet-cute. A match made in architectural heaven, he would tell his kids one day. They had mistakenly picked up each other's glasses (double vodka sodas with a hint of lime juice) and then bonded all night over their mutual love for the *Big Little Lies* soundtrack. Before the party ended, they picked up each other's Instagram handles.

After a whirlwind first date at a local bistro, Zishaan texted Sumit telling him that he wanted to see him again. And again. And again.

After the second date – an indie movie at a derelict single-screen – Zishaan messaged with a stream of endearing heart emojis.

After the third, the designer made a joke about the chocolate chip sundaes they had just shared right after he kissed him goodbye under the starry sky. He'd use that one in his wedding speech, Sumit thought to himself later that night.

Sumit had met a lot of men in his life. There was the 'it boy' he had spent months chasing (who dumped him for a socialite prince), the gym freak he had joined the gym with (who believed in free weights and free love), the hipster he had gone vegan for (who ditched him for an Alt-J's concert), the sapiosexual who made him do crossword puzzles (and realized he was not as good), and lastly, the fuckboy who said he wanted to give Sumit all his love (but gave him genital crabs instead). So many men, but none had made him feel this way.

With his broad grin and broader shoulders, Sumit rightfully thought Zishaan was the One. He was charming, he was funny, he was full of those soul-stirring words that made Sumit dream of Disney musicals. Plus, he didn't have genital crabs.

But the one thing he was *not*?

Available.

Five dates in, Zishaan was always busy. He was always swamped with work. He was always attending a friend's birthday. He was always a 'let's just chill next week?' text away.

In retrospect, Zishaan was the quintessential heartbreaker, and like many others like him, he eventually pulled a Houdini, and disappeared without a trace from Sumit's life. The Disney musical sadly couldn't even make it to its second act.

What Makes a Heartbreaker?

Like Zishaan (and other self-proclaimed misunderstood men), the heartbreaker is the junk food of the dating pool – good for a quick bite, but bad for your long-term health. But when there's no Happy Meal, can you really tell your Disney prince from the douchebag?

It's simple. Wave away all that fairy dust and scroll through this list before you start planning your tropical bae-cation in Aruba. If the object of your affection checks five items on this list, he gets a yellow card; if he checks seven, he gets a red card; and if he gets more than ten, stop reading this list and send him a goodbye text right away.

Because there's a chance he never will.

- The heartbreaker wears his own line of perfume. It's clean and invigorating, and has notes of cypress combined with hints of cardamom, cedarwood and a base of vetiver root, resulting in a blend that's 'comfortingly familiar and mature'.
- He calls it *Heartbreak* by 'Me'.
- The heartbreaker will look at you endearingly and tell you that 'he's never felt this way about anyone else before'.
- He's probably also said this to three other boys in the past week.
- The heartbreaker is quick to christen you with a pet name. It's usually a variation of his favourite dessert.
- It's also a tactic because he doesn't remember your name.
- The heartbreaker disables his read receipts on WhatsApp because it's so 'exhausting' to keep a tab on all the conversations.
- The heartbreaker flakes like he Instagrams.
- Incessantly.
- The heartbreaker's favourite adjective to describe himself is also the working title of his autobiography.
- *Misunderstood.*
- The heartbreaker calls himself a 'lone wolf'. The alpha of a one-man army. He never talks about his family, friends or anyone really significant, and seems committed to keeping it that way.
- Yet, he's always hanging out with them when you try making a plan.
- As he hand-feeds you breakfast one day, he'll laugh and tell you how everyone will warn you that he has a bad reputation.
- Only he's not joking.
- The heartbreaker doesn't roll up his sleeves, because that's where he 'wears his heart.'
- Only this time, he's joking.
- The heartbreaker only wants to 'hang out'.
- The heartbreaker leaves a trail of likes through three years worth of your Instagram pictures.

- But he still won't request to follow you.
- You spend more time talking *about* the heartbreaker than *to* him.
- The heartbreaker doesn't like to '*plan*'; he'd rather just '*live*'.
- In the confines of his living room, with pre-mixed cans of gin and tonic.
- The heartbreaker flits through relationships like you flit through magazines at the dentist's. In fact, he ended his last relationship just while you were ending your workout for the day.
- When he asks you to come over for some #NetflixAndChill, that's all that he wants to do – binge-watch a Netflix original and chill with canapés and a bottle (or two) of expensive wine.
- Bonus points if it's a bottle of York Sparkling Cuvee Brut.
- Additional bonus points if he makes the canapés himself.
- The heartbreaker is too conflicted/damaged/busy to be 'in a relationship'. He wears it like a badge, nonetheless, and uses it to introduce himself at mixers. It works like a charm, especially when he mistakes your double vodka soda for his.
- The heartbreaker isn't necessarily a bad person. He's just a bad person for you.
- See, but that's the thing about our guy. He'll tell you he's not a heartbreaker.
- And that's exactly what makes him one.

So pull out those Band-Aids. You'll need one.

Number Sixty-five: The Taken
Does It Count If No One Was on a Break?

March 2016 / January 2017 / October 2018 / September 2019

Sixty-five is an investment banker with a high profile bank in the suburbs. **Sixty-five** is a consultant with a global MNC that operates out of an industrial estate. **Sixty-five** runs a family business of jewellery imports but secretly aches for a trust fund. **Sixty-five** is a network producer who shoots celebrity interviews. And from one time, **Sixty-five** is a failed television actor who's waiting for his big break.

Sixty-five is a template. He wants to meet casually first. 'Would you like to get a drink sometime?' he asks nervously. Sex is not mentioned. The idea pops its head eagerly, but we ignore it.

'Sure, why not?' I agree, but we both know that drinks will never happen.

I meet him in hotel rooms and lounges, and on two separate (and equally shameful) occasions, I meet him at his house. **Sixty-five** is not a man with many faces. **Sixty-five** is a face for many men.

'So … can we be friends?' he asks me once we are done, wiping the guilt off his brow as he unlocks the doubly latched bedroom door. The drinks didn't happen.

It's time to address the elephant in the room.

His wife. (And no, she's obviously not in the room.)

Sixty-five is married, and often has kids. **Sixty-five** is happy, but he's 'not living a lie'. **Sixty-five** doesn't think this is cheating, because 'you are not a woman, so does it even count?' **Sixty-five** thinks that I will never get what he's going through. **Sixty-five** wants to know if I'd like to 'continue being friends and maybe meet him for drinks sometime'. We both know that drinks will never happen.

'Why don't I call you?' I smile, as I book my ~~walk of shame~~ cab back home.

We both know that I won't.

12.2 Am I Picking the Wrong Men?

All the Reasons You Need to Break It Off Right Away

For every relationship that works, there are dozens that don't. In his many (short-lived) romances, Kartik's had a lot of experience with the latter. Before I comment on his knack for always choosing the wrong men, he counts them down on his fingers himself.

There was the boy who got passive-aggressive. The one who said he could never stay in a monogamous relationship. The one who had a drinking problem. The one who had a problem with him drinking. The one who fought a lot. The one who stared a lot. The one who hated his dog. The one who treated him *like* his dog. The one he had nothing in common with. The one he had family in common with. He's run out of fingers to count on now. The list is endless, but the signs were not.

They were all breaking him. Breaking his spirit. Breaking his worth. Breaking his ability to believe. And in the case of one extremely toxic fitness blogger, they were also breaking his back.

All he had to do was break up with them.

But when has life ever been that easy?

Kartik believes he's always lived life on the edge. He likes playing with fire, he once told me. I pass. I don't even like playing with matches.

Do any of these men come with warning labels, I want to ask, but I stop myself.

If they did, wouldn't we find them in a supermarket?

'Thankfully, now I know what to look for,' he says. 'You know, if I had the time, I'd even write a book.' I don't tell him I'm already working on one. I'll put him in the acknowledgements.

So this one's for him. As Kartik would like me to tell you, the next time you come across any of these indicators, pull up your socks and pull the plug instead.

1. **The ex whisperer**

During fights. While having breakfast. While eating sushi. At brunch. On the phone. At your sister's birthday. At a drunken night out with friends. In bed. Out of bed. And most importantly, when you propose.

Any man who brings up his ex every other instant needs to be dropped in an instance. Before he drops you for the ex (which he will).

2. **The suspect**

Ring the alarm bells when someone acts suspicious as you reach for their phone, because these are the only reasons why your boyfriend should have the nervous sweats when you are casually using his mobile:

a) He's a secret agent.
b) He's planning your surprise birthday party.
c) He has diarrhoea.
d) It's actually *your* phone and he stole it – in which case, you should still dump him.

3. **The fake**

If he gushes over your mum's chocolate cake at a family dinner and then complains about how he's never liked desserts, it's time you desert the two-faced liar. Building on the classic Indian trope of 'family comes first', never trust a guy who badmouths yours. Why not?

He's probably doing the same for you, even when you are not baking him cake.

4. **The fighter**

Remember one thing, boys. If you are in a relationship with someone who always picks a fight, it's time you pick up your bags and leave.

5. **The substitute**

Have you ever had dosas with mustard sauce because you couldn't find your jar of chutney? Winging a relationship that isn't heading anywhere ('because something is better than nothing') feels the same way. Only in this case, you end up with a bad case of emotional indigestion.

Never date a guy because there's no other man on the horizon; date a guy because you think he *is* the horizon.

6. **The wanderer**

He's always trying to 'find' himself. In fact, he'll wander around the world looking for answers – he'll shack up with Samuel in Spain, jam with Jeremy in Jamaica, cruise with Colin in the Caribbean and binge drink with Benjamin in Berlin – but the only thing he'll end up finding is chlamydia.

7. **The trigger**

You came to this book looking for a sign to break up with him. But if you've just gone through an instruction manual for finding love, you are not in the wrong place; you are simply in the wrong relationship. Dump your boyfriend before he finds out the hard way while snooping through your bookshelf.

Number Sixty-six: The Pianist
Ex and the City?

September 2014

Breaking up can be difficult. Ask me; I've been there. A relationship is a long, arduous climb up a rather rickety ladder. A break-up is the evil person who pushes the ladder down when you are midway. Sometimes, if you are lucky, the end of a romance can result in a friendship that no fall can ever break. Your ex will move on and be happy, and that in turn will make you happy.

But not when you are **Sixty-six**. He's a musician who plays the piano for money and solves complex math equations for fun. Over steak sandwiches and Sudoku puzzles, we gently nudge our way into talking about our exes – a first-date topic that is usually controversial, and almost as complicated as trying to solve an integral equation blindfolded. (Why anybody would want to solve an integral equation blindfolded is beyond me.) What if we have friends in common? Or worse, exes?

But not when you are **Sixty-six**. He makes it light and breezy, and I find myself joking about all my misadventures with him. He chuckles at all the right moments, and his eyes crinkle in delight when I tell him about all the times I've had to wipe the proverbial footprint off my forehead. I'm not very good at math, but I know that our equation is rather balanced.

'Should we go back to your place?' I ask him at the end of the date, hopeful that he can teach me more about integration.

'Sure, but let me just check up on my roommate? I need to see if he's home …' he says, brandishing his phone. Roommate? I didn't know he had a roommate.

'Yeah, it's my ex, he hasn't moved out yet …' He grins sheepishly.

They broke up eight months ago.

And just like that, I break out of the equation.

12.3 A Beginner's Guide to Breaking Up

'It's over. It's *really* over.'

It's a Sunday night, but Aneesh isn't talking about the weekend.

He's talking about his relationship with Vir.

In the months to follow, he'll obsess over *why* it happened. Was it the sex? The glaring physical distance? The (even more) glaring wage gap? Their first fight from nine months ago? Their last holiday from three months ago?

For now, he's obsessing over *how* it happened. He'd felt the cracks in the wall; the slight tremors you feel at the beginning of a crumbling relationship. Kartik calls it an emotional earthquake – a solid 7.5 on the Richter scale of romances.

Yes, he could sense something was wrong, but he assumed it had to do with the lull in their relationship. Not every day had to be a romedy special. Not every day was full of fireworks. There were good days, and then there were bad days.

'But what relationship doesn't have cracks?' he asks, 'What relationship is a bed of roses?'

Aneesh chooses to ignore that the last few months were only full of bad days.

And yet it happened. Vir called him while he was on a business trip. They hadn't spoken for three days. ('I was busy with work,' says Aneesh, 'and he was busy showing his friends around.') Which is why the call had felt like a breather; a breath of fresh air at the end of a really long day of conferences and PowerPoint slides. It was supposed to be them starting over.

'I can't do this any more ...' Vir's voice crackled over the phone. Aneesh doesn't remember the rest. He blames connectivity issues.

Somewhere, the cracks led to fissures, and the relationship saw its due course. Their love story fell to dust. A twenty-minute call ended their two-year-long romance. Just like that, the breath of fresh air had been taken away. The fireworks had fizzled out. Their romedy special had been cancelled.

Breaking up with someone is no bed of roses. Nicely put, it's a sledgehammer to the head. Or, in Aneesh's case, it was an extremely expensive ISD call.

Is there really a nice way to tell someone that things are not working out any more, and that you might want to see other people instead? Maybe a cake that says 'sorry' in butter-cream frosting and a chilled bottle of champagne monogrammed with his initials (and his alone)?

Most definitely not. But there *are* many different ways to bubble wrap that blow that often accompanies a break-up. You just need to know when (and how) to do it.

When Is a Text Message Okay?

Breaking up via text message has so much bad press, it's like the Paleo diet – it's the 'leaving him at the altar' version of short-lived flings.

But that's exactly what short-lived flings need – a swift, final blow that is as easy as it is bloodless. It helps you get straight to the point, be emotionless (and still not sound like a cold-blooded killer) and is free of hassles such as tears, long bills at the restaurant or a swift punch to the face that is sure to break your nose.

You can be lying through your teeth or hiding what you really want to say, but in all honesty, a break-up text is your 'get-out-of-jail-free card – especially when you want to make sure that you don't have to endure a humiliating public break-up in front of your friends.

How do I do it?

The key to tactically breaking off a relationship through a well-worded text is to *not sound like a douchebag*. It's that simple. Pull that plug with those crucial 160 characters, but make sure you do it right – men can be taken back, but texts can't.

The last thing you would want is a spurned lover to screenshot all your shoddily written words and post them all over social media for the world to ~~see~~ judge:

Some appropriate things to say:

- 'I really don't think it's working out.'
- 'We've lost our spark, haven't we?'
- 'I think I need some time for myself. I am sorry.'

- 'I think we've both been trying to make this work. Can't we just be friends instead?'

... and some things that would sound inappropriate:

- 'I think you are really ugly, and the sex was terrible.'
- 'No more see you later, alligator.'
- 'I've moved on, mate.'
- 'Didn't you get the memo? We are done!'
- 'I am currently in bed with your best friend, bud. Don't H8! ☹'

When is it okay?

- You've gone out on a few nondescript dates.
- You've seen each other a few times, but it's been gradually fading into nothingness.
- The last time you saw each other was a little more than two weeks ago.

When is it not?

- You just finished your two-year anniversary.
- He's waiting for you at the airport.
- You are on your way to his sister's engagement party.

When Is a Phone Call Fine?

While a break-up text lets a person cope with the death of a relationship in their own way (crying in the shower, writing dark love sonnets, getting a fabulous makeover, etc.), a phone call helps make it *slightly* more personal.

How Do I Do It?

Know where you are going to be making the call from – preferably a quiet place, like your bedroom. It's probably not a good idea to get on the call when you are on a bathroom break at work, getting a haircut at the salon or buying farewell shots for your friends at the bar.

At the same time, make sure they are in the right place (and the right frame of mind) to hear the bad news. You don't want to catch them at an odd time, especially when they are in the middle of an important work presentation, burying their recently deceased dog, or worse, watching the series finale of *Game of Thrones*.

What happens after you tell them? Do you wait for them to ~~reason with you~~ voice out their reactions, which can feature anywhere between a compendium of expletives that are hurled at you, to a heartfelt, whimpering plea to take them back?

You can hear them out, but remember to bear the brunt of their emotionally charged response. If you want to cut the call short, be polite. In the end, dismissing a huge phone bill is okay, but dismissing a broken heart is not.

Some appropriate things to say:

- 'I think it'll be good for the two of us if we break up.'
- 'We haven't been working out …'
- 'I might not be the right person for you.'

… and things that would sound inappropriate:

- 'I want to break up with you. Right now.'
- 'The truth is, your breath stinks. Can I send you an email instead?'
- 'Are you at your mother's funeral? Oh, I wanted to tell you something …'
- 'Can't hear me? Hello? Hello? Which club are you at? I have to tell you that …'

When is it okay?

- You've been seeing each other a few weeks, but he's been too busy to meet you lately.
- The last time you met each other was such a disaster that you are just too embarrassed to do this face to face.

When is it not?

- You are prepping a party for your ten-year-long relationship.
- He's waiting for you at your friend's party.
- He just co-signed a lease for an apartment with you.

When Do I Need to Do It in Person?

Breaking up with someone in person is like taking the JEE exam hungover, but with a rock concert playing in the background.

Only, there are no multiple-choice questions.

When you break up with a man face-to-face, the snug security blanket that comes with letting go of someone over text (or a phone call) is snatched away. Not only do you need to choose *your words* carefully, but you also need to *look* like you mean them (even if you don't).

How Do I Do It?

Saying 'we should break up' or even a succinct 'I don't think we are working out' works better than the rather cold (and equally accusatory) 'I want to break up with you' – *especially* when you are the one who's ripping out his heart and flinging it far into the sea of heartbroken men.

By saying 'we', you are taking part of the blame on yourself (as you should), ensuring you don't end up with a broken nose, bad karma or a face full of red wine (or all three). Tell him why you are breaking up with him, but don't make it too real. If you want to cut the cord because you think someone's voice is too shrill or they chew funny, it's best you keep it to yourself. Be politically correct in a way that it doesn't look like you are trying to be polite.

Once the talk is done, smile at them sadly, and if you are in a place where neither of you wants to kill the other, hug it out. And then let go.

Walk away, but don't turn back. Let them move on, because you need to move on too.

How Do I Respond to a Break-up?

Breaking up in the Time of Social Media: Bonus Feature

Millennials would agree that pulling the plug on your ex's social media is the final speed bump you hit after you end a relationship. If *Black Mirror* has taught us anything (besides the fact that technology can *end* you), it's that feelings might fade but feeds don't.

Break-ups are tough. But it's the aftermath that's much worse. This isn't the '90s, where interactions with your ex fizzled out as soon as your relationship did. We live in the time of social media, and your ex is *everywhere*. Popping up on your Facebook timeline with a new relationship update. Sliding into your Instagram grid with a happy picture. Sneaking into your Twitter thread with a tweet about the #SingleLife.

The *only* place they are not?

With you.

'But I don't mind having my ex on my social media,' you'll try to reason. Isn't that the healthy way to end a relationship?' Yes, but this person is categorically not a friend who's turned sour, it's an ex.

Do you want to see them doing shots at the bar just *mere weeks* after they took shots at you? I guess not. When you break up, it's crucial to see as little of their public information as possible, so avoid all their handles like you would avoid genital herpes. Nothing can ruin a day like seeing an Instagram story of him canoodling with a ~~boyfriend-stealer~~ new guy at your favourite restaurant. One minute you are casually stalking his profile, and before you know it, you accidentally like a picture three grids down his best friend's dog's

Instagram page. From there on, it's a downward spiral of double taps and retweets.

Social media is like that common friend who's always updating you about your ex's life (even if you don't want it) while listing out all the reasons you shouldn't get back together in the first place (even if you do want to). No one needs friends like that. It's time to say goodbye to this common friend.

But listen, you don't need to close all your social media accounts to find closure in real life. Just follow this simple three 'U' strategy to unleash the ~~next~~ best version of you: Unfollow. Unsubscribe. Understand.

Want to know how this works? Here are some quick tips to follow for social media Break-ups on the most popular apps of today.

Facebook

Do stay friends on Facebook, but unfollow his posts. That way, you don't look bitter and can still avoid seeing things you don't want to see: his new relationship updates, for instance.

Instagram

Nothing triggers one more than their ex's Instagram feed. Instagram's mute feature is a solid way of ex-proofing your life, because while you no longer see his ~~fabulous life~~ pictures, you can continue driving him crazy as you live your best life ahead.

Clubhouse

Block them right away, because the last thing you need is getting notified every time they step into a 'Shoot Your Shot' room with self-proclaimed hot gay singles (and we all know how they all turn out).

Google+

The fact that your relationship has become redundant is only because Google+ no longer exists.

TikTok

If your ex came with a TikTok channel, there's a reason this Break-up was meant to happen. Revel in it.

Snapchat

Unfollow right away. Snapchat is a cesspool of regrets and #NSFW thirst traps, and you don't want a picture of his junk burning your eyes any more (than it did before).

Twitter

It's better to just avoid Twitter completely, because when have your angst-ridden tweets throwing shade at an ex ever been attractive?

Whatsapp

Three words: Delete. That. Number.

Every once in a while, you'll have this sudden urge. It will hit you in the middle of the night as you toss in bed, or when you are answering emails at work. It might even sneak in when you're writing out a birthday card for the best friend. It most often comes for you when you are drunk and feeling your most ~~confident~~ vulnerable self at the bar. This is the urge to reach out to your ex with a well-worded WhatsApp text, and ask them to take you back. You'll beg, you'll plead, you'll reason, and you'll hate. You'll sound desperate, even though you think you sound rather *dashing*.

For this alternate universe to play out, you need their number. Cut that cord right where it begins. You know how this works.

LinkedIn

Wait. Why are you even on each other's LinkedIn?

12.4 What Do We Do with a Broken Heart?

The concepts of love and heartbreak are like two sides of the same coin. They both pop up their heads in the middle of the night, bringing with them a constant state of distress and an almost surreal craving for double chocolate chip ice-cream. The only difference?

When you know you are in love, you know it gets better. The latter, not so much. But that's the thing: while getting your heart broken might seem like it's a bad thing, it's not. It makes you more real and more empathetic. In fact, once you've had your heart irreparably damaged, there are fewer chances of you doing that to someone else.

Not that it stops the best of us.

Kartik understands why a broken heart is a part of growing up. If you've been reading this book end to end, you'd know that he flits in and out of love every other month, flashing dimples from boy to boy, and picking up stories and tabs at various bars across the city. He says he's hardened now, and keeps his heart in check for charming boys, just like he keeps it in check for cholesterol.

'How many times have you *really* fallen in love?' I ask him.

Twice.

'How many times have you had it broken?'

Seven.

The first time he fell in love, it felt like everything before had been black and white: it was a giant Rorschach drawing full of inkblots and other things that didn't make sense. Kartik says he understood how a colour TV must have felt in the early '80s.

But in 2012.

Lakshman, a musician in his mid-thirties, was straight out of a Jane Austen novel. He was charming, attentive and everything a Darcy-loving twenty-three-year-old would want.

Mr Darcy on *drugs*, that's what he, was. It was love that was chemical. A constant burst of over-the-counter oxytocins and dopamine, Kartik's love grew in a fug of cigarette smoke and strains of marijuana straight from the hills. The love affair went on for seven months – a 'will they, won't they' saga that we've grown to love on television. But there was no season finale, and no ratings to vie for. He finally decided to take the plunge and tell Lakshman how he felt.

And he did, on a long phone call that changed day to night.

There was radio silence on the other side.

For two days, he didn't hear back. He kept his distance, wanting to give Lakshman time to react. You can't make such grand decisions overnight, can you? Rome wasn't built in a day, so there's no way that love stories could brew overnight. Sometimes, it takes seven months. Sometimes it takes seven months and three days.

On the third day, his phone beeped.

It was a text from Lakshman, telling him to never text back. It was over.

Things were moving too fast, and he didn't like it.

Kartik cried till he had a headache that day, followed by the first of many sleepless nights – nights where he imagined a multiverse of what ifs. What if they had never met? What if he never told Lakshman how he felt? What if he pleaded to go back to being lovers? What if it was never really a relationship to begin with? What if he would never fall in love again? What if he would never heal? What if he did?

I can't get myself to tell him that heartbreak is like any other pain; it takes time and space to heal. You can't leave a broken heart at home when you go to work. It's not a pet that can be cared for by a neighbour; it needs to be fed repeatedly and taken to the beach for long walks by the hour. You need to call in sick and nurture it.

The heartbreak lasted all of four months and seventeen days (he knows because he counted), till one day he realized he needed to move on. The Jane Austen novel had ended, and he needed to go get ice cream.

And he did.

'What changed?' I ask him.

Like most things in this world, his heartbreak had reached an expiry date. The road to a fulfilling life is littered with broken hearts, memories, and feelings that will never truly heal.

He broke his first heart shortly after – the first of many. 'It's funny how one man's hero can be another man's villain,' he half jokes.

Kartik met Purab, twenty-five, an English professor on Facebook. Like most English professors, Purab was sensitive and beautiful. 'He looks like an Indian Tom Cruise,' Kartik tells me, and I can instantly tell that the story has a bittersweet end. Most tales involving Tom Cruise do. I expect nothing less from his doppelgänger.

One poke led to another, and before they knew it, they were texting deep into their pillows into the depths of the night. And like most love stories that succeed the death of a broken heart, it was fast (and equally furious).

Was Purab filling the Lakshman-sized hole in Kartik's life?

It felt like the same fug of fumes; the same sonnets of cigarette smoke.

Well, almost.

They shared a quick life-changing kiss on their second date, a rum-filled extravagance at a local bar, and by their fourth – a long winding walk by the beach – they'd exchanged brisk I-like-you over a post-date phone call.

Yet, something felt amiss. There were oxytocins and dopamine, constant bursts of it, but they felt borrowed, as if they hadn't been actually prescribed. The affair felt staged, he tells me – 'like we were playing with string puppets.'

Not the right term of endearment for an ex, but I don't tell Kartik that.

Kartik felt detached, but he had to end things before hearts (and his face) were broken. Kartik couldn't be a Lakshman. It was a long coffee date. Words were exchanged, numbers were deleted, and abuses were hurled. It was dirty, but it had to be done.

'Is that how it ended?' I ask. I am not very sure his dimples can help him out any more.

This is the moment where I take a break from ~~Kartik's tale of douchery~~ regular programming and remind you that we aren't reading a short story. This is still a book, reader, and it's not forgotten its one true purpose of helping you cope with heartbreak. We'll be back with a follow up to this thrilling ~~trainwreck~~ tale, but first, we take a quick detour.

Back to the goal of this guide.

As for Kartik?

He smiles and goes to get another cup of coffee.

Number Sixty-seven: The Copywriter
Fresh Hearts Make for Easy Targets for Love Bombs

October 2013

Another writer, another day, another boy, another bar.

It takes me four drinks to realize that **Sixty-seven**, a copywriter visiting from Bangalore, is a textbook romantic. He's two minutes away from telling me that he thinks the One exists.

'How are you so charming?' he slurs, with rum running down his embroidered shirt.

Sixty-seven is also very drunk. He's twenty minutes away from vomiting all over the sidewalk outside, but I am already blushing.

'Oops,' he exclaims, as his winding arms knock down one of the glasses off our table. I don't react negatively to any of it. Unlike the rest of them, he's not cynical: he fills me with optimism that almost feels alien. There are no mind games at play, just a constant stream of witty banter and throwaway compliments. Plus, we both like the same books (and also, alcohol). The horizon seems promising, and I can't see a red flag for miles. It's surprising how perfect I think he is ...

Until I realize that he's also two hours away from telling me that he's already fallen in love with me, and three hours away from vomiting all over my shoes.

12.5 How Do You Survive a Break-up?

The Single Survival Checklist for Men Who've Recently Let Go of Their Relationships

So here we are.

Like Aneesh, you've just gone through (what you feel is) the worst break-up of your life. You're standing all alone in your apartment, with your no-longer-jointly-owned cat, half of your belongings and some bits of your heart. You're single and stressing out over waking up to an empty bed and an emptier life.

But here's the thing. You're obviously going to get through it. All you need are a few essentials to start over before you get back in the game. So how about you prep your house (and your heart) with this essential (Recently) Single Survival Kit?

❒ Crisp white sheets

Nothing screams the single life louder than brand new white sheets, completely devoid of the stains and smells of your monstrous ex. It makes your dull, depressing apartment (and you) appear larger and brighter, and is the perfect background for the various flings you'll bring back home over the weeks to come.

❒ A super-sized box of condoms

All the flings that you bring back home aren't going to cover themselves.

❒ Instant noodles

You'll need packets and packets of instant noodles, because you won't feel like cooking anything more complicated. It's your 4 a.m. friend, and you can douse it with everything you've got – the spare bit of ricotta cheese, some tomato ketchup, a little smidgeon of Tabasco, oregano that you painstakingly collected over years of pizza deliveries, a healthy drizzle of soy sauce and the dozen expletives you didn't use in your goodbye email.

And as you wait for those two minutes for the water to boil, you can cry. Because that's enough time to cry your heart out.

❒ A tub of your favourite ice-cream flavour in the fridge

Ice cream solves what therapy can't. Enough said.

❒ A therapist on speed dial

Just kidding, ice cream can only help in some ways.

❒ A set of spoons

But you'll need all the help you can get to finish that ice cream.

❒ An emptier smartphone

Delete the texts, the pictures from your vacation last year, the bill receipts from your dates, the sexts you sent each other on your anniversary and the screenshots you saved to use in a fight later (and did). Delete it all. Cleanse your phone, and then use it to call a friend over. Call all your friends over. Share your ice cream and your instant noodles with all of them. Repeat till you are happy.

❐ A Netflix account with high-speed internet

The only remedy to the perfect post-break-up life is HD quality television, free of commercial breaks (that will make you consider going back to your vile ex.)

Good luck binge-watching five seasons of *Money Heist* as you try your best to chew on your lukewarm instant noodles from last night.

❐ A bottle (or crate) of Cabernet Sauvignon stacked away in the closet

There's nothing like some wine loving to get you out of your slump and into bed with the cute writer you've been flirting with all of last week.

❐ A yoga mat

At some point, you'll open the blinds and want to lose all the ice-cream-induced weight. You'll want to get back into the dating game. You'll want to look like the best version of yourself.

On that day, you'll buy yourself a yoga mat (because deep down, you know you'll never commit to a gym membership right till the very end). You'll effectively end up using the mat as a background for your next Grindr picture.

❐ Optimism

One day, after an hour's worth of Pilates on your new yoga mat, you'll sit up straighter than before and tell yourself that this *isn't* the worst moment of your life. You'll throw out the leftover ice cream and drink the last bottle of wine. You'll wash the noodle-stained vessels and put them away. You'll tell yourself that you'll be okay.

You'll eventually start believing it.

Because you *will* be okay.

Number Sixty-eight: The Assistant Director
But Where Do Broken Hearts Go?

May 2013

Afternoon dates are always risky. Daylight can be unforgiving, and going for a drink in the middle of the day reeks of a bad decision that's waiting to put you under the interrogatory spotlight. But I clearly haven't learnt a lesson from my dates with **One**, **Ten**, **Twenty-eight** and the others.

Here we are, guzzling down glasses of Jack Daniels at half-past three. He's an assistant director who moved here with the dreams of making it big; you would assume he's a stereotypical cutout of thousands like him – men who want to ditch the commercial route to make something *meaningful*. 'I want to make real cinema,' they all say at film festivals, waiting in line to meet commercial film directors.

Yet, unlike all of them, he's different. I don't know whether **Sixty-eight**, with his intense green eyes and his cocky personality, gets to me or gets me. His jokes are sharp, but laced with sarcasm. If I touch one, I am sure I'd cut myself.

So I don't.

Instead, I humour his ego and play along. Every time he throws a snarky jibe my way, I gift-wrap it into a compliment and throw it back. Why can't you make eye contact? *It's because you make me nervous*. How have you never seen *Good Will Hunting*? *Maybe I can watch it with you*. Are you always so chatty? *Yes, but only when I feel a spark*.

I can make a living out of this.

Sixty-eight is wry enough not to leave a dry taste in your mouth. I'd gulp him down with a quick glass of Chardonnay. It's too hot for whisky at the moment … maybe I *should* shift to Chardonnay …

I can tell that the man was a hopeless romantic once. You can always tell by their eyes – bright and sparkly, but *also* shrewd. Over time, I'll find out that he's had his heart broken multiple times, which makes him jaded like thousands of gay men like him. He makes a joke about how I add too much whisky to my coke, and grins broadly like the Cheshire cat. His smile goes end to end, reaching his eyes.

But unfortunately, it doesn't reach mine.

12.5 This Is Why Everybody Needs a Broken Heart

Kartik always assumed that when someone breaks his heart, he'd cry for months and write long-winded emails begging them to take him back, like they do in the movies.

But it didn't happen.

In real life, he cried for a week and switched off his phone. A week after the dreaded text message from Lakshman, it wasn't sadness that he felt; it was the emptiness that stayed – the emptiness of knowing who he was *without* Lakshman. It stayed for months – sharing cups of tea, going for morning runs and watching the occasional late-night movie – till it faded away into nothingness. It took a part of him with it, like taking a goodbye gift.

Kartik got his heart broken multiple times over in the years to come; a string of boys with a series of red flags to their name – Harsh, a performance artist from the Gulf (turned out to be bisexual); Anirudh, a high-flying arbitrator from town (left him for his best friend); Rajesh, a struggling actor who stayed two states away (broke up with him while on vacation); Carl, the fashion manager from across the street (already had a boyfriend); Vaibhav, a yoga entrepreneur from New York (ghosted him after three spectacular dates); Saurabh, a lawyer from Delhi (wanted to remain discreet); Raghav, a sales associate from the hills (spent the night and never called back); and Puneet, a wry assistant director from the suburbs (friend-zoned him after a hookup). His trail of heartbreak runs 10x longer than Leonardo Di Caprio's Oscar acceptance speech.

But unless he decides to make an equally riveting speech about global warming and climate change, how does having a broken heart help?

Tremendously. He might not know what he wants from a relationship any more, but he knows what he doesn't; and he has a string of Lakshmans, Anirudhs, Harshs, Carls, Vaibhavs, Raghavs and Puneets to thank for that.

It's easy. At some point, he fell out of love with each of them. It took him days for some, weeks for others, and even years for a couple. But the feelings gradually faded away like ink stains on a white shirt. Each mistake became a memory. They all took souvenirs from his deteriorating heart, nonetheless. Someone needed closure. Someone wanted to show it to a friend. Someone wanted a bit of him to remember him by. Someone thought it was a nice shade of crimson.

I feel so bad; I offer him my almond biscuit. He's no hermit though, he says. He's collected his fair share of souvenirs too. I take back my almond biscuit.

As gay men, do we just collect broken hearts? Trading one for another till you find that kitschy one at a garage sale that you haggle over, and ultimately buy for half its price and take back home forever. It looks great by your computer – a patchwork of fuckboys, cowards and ghosts who disappeared in the dark – doesn't it?

In that case, should we just settle for this Mobius strip of heartbreak? One broken heart leads to another, till all that we are left with are emotionally damaged men who exchange pictures first, names and numbers later.

Not Kartik though.

People have different ways of coping with having their hearts splattered all over the floor. They join the gym. Start eating healthy. Write love ballads. Work on their button poetry. Grow a herb garden. Get a fabulous haircut. Take up jazz lessons. Learn Spanish. Listen to Taylor Swift's complete discography. Practise the flute. Paint an impressionist painting. Adopt a kitten (or two). Win a Grammy (or six).

Or just become Taylor Swift … Kartik just falls in love again.

But then again, he's not the same Kartik from 2012. He feels he's hardened now; it has helped him with the failed dates and the 'string of above-average men' that has been his life for the past few years. He knows he'll eventually find his way.

How does it help?

Because he's found a bit of himself every time he's lost some. Every time he had his heart broken, he rediscovered what he had lost to some other person. Lakshman's departure taught him that he despised cigarettes. Anirudh's exit made him a conversationist. Harsh's made him a believer. Rajesh's got him to join a gym. Carl's made him a better friend. Vaibhav's drove him towards escapism. Saurabh's led to his love for gin. Raghav's pushed him towards better grooming. Puneet's pushed him towards stand-up comedy. They all made him as they broke him.

But what happened to Purab? His absence unnerves me, but it seems to have no effect on Kartik. Is he also lost in the sea of cynical men and lost souls, with all the other above-average men that Kartik's been complaining about?

Kartik smiles again. His dimples need no GPS; they know their way.

He eventually did run into Purab at a bar, two months later. He was with someone else – a handsome man in his late thirties, with curly hair and a curlier smile. A banker. They even bought Kartik a drink. The English professor was in a better place with a better man.

Purab had found his ice cream.

And that makes Kartik believe that he will too.

12.6 What About Closure?

The Ultimate Handle-Your-Heartbreak Bucket List for Men Who Can't Let Go

It's over.

You've cut the cord, the phone calls and your heartstrings. You've had two tubs of ice cream at once. You've not showered for days. You've used up three cans of deodorant to mask it. You've blamed everyone, from your mother and your best friend to that boy who sat behind you in the seventh standard. You've heard (or wept to) Ariana Grande's entire playlist on loop. Thrice.

See, dealing with a break-up is only half the battle won, because getting over heartbreak is where you need to get all your troops out (unless you are Grande, in which case you'll just write another hit song about it).

Let me tell you this. Mending a broken heart is worse than trying to put together a torn Ralph Lauren gift voucher. While glue can be therapeutic (have you never spread it on your palms and peeled it off?), you'll need time and space, and multiple bottles of self-belief, to walk out of your shell. But hey, listen. While it might seem tough, it's not impossible. What do you do to soften the blow of a break-up?

Read this book. You've been doing it all along just fine.

Now heal away with this extremely helpful handle-your-heartbreak bucket list and fall in love with yourself (and someone else, hopefully) sooner than you can drunk-dial your ex on a lonely Tuesday night.

Get a haircut.
Deal with the split and the split ends with a quick makeover; one that probably doesn't cost as much as a wardrobe do-over.

Take a weekend trip.
You don't need to go to Hawaii or Paris to find yourself. Head off to the nearest vacation hotspot and drown your worries in draught beer.

Take up a sport.
Any sport. Preferably one that involves balls, so that you imagine your ex's face every time you hit it.

Clean up your house.
Remove all the letters, clothes, toothbrushes and love notes he left behind. Donate. Cleanse. Repeat till happy.

Find a new favourite restaurant.
Remember sharing maki rolls and miso soup at your favourite sushi bar? Feeding him wasabi peanuts and grinning like idiots over sake shots every Saturday night? You don't need to any more. It's time to make new memories with a new menu card.

Find a new favourite wine (or beer).
Because you'll need a fresh crate every weekend.

Read the biggest book you can find.
It'll save you a lot of time thinking about him.

Spend a day in bed.
Watch as many internet fail videos as you can.

Try out a class.
Channel all your angst into a class. Any class. Try something that interests you. Maybe try poetry. Although your chances of turning into Pablo Neruda overnight are very low, you'll have something to laugh over next year.

Cook up a fancy meal.
You'll need to get used to those.

Get all your STD tests done.
If you are going to start over, you better start clean.

Buy yourself a gift.
And post it to your home address. Act surprised when you receive it. Repeat till you believe.

Call your best friend.
But make sure they aren't in a patronizing mood.

Buy healthier food at the market.
Multigrain buns are better than your man's buns.

Make a playlist.
And fill it up with all the songs that your ex hated. Let that be a constant reminder to never go back.

Join a gym.
If you are going to be working up a sweat every time you think about your break-up, you might as well burn calories while you're at it.

Start running.
Learn to run fast, not run away from your problems.

Write an email to the ex.
Pour your heart out – about all the good and the bad things. Talk about that one time he puked all over your shoes after his thirtieth birthday, and how he got you cupcakes to make up for it the day after. Chuckle over that night you spilt wine all over his favourite shirt. Mull over the great sex. Vent out your anger. Laugh at your in-jokes. Tell him everything you ever wanted to say; cry about it after, and just when you are about to hit 'send', delete it.

Read a book about getting back in the game.
Just like this one.

And finally, get back in the game.
But only when you are ready.

Number Sixty-nine: The Last One

How to Be Single in Your Thirties … and Where Do We Go from Here?

Here we are.

Right at the very end of ~~your biggest life lesson ever~~ this book.

Congratulations on getting here, kid. You did it. You can bring out those tequila shots, because you now know everything there is to know about love, relationships and living life as a gay man in the country (or at least, everything that I know).

All the advice you got here is based on my ~~dating mistakes~~ real-life experiences and the stories I've heard over the years. Does that mean you need to memorize this guide and make it a part of your morning mantra? Well, I'd take at least *some* of it with a pinch of salt, because honestly, I made up a few of these rules.

Wait … *what*?

Before you throw this guide out of the window because you feel cheated, remember this – brushing your teeth is important; brushing this book aside is not. A lot of the stuff you read here is based on things that have happened to me, and they worked for me in the end (or at least some aspects of them did). But that also means there will *always* be exceptions to the rules that have been set in this book. There will always be anomalies. There are more than ten million queer men in the country, and at least ten of them will text you back even though you ghosted them after a drunken night of debauchery (none of them texted me back, but like I said – my story, my rules). All that aside, this book mostly comprises ~~cool things~~ hard facts that will work for you a *minimum* of 98.3 per cent of the time. Did I just make up these statistics?

You bet I did. Dating as a gay man is a lot about making these rules along the way. You do what works for you best. You adapt. You evolve. But most importantly, you survive.

Over the past decade, I met a lot of men who made it to these stories. Men with daddy issues, men with commitment issues, men with intimacy issues, men with drug issues, men with anxiety issues and the occasional man with no issues. And whether it worked out with them or not, I found out that each story had a definite ending. I didn't go back to any of these men (because what's the point of repeating the same mistakes again?), but I know that a lot of them found their own version of a happy ending. For some of them, it's still a work in progress. For the rest, it's a distant dream, but they haven't given up. Yet.

One is currently engaged. It's a new girlfriend. **Fifty-five** and **Fifty-six** broke up, but there are no new boyfriends. **Fifty-two** and **Fifty-three** are still together, but there's a new house. **Thirty-seven** finally quit his horrid job and joined the environmental law firm of his dreams. He's still dating his best friend, and they've reached a mutual understanding to take more selfies together. **Three** is dating a young up-and-coming filmmaker, and they've reached a mutual understanding to learn how to enjoy sex together.

Twenty-eight wiped those tears, moved to Berlin and fell in love with a French expat. **Thirty-nine** wiped himself a clean slate, and got out of rehab. **Fifty-two** bought a bit part in a movie. **Fifty-nine** bought his third house in the city. **Twenty-two** abandoned his dreams of becoming an actor and has traded the set life for a discourse on spirituality back home. **Thirty-one** traded his cushy law job (and cushier life) to run a bar and grill in Goa. Neither regrets their decision. **Fifty** texts often, but **Thirty** never replies. **Sixty-five** texts from time to time, but I never reply. **Six** switched jobs and boyfriends and has never been happier. **Seven** switched dating apps, but still hasn't found the right one that makes him happier.

Five's journey to find his heart a permanent home persists, but his oil paintings have found many new homes. **Forty-six** is also on the lookout for a landlord for his heart, but he's also on the lookout for a bottom that can accommodate his girth down under. I never ended up working with **Thirty-four** or meeting **Thirty-two**. I never ended up forgiving **Thirty-six. Sixty-one** never ended up forgiving me.

Twenty-one continues to fall in love with new Wet Dreams and is currently besotted with a fitness expert in the city. **Ten** revealed his name; **Forty** revealed his dealer's number; and **Thirty-five** finally revealed that he lied about being a prince. **Twenty-three** finally sent me that follow request and is currently the star of a popular reality series on the web.

Fifty-eight moved out of his mother's house, and **Sixty-six** moved out of his ex's. **Twenty-six** moved to Dubai to be with his boyfriend and is working on his commissioned cookbook. Word has it that it's already a bestseller. **Sixty-two** ditched the domineering boss and found solace in a postgrad degree in public policy in Toronto. **Forty-eight** ditched his expat status and moved back to Greece. **Forty-nine** ditched the dating app he was working on. **Forty-four** ditched the closet and found solace in the arms of a surprisingly accepting family. **Forty-seven** got that job in Singapore. But he never sent me tickets to come visit. **Nine** moved out of Singapore. **Sixty-four** is still selling his art at astronomical rates, finding new muses over strains of marijuana. He's not found himself yet.

A few others went on to start their own ventures, a couple moved away to different countries and some to different men, and two even found love with each other. One adopted a child, another adopted six stray cats. A few met each other and bitched me out on dates. A couple of them even got married (to other men). And what about ~~the stars of this book~~ my friends who made their way to this guide?

Aneesh moved to Goa and jumped right back into the dating pool. He's living his best life. Kartik ditched all the dating apps and decided to start over, but he continues collecting little pieces of hearts like he has been doing for the past few years. Urvaksh has chlamydia. He's currently under treatment. He's deleted Tinder. No comments.

But … **sixty-nine**?

Oh well, I thought you'd never ask. Time to get to the last one in the long line of first dates. Time to go back to **March 2020**.

There I am, waiting for him right by the sea. I can smell the anxiety in the air; it's a nervous tingling that radiates with the sea breeze. There are no hawkers haggling for prices, no late-night joggers sweating out their pedometers, no nervous couples trying to steal a quick snog under the moonlight. The whole world is on the brink of a global shutdown. We are one week away from knowing that we're in the middle of a pandemic.

Sixty-nine is running late. It's okay, because I have all the time in the world today. We've reached the end, after all.

This is the twelfth time I'm seeing him over the eighteen-odd months I have known him. The fifth time we've matched on Tinder.

And yet, this is not a date. Like the man from sixty-eight dates (and nine years) ago, **Sixty-nine** is a man with many jobs. He's been an entrepreneur, an event manager, a marketing guru, a shoemaker, a filmmaker, an Instagram activist, a production whiz, an all-around party boy and most importantly, a serial heartbreaker.

You'd think that after a trail of sixty-eight different men, I'd have some common sense. But I've always only had one motto in life: 'As long as I love someone I can't have, I'll never put myself at risk.' My romantic inconsistencies are not a flaw to be corrected; they are a trait to be accepted. Does that mean I don't feel nervous?

There he is, right on cue. He's grinning apologetically, blaming the Bombay traffic (and the Bombay weather) for being fifteen minutes late. His tonsured head is glistening with evening sweat, and yet, I am the one feeling hot under the collar.

It's suddenly really warm, even though we are in the middle of winter. Our chemistry had always been electrifying; purely exothermic, you could call it – like concentrated HCL with Sodium Hydroxide. *Boom*.

And yet here we are, eighteen months (and fifteen minutes) later. Our chemical apparatus has been sold and dusted off. The lab is officially out of business.

Today, we meet as friends. Not 'let's-mute-each-other-on-Instagram-and-send-the-periodic-birthday-wish' friends, but actual 'two-adults-who've-made-peace-with-the-fact-that-they've-run-their-course-but-still-want-to-be-a-part-of-each-other's-lives' friends. We've reached our (fri)end goal.

'The first two rounds are on me,' he promises. Years of conditioning have taught me to reject his offer with a shy chuckle and offer to split the bill like the self-serving gentlemen that we are. He'll try to argue, but I'll shut him down with a smile and a suggestion that he can pay next time. A carousel of first dates (and encounters) later, it's a template I'm *expected* to follow. But, instead—

'The first two? *All* the rounds are on you ...' I roar.

As you've already guessed, **Sixty-nine** isn't the One. **Sixty-nine** is **Sixty-nine**.

Here's the plot twist. **Sixty-nine** could be ... *anyone*. If you thought that this was the kind of book where I end up with the last blind item date I write about, then I'm sorry to tell you but YOU HAVEN'T BEEN PAYING ATTENTION.

There's a reason the men listed here are referenced by numbers and not real names (apart from being a ruse to avoid the hypothetical lawsuits). There's going to be many more men. There's going to be a seventy. An eight-eight. A ninety-seven. A two hundred and thirty-nine (but let's hope not).

We live our entire lives trying to find that one special person who is perfect for us. But once you've been through multiple serious relationships (such as myself), you begin to suspect that there's no such thing as the right person, only multiple versions of wrong.

It's only then that you know what you are really (not) looking for. We are looking for the wrong person. But this isn't just any wrong person – it's the most perfect version of a wrong person there is. You can be eighteen or eighty and still not understand your self-worth because this realization doesn't just happen overnight. It takes years (or sometimes, even a decade) of exhausting love affairs and lonely months to just wake up one day and realize that you are not, in fact, alone. You have the most important person in your life right now.

You have you. And me?

I have this book.

And I have you, reader.

If you didn't drift off while you went through this incredibly long book, you'd realize that each man found ~~his happy ending~~ a decent end to his story, or at least some version of it. One thing I have learnt is that there are three things that are certain in life: death, holiday weight and the importance of loving yourself. Other dating guides will tell you that society views singlehood as a state of incompletion. A problem that needs a solution. An anomaly that needs to be fixed. An equation that needs to be balanced. A jigsaw puzzle that needs to be completed. A B-Grade Bollywood movie that desperately needs a plot.

In fact, there's a strange undecipherable sadness that people look at you with when you tell them you're single – one usually reserved for missing dog posters and stage-4 cancer patients – are you going to be okay, they ask. Sometimes, they'd even pat you on your back sympathetically.

It's a tale as old as time. Ever since humanity began archiving history, people have always frowned upon singledom. If you voluntarily choose to be single, there must be something *irrevocably wrong* with you.

Do you have commitment issues? Are your standards too high? Do you get very dismissive of romantic relationships? Are you emotionally distant? Were you unloved as a child? Could you have abandonment issues? Do you have a bad body odour? The list of possible suggestions for your 'conscious decision to remain single' is endless.

As ~~the author of this book~~ a thirty-something self-sufficient gay man, I blame mainstream media for the disdain with which people usually approach singlehood. The Disney-style romance has been packaged so well, that if you were to find it at a supermarket marked up to 200 per cent of its price, you'd still buy it. That's how highly society thinks of being coupled up. The world wants you to believe that unless and until you've found the Yin to your Yang, you can never be truly complete. Happy? Probably. But wholesome? Definitely not.

But LESSON #7 (Yes, I've been keeping count right from the very beginning): you no longer need to arrange your life around that empty man-sized hole in your heart (or your bed), because – plot twist – there isn't one. Settling down doesn't mean finding a soulmate, romance or even lifelong companionship.

It means settling into your own. Get this – the perfect man is a lot closer than you think he is. He's actually reading this book right now.

It's **you**.

If you've been reading this book with the same dedication with which I wrote it, you'll realize that the point of this book isn't to help you find the One. It is to help you *become* the One. Find your spirit, wrap it around yourself tightly and snuggle in.

You deserve every bit of it.

Now get out of this book.

You could do with some sunshine, love.

Acknowledgments

Phew.

That's it. We're done. Congratulations, you've made it to the very end of this book, and chances are that if you're actually reading the acknowledgments, you don't think the book is *half bad*.

I'd like to begin by thanking the most important person who's responsible for this book. It's me. Don't act all surprised, if you've read this book cover-to-cover, you know that I'm quite the self-entitled twat. Just kidding. There were days when I wanted to quit, days when I wanted to send my publishers an apology email for giving up midway, days when I wanted to pretend I'd never thought of this book, and that 'one' day (okay fine, it was three separate occasions) when I sobbed uncontrollably in the shower because it just wouldn't end. But I'm glad I didn't.

Okay, let's start over. I'll kick off with Shreya Punj, for sending me the email I think I've been waiting for all my life. For replying to a drunken DM back in July 2018, and having enough faith in an absolute stranger (that would be me) to actually commission them a book based on a 200 word (mildly euphoric) pitch. You wouldn't be reading this page in the flesh if it weren't for her, and I'm glad I found a friend for life. A special shoutout to that bottle of cheap wine that egged gave me the liquid courage to send that drunken DM in the first place.

To Swati Daftuar (and the entire team at HarperCollins India) for being kind and patient and brimming with enthusiasm – and for being an insightful editor who believed in the book more than I did. I'll gladly skip over the part where she politely replied to every exasperating text I sent her over the past two years. Thanks for helping turn my tears, blood and sweat (and yes, words) into a healthy, breathing baby 100% real 'wow, I can touch the pages' book. To Srishti Guptaroy for designing the most breathtakingly gorgeous cover ever. For reestablishing that 'yes, sometimes you can actually judge a (great) book by its cover'.

I'd like to thank my parents (but mostly my mom) for tolerating the absolute man child I was while writing this book, and for sending daily reminders asking me whether I had finished writing it yet (sometimes she sent them twice a day). My dad, for his accompanying nods and grunts. Much love to Amrita Mahale, who told me time and time again that I need to improve my writing and my math, and has been my one true critic ever since I wrote my first story back when I was twelve years old (it was terrible and I used too much punctuation). I still can't solve a differential equation, but I hope this one's up to her standards.

To Avanti Desai, whose illustrious (but tragically short) life set in motion a series of events that made me the person confident enough to even think of pitching this book - instead of letting it be one of my (many) unrealised dreams. To Akshay Saxena, who made at least a half of those dreams see the light of day. To Advait Azad, my lone glimmer of joy during the pandemic.

To all my close friends (there's a huge list, and I'm already well past my word count), for forgiving me for those minor lapses of judgement when I'd forget to reply to texts or wish them on their birthdays - or sometimes even ghost them for months at end. For understanding that I wasn't being a terrible friend (not entirely), but just concentrating on something that was really special to me. And for that, they'll all be special. Each and every one of them.

To every family member, colleague and acquaintance (and those countless strangers in my favourite bar) for making it easy for me to come out to them over my decade long journey as an out-and-proud gay man. Every single ounce of acceptance that has been shamelessly poured my way made this book a possibility, instead of (forever) remaining an anonymous blog that would never go viral.

To all the gay men I've known and loved, ghosted and shunned, the dates, the lovers, the one night stands and (especially) the *one that got away, this book wouldn't have worked out if things between us had. To the three men that Aneesh, Karthik and Utkarsh are (very loosely) based on, for the drinks and the anecdotes that helped make this book twice as fun (and half as one dimensional). To the man who reads this book, and finds me witty, charming and an absolute delight, and eventually slides into my DM's with an opportune pun.*

I'd also like to thank Rahul Khanna for existing (and also because I'm confident that he'll never ever read this thank you note). Most importantly, I'd like to thank you for actually buying this book (we'll pretend you didn't borrow this from a friend), and for funding my eventual trip to Paris with the royalties that I earn from writing this manuscript.

Peace out.